Liquidated

A JOHN HOPE FRANKLIN CENTER BOOK

KAREN HO

Liquidated

AN ETHNOGRAPHY OF WALL STREET

Duke University Press   Durham and London   2009

© 2009 Duke University Press
All rights reserved.
Printed in the United States
of America on acid-free paper ∞
Designed by C. H. Westmoreland
Typeset in Chaparral
by Keystone Typesetting, Inc.
Library of Congress Cataloging-
in-Publication Data appear on the last
printed page of this book.

For my daughter and son,
Mira and August, in the hope that
their generation will see greater
socioeconomic equality.

Contents

acknowledgments   ix

Introduction: Anthropology Goes to
Wall Street   1

1   Biographies of Hegemony: The Culture of
Smartness and the Recruitment and Construction
of Investment Bankers   39

2   Wall Street's Orientation: Exploitation,
Empowerment, and the Politics of Hard Work   73

3   Wall Street Historiographies and the Shareholder
Value Revolution   122

4   The Neoclassical Roots and Origin Narratives of
Shareholder Value   169

5   Downsizers Downsized: Job Insecurity and
Investment Banking Corporate Culture   213

6   Liquid Lives, Compensation Schemes, and the
Making of (Unsustainable) Financial Markets   249

7   Leveraging Dominance and Crises
through the Global   295

notes   325
references   353
index   369

Acknowledgments

An intellectual commitment to social and economic justice first galvanized this book's journey. My search to understand the massive sea changes occurring in American business practices during the past three decades took me to the doorstep of Wall Street investment banks, an unconventional site for anthropological research. This project found a champion in my graduate advisor, Emily Martin, during a time when studying centers of power within the United States was still uncharted territory for most anthropologists. I still remember how, after I was offered a job at an investment bank, I called Emily in a panic as Wall Street demanded my immediate response, leaving me little time to think through how to negotiate a job with potential fieldwork. Her voice registered excitement and concern simultaneously, and she knew instinctively what I should do. "Take it," she answered, sensing the opportunity and trusting my ethnographic and ethical sensibilities. Upon accepting the job, I took a leave of absence from graduate school and informed my coworkers of my future research intentions. Despite the tendency for disciplines to reproduce caution, Emily believed that ethnography was about challenging the status quo, literally putting one foot in front of the other. She taught me that passion and desire for social change are not irrational noise to the scholarly temper, but rather constitutive of pathbreaking research.

The job on Wall Street led me directly into the belly of the financial markets; taking this path made the book possible. I am thus also deeply indebted to the Management Consulting Group at Bankers Trust, where I worked as a business analyst before I began my fieldwork. I want to thank in particular Tony Brown, Richard Gibb, and Kimberly Thomas. Not only were they instrumental in hiring me, but they graciously introduced me to a number of influential contacts from which I built a strong web of informants. Of course, I owe an incredible thanks to all my Wall Street interviewees and informants who shared with me their experiences, introduced me to their networks and coworkers, and allowed me to understand aspects of their worldviews, values, and practices. I am grateful to a few Wall Street organizations, such as the Securities Industry Association and Jesse Jackson's Wall Street Project, who waived their hefty conference fees for a graduate student. I also want to thank especially Angel Lau, a Wall Street veteran, a dear friend, and a fountain of knowledge, who answered and clarified thousands of my clueless questions about finance.

Living in Brooklyn to conduct field research was an adventure of a lifetime. It was made possible in part by the good fortune of answering an advertisement for an apartment share in the Cobble Hill neighborhood, and my future roommate Regina Weber's deciding that I, a complete stranger, was sane and potentially interesting. Little did she know that she would have to put up with endless boxes of books, fieldwork documents, and phone calls from informants for almost three years. For her patience and generosity, I am deeply grateful. I also want to thank old college friends living in New York City at the time, Beatrice Hastings-Spaine, Eunice Lee, and Irene Jeng, who brought endless laughter and much-needed respite from fieldwork.

Fieldwork turns into a successful dissertation only with the help of a supportive department and community. With a generous graduate fellowship, the Department of Anthropology at Princeton initiated me into the discipline. I offer my gratitude to Rena Lederman, Carol Greenhouse, Vincanne Adams, Jim Boon, Gananath and Ranjini Obeyesekere, Larry Rosen, Kay Warren, and especially Carolyn Rouse, for their counsel and academic stimulation. I am indebted to Carol Zanca, the department administrator, whose support and organizational expertise saw me to graduation. I also want to thank a broader Princeton intellectual and friendship community that sustained me throughout graduate school: Sylvie Bertrand, Miguel Centeno, Frances Chen, Jane Chen, Rebecca Clay, Heddye Ducree, Cheryl Hicks, Alison Lake, Lauren Leve, Jose Antonio Lucero, Wende Elizabeth Marshall, Tony Monsanto, Nell Painter, Samuel Roberts, and Ellen Thorington. The Center of Domestic and Comparative Policy Studies and the Fellows program at the Woodrow Wilson School at Princeton University as well as a National Science Foundation Cultural Anthropology Dissertation Improvement Grant provided the research funds necessary to complete fieldwork.

It was at the University of Minnesota that the dissertation was transformed into a book. I thank the faculty in the Department of Anthropology as a whole for their collegiality and support of my research; I am also deeply indebted to the administrative support and skill of Terri Valois, Amy Nordlander, and Susan Laska. My research assistants, Ava Rostampour and Jennifer Walker, were invaluable in helping me prepare this manuscript for production. They painstakingly organized files and searched for references; their dedication was exemplary. I have been very fortunate at Minnesota to have received a variety of grants that allowed this book's completion: the President's Faculty Multicultural Research Award, the Faculty Summer Research Fellowship and McKnight Summer Fellowship, the Institute for Global Studies Intellectual Collective Grant, the College of Liberal Arts semester leave, and research grants from the Humanities Institute and the Asian American Studies Program. I especially want to thank the faculty residential fellowship program at the Institute for Advanced Study and the McKnight Land-Grant Professorship at the University of Minnesota for providing funding and crucial leave time for making revisions and compiling the final draft of this manuscript. My senior colleagues in the Department of Anthropology were instrumental in supporting my candidacy for the McKnight Professorship: I especially owe thanks to Gloria Raheja, William Beeman, John Ingham, Sally Gregory Kohlstedt, and Martha Tappen.

At Minnesota, I have been blessed to find a community of scholars and kindred spirits both within the Anthropology Department and beyond that have sustained this project. I first want to thank members of my writing group, which has changed in composition over the years, but has never lost its intellectual verve or collegial warmth: Bianet Castellanos, David Chang, Tracey Deutsch, Kale Fajardo, Malinda Lindquist, Scott Morgenson, Keith Mayes, Hiromi Mizuno, Kevin Murphy, Rachel Schurman, Hoon Song, Dara Strolovitch, Shaden Tageldin, Karen-Sue Taussig, and David Valentine. I am indebted to Tracey Deutsch and George Henderson, who endured for almost five years co-organizing with me the "Markets in Time: Capitalism and Power" research collaborative, which provided a stimulating environment to think through interdisciplinary approaches to financial markets. Presentations and generous audience feedback from the departments of American Studies, Sociology, and Gender, Women, and Sexuality Studies at Minnesota allowed me to think through sections of the manuscript. I am also grateful for the mentorship of many throughout the university, especially Josephine Lee, Jigna Desai, Roderick Ferguson, Jean Langford, and Karen-Sue Taussig.

I began this project with the grand hope that I would be able to unpack markets ethnographically from the ground up, and in so doing, counter social-scientific tendencies to approach markets as undecipherable, abstract, totalizing, and all-powerful. In the process, I sometimes found myself caught up in the very black-box assumptions I sought to critique, and it was the scholarship, wisdom, and invaluable advice of Bill Maurer, Anna Tsing, and Sylvia Yanagisako that helped me grasp the slipperiest aspects of finance capital. They have collectively left an indelible mark on this book, and I owe them a special debt which cannot be repaid. I can only hope to pass on their intellectual generosity to my students and colleagues.

Parts of this manuscript have also benefited from the feedback and conversations with many scholars during the course of panel discussions and the process of article revisions, among them Ann Anagnost, Tom Boellstorff, Jessica Cattelino, Julie Chu, Paulla Ebron, Julia Elyachar, Ilana Gershon, Jane Guyer, Michael Fischer, Melissa Fisher, Alan Klima, Mae Lee, Lorna Rhodes, and David Valentine. I would like to thank the departments of Anthropology at the University of California at Berkeley, the University of Chicago, and Cornell University for their generous and insightful comments on sections of this book.

I owe my family an enormous debt of gratitude. It is impossible to thank them sufficiently. My parents Jiunn H. and Jene Y. Ho have been pillars of strength, nurturing and encouraging me every step of the way. Even in moments when I did not trust in this project's completion, they had enough faith to make the difference. I would also like to acknowledge my parents-in-law T. N. and Joan Chen for their generosity and support throughout the years. I am very grateful for my sister Chanda Ho and my brother Ralph Ho, who have been my best friends and have always shown me unconditional love; I am a better person because of it and strive to be worthy. My husband, Jeff Chen, who often shows his excitement and interest in this research by surprising his colleagues in the business world that his partner is studying "us," has long been my biggest champion. He has been there for me throughout every stage of this journey, and I thank him with a grateful heart. Our daughter Mira Ho-Chen, who is four years old, has witnessed two sets of revisions of the book. Her intense joy, curiosity, and engagement with the world have inspired the necessary creativity and energy to complete the final version. My son, August Ho-Chen, born just in time to see this book go into production, motivated me to finish as much as possible before his birth.

My friends have supported and cheered me on throughout this process. Hearing their voices never fails to hearten me, and I am especially grateful for the laughter, advice, and encouragement of Christina Chia, Jason Glenn, Irene Jeng, Nicole Johnson, Angel Lau, Mae Lee, George McKinney, Cliff Wong, and many more.

Last but not least, I am deeply indebted to the intellectual and emotional labors of Gary Ashwill and David Valentine. Gary, my freelance editor, has generously read and endured multiple versions of this manuscript. His keen editorial eye, exceptional wit, and pervasive calm have propelled this manuscript forward and encouraged the author to persist. David, an extraordinary anthropologist, has also engaged deeply with this manuscript, helping me through many an impasse. An abundant spirit and listener, he has been a dream colleague, and even lent me his kitchen timer and lucky pencil.

And, to Ken Wissoker and the editorial team at Duke University Press (Tim Elfenbein, Cherie Westmoreland, and many others), thank you for your confidence in, and patience with, this book. Ken's bold enthusiasm and support have helped to make this book a reality.

Introduction:

Anthropology Goes to Wall Street

I first became interested in studying Wall Street on 21 September 1995.[1] AT&T had just announced that it would split into three different companies, engendering one of the largest dismantlings of a corporation in U.S. history: 77,800 managers received "buy-out offers" and 48,500 workers were downsized. Living in New Jersey at the time, I was dismayed by the extent of downsizing-induced worker trauma and even more troubled to hear that, on the first day of the announcement, AT&T stock leaped 6.125 points to 63.75, or 10.6 percent of its total value, "growing" another $9.7 billion. But what shocked me the most, upon further investigation, was that the stock prices of Wall Street investment banks also rose. What was the connection?

This seemingly counterintuitive relationship between AT&T's massive downsizing and its soaring stock price was not an isolated case. According to the *New York Times* on the day of the AT&T restructuring, during this period of increased merger and reorganization activity and in anticipation of future telecommunications industry restructurings, the stocks of the Wall Street investment banks that initiated, organized, and gave advice on these deals also rose. "Brokerage stocks were one of the session's stronger groups, with analysts citing their belief that volume growth is sustainable and merger activity will continue" (Sloane 1995). The stocks of Morgan Stanley, Merrill Lynch, and Lehman Brothers all rallied with the assumption that if AT&T, a bellwether for the telecommunications industry, restructured and downsized, then other companies would follow that "economic fashion," thereby bringing in more business for Wall Street investment banks (Klein 2000, 199).[2]

For the past three decades it is precisely these kinds of inversions that have dominantly characterized the corporate landscape and the relationships among layoffs, corporate profits, and stock prices. In this period, which includes what has been proclaimed as the greatest economic boom in U.S. history (early 1990s–2000), the economy experienced *not only* record corporate profits and the longest rising stock market ever, *but also* record downsizings (O'Sullivan 2000). Research reports by Challenger, Gray, and Christmas, a Chicago outplacement firm, found that in 1994, 516,000 workers were downsized "when American corporations recorded their best profits in years; for 1995 it was 440,000 when profits were even better; and for 1996 and 1997 the totals were 447,000 and 434,000, respectively, when profits were better still" (O'Boyle 1999, 219). While the U.S. stock market, as measured by the Dow Jones Industrial Average, boomed from just above 4,000 points in February 1995 to over 7,000 in February 1997, then to 11,000 in 1999, job insecurity also spiked as corporations, on average, downsized over 3 million people per year (Oldham 1999; New York Times 1996). To give another example of this new cultural code of conducting business, in 1995, Mobil Corporation announced unprecedented earnings of $626 million for the first quarter, a reversal from a $145 million loss a year earlier, then a week later announced plans to eliminate 4,700 jobs. Wall Street analysts, reacting "enthusiastically to the news," praised Mobil's aggressiveness: they were pleasantly "surprised" when layoffs were not only higher than expected but also included refining and marketing personnel in the United States, who were paid more. Wall Street institutional investors demonstrated their confidence in Mobil by bidding up shares to a fifty-two-week high (Ritter 1995; Fiorini 1995).

What was so arresting about Wall Street's approach to corporate downsizing was its celebratory tone, its rejoicing in the very fact of corporate restructuring.[3] Throughout the mid-1990s, countless financial news articles demonstrated what seemed to be a new "structure of feeling." To continue with the case study of AT&T, a few months after it announced that it would fundamentally restructure and divide itself into three different companies, a move Wall Street analysts generally applauded, AT&T announced in January 1996 that it planned to eliminate forty thousand jobs over the next four years. According to the *Wall Street Journal*,

> The magnitude of the cuts stunned even some veteran AT&T-watchers. It broadly signaled that, for many major U.S. corporations, the eagerness and urgency for wholesale restructuring continues unabated. For AT&T, in particular, it also underscored that—even after trimming some 85,000 people in the decade since the breakup of the old Bell System empire—AT&T still employs far too many workers. . . . "This is a big number—a very, very big number," said Blake Bath, an analyst at Sanford Bernstein & Co. "It's a lot bigger than Wall Street had been anticipating." Wall Street responded well, sending AT&T shares up $2.625 yesterday to close at $67.375. (Keller 1996)

In fact, Wall Street was so excited about the magnitude of these layoffs that Salomon Brothers' infamous superstar telecommunications research analyst Jack B. Grubman thought it necessary to temper investor enthusiasm, cautioning that "investors shouldn't expect a huge jump in earnings from the cost cuts, as AT&T reinvests much of the savings to accelerate forays into wireless and local service." He did state, however, that "it's a good aggressive move, but the earnings impact going forward will be much, much less" (Keller 1996). In other words, AT&T, in the near future, would need to find even more ways of boosting its share price. Then, in March 1996, the company retracted its initial claim of forty thousand jobs cut, announcing it planned "only" eighteen thousand layoffs. An article in *USA Today* noted that "observers say AT&T deliberately inflated its initial layoff estimates to *impress* Wall Street, which sees job cuts as increasing profit. AT&T's stock price jumped almost 6% in the two days following the January announcement" (D. Lynch 1996, my emphasis).

While the desire for profit accumulation is certainly not new, what is clearly unique in the recent history of capitalism in the United States is the complete divorce of what is perceived as the best interests of the corporation from the interests of most employees.[4] Only twenty-five years ago, the public corporation in the United States was mainly viewed as a stable social institution involved in the steady provision of goods and services, responsible for negotiating multiple constituencies from employees to shareholders, and judged according to a longer-term time frame that went beyond Wall Street's short-term financial expectations to unlock immediate investment income (O'Sullivan 2000).[5] Today, in contrast, the primary mission of corporations is understood to be the increase of their stock prices for the benefit of their "true owners," the shareholders (that is, to create shareholder value). Employees, located *outside* the corporation's central purpose, are readily liquidated in the pursuit of stock price appreciation. Whereas, under the assumptions of post–Second World War welfare capitalism, workers struggled for and (sometimes) received their (unfair) share of corporate earnings, today even this traditional capitalist hierarchy has been largely eliminated such that employees often no longer benefit at all (or even suffer) when the corporation makes a profit. It is this new logic which I encountered on Wall Street that I investigate throughout this ethnography.[6]

In light of a celebratory Wall Street, what does the ostensible dominance of finance capital, which I would argue has centrally characterized our times, mean concretely? How might an in-depth ethnographic analysis of Wall Street investment banks, and the processes leading to their ultimate demise, provide a key to understanding the sea change occurring in corporate America? How do investment bankers actively *make markets*—that is, produce the dominant sensibilities of the stock market and Wall Street financial norms through their daily cultural practices?[7] How do Wall Street investment bankers negotiate the relationship between massive downsizing, shareholder value, and the production of market crisis, which leads not only to the overhaul of mainstream business values but ultimately to the liquidation (and reinvention) of Wall Street itself? Given my assumption that the measure of corporate health has something to do with employment—an understanding bolstered by my academic training and political beliefs and supported, I thought, by mainstream American culture—how could it be that a time of record corporate profits and soaring stock prices could also be an era of record downsizings and rampant job insecurity? More broadly, how have the severe social dislocations social scientists have usually attributed to global capitalism at large—the dismantling of corporate and governmental safety nets; the wave of corporate downsizings, mergers, and restructurings; the changing nature of what it means to be a successful worker; the growing concentration of wealth at the top; the social violence of financial booms and busts—been actualized? These questions propelled me to conduct fieldwork on Wall Street to investigate what role the stock market and investment banks played in these radical socioeconomic shifts.

Wall Street Habitus: The Cultural Production of Liquidation

My central purpose in this ethnography is to analyze both Wall Street's role in the reshaping of corporate America and its corresponding effects on market formations, *and* how Wall Street helped to instantiate these changes.[8] By Wall Street, I mean the concentration of financial institutions and actor-networks[9] (investment banks, pension and mutual funds, stock exchanges, hedge funds and private equity firms) that embody a particular financial ethos and set of practices, and act as primary spokespeople for the globalization of U.S. capitalism.[10] I examine in particular the relationship between the values and actions of investment banks, the corresponding restructuring of U.S. corporations, and the construction of markets, specifically financial market booms and busts. I ask how exactly Wall Street investment bankers and banks, at the level of the everyday, helped to culturally produce a financially dominant, though highly unstable, capitalism: what kinds of experiences and ideologies shaped investment banker actions, how they were empowered to make these shifts, and how these changes were enacted and understood to be righteous. As such, this book will contribute to contemporary anthropological understandings of the globalization of U.S. capitalism through an "on the ground" ethnographic approach that counters the widespread conception of capitalist globalization as an abstract metanarrative and homogenizing force too unwieldy for ethnographic translation.

Multiple key functions and institutions constitute Wall Street and the financial markets in the United States. Aside from investment banks there are asset management companies (hedge funds, pension and mutual funds, and private equity firms), and the securities exchanges themselves. Financial firms contain departments that deal with trading and sales, corporate finance, mergers and acquisitions (M&A), research, and investment management, each with slightly divergent goals, methods, and perspectives. From this broad landscape I chose as my primary field sites the central, iconic institutions of Wall Street, the major investment banks such as Morgan Stanley and Merrill Lynch. Within the banks I focused on those functions commonly considered investment banking proper—corporate finance and M&A—because they directly demonstrate the interconnections between financial and productive markets, between financial and corporate institutions. Through their middlemen roles as financial advisors to major U.S. corporations as well as expert evaluators of and spokespeople for the stock and bond markets, investment bankers work to transfer and exchange wealth from corporations to large shareholders (and their financial advisors), hold corporations accountable for behavior and values that generate short-term shareholder value, and generate debt and securities capital to fund these practices. It is in the activities of these corporate-finance-related departments that we most clearly see the imbrication of the productive economy, investment banks, and the financial markets. The work of Wall Street does not consist only of trading and exchange in the global financial markets; it is also linked to corporate restructurings and attendant shifts in corporate values.

It is important to understand both the connections and distinctions between Wall Street investment banks and corporate America. Although investment banks are corporations in an organizational sense with specific corporate cultures, they also possess a supplementary role as the voice of the financial markets, and claim to speak for millions of shareholders as well. They thus occupy a unique social position: investment banks represent both "the market" and the corporate entities that are subject to the market. Locating the supposedly abstract market in sites with particular institutional cultures localizes the market, demonstrates its embodiment, and shows how it is infused with the organizational strategies of investment banks.[11]

Despite the recent, much-proclaimed "death of Wall Street," it is important to understand that the financial culture that I generally denote by the term "Wall Street investment banks" does not always map neatly onto particular institutions. I use the designation to broadly signify an ethos and set of practices that continue to be deeply embedded in the intricate network of institutions, investments, and people we call high finance. Moreover, I argue that the supposed end of investment banking does not signal the permanent vanquishing of Wall Street ideologies or practices. Rather, instability and crisis fundamentally characterize this particular culture of liquidity, and signal not the decline but the influence of Wall Street values and practices. During the latest period of finance capital dominance of American business, Wall Street—the names, physical locations, and institutional identities and structures of almost all Wall Street investment banking firms—has continually transformed itself through mergers, acquisitions, bankruptcies, and failures.

This observation is methodologically and theoretically crucial to the argument of this book: it demonstrates that Wall Street investment banks have incubated, promulgated, and themselves undergone the very radical shifts they imposed and recommended for corporate America. The very particular cultural system that Wall Street has constructed and nurtured —one that promotes the volatile combination of unplanned risk-taking with the search for record profits, constant identification with the financial markets and short-term stock prices, and continual corporate downsizing—has not only been imposed on corporate America but also fundamentally characterizes and affects Wall Street itself. In fact, investment banks' self-effects are perhaps even more pronounced than their restructuring of other corporations as they consider themselves to be the incarnations of the market.

Wall Street's vanishing acts are indicative of its corporate culture; a glance at its recent history is telling. Even during the time of my research from 1996 to 1999, concurrent with the longest rising bull market ever, the institutional identities and locations of many of my central field sites radically shifted. For example, in 1997, Bankers Trust (BT) bought boutique investment bank Alex Brown and was in turn acquired by Deutsche Bank in 1998; BT was then merged out of existence. In 1993 Travelers

Group, an insurance and financial conglomerate, bought Smith Barney, a brokerage and mid-size investment banking firm, then in 1997 purchased major investment bank Salomon Brothers to form Salomon Smith Barney; in 1998, Travelers merged into Citicorp to create the behemoth Citigroup, a bank holding company. In 2000, J. P. Morgan and Chase Manhattan Bank merged to create J. P. Morgan Chase. With the formation of Citigroup and J. P. Morgan Chase, major investment bank Salomon Brothers effectively disappeared, and J. P. Morgan, already a "hybrid" investment and commercial bank,[12] solidified its status as a bank holding company—which is also what Goldman Sachs and Morgan Stanley changed their status to in September 2008. Not surprisingly, the mergers and acquisitions (M&A) mania, the bull market, and the dot-com bubble of the late 1990s led, not only to the millennial crash and record downsizings, but also to the corresponding restructuring of a majority of the Wall Street investment banks I researched (see Map 1 and 2).

It is important to mention that while I argue that these dismantlings germinate out of the specific corporate culture of investment banking, massive governmental deregulation and the shareholder value revolution helped to catalyze this cultural system. The late 1990s Gramm-Leach-Bliley Act ensured the rollback of most of the stipulations of the Glass-Steagall Act, which was passed during the Great Depression to prevent deposit-taking commercial banks from speculating in the financial markets. It had sought specifically to segregate investment banking, which engages in the "risky" capital markets, from the businesses of everyday banking and insurance, which are supposed to safeguard savings and provide loans. However, given the rise in stature, power, and profitability of Wall Street investment banks since the 1980s, retail and commercial banks—the titans of "low" finance—were eager to acquire investment banking capabilities and presence. Moreover, many investment banks were themselves pressured by the M&A boom to become gigantic, "one-stop shopping" institutions for corporate clients, which was deemed to increase shareholder value, not to mention the fact that senior executives received astronomical financial incentives for advising and participating in as many deals and transactions as possible. In this climate of regulation *for* the latest trends of the financial markets, investment banks participated in their own dismantling—that is, they relinquished a "purist" notion of investment banking—and financial institutions were allowed to "have it all," both commercial and investment banking ambitions.[13]

Not ironically, then, the very influence and success of Wall Street—its ability to globally market and proselytize both its products and its ethos—

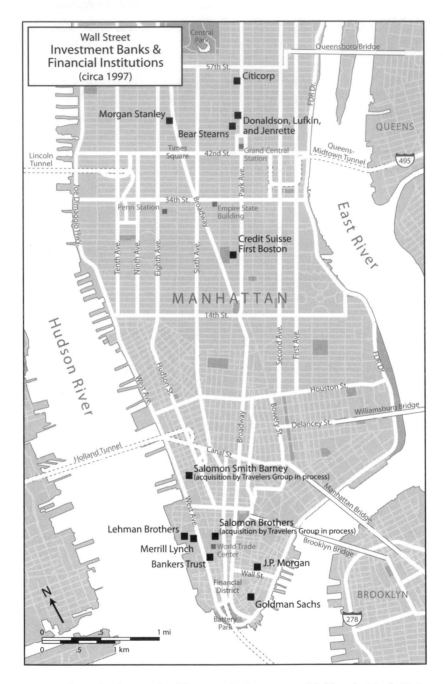

**Wall Street
Investment Banks &
Financial Institutions
(circa 1997)**

Central
Park

Queensboro Bridge

57th St.

Citicorp

QUEENS

Morgan Stanley

FDR Dr.

Donaldson, Lufkin,
and Jenrette

Bear Stearns

Times
Square

42nd St.

Grand Central
Station

Queens-
Midtown Tunnel

495

Lincoln
Tunnel

Park Ave.

East River

34th St.

Penn Station

Broadway

Empire State
Building

Joe DiMaggio Hwy.

Tenth Ave.

Ninth Ave.

Eighth Ave.

Sixth Ave.

Credit Suisse
First Boston

MANHATTAN

Hudson River

14th St.

West Ave.

Hudson St.

Second Ave.

First Ave.

FDR Dr.

Houston St.

Broadway

Bowery St.

Williamsburg Bridge

Delancey St.

Holland Tunnel

Canal St.

Salomon Smith Barney
(acquisition by Travelers Group in process)

Manhattan Bridge

West Ave.

Lehman Brothers

Salomon Brothers
(acquisition by Travelers Group in process)

Brooklyn Bridge

Merrill Lynch

World Trade
Center

Bankers Trust

J.P. Morgan

Wall St.

Financial
District

BROOKLYN

Goldman Sachs

278

Battery
Park

N

0   .5   1 mi

0   .5   1 km

Map 1. The author's central field sites at the beginning of fieldwork. *Map by University of Minnesota Cartography Laboratory.*

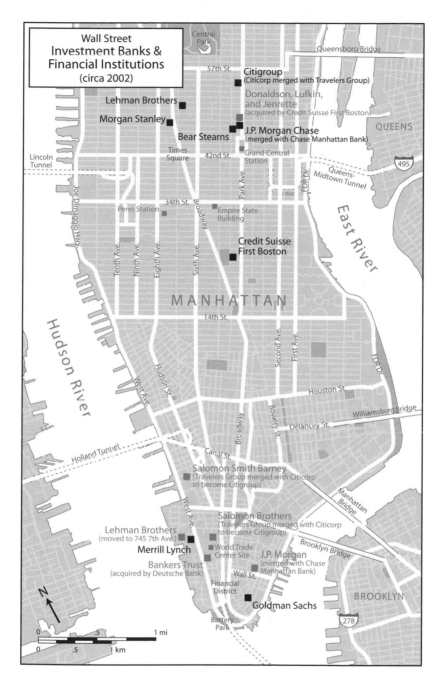

Wall Street
**Investment Banks &
Financial Institutions**
(circa 2002)

Central Park

Queensboro Bridge

QUEENS

57th St.

Citigroup
(Citicorp merged with Travelers Group)

Donaldson, Lufkin, and Jenrette
(acquired by Credit Suisse First Boston)

Lehman Brothers

Morgan Stanley

Bear Stearns

J.P. Morgan Chase
(merged with Chase Manhattan Bank)

Times Square

42nd St.

Grand Central Station

Lincoln Tunnel

Queens-Midtown Tunnel

495

Joe DiMaggio Hwy

Penn Station

34th St.

Empire State Building

Credit Suisse
First Boston

East River

Tenth Ave.

Ninth Ave.

Eighth Ave.

Sixth Ave.

Broadway

Park Ave.

FDR Dr.

MANHATTAN

14th St.

Second Ave.

First Ave.

FDR Dr.

Hudson River

West Ave.

Hudson St.

Broadway

Houston St.

Bowery St.

Williamsburg Bridge

Delancey St.

Holland Tunnel

Canal St.

Salomon Smith Barney
(Travelers Group merged with Citicorp to become Citigroup)

Manhattan Bridge

Salomon Brothers
(Travelers Group merged with Citicorp to become Citigroup)

Lehman Brothers
(moved to 745 7th Ave.)

West Ave.

World Trade Center Site

Brooklyn Bridge

Merrill Lynch

Bankers Trust
(acquired by Deutsche Bank)

J.P. Morgan
(merged with Chase Manhattan Bank)

Wall St.

Financial District

BROOKLYN

Goldman Sachs

Battery Park

278

N

0   .5   1 mi

0   .5   1 km

Map 2. After five years. *Map by University of Minnesota Cartography Laboratory.*

has generated not only record profits but also volatility, crisis, and a continual existence on the brink of annihilation (for itself as well as corporate America). For example, just as the M&A and internet bubble was the nineties analogue to the millennial subprime boom and bust, the leveraged buyout movement of the "ga-ga" eighties led, not only to the insider trading scandals, junk bond crisis, and stock market crash of 1987, but also to the bankruptcy of one of the largest investment banks of the time, Drexel Burnham Lambert, and the eventual liquidation of the investment bank Kidder Peabody. Over the past three decades, then, given the continued resurgence of Wall Street practices, I would argue that Wall Street's self-annihilation, even cannibalization, has not so much led to the disappearance of its particular cultural practices or power over American business as it has to constant financial crisis and ever widening socioeconomic inequality. Although the enormous scale and scope of what is currently being dubbed the worst financial crisis since the Great Depression—the federal bailout of Wall Street brought on by investment banks' engendering of the subprime debacle, which has in turn caused a global credit panic—is certainly extraordinary and has instigated a groundswell of reform and regulation, it remains to be seen whether Wall Street's particular investment banking ethos will disappear or will resurge in new and varied institutional forms, as it has regularly done since the 1980s. As Andy Serwer, managing editor of *Fortune* magazine, has observed: "The party is over on Wall Street—until it comes back again. . . . I've been around long enough to see that we have these cycles. These guys get their cigars and champagne. They have a great time. The whole thing blows up. But then they re-emerge years later. This one is a really, really bad one. But I don't think Wall Street is dead" (Boudreau, Fitzpatrick, and Zamost 2008).

The ostensible demise of my field site—Wall Street investment banking—in 2008, then, is not so much a radical turn of events as the fairly predictable outcome of a peculiar corporate culture. A central tenet of this ethnography is that the everyday practices and ideologies of investment bankers (which have solidified and gained currency since Wall Street achieved dominance over corporate America and global influence) continually set the stage for Wall Street's possible liquidation—and reconstitution. Yet this insight is rendered invisible precisely because Wall Street investment bankers as well as academic and popular analysts of finance often resort to an abstraction they call "the market" to explain these crises. Junk bonds, merger crazes, internet bubbles, highly leveraged housing meltdowns, and subprime debacles are mistaken for, and understood to be the organic results of, market cycles (what goes up *must* come down) with a dash of greed and hubris as human nature thrown in. As such, the construction of booms and busts are simply conflated with "the market" and are not understood as arising from the particular work-place models, corporate culture, and organizational values of Wall Street financial institutions (investment banks in particular) or the specific and personal experiences of those who work for them.

In this book, I make the case that accessing the central ideas and prac-tices of investment banking culture allows us to unpack the very process of market making and will give us insight into the cultural workings of the so-called market. To do so, I take inspiration from Pierre Bourdieu's no-tions of "disposition" and "habitus," where "disposition" refers to a "way of being," "inclination," and "predisposition," often of the body, which collectively constitute the habitus, "a system of dispositions," which in turn organizes action, "produces practices," and constructs social struc-tures and worlds (Bourdieu 1990, 73–87, 214). Specifically, I examine the structure and formation of investment bankers' habitus—how they have developed an investment banking ethos and set of experiences that frame and empower them to impose regimes of restructuring and deal making onto corporate America and, ultimately, help to engender financial market crisis. I demonstrate how, for example, the personal biographies of invest-ment bankers play into, and converge with, job status and workplace experiences to shape a "common-sense" understanding of the righteous-ness of Wall Street analyses and recommendations. Recruited from elite universities and represented as "the smartest," investment bankers enter into a Wall Street workplace of rampant insecurity, intense hard work, and exorbitant "pay for performance" compensation. Forged in these experi-ences is a particular investment banker habitus which allows them to embrace an organizational model of "employee liquidity" and to recom-mend these experiences for all workers. Wall Street work environments, it turns out, are notorious for downsizing privileged investment bankers, even during bull markets, multiple times a year. To answer why constant corporate liquidation, including the downsizing of employees, has been celebrated and justified on Wall Street, it is necessary to understand how the people heralding downsizing themselves experience it.

And yet—Wall Street investment bankers understand the necessity of constantly performing in notoriously insecure work environments not as a liability, but as a challenge. Bankers, recruited as they are only from the Ivy League and a few comparable schools like MIT and Stanford, are trained to view themselves as "the best and the brightest," for whom intense deal-making through insecurity becomes a sign of their "smartness" and superiority as well as a way to cope with an anxious environment. Empowered by cultural capital, extensive elite networks, and an organizational structure of exorbitant compensation premised on numbers of transactions, investment bankers often successfully weather and negotiate (and create) crises until the next resurgence. They understand their lack of employment security as testing and developing their "mettle."[14] In this context of privilege and insecurity, investment bankers, on a practical level, are incentivized and learn to relentlessly push more deals (usually short-term transactions intended to boost stock prices) onto corporate America. By thus pressuring corporations, bankers transfer their own models of employee liquidity onto corporate America and set the stage for market crisis. Buttressed by the shareholder revolution, which I chronicle, Wall Street is empowered to shape and discipline corporate America, and such a relationship allows Wall Street to impose its own organizational practices—the very particular industry culture of banking —onto corporations at large. Instead of recognizing constant deal-making and rampant employee liquidity as their own local culture, my Wall Street informants conflated their organizational practices with their cultural roles as interpreters of the market and saw themselves, not as describing their own work and life circumstances, but as explaining "natural" market cycles and economic laws.

Bourdieu's models are prescient: these everyday practices of anxious deal-making and performance of smartness and market immediacy serve as the link between habitus and field, between the cultural structures and habits, anchored in individual's and group's bodies and minds, and the larger "fields" of social relations in the world. I thus approach the daily practices and corporate cultural values of investment bankers in the workplace as the site which links the cultural frame, dispositions, and habitus of investment bankers with broader U.S. corporate restructuring *and* the construction of financial market booms and busts (Bourdieu 1990). The very organization of this book—starting with biographies, delving into powerful ideological and institutional transformations, and ending with crises—mirrors this goal of demonstrating empirically how Wall Street's subjectivities, its specific practices, constraints, and institutional culture, dynamically intersect to constitute powerful systemic effects on U.S. corporations and financial markets, and beyond. It seeks to unpack the cultural labors necessary to construct a social and historical phenomenon— the dominance of Wall Street models and actors of finance capital.

It is not my intention, however, to assert that the Wall Street financial community, a heterogeneous site itself, single-handedly caused these massive corporate transformations, as multiple actors and institutions beyond investment banks, securities exchanges, and investment funds were critically involved, among them: governmental policies and federal "reregulating" of corporations, a neoliberal resurgence in departments of economics and business schools, various crises in the rate of corporate profits and the choices made by corporate managers, the invention and popularity of new financial instruments from junk bonds to mutual funds, and the compromising of labor movements punctuated by racialized and gendered inequalities. It is therefore beyond the scope of this project to document all the myriad and complex conditions and practices that have enabled financial market values and actors to consolidate their influence over corporate America and have helped to solidify shareholder value as a dominant measure of business success.

Wall Street Institutional Culture: Access, Initiation, and Method

My particular strategy in "studying up," to break through the barriers of security and public relations, was based on institutional kinship.[15] To enable this research, I leveraged my socioeconomic background and connections with elite universities—the only sites from which Wall Street investment banks recruit and hire. I was first introduced to investment banking as a career option while an undergraduate at Stanford University, although admittedly Wall Street was not the destination of most of my network of friends (graduate school, nonprofits, and, of course, Silicon Valley were bigger draws). (When I began fieldwork, I also relied on Stanford alumni who worked on Wall Street as contacts and potential informants.) I then became a graduate student at Princeton University, a recruiting hotbed for investment banks. There, I had the opportunity not only to make contacts with alumni but also to participate in the job recruitment process itself. My path to Wall Street was made possible by the institutional, elite "familial" connections between particular universities and Wall Street investment banks, where alumni from prestigious universities have an inside-track into Wall Street. It is thus not far-fetched to argue that elite kinship creates a bridge or network to access finance capital. As Sylvia Yanagisako points out, framing kinship and family as dichotomous with, or external to, the very processes of capitalist formation ignores the centrality of the connections and sentiments of kinship that make capitalist production possible (Yanagisako 2002).

My particular strategy for accessing the elite lifeworlds of investment banking relied on research methods that blurred the boundaries of anthropology and sociology. I got a job at a Wall Street investment bank, a strategy with sociological precedent, while still following anthropological ethical norms, as I did not conduct ethnographic research covertly. In 1996, I participated in the spring career services recruitment process at Princeton. It was during the grueling interview process that I first recognized that anthropological discourses about globalization were not only appreciated by, but also similar to, those of Wall Street investment bankers. That June I was hired by Bankers Trust New York Corporation (also known as BT),[16] a "hybrid" investment and commercial bank, as an "internal management consultant" analyst, part of a group that acted as an "agent and advisor of change" for the different businesses within the bank.[17] Upon receiving the job offer, I told my boss (and when I began work, my colleagues) that I was taking a leave of absence from graduate studies to work at BT for two reasons. First, I was genuinely interested in learning more about the world of finance and acquiring "real world" work experience. Second, in the future I wanted to return to graduate school to study Wall Street culture. At BT, I was an employee first, friend second, and a fieldworker third; thus, while I learned much from my time there, my fieldwork mainly took place after I left my job. I did not secretly conduct fieldwork in my workplace; instead, in order to record the initial strangeness and surprises of the ethnographic encounter, the awakening into Wall Street life, I kept a journal of personal reflections and experiences, taking care not to describe in detail the thoughts and actions of my coworkers and friends who—although they knew of my research interests —were "on the job." As such, the experiences that I relate from this period are based on my observations and journal writing and not on any information that was considered private or proprietary.

As an "internal management consultant" at BT, I rotated through the many businesses of the bank to advise on a number of projects on strategy, workflow efficiency, operations, and change management. Although I did not work directly in the investment banking businesses (such as the corporate finance department), as a financial-services consultant within an investment bank, I was trained and immersed in the perspectives and mores of Wall Street financial practices. My role as a consultant allowed me to access and make contacts in multiple parts of the bank, as well as with young investment bankers throughout Wall Street. By participating intensely in conferences and financial networking events, as well as the after-work social lives of my coworkers, I also extended my contacts across multiple institutions. My goal for the year was to imbibe the general, taken-for-granted language and landscape of Wall Street, usually gathered during intense participant observation, as well as to establish a web of informants for "actual" fieldwork when I quit my job.

Living in a two-bedroom apartment share in the Cobble Hill/Carroll Gardens neighborhood of Brooklyn, New York, where I paid lower rent ($425 a month) than at Princeton, gave me the emotional sustenance to both work at BT and conduct this fieldwork. Although today my friends tell me that my old neighborhood is "the place to be" among young professionals, Wall Streeters included (with one-bedroom apartment rents now pushing $2,000 a month), in the late 1990s it was precisely the fact that almost no one from Wall Street lived in my overwhelmingly Latino, white ethnic, and Arab American neighborhood that enabled me to put on a suit for three years and take the F train into a highly sanitized world of shareholder value proponents spouting the bull market hubris of Wall Street. I could come home to the smells of cubano sandwiches and pizza so juicy it had to be folded in half. Walking home around 8:30 p.m., I enjoyed making small talk with the porch and sidewalk crowd, who wondered why I always came home so late, looking quite forlorn, although my hours were early by Wall Street standards.

Toward the end of my time at BT, I was hitting my stress limit at work. Under constant pressure to vie for more and more projects in order to demonstrate my smartness, my capacity for hard work, and my ambition for deal-making responsibility, I was expected to demonstrate the desire for more money as evidence that I had properly imbibed these new sensibilities. As a graduate student used to living on $1000 per month, whose main purpose—seriously—was ethnographic knowledge and connection, I was reluctantly pushed into an alternate conception of space and time. Then the urgency (not to mention desperation) motivating everyone else hit me.

In January 1997, after a mere six months of employment in the Management Consulting Group (MCG) at BT, I was canned. In the midst of prefieldwork, preparing myself to undertake research on investment banks' role in the downsizing of corporate America, I abruptly found myself downsized, along with many of my potential informants. The rationale given by BT for eliminating MCG was that we were a fixed expense that detracted from shareholder value. Management consultants internal to BT were on the permanent payroll, giving the bank a steady source of oversight and advice on business strategy and streamlining work processes. But key senior managers had decided that our work could be contracted out to external consultants. Our salaries were an unnecessary drag on shareholder value.[18] Two years later, BT itself was bought by the German monolith Deutsche Bank and was itself, as the lingo goes, "absorbed."

The moment appeared rife with ethnographic significance: financiers, the instigators of mass corporate restructurings throughout the United States, were downsizing themselves. BT's loss was ironically the anthropologist's gain. These seemingly mundane experiences of downsizing and job insecurity, everyday occurrences at investment banks, might yield crucial insights into the contemporary moment of financial crises and globalization. I learned that bankers' institutional culture and their own personal experiences of downsizing could reveal how the goals and practices of Wall Street not only reshaped global capitalism but also reverberated within. Investment bankers were subjected to, and suffered from, the same concepts and practices they imposed on others.

Two months after the announcement of my own downsizing, a vice president in my group, Lacey Meadows, called me into her office. She was leading "The Account Services Project" and wanted to inform me that she had chosen me to be her analyst on the project, her "right hand." "Do you want to know why I chose you?" she offered. When I shrugged, feeling slightly apprehensive about what was to come, she answered, "Because you are so nice; you're an anthropologist, and you can understand and empathize with how other people are feeling. We need someone they can talk to, and you'll be able to gain their trust." Needless to say, by the time she uttered "empathize," I was already dreading my soon-to-be role as potential collaborator, or put bluntly, her fellow axe man. I had just been called upon to streamline a "back office" department at BT that played a support role for the investment management "front office," processing trades, managing ledgers, and fielding customer accounts. Given the hierarchical structure of investment banks, front-office workers, such as investment bankers, traders, and investment managers who take credit for all profits and deals done, depend on the back office for daily support, all the while looking for ways to restructure these "cost centers." I knew immediately that I would resist; for me, this was the freedom of being a future fieldworker.

Specifically, I was asked to conduct a Taylorist time-motion study of their workday, actually charting and measuring the kinds of tasks and the time needed for completion to judge how many workers were necessary. I firmly intended not to recommend any downsizing. While interviewing the workers, who were overwhelmingly people of color and white women, I occasionally tried to assure them that my findings would bolster the necessity of their labor and protect their jobs. (Of course, I also recognized that given the role of investment bankers and consultants as agents of restructuring, this could have been viewed as trickery, as attempts to "soften them up.") When talking to my team members (both of them higher up in the Wall Street hierarchy—a vice president and an associate with an MBA), I carefully asserted evidence that cast doubt on the very agenda of this project: why aren't these workers needed, who would do the job if they are "restructured," and does BT actually have a plan in place to make these changes? My fellow consultants, not to mention all the investment bankers whose reactions I solicited, were unclear as to why I defended the workers in Account Services. To say that Wall Street had little respect for back-office workers is an understatement. Although they were not openly disparaged, they were casually dubbed career nine-to-fivers; their work ethic was questioned, as was their smartness, drive, and innovation. Were they really "adding value," defined as directly boosting revenues or stock prices? The associate on the team wondered why we were wasting so much time there; in addition to being low prestige, the Account Services project was certainly not representative of the sort of financial deal-making he had hoped to be involved in.

At the same time, I was at a loss to explain why Wall Streeters, especially those in my group who were just downsized, were not more sympathetic to the concerns of these about-to-be canned workers. It was as if these privileged bankers and consultants hadn't really lost their jobs, as if restructuring did not apply to them in the same way, as if the anxiety of constant insecurity did not cause them to doubt their financial prowess or desirability to employers. Exploring this quandary would take center stage during fieldwork. I would come to understand that, not only were investment bankers' experiences of downsizing qualitatively different than that of most workers, but also that Wall Street investment banks' institutional culture helped to produce a model of workplace relations that was crucial to analyzing and understanding finance capital's approach to both American employment writ large *and* the making of markets. Given that recent work in social studies of finance has demonstrated that economists and financial models and theories, not only describe and analyze financial markets, but also perform and produce them (Callon 1998; MacKenzie 2006), it thus seemed a distinct possibility that studying the personal crises of investment bankers could provide a unique insight into the production of corporate restructuring and financial crises. Far from being only the perpetrators, investment bankers have themselves been subjected to the revolving-door model of employment that they recommend for other workers, although their particular mix of privilege, pedigree, compensation, and networking affords them a very different "lesson learned" from the experiences of downsizing and insecurity. By investigating Wall Street's own culture of employment, I examine how and why elite financial actors have over the past few decades radically altered the nature of American corporations, ultimately helping to shape a world of socio-economic inequality, insecurity, and crisis.

As for my role in the Account Services project, after many sleepless nights and acne breakouts worse than a teenager's, I created a spreadsheet demonstrating that although communications channels and repetition could be reworked to flow better and some discrete tasks could be combined, there continued to be as many labor hours needed to accomplish necessary work as there were people. In other words, I concluded that the amount of labor equaled the number of people employed. Upon reviewing my spreadsheet, my vice president inquired, "How come everything fits together so neatly! Are you up to something?" I replied, "BT doesn't have its own house in order; we just got downsized, so I think it would create more inefficiency to restructure Account Services than any real long-term savings." In the end, Account Services was not downsized. I suspect it had less to do with me—though our group offered BT no justification for such action—than with Wall Street investment banks' notorious lack of planning and follow-through even in their search for short-term gains.

A year after my downsizing,[19] I undertook seventeen months of fieldwork, from February 1998 to June 1999, among differently positioned investment bankers working at most major Wall Street financial institutions. I drew on university alumni connections and a web of contacts that I had made during my prefieldwork job, which allowed me access to a number of investment banks as well as other fieldwork sites, from bars to outplacement agencies, conferences to panel discussions. I conducted participant observation and over one hundred interviews. Had I relied solely on my alumni contacts to create a network of informants without getting a job, my toolkit would have been mainly limited to interviews. Had I relied primarily on my job and contacts at BT, I would have learned the language and mores of finance, but my ethnography would have been contained within the walls of one investment bank and could not have addressed Wall Street as a broad occupational community.[20] Since the goal of my research was to analyze key financial agents making markets and their effects on socioeconomic inequality, I designed a methodology that combined immersion with movement, broad enough to access Wall Street worldviews and practices, yet particular enough to understand how such norms were constituted on a daily basis within particular institutions. Given that the fieldwork process constitutes and constrains one's ethnographic findings (methodology is theoretical after all), in this field space, I was able to focus my study not only on "the interior lives of experts as an elite as such, but rather to understand their frame . . . a project of tracking the global, being engaged with its dynamics from their orienting point of view" (Holmes and Marcus 2005, 248).

Partly planned and partly fortuitous, my access to Wall Street lifeworlds resulted from exploring and combining multiple sites and techniques of fieldwork, similar to what Hugh Gusterson has called "polymorphous engagement." He de-emphasizes participant observation as an often impossible method in studying up. Instead, he writes, the ethnography of the powerful needs to consist of "interacting with informants across a number of dispersed sites, not just in local communities, and sometimes in virtual form; and it means collecting data eclectically from a disparate array of sources in many different ways [such as] . . . formal interviews . . . extensive reading of newspapers and official documents . . . careful attention to popular culture," as well as informal social events outside of the actual corporate office or laboratory (Gusterson 1997, 116). This is not to say that immersion is no longer an indispensable anthropological staple in a varied toolkit; rather, such a methodology has been constituted via particular ways of imaging culture and the proper anthropological subject. The very notion of "pitching tent" at the Rockefellers' yard, in the lobby of J. P. Morgan, or on the floor of the New York Stock Exchange is not only implausible but also might be limiting and ill-suited to a study of "the power elite."[21]

Although I was able to incorporate substantial participant observation during fieldwork, the majority occurred during "prefieldwork" since I did not (nor was it my goal to) obtain investment banks' official permission to "hang out" within their workplaces. Such a strategy would have led me directly to their public relations office. During "actual" fieldwork, I relied mainly on interviews, some "shadowing," and attendance at industry conferences, panel discussions, formal networking events, and informal social events. The circumstances, connections, and affiliations that allowed (as well as circumscribed) my access to potential informants are instructive to lay out. First, because of my job at BT and subsequent experience of downsizing, I had little trouble creating a sizeable network of informants, especially through the process of direct referral. Employing this method through Wall Street insiders might normally have led me to a rather homogenous, mainly white male crowd. But, as it happened, I was a member of the internal management consulting group (MCG), one of the most diverse departments in the front and middle offices of BT. The head of MCG was an African American managing director who made a concerted effort to build a group with half women and one-third people of color. My coworkers' referrals often reflected this diversity. For example, through our head, I met Thomas Douglass, an African American managing director at BT who in turn introduced me to Corey Fisher, an African American managing director at Vanguard Investments, and Roy Allen, a white managing director at Fidelity Investments. Julie Cooper was a former white associate in my internal management consulting group, yet when we were all downsized, she secured a job in the high-yield investment banking division and introduced me to her entire team, which included John Carlton, a white managing director, Christine Chang, an Asian American vice president, and Chris Logan, a white analyst. Luckily, these connections often snowballed.

I also relied on alumni and friendship networks. While at Stanford, my social network did not include many business types, but I was actively involved in Ethnic Studies organizing as well as various Asian American student organizations. I also lived in both the Asian American and African American issues "theme" dorms. As such, I had over the years formed a handful of fairly close relationships (on my own and through friends) with a few professional Asian American and African American informants such as Joseph Tsai, associate at Donaldson, Lufkin and Jenrette (DLJ), Malinda Fan, senior vice president at Lehman Brothers, Joannie Trinh, an associate at Morgan Stanley, Raina Bennett, an analyst at Lehman Brothers, and Jason Kedd, an associate at DLJ. Many of them referred me to their bosses (most of whom were white), as I was eager to hear from more senior bankers, as well as their friends (many of whom were quite diverse). Unfortunately, at Princeton, despite the fact that almost 40 percent of the undergraduates go to work on Wall Street, as a graduate student I hardly knew any of them. Furthermore, since Princeton does not have a business school, I was unable to network via the MBA program, and since most of my Stanford acquaintances had not yet finished business school in the late 1990s, I could not tap into a potentially rich network of elite MBA graduates—although, for example, Jason Kedd did introduce me to two of his Harvard Business School classmates who worked in investment banking. There were of course acquaintances of mine from both Stanford and Princeton who knew me as a student activist and feminist studies/anthropology major and were suspicious of my research: one had established a vast network of Wall Street investment bankers, but proved reluctant to help.

My attempts at "cold-call" socializing with investment bankers while living in New York City were hit and miss. In some cases, I found some affinity with fellow Asian American women and men, especially those who were struggling with issues of what it meant to be an Asian American professional (expectations of upward mobility, relative class privilege, racial discrimination and stereotyping at work, bicultural identity formations), and they often agreed to be interviewed. In other cases, I left large events or conferences with rich, informal anecdotes gained from chatting, yet no one had been willing or able to sit down for further conversation. In one unexpected encounter that happened while volunteering for an economic justice organization in New York City, I met a white feminist minister whose partner, Jacob Carnoy, used to work on Wall Street. It turned out that he had graduated from Princeton in the 1980s and offered to introduce me to "fellow Princeton grads" such as two senior investment bankers at Goldman Sachs who, according to him, were "complaining that they only made 20 million that year." Unfortunately, I was only able to converse with them via e-mail. Finally, through my participation in SEO (Sponsors for Educational Opportunity, which focused on supporting minorities from elite campuses to enter investment banking and management consulting) conferences, I became close friends with a small network of young African American investment bankers. Through these various interconnections and chance encounters, I was able to assemble a diverse financial crowd at multiple levels of the Wall Street hierarchy. Around 40 percent of my informants were people of color, with a slim majority of them men.

As I have footnoted, all of my informants have been given pseudonyms, and although I struggled with whether or not to disguise the financial institutions themselves, I ultimately decided not to. First, this project focuses on Wall Street investment banking culture broadly conceived; as such, I am interested in general ethnographic data, not information on specific banks that might be considered proprietary. Furthermore, precisely because I seek to confront and unpack powerful globalizing institutions that also claim to speak for the markets and corporate America, it makes sense to name these institutions and call attention to their pronouncements, strategies, and influence, as I do with the speeches and announcements by Wall Street CEOs and senior management made during major events and conferences covered by the press. It is also instructive to note that providing pseudonyms for Wall Street financial institutions is practically a futile exercise given the prevalent cultural norms of the financial market where corporate names statuses, and identities constantly shift over time. For example, in 1997, Dean Witter Discover, a retail brokerage, merged with prestigious investment bank Morgan Stanley to form Morgan Stanley Dean Witter Discover; yet, by 2001, to reclaim prestige and name recognition, the firm, which had already dropped the name "Discover," renamed itself Morgan Stanley.

Shareholder Value, Decentering Privileged Models and Histories, and the Politics of Ethnographic Representation

When I rode the subway to the field,[22] determined not to allow "the study of the stock market" to be "left to economists" (Hertz 1998, 16), I was bombarded by images and representations of the United States as a nation of stockholders and investors, and of the stock market as a populist site of economic empowerment for all Americans. President Bill Clinton gave numerous speeches about the "New Economy," locating our unprecedented national prosperity on the shoulders of the longest bull market in history and on the fact that more Americans owned stocks than in any other time (albeit largely through pension and retirement funds). The White House's figures for stock market ownership hovered around 150 million Americans, and the rising stock market was seen as a primary indicator of the improved economic lives of most Americans. A cover of *Fortune* magazine in 1999 proclaimed America "a Trader Nation": "At work, at home, all day, all night: Everybody wants a piece of the stock market." Inside, the article claims that "there's a revolution under way, and it's changing the way we invest and work and live. Our money is no longer with some broker or fund manager. Our money is with ourselves" (Serwer 1999, 116). We see an illustration of four fists, three clutching computer mice, tearing down a sign that reads, "Wall St." Such representations of "revolutions" were rampant in the late 1990s (Serwer 1999, 118).

In Wall Street's new rhetoric of market populism via shareholder value, "each mass-market success by a bank or brokerage [was declared] a victory for a democratic 'revolution'" (Frank 2000, 125). To take just one example, Thomas Frank describes how E*Trade appropriated the language and imagery of the civil rights and feminist movements. "In its 1999 annual report, entitled 'From One Revolution to the Next', E*Trade used photos of black passengers sitting in the back of a bus," with a caption reading "They Said Equality Was Only For Some of Us" to signal their role in the destruction of exclusionist and elitist Wall Street and the mass triumph of the individual investor (Frank 2000, 91). Wall Street thus allied itself with the "common people," constructing a pro-Wall Street populism and incorporating the disenfranchised into a cool new image opposed to its older, stodgier self.

In parallel, I also encountered Jesse Jackson's "Wall Street Project," a division of his Rainbow/PUSH coalition based in New York City, articulating a strategy of incorporating African-Americans and other excluded groups into the stock market. This project, founded in 1997, began as a coalition challenging Wall Street on three fronts: diversity and representation in corporate America and on Wall Street, stock market democratization, and access to capital for "inner cities" and Appalachia.[23] In his speech at the Wall Street Project Conference held at the World Trade Center in 1999, Jackson posed the question, "Why are African Americans continuing to 'invest' in the bear lotto when they need to be included as participants in the bull market? Why are our youths buying hundred dollar Nike shoes instead of Nike stock?"[24]

Perhaps not so ironically, it was precisely at the moment when Jackson advocated the incorporation of marginalized communities into the so-called shareholder value revolution that my Wall Street informants began to suspect the impending burst of the bubble. Many subscribed to the old Wall Street adage: When cab drivers start asking for investment advice and stock picks, its time to get out of the market. As Wall Streeters understand it, by the time stock market knowledge seeps to the masses, the bull market has turned into a bubble economy. This assumption only makes sense, of course, if success in the stock market depends on a delicate balance of insider knowledge, market hype, and timing.[25] Wall Street, then, views the democratization of stock market participation as a bellwether of oversubscription and as a signal for insiders to sell, meaning "latecomers" to the market tend to bear the brunt of crashes.

Despite Wall Street's and corporate America's proclamations about putting shareholders' interests above all other constituencies of the corporation, the very practices that constitute the shareholder value repertoire do not necessarily enrich owners of corporate stock or empower shareholders to make corporate management decisions. On 25 February 2002, chronicling the continued dot-com stock market bust, *Business Week* ran a cover story on "The Betrayed Investor," which documented how the "true believers" in the stock market—the new investor class of the 1990s, comprised of "predominantly middle-class, suburban baby boomers"—had lost "$5 trillion, or 30% of their stock wealth since the spring of 2000" and were now beginning to doubt that the stock market "treats average investors fairly" (Vickers and McNamee 2002, 105).[26] The quintessential case is Enron, where shareholder value was proclaimed by Enron senior executives, Wall Street investment banks, and accounting firms such as Arthur Anderson as the central goal, yet their actions mainly benefited themselves. To keep the stock price "artificially" high, top management, who were paid via stock options (and sold their shares before the crash using inside information), worked with investment banks, who received millions in advisory and transaction fees, to find and invent new financial structures and "hypothetical transactions" to both project windfall profits and keep the massive debts off the balance sheet. When Enron imploded, not only did employees lose their jobs and savings, but the investing "public," that is, the shareholders, lost an estimated $200 billion (McClean and Elkind 2003).

If the shareholder value revolution was not sustainably enriching the average investor, who may also have been facing unemployment as his or her 401(k) appreciated a few hundred dollars (if that), then was Wall Street not increasing the stock price of corporations—their stated central mission? When I worked at BT, I certainly heard of corporations drastically cutting costs, whereupon their quarterly earnings and stock prices immediately jumped, but research and development suffered, productivity gains were negligible, and shareholder value over a longer time horizon did not increase and even declined. But it was during fieldwork that the full contradictions of shareholder value hit home.

To return to my earlier discussion of AT&T: the little-known backstory to the massive breakup of AT&T in 1995 was the disastrous acquisition of National Cash Register (NCR). This prehistory is crucial because four years prior in 1991, AT&T, also under the advisement of Morgan Stanley (a connection buried after the failure of this deal), acquired NCR in a hostile takeover for $7.4 billion (Zuckerman 1995). This aggressive act not only generated massive downsizings and insecurity in NCR's hometown of Dayton, Ohio (once a stable, thriving "company town"), but was also an utter disaster for AT&T, which "lost a half-billion dollars in the first nine months of 1995 alone" (Rimer 1996). In a desperate move to push up its stock price, CEO Robert Allen decided to spin off the ill-conceived purchase of NCR in the "trivestiture" of 1995. Yet, by 1997, less than two years after this "bold" breakup, AT&T's stock was performing dismally, trading at $33.625 a share. Allen stepped down in the face of persistent questions about the profitability of long-distance service in the new economy, which the restructurings in 1991 and 1995 did not address but exacerbated. Allen, however, continued to defend "the breakup on the grounds that AT&T unlocked almost $40 billion in shareholder value," insisting that "the whole idea was to avoid [its] destruction" (Landler 1997).

Morgan Stanley's advice, intended to bolster shareholder value, actually damaged AT&T's stock price in the long run, despite the fact that this deal making helped to generate an explosion of wealth for shareholders primed to cash out during the short-term price spikes. It is important to remember that investment bankers always receive high compensation for the deal *no matter the result*. The higher the risk, the bigger the deal, the more radical the change, the more money Wall Street makes, even though a merger or restructuring of a large company is precisely the kind of transaction that leads to a deterioration of long-term shareholder value. Many mergers have failed to deliver the expected profits due to unforeseen difficulties in integrating the companies.[27]

Despite the missteps that AT&T had taken under the advice of Morgan Stanley, in 1998, Credit Suisse First Boston (CSFB) and Goldman Sachs advised new AT&T CEO Michael Armstrong in the acquisition of TCI *and* the subsequent purchase of MediaOne, both among the largest cable television and modem companies in the United States. These deals were both named "Merger of the Year" by Wall Street trade magazine *Investment Dealer's Digest* (for 1998 and 1999, respectively). Although AT&T's acquisition spree in the late 1990s is generally blamed as much on the trigger-happy, "acquisitive" Armstrong as on his Wall Street advisors, it is crucial to note that the investment banks made over $100 million on these mergers, and that by 2000, AT&T announced that it would once again split into four separate companies, thereby breaking up and undoing the previous two years (Stokes 2000; Waters 1999). Scott Cleland, "telecommunications analyst at . . . an independent research firm," called the deals "a multibillion-dollar oops" (Hiltzik 2001). Armstrong spent over $112 billion in acquisitions and expansions, yet by 2002 had losses of $60 billion to show for it. AT&T's stock was at $13.51 in 2002, "well below their 1999 high of $49.77," and by April 2004, the once-storied AT&T was actually delisted from the Dow Jones Industrial Average (S. Lynch 2004).

A central question for this book, then, becomes: why do Wall Street investment banks continually fail to achieve their raison d'être? How can investment bankers do what they do and engage in seemingly irrational practices, such as proclaiming shareholder value while engaging in actions that not only undermine it but produce corporate and financial market crisis? How does shareholder value maintain cultural legitimacy despite the inconsistencies and failures of its champions?

Addressing such questions is complicated by dilemmas in ethnographic representation and methodology encountered when studying the powerful. For example, part of the crisis of representation and the turn toward greater anthropological reflexivity was the realization that anthropologists were unable to see "the objects of social analysis" (usually the marginalized) as "also analyzing subjects"; furthermore, ethnographers did not sufficiently locate or recognize their gaze, influence, or dominant authorship (Rosaldo 1989, 207). These historical mistakes, however, only make sense with a "typical" power configuration in mind, such as that of the Western white upper-middle-class male anthropologist studying the less-powerful "native" in the context of the colonial and postcolonial encounter. Underlying this politics of representation is the notion of the invisible expert and the marked subject. To rectify these mistakes, many anthropologists, in their attempts to "give voice" to their subjects, "run the risk of merely shifting the burden of representation from the anthropologist to the subject," making the representations of subjects the "privileged 'reality'" (Yanagisako 2002, 48). Given the historical imbalance between the native's voice and that of the ethnographer, this strategy is understandable. However, when one is studying the powerful, this approach is no longer appropriate, as it can overprivilege the informant.

My informants' representational power, influential models, historical interpretations, and prolific theorizing on capitalism, markets, and globalization rendered their voices loud and clear, even in relation to the anthropologist studying them. The task is *not* simply to "recognize" Wall Streeters as subjects acting in the world, but rather to situate and critique Wall Street worldviews in relation to other cultural models, histories, and voices. For instance, throughout much of my fieldwork, I was myself entranced by Wall Street's dominant model of shareholder value. Delving into the intricacies of bankers' proclamations and explanations of shareholder value as objects of importance in and of themselves, I did not always locate these discourses within the corporate culture through which they speak. Eventually I came to realize that Wall Street investment banks do not so much enact an ideal or model of shareholder value as perform a particular version of it, mediated through their corporate culture and experiences as investment bankers—one that in many cases actually undermines their very proclamations of shareholder value.

Similarly, I found that part of what imbues the presentist shareholder value ideal with such explanatory power is its rootedness in dominant historical narratives that legitimize Wall Street's identity as guardian of shareholder value and empower its role and practice in shaping corporate America.[28] The use of shareholder value is part and parcel of a broader project of laying claim to a restorative narrative of entitlement and succession, through which Wall Street investment bankers have been able to define their professed beneficial social contributions to our economy. Wall Street cultural legitimacy and shareholder value are naturalized through "origin myths," particular interpretations of neoclassical economic thought, and investment banking histories of shareholder rights.

Specifically, my informants viewed themselves as gatherers and purveyors of the capital that forms the foundations and enables the growth and expansion of our largest corporations and public and private works. Not surprisingly, much of the academic literature on Wall Street, in disciplines ranging from business administration to law, replicate and perpetuate investment bankers' assumptions about themselves and the history of their profession. The presumption is that investment banks financed the very creation of the U.S. corporate system and have throughout history been the primary suppliers of fresh capital to maintain and expand it. So ingrained are these notions that even the project of delineating "what Wall Street actually does" proved a much more intricate endeavor than I had realized precisely because most of the literature (popular, "native," and academic) about Wall Street is framed by this dominant, taken-for-granted narrative of its roles and responsibilities, one which relies on a particular interpretation of American corporate and financial history. Michael Jensen's idealized portrait of investment bankers in *The Financiers* (1976) is indicative of mainstream culture's approach to Wall Street as both highly secretive and esoteric as well as crucially important for the functioning of our capitalist system:

> They are the elite of Wall Street. Their offices are furnished with expensive antiques and original works of art. They dress in conservatively cut $500 suits, and are as quick to place a telephone call to Rome or Zurich or Frankfurt as most Americans are to call their next-door neighbor. . . . They engineer multimillion dollar transactions and, although they render middleman services only, enough money remains in their hands to make them the richest wage earners in the world. They are the investment bankers of Wall Street; the men who raise billions in cash for America's giant corporations. . . . Unknown to the general public, as dissimilar to the neighborhood savings banker as Harold Geneen of ITT is to the owner of a neighborhood delicatessen, the investment banker is an invisible man. Most Americans have only the vaguest notion of what he does. . . . His art is arcane. But just as the rainmaker promised to draw from the sky the drops that nourished the farmers' crops, so these latter-day rainmakers draw from the people and institutions around them the dollars

that are needed to build the nation's factories. . . . What is investment banking? Simply the art of raising money for a client. (Jensen 1976, 1–2)

One of the key ways in which Wall Street investment bankers control their
present and future representation as a fountain of capital that "build[s]
the nation's factories" is to strengthen their hold on the past. Such a
storied role allows them to spin the pursuit of seemingly selfish goals as,
in the end, a force for social good, arguing that the incentive of personal
gain leads to an efficient economy, greater innovation, and better jobs.

To address the inconsistencies, failures, and ramifications of Wall Street
investment banks' approach to shareholder value while paying attention
to its explanatory power necessitates a multiprong approach that decen-
ters the models, histories, and discourses of Wall Street. First, to inter-
rogate the gaps in their dominant models of shareholder value, it is crucial
to build on research in social studies of finance on the mundane cultural
details and failures of finance, as well as on finance's productive effects
and the (often unpredictable) relationship between financial models and
their instantiation (J. Guyer 2004; Maurer 2002; Miyazaki 2003, 2006;
Miyazaki and Riles 2005; MacKenzie 2006). As Jane Guyer (2004, 4)
points out, "people's exchanges" are not only constructed out of "essential
or archetypical" models or transactions, but also through "popular con-
ventions" and "market experience," thus the importance of examining the
interface between model and effect. As Hirokazu Miyazaki and Annelise
Riles (2005, 320) observe, given the "series of high-profile financial failures" and continued examples of financial market collapse, for "market
participants," "the failure of economic knowledge to predict, plan, and
regulate the market seems self-evident." The question for my purposes,
however, is *how and why* my informants continually construct failure, not
only against their own stated values of shareholder value, but also in such
a way that promotes and validates their own job insecurity.

Drawing from the scholarship on models and performativity in social
studies of finance also allows for the productive analysis of both the
powerful influence *and* the failures of shareholder value and other dominant models and ideals on Wall Street. Given that these theories and
models are "our culture's most authoritative forms of knowledge of financial markets," it is crucial to interrogate *how* they perform and what they
actually do in the world (MacKenzie 2006, 275). Donald MacKenzie and
Bill Maurer point out that financial models, in my case the ideal of shareholder value, both shape the construction of markets *and* have their limitations. "Keeping performativity in mind reminds us also to ask: if the

model is adopted and used widely, what will its effects be?" Further, are these models "accurate" and "what sort of a world do we want to see performed" (MacKenzie 2006, 275; Maurer 2006)? Given the limits of the shareholder value model and the gap between the ideal and the effects, my approach to shareholder value inquires what other financial cultural values and norms, beyond the "most authoritative" and dominant, shape Wall Street investment banks' restructuring of corporate America and financial markets.

Second, to directly investigate why and how these particular representations of Wall Street hold such explanatory and naturalizing power, I approach Wall Street historiographies of shareholder entitlement and Wall Street's conception of itself as fundraiser to the world as origin myths, indicative of a particular worldview and socioeconomic interest rather than objective statements of fact. Articulating the relationship between myth and social practice, Bronislaw Malinowski (1948, 96) writes that "an intimate connection exists between the word, the mythos, the sacred tales of a tribe, on the one hand, and their ritual acts, their moral deeds, their social organization, and even their practical activities, on the other." I document how Wall Street, through strategic alignments with long-standing neoclassical desires entrenched in American cultural norms, evokes nostalgia to construct a "restoration" narrative central to its "rightful" succession.

In a similar vein, to particularize Wall Street voices and global claims and decenter their realities, I analyze investment bankers' narratives of shareholder value alongside the narratives of those in the business community who have historically struggled with Wall Street's finance-centric approach to corporations.[29] Delineating the differences and contestations *between* capitalists serves as a foil to better situate and historicize investment bankers' universalizing and taken-for-granted assumptions. By examining the contestations between competing capitalist worldviews and practices of the postwar era, I write against assumptions of a singular, static, totalizing capitalist worldview, promulgated by homogenous capitalists. In her ethnography of Italian capitalist family firms, Yanagisako points out that in studies of the powerful who have considerable access to interpretive control over the terrain of meaning and self-representation, it is pivotal to go beyond their "official" versions in order to "supplement, challenge, and interpret" their dominant and authoritative discourses with other understandings.[30] At issue in the task of "describing" Wall Street is why particular narratives and social groups have come to be dominant and what is at stake in their varying visions of the world.

Finally, the politics of ethnographically representing and interpreting the powerful goes beyond decentering their models and histories; how their voices are methodologically accessed also shapes ethnographic findings. In a "studying up" context, for example, interviews are oftentimes the most accessible form of evidence: in my case, most of my written ethnographic data is in the form of interviews drawn from prearranged meetings with investment bankers, supplemented by field notes based on participant observations and my own experiences working on Wall Street. As such, much of my recorded fieldwork focused on the "talk" of investment bankers, which I both embrace and problematize. On the one hand, Michel de Certeau (1984, 77) writes, "If the art of speaking is itself an art of operating and an art of thinking, practice and theory can be present in it." He further explains that "stories" serve to "authorize" and "found" a set of social practices, to delimit and carve out "a theater of actions" (Certeau 1984, 123). Similarly, Teresa Caldeira (2000, 19–20, 78) demonstrates that the "talk of crime," through daily "repetition of histories" and stereotyping to "establish order in a universe that seems to have lost coherence," resignifies "segregation and exclusion as central logics of urban space and movement," reestablishes "a static picture of the world" that is "expressed in very simplistic terms, relying on the creation of clear-cut oppositional categories," and shapes "the scenario for social interactions." I argue similarly that Wall Street's narratives of shareholder value resignify the business landscape, creating an approach to corporate America that not only promotes socioeconomic inequality but also precludes a more democratic approach to corporate governance. Banker talk of shareholder value simplifies corporate history, limits others who may have claims on corporate profits, and forecloses a range of more equitable corporate practices. Just as the "talk of crime" Caldeira encountered was "not meant to describe the world accurately but to organize and classify it symbolically," bankers' shareholder value discourses do not reflect the complex histories of the struggles for corporate resources, but rather reorganize corporate history and values such that certain interests hold a monopoly on corporate decision-making and profits. Through circulation and repetition, these stories "delegitimate" the corporation as a social institution and "legitimate" the corporation as a private investment vehicle for the few (Caldeira 2000, 38).

On the other hand, the focus on privileged talk can be methodologically limiting, as it was often easy to detach what my informants said from what they did; such was the nature of interviewing powerful informants without a corresponding referent and constant access to participant observation. Focusing on the discourses, logics, justifications, and talk of shareholder value without a corresponding analysis of how investment bankers actually go through with it—the practices through which a particular version of shareholder value comes to have power—is not only ethnographically flat but also assumes the self-actualization of a self-serving model and discourse of the world. Recognizing that cultural effects and production are never as neat as their powerful, legitimating logics, I worked to include and juxtapose multiple observations, field notes, situations, and experiences—which I had access to due to the particular combination of my network, Wall Street job, and fieldwork—into the same analytic frame. I thus realized that embracing the interfaces, gaps, and frictions[31] constitutive of "worldviews-in-action" was crucial in examining the cultural productions and influence of Wall Street. Though admittedly intriguing and rewarding, having my hard-to-access informants "tell all" was only one piece of the puzzle, not the analytic goal. Given often unchallenged Wall Street discourses of shareholder value and market truths, the strength of what anthropology can contribute to unpacking Wall Street lies in its ability to demonstrate ethnographically how Wall Street's institutional practices produce experiences that then make discourses come alive, more than the other way around.

Countering Abstraction, Constructing Financial Markets, and Particularizing Global Capitalism

What would it mean for anthropology to resist top-down categories, distinctions, and definitions of what "markets," "capitalism," and "globalization" are or should be? What if anthropologists approach the market as a set of daily, embodied practices and models? Given the resurgence of neoliberal discourses and practices in the mid- to late 1990s, where "the market" (often referring to financial markets) occupies in mainstream, financial, and social-scientific understandings an increasingly dominant, globalizing, and normative space, this book examines the building blocks of these macro structures. Because Wall Street investment bankers are highly visible in terms of their own self-representations and claims to truth and authority, yet culturally invisible in terms of their everyday practices and assumptions, by directly accessing key agents of change on Wall Street, a site widely deemed the epitome of global capitalist markets, I attempt to localize the very actors and institutions with a world-making influence on the global economy, and thus on the livelihoods of many.

The push to explain the massive socioeconomic inequalities generated by new configurations of financial markets in this neoliberal moment has invigorated in anthropology an approach to understanding finance that could hinder the cultural analysis of influential financial actors and reproduce power-laden assumptions about the "winners" and "losers" in the global economy. By taking as central the assumption that finance capital is abstract and abstracting—that is, separated and decontextualized from concrete lived realities, in turn shaping and corroding social relations in mystifying ways—we run the risk of allowing elite players in the global economy even more space to define and decipher our socioeconomic lives (see Gregory 1998; Tsing 2000a). Of course, it is crucial to remember that anthropologists have long been at the forefront of culturalizing the economy, in particular critiquing neoclassical economic theories as narrow ideological models divorced from and unable to represent the on-the-ground complexities of economic reality, especially in "non-Western" societies (Dalton 1961; Dilley 1992; Gudeman 1986; Sahlins 1972). This legacy stems in large part from the work of Karl Polanyi, who challenged the "'economistic fallacy' of liberal economic thinking, in which market relations . . . come to be viewed as universal models of human conduct," and argued that economic practices are embedded in social networks, relations, and institutions (Slater and Tonkiss 2001, 94). The multiple dichotomies, however, upon which Polanyi and many social scientists after him rested their analyses continue to have reverberating effects. Whereas nonmarket, premodern economies are assumed to be embedded in social relations, markets in modern industrial society are frequently imagined as operating according to formal and abstract economistic models. In this formulation, binaries of concrete/abstract, embedded/disembedded, and culture/economy are implicit and perpetuated.

Recent anthropological and sociological works have challenged many of these taken-for-granted dichotomies, demonstrating that economic practices take place in complex webs of social relations, which change in form and degree over time. Just as "nonmarket" gift exchanges are characterized by a high degree of formal calculation, "market economies are more fully embedded in social networks than Polanyi's strict separation allows" (Slater and Tonkiss 2001, 101).[32] The "actual practice[s] of economies" defy top-down notions of market: "high finance is largely concerned with personalities, private perks and little interest groups, prestige, imagination, almost anything but what might be called a market" (D. Miller 2002, 224, 228). Also, anthropological investigations of "the free market" have deconstructed the concept of the market in Western culture, demonstrating how market ideology in the West is intimately tied to British and American notions of individualism, property, and neoclassical economics (Carrier 1997).

Despite these important contributions, given the rise of neoliberalism and its resurgent representations of abstracting and globalizing markets, many scholars, especially when referring to Western money and finance, revert back to our legacy of binary assumptions where the financial dominance of investment banks are often attributed to abstract, all-powerful global markets. In moments when finance and the stock market are the ruling paradigms of capitalist practice, many academic critics of market fundamentalism inadvertently take as foundational the notion that the economy has become "disembedded" from society, that financial market logics—as utopian ideals—are being used to abstractly shape social relations, leading to social violence and inequality on a global scale (Arrighi 1996; LiPuma and Lee 2004; McMichael 1998). Neoliberal actors and institutions are restructuring social worlds according to virtual economic models which privilege elite institutions and transnational corporations (Carrier and Miller 1998).[33] Taken to the extreme, these narratives of money and finance predict a homogenized and reductionist "global" world where the complexities of "local" social relations are narrowed to, and judged against, an abstract and singular bottom line, where the world is remade in the image of financial logics. I describe these academic critiques of neoliberalism as "neoliberal exceptionalism," where the confrontation with conditions of socioeconomic inequality encourages scholars to privilege distant logics over particularity and grounded cultural analysis, which (ironically) overempowers neoliberalism.

So, what is at stake in these evolutionary narratives of increasing abstraction? Overarching scripts of universalizing financial logics and capitalist globalization not only obscure the heterogeneous particularities of Wall Street practices and effects and prevent the interrogation of Wall Street investment banks' hegemonic claims, but also ironically parallel the marketing schemes and hyped representations of Wall Street capitalist promoters.[34] Recent innovative research in social studies of finance, by taking as their subjects (and objects) of study key sites in the construction and globalization of financial markets, have been central in addressing these dominant rubrics by making powerful actors in finance culturally knowable and embedded in novel forms of sociality.[35] Bill Maurer (2006, 15, 19) rightly points out that the notion of money as abstract and deracinating is a dominant "Western folk theory" and in analyzing markets, money, and finance, "anthropology . . . too often repeats the same story of the 'great transformation' from socially embedded to disembedded to abstracted economic forms." Demonstrating the naturalization of this logic in the narrative of money, Maurer writes: "The story of money is repeatedly told in venues scholarly and popular as an evolutionary tale of greater and greater distance from actual things, of greater dematerialization, in a linear trajectory from barter to metal coin, to paper backed by metal, to paper declared valuable by fiat, and finally, perhaps to complex financial entities like derivatives, with future, not anterior, backing" (Maurer 2005, 100). Similarly, Hirokazu Miyazaki and Annelise Riles (2005, 321) have observed that the scholarly preoccupation with "the mystique of finance" has prevented giving "ethnographic attention to the mundane quality of the mundane." Given that finance and money may be anthropology's "new exotic," demonstrating the quotidian particularities and insufficiencies of finance becomes all the more crucial (Maurer 2006, 18).

Put simply, allowing finance to be simply abstract lets it off the hook. I make the case that massive corporate restructurings are not caused so much by abstract financial models as by the local, cultural habitus of investment bankers, the mission-driven narratives of shareholder value, and the institutional culture of Wall Street. While I am sympathetic to explanations of corporate downsizing and rampant job insecurity as the intensification of abstraction, my intervention is to demonstrate that what seems like abstraction can actually be culturally decoded. Critics resorting to abstraction are well reminded not only of our own legacy (of binaries) but also that of neoclassical economics, where there is the "attachment of great value to detachment; in its passion for dispassionate analysis" (Nelson 1998, 78). At the level of ethnographic interpretation, it is crucial to recognize that a finance capital-led version of capitalism, which privileges downsizing, stock price, and market crisis, is perhaps not so much about disembedding as it is about power relations and unequal clashes of differently valued social domains with diverging visions of the world. But I first want to recognize that abstraction is a powerful explanatory tool in light of pressing social problems.

There seems to be little question that particular economic measures from prices to interest rates to the Dow Jones industrial averages shape our lives, that powerful knowledge producers from financial economists to corporate executives to Wall Street bankers have over the past two decades used and relied even more heavily on these indicators to make top-down decisions about jobs and policies. Tackling these profound changes, anthropologist James Carrier explains that abstract neoclassical economics, armed with greater institutional power, is engaged in "the conscious attempt to make the real world conform to the virtual image." It is precisely this "move to greater abstraction and virtualism" in economic thought that is creating a prescriptive model for reality, a "virtual reality" that is reductive, dislocating, and divorced from responsible and engaged social relationships (Carrier 1998, 2, 5, 8; Carrier and Miller 1998). Specifically, given that we now live in a business environment where corporate decisions are based less on strategic knowledge produced within the organization on the ground, but rather are dictated by financial measures, stock prices, and the expectations of Wall Street investment banks, does not abstraction seem like the appropriate diagnosis?[36] As Carrier (1998, 4) claims, "It is not too far-fetched to see the disaggregation of firms and the increasing use of outsourcing and temporary workers as a kind of disembedding, for economic activities that had occurred within the structure of the firm and the durable employment and institutional relations contained within it, move outside and are acquired through relatively more impersonal and transient market relationships." These examples do seem to demonstrate that "external" forces, "disembedded" from local and organizational contexts, with allegiances only to abstract financial markers like stock price and profit accumulation, are not only loosening social ties but also generating conditions of supreme socioeconomic inequality by obliterating any concern for the daily lives and dilemmas of everyday people.

Part of my argument here is that the construction—the feeling—of abstraction is absolutely about power and hierarchy in that powerful changes stemming from very different values, priorities, and interests "feel like" the triumph of a penetrating, alien abstraction from the point of view of the marginalized. For example, many downsized workers have argued that the stock price is just one value among many, and that other values such as a stable job and the American Dream are more important. From the stance of the disenfranchised, financial parameters like the stock price are understood as *overtaking* other values and affecting differently positioned people unequally. The unequal conflict between the priorities and agendas of the powerful versus the powerless, not to mention the dismissal, may in turn be experienced as being "turned into a dollar sign from above," yet such a phenomenon is perhaps better explained as the social effect of concrete manifestations of power relations, not abstraction.

Similarly, when one directly interrogates the powerful, what gets dubbed as abstract is about very particular values, interests, and origin myths.

From my natives' point of view, their use of stock prices as the primary measure of evaluating corporations is not about heralding abstraction, but about reclaiming the "rightful" capitalist unity between ownership (of stock) and control over corporations that had been sundered during the heyday of managerial, "welfare" capitalism, which in turn fosters the values of responsibility, efficiency, and individual proprietorship. Fixation on the stock price is a mission-driven cause, not a cold abstraction, that counters and overcomes the wrongful allocation of capital. Representing a host of values, shareholder value allows bankers to translate their particular values into a number, which acts as its own explanatory force. It is a discursive strategy used by powerful financial institutions to articulate their vision of the world and fight for their elite interests by utilizing a shareholder value worldview to impose short-term, financial market-based decision-making on corporations. Simultaneously, shareholder value, Wall Street investment bankers' central worldview, is often not enacted or actualized. While I would argue that downsizing workers based on stock prices is not about liquidating local values for the sake of abstract numbers, I would also make the case that Wall Street does not downsize based only on stock prices: other models and cultural and institutional norms are at play.

Given that on Wall Street, financial models are not fully actualized in practice, the interstitial space between "virtual" models and its "real" effects is a crucial analytical site. The heated academic debate between Michel Callon and Daniel Miller is instructive here. Callon has suggested that the models and theories of financial economics are not virtual, as Miller claims, but "real" in the sense that economic practices actually perform and enact "homo economicus" on a daily basis. Economic practice socially constructs the kinds of conditions and frames which allow economic thought to be actualized. In this vein, Callon (1998) refuses the dichotomies of abstraction/real. I would argue, however, that both Callon and Miller take as their defining assumption either the distance or lack thereof between economics and markets, between theory and practice. Whereas interpretations along the lines of Callon and Miller might see the current dominance of shareholder value as evidence *either* that homo economicus now exists, as financial economics has converged with market practices, *or* that market mechanisms have abstracted social relations according to virtual, utopian capitalist fantasies, I demonstrate that economic ideals are neither wholly performed and instantiated into reality *nor* virtual substitutions for "real life complexity." Analyzing what Wall Street investment bankers actually enact necessitates attention to the interface between virtual and real, model and effect, as well as the existence of other key cultural contexts that would influence this interaction.

When Wall Street's actions in the world are framed and translated as "people got downsized because of stock prices" or shrugged off because "markets crash," investment banking practices are represented and interpreted as abstract, cordoning "the market" off from social decisions. Socioeconomic dislocations are less cases of abstraction than instances of power being experienced and enacted. When conflicts between unequal values and interests are interpreted mainly in terms of abstraction, which in turn is refracted back as a core characteristic of finance, such assumptions further obfuscate the task of grounding Wall Street actors.

This discussion of abstraction and power is incomplete without an analogy to the power of whiteness as a racial construct. Richard Dyer (1997, 38–39) has written that one of the central markers of white identity is "the attainment of a position of disinterest—abstraction, distance, separation, objectivity." Yet, while privileging the notion of universality, abstraction, and invisibility, whiteness paradoxically also claims individuality, a particular display of spirit and character, as well as a sort of privileged "race." Dyer (1997, 39) argues that the representational power of whiteness—its flexibility, productivity, covetedness, and exclusivity—stems from its ability "to be everything and nothing, literally overwhelmingly present and yet apparently absent." Not surprisingly, part of the discursive power of the financial market is precisely its representation as abstract, its seeking to be everywhere and claiming to be nowhere *coupled with* its particular mission and claims to freedom, democracy, property, and prosperity. Market power thrives on this representational flexibility: though its beneficiaries can emerge as an interest group when necessary, usually this kind of power is cloaked in its abstraction and universality. It is instructive to compare, then, Dyer's claim that the power of whiteness can be challenged by "locating and embodying it in a particular experience of being white" (Dyer 1997, 4). In this ethnography, I intervene against the flexible and productive power of markets by rendering it concrete and by demonstrating that investment banking decisions and the very experiences of the investment bankers themselves are thoroughly informed by cultural values and the social relations of race, gender, and class. I hope to portray a Wall Street shot through with embodiment, color, and particularity.

The dual work of studying ethnographically the globalization of capital markets and the values and strategies of financial actors is to both recognize their power and demonstrate their locality and instability, even their fragility.[37] On the one hand, I emphasize the location of Wall Street practices in the United States and how specific investment banking subjectivities and actions work to produce American hegemony through their brand of finance. As such, Wall Street finance is distinct from global finance, and the interests of the United States, though powerful and globalizing, should not be conflated with those of the world. On the other hand, investment bankers and banks located in the United States often do *claim* the entire globe: they effect rippling, global changes and self-represent themselves as the ultimate global actors promoting global capitalism. As Douglas Holmes and George Marcus (2005, 237) write, the "contemporary system of technocratic expertise . . . conceives and produces the idea of the global as daily practice. Central banks operate not merely under the sway of fast-capitalism; they have played a direct role in creating and mediating it."

Of course, although these actors do strongly shape social relations, part of the project of localizing Wall Street involves emphasizing the hype, miscalculations, and discrepancies of global strategies and practices, especially given the central role that boastings of global reach and power play in the self-representations of investment bankers.[38] We can acknowledge the global spread and influence of Wall Street's investment banking practices and worldviews without assuming that the actors' plans are flawlessly conceived and executed. As Michael Fischer points out, the global is "polycentric": however homogenizing, it is multiply situated, dynamic, local, and productive of odd ethnographic juxtapositions (Fischer 2003). Experts and cultures of expertise can make blunders, spinmeisters can fall prey to spin, and masters of the universe can be undermined by hubris. My approach to Wall Street investment bankers writes against this tendency to attribute infallibility and necessity to their cultural practices by investigating the fragilities of market practices and the inconsistencies of expert opinions, especially instances when encompassing global logics of shareholder value break down. It is precisely this global confidence in their capabilities that allows them the freedom to act unimpeded.

1

Biographies of Hegemony:

The Culture of Smartness and

the Recruitment and Construction of

Investment Bankers

When I began to conduct fieldwork in 1998 and 1999, delving into the network of contacts, coworkers, and friends I developed at Stanford, Princeton, and Bankers Trust (BT), it struck me how often my informants ranked and distinguished themselves according to their "smartness." The term seemed fundamental to the Wall Street lexicon. My informants proclaimed that the smartest people in the world came to work there; Wall Street, in their view, had created probably the most elite work-society ever to be assembled on the globe. Almost all the front-office workers that I encountered emphasized how smart their coworkers were, how "deep the talent" was at their particular bank, how if one just hired "the smartest people," then everything else fell into place. Chris Logan and Nicolas Bern, recent Princeton graduates working at BT and Merrill Lynch respectively, explained that from their relatively fresh perspective, what was most culturally unique about Wall Street was the experience of being surrounded by, as Bern put it, the "smartest and most ambitious people." Logan added that the three qualities of success on Wall Street are to be "smart, hardworking, and aggressive. Everything else is considered tangential." According to Kate Miller, a Spelman College graduate and former analyst at Morgan Stanley, interviewees are typically told they will be working with "the brightest people in the world. These are the greatest minds of the century."

Such sentiments were not confined to eager young analysts or investment banking representatives talking up their industry to overawed recruits. Julio Muñoz, who received his MBA from Harvard and was an associate in investment banking at Donaldson, Lufkin and Jenrette (DLJ), a prestigious boutique investment bank which has since been bought out by Credit Suisse First Boston (CSFB), claimed that the most distinguishing features of investment banks are their smartness and exclusivity:

> People are really smart. They really don't hire any—the hiring standards are
> pretty good. That's one thing they really focused on doing, and that differenti-
> ates investment banking from other working environments in that they really
> do target the experienced individuals with good academic background. . . .
> [This] really brings to the investment banks a very elite society—somebody in
> society that had the means to study in X universities. If you really narrowed
> down the universities where the investment banks recruit, your number prob-
> ably will not exceed fifteen to twenty universities.

Similarly, John Carlton, a senior managing director at BT who had worked
at multiple investment banks such as Kidder Peabody and CSFB, stated
that the key characteristics of Wall Street investment bankers are their
smartness, aggressiveness, and self-confidence: "There is always a premium on having smart people . . . so, it is highly competitive. What
happens is that a lot of people say, 'Look, some of the best and brightest
people are going to Wall Street. I'm pretty smart myself; I should go
[there] as well. And, by the way, I get paid very well.'" Remarking on how
hedge funds attract the most brilliant minds from investment banks,
Robert Hopkins, a vice president of mergers and acquisitions at Lehman
Brothers, exclaimed, "We are talking about the smartest people in the
world. We are! They are the smartest people in the world. If you [the
average investor or the average corporation] don't know anything, why
wouldn't you invest with the smartest people in the world? They must
know what they are doing."[1]

The "culture of smartness" is central to understanding Wall Street's
financial agency, how investment bankers are personally and institutionally empowered to enact their worldviews, export their practices, and
serve as models for far-reaching socioeconomic change. On Wall Street,
"smartness" means much more than individual intelligence; it conveys a
naturalized and generic sense of "impressiveness," of elite, pinnacle status
and expertise, which is used to signify, even prove, investment bankers'
worthiness as advisors to corporate America and leaders of the global
financial markets. To be considered "smart" on Wall Street is to be implicated in a web of situated practices and ideologies, coproduced through
the interactions of multiple institutions, processes, and American culture
at large, which confer authority and legitimacy on high finance and contribute to the sector's vast influence. The culture of smartness is not
simply a quality of Wall Street, but a currency, a driving force productive
of both profit accumulation and global prowess.

The key criterion of smartness is an ability to "wow" the clients—

generally speaking, the top executives of Fortune 500 companies. In this sense, although technical skill and business savvy also help to constitute smartness on Wall Street, they are often considered secondary, learnable "on the job." "The best," "the greatest," and "the brightest" minds in the world are sorted and recognized through a credentialing process that is crucially bolstered by image and performance. In other words, smartness must be represented and reinforced by a specific appearance and bodily technique that dominantly signals that impressiveness; not surprisingly, such characteristics as being impeccably and smartly dressed, dashing appearance, mental and physical quickness, aggressiveness, and vigor reference the default upper-classness, maleness, whiteness, and heteronormativity of ideal investment bankers. Though here I focus mainly on the specific elitism that is the key valence of smartness, in the next chapter, I further analyze "the total package" through which smartness is recognized and delivered.

What allows investment bankers to claim smartness, what defines and legitimates them as smart in the first place, and what particular kind of smartness is being deployed? Where these questions become especially clear is during the process of investment banker identity and social formation: the recruiting, training, and orientation of freshly minted college graduates and MBAs, their initiation into the world of Wall Street. Here it is possible to discern, in starkest relief, Wall Street's cultural values in action, particularly the construction and maintenance of the hegemonic elitism that produces "expert" knowledge of financial markets. Through the continual praxis of recruitment and orientation, the Street enacts and regenerates the very foundations of its legitimacy.

Through the process of recruitment and orientation, investment banks define their notion of both what it takes and what it means to be a successful subject in an age of global capital. To play the role of "master of the universe" requires not only especially strong doses of self-confidence and institutional legitimation, but also a particular set of beliefs regarding Wall Street's role in the world and one's own role on Wall Street. Investment bankers, trained to view financial markets and corporate America through particular, highly ideological lenses, are also imbued with a sense of their own personal exemplariness as agents of *and models for* socioeconomic change—a sense that must be embodied, believed in, and continually "pumped up." In approaching the question of how investment bankers become empowered to advise and influence the direction of corporations in the United States and globally vis à vis their personal trajectories, qualities, connections, associations, and identities, I make the case for the importance of the biographical and the institutional in enacting global capitalist change. The building blocks of dominant capitalist practices are also personal and cultural; people's experiences, their university and career tracking and choices, are constitutive of capitalist hegemony; and the financial is cultural through and through.

In particular, I focus on the construction of "the smart investment banker": a member of an extended "family" network of elite university alumni and a living symbol of know-how and global agency. Their impressiveness and financial influence are further cemented and proven by surviving brutally intense hard work and an insecure job environment, which in turn allows them to internalize the merit of their analyses and recommendations. Through the institutional culture of Wall Street broadly conceived—where job experiences and workplace incentives map onto elite biographies—investment bankers not only imbibe a particular ideology of shareholder value and spread it across corporate America, but they are also pushed to refashion and reconstruct the working lives of millions in the image of their own.

By investigating investment bankers, as individuals and as collective agents of change, I do not assume a priori that "the market" always already exercises power, but rather that the particular biographies, experiences, and practices of investment bankers, who are both empowered and constrained by their cultural and institutional locations, create social change and financial hegemony on a daily basis. Just as "it is through the 'small stories' that one can begin to unravel and challenge homogenizing discourses embedded within concepts such as globalization, 'the' market, and 'the' state," it is possible to decenter the market as an abstract agent and powerful force by demonstrating that it is only through the small and the everyday that we can understand the creation of hegemony in all its particularity and contextuality. Otherwise, we risk privileging, homogenizing, or taking for granted the metanarratives of the market, the big stories (Crossa 2005, 29; S. Smith 2005).

Recruitment

I first entered the cultural world of investment banks through the herculean recruiting efforts that Wall Street undertakes at the most elite universities. Despite my own ambivalence and feelings of mystification about Wall Street as an anthropology graduate student, this direct link—the pipeline between Princeton University and investment banks—enabled my very access to each step of the recruiting process, not to mention the field site itself. Wall Street, in a sense, came to me. Although I hardly recognized it at the time, Wall Street's ubiquity on campus, as well as the intensity of undergraduate interest in investment banking, meant that merely being a student at Princeton allowed, in a sense, automatic participant observation of this world. After fieldwork, I returned to Princeton to write the dissertation, thinking I would be getting away from Wall Street, retreating to an ivory-tower refuge in order to do some serious thinking and writing. Instead, it was more like reentering the belly of the beast. I was a graduate advisor at an undergraduate resident hall. Two weeks into the job, taking a walk after dinner I crossed paths with an undergraduate crowd (two of whom lived in my residence hall) headed toward Nassau Hall. Before I knew it, they had steered me into a Merrill Lynch presentation! The masses of students converging on these recruitment presentations and information sessions are akin to the campus traffic generated by the gatherings and dispersals of concert crowds. Already a veteran of the actual recruitment process back in 1996, now, almost four years later, after campus recruiting had even further intensified as a result of the bull market, I found myself participating in countless dining hall discussions about investment banking, attending still more presentations, and reading endless investment banking advertisements, updates, news, and opinion pieces in the pages of the *Daily Princetonian*. In 2000, I also had access on a regular basis to many of Wall Street's cultural representations and practices at Harvard University because my younger sister was an undergraduate there at the time. She introduced me to friends going through the recruiting process and kept me continually updated on how many of her acquaintances had suddenly, in their senior year, found their true calling as Wall Street investment bankers or management consultants. As many of my previous investment banking informants were also Harvard graduates, I have been able to make detailed observations of Wall Street's interactions with two elite universities.

More so than even the other Ivy League schools, Harvard and Princeton are the "prime recruiting ground for all of the most prestigious Wall Street, management consulting and other types of firms that offer the most sought after jobs. . . . The Princeton badge is a powerful currency that buys access" (Karseras 2006). As many of my informants have elaborated, "If you go to Harvard, Yale, or Princeton, there are really only two career fields presented: banking and consulting" (Duboff 2005). This shocking narrowness was verified throughout my time at Princeton and on Wall Street: I found not only that most bankers came from a few elite institutions, but also that most undergraduate and even many graduate students assumed that the only "suitable" destinations for life after Princeton—the only sectors offering a truly "Princeton-like job"—were, first, investment banking, and second, management consulting.[2] With its extensive alumni network and juggernaut recruitment machine, Wall Street is the "de facto home away from Princeton for recent graduates, many of whom continue living together even as they take on new responsibilities and lifestyles" (Hall 2005).

As perhaps the most important feeder school to Wall Street, Princeton sends astounding numbers of recruits into financial services in general, and in particular investment banking. According to the Office of Career Services, 30 percent of the class of 2001, 37 percent of the class of 2003, and 40 percent of the class of 2005 and 2006 entered financial services after graduation (Chan 2001; Creed 2003; Easton 2006; Henn 2001). Whereas from 2000 to 2005, 470 Princeton students pursued law or medical degrees, "520 Princeton students—about 40 percent of Princeton students choosing full-time jobs directly after graduation—decided to work in the financial services sector," amounting to the largest percentage in a single industry (Hall 2005). At Harvard University, which rivals Princeton as the primary producer of Wall Street recruits, investment banking (as well as management consulting) also provides the majority of jobs for its students upon graduation (Lerer 1997). According to Harvard's Office of Career Services, in 2005, close to half of Harvard students go through "the recruiting process to vie for investment banking and consulting jobs" (Huber 2006).

As Devon Peterson, an undergraduate writing for the *Daily Princetonian*, observed in 2002, "It's been common knowledge that many of [Princeton's] undergraduates join the financial realm every year, creating a kind of lighthearted, self-deprecating joke about Philosophy majors becoming I-bankers and once hopeful novelists heading to Wall Street" (Peterson 2002). How do so many undergraduates who enter these institutions without any prior knowledge of investment banking, who once aspired to become, say writers or teachers, "realize" by the time they graduate that they have always wanted to go to Wall Street? How do these talented and well-connected students, with access to a wide range of possible futures, come to believe that investment banking is one of the *only* prestigious job options available post graduation? I argue that such changes in life courses and the attendant discursive transformations must be unpacked in order to understand the particular worldviews, cultural associations, and orientations the recruiting process demands and calls into being.

The forces that push these college students toward investment banking are obviously multiple: the particular college environment, the strength of alumni and peer networks, the cultural linking of success and smartness with Wall Street, the hierarchical narrowing of career options and what constitutes prestige, to name a few. Perhaps the most self-evident reason for Wall Street's recruiting monopoly is simply that its presence dominates campus life: recruiters visit the university virtually every week, even on weekends; they show up in the greatest numbers at career forums, panel discussions, and social events; their advertisements for information sessions, "meet and greets," and free drinks and hors d'oeuvres dominate the campus newspapers daily; their company literature and application forms are easily accessible, either at campus locations or online.

The recruiting process saturates almost every aspect of campus life from the very first day of the academic year. Investment banks and consulting firms dominate the early fall career fairs, setting the terms for what constitutes a successful career (and what it looks like), and monopolize the attention of the student body by showing up with the most polish, fanfare, and numbers. They hand out the best goodie bags, the most titillating magnet sets, mugs, Frisbees, water bottles, caps, and t-shirts, and in a matter of days, thousands of students become walking advertisements as their logos disperse into campus life. At the 2006 Princeton Career Fair, 60 of the 104 firms represented were in financial services or consulting (Rampell 2006). At the 2003 Harvard Career Forum, more than half of the close to one hundred firms in attendance were in investment banking, general finance, and consulting (Urken and Habib 2003). Marketed as general career exploration meant to attract a diversity of students and pathways, these forums actually constitute "recruitment on a grand scale" for the investment banking and consulting industries (*Harvard Crimson* 1995). This early and intense branding of Wall Street careers as the symbol of arrival, the equating of investment banking with "career" in general, serves to narrow students' notions of success and gives the impression that for graduates, there's nothing else out there besides investment banking and consulting (N. Guyer 2003).

Taufiq Rahim, a *Daily Princetonian* columnist, wrote of what he called the "hunting season": "They're here. I can see them. I can smell them. They're in my inbox. They're in my mailbox. They're on my voicemail. They're outside my door. They're on campus, and they smell blood. . . . They're the investment banks, the consulting firms: McKinsey, Goldman Sachs, Bain and Company, Merrill Lynch" (Rahim 2003). Below I reproduce Goldman Sachs's "Recruitment Calendar" for Harvard undergraduates at the millennium (see table 1). The recruitment schedule is painstakingly detailed,

Table 1. Goldman Sachs Recruitment Schedule at Harvard University, 2000–2001.

DIVISION	DATE	EVENT
Firmwide	September 6, 2000	Thirteenth Annual Women's Leadership Conference Panel Discussion, 10:00–11:30 a.m.
Firmwide	September 14, 2000	HSA Business Leadership Dinner The Charles Hotel, 6:00–8:00 p.m.
Firmwide	September 27, 2000	Resume Writing Workshop Office of Career Services, 12:00–3:00 p.m.
Firmwide	September 27, 2000	Firmwide Information Session The Charles Hotel, 6:00–8:00 p.m.
Investment Management	October 2, 2000	Divisional Presentation The Charles Hotel, 6:30–8:00 p.m.
Investment Banking	October 3, 2000	Divisional Presentation The Charles Hotel, 6:30–8:00 p.m.
Equities	October 5, 2000	Divisional Presentation Faculty Club, 8:00–9:30 p.m.
Firmwide	October 11, 2000	HSA Career Week Panel Discussion on "My Career"
Firmwide	October 13, 2000	Career Forum Gordon Track and Tennis Center
Sales and Trading	October 16, 2000	Divisional Presentation The Charles Hotel, 6:30–8:00 p.m.
All Divisions	October 19, 2000	Resume Drop
Corporate Treasury	October 25, 2000	Resume Drop (open)
Corporate Treasury	October 27, 2000	2 Open Full-time Analyst Interview Schedules
Firmwide	October 30, 2000	Minority Event (tentative)
Fixed Income, Currency & Commodities	October 30, 2000	Resume Drop (open)
Fixed Income, Currency & Commodities	November 1, 2000	1.5 Closed Full-time Analyst Interview Schedules 1.5 Open Full-time Analyst Interview Schedules
Investment Banking	November 2, 2000	3 Closed Full-time Analyst Interview Schedules

Continued

DIVISION	DATE	EVENT
Equities	November 3, 2000	3 Closed Full-time Analyst Interview Schedules
Investment Research	November 9, 2000	2 Closed Full-time Analyst Interview Schedules (1 Schedule for London)
Investment Management	November 9, 2000	2 Closed Full-time Analyst Interview Schedules
Firmwide	December 4, 2000	Women's Event (tentative)
Firmwide	December 14, 2000	Resume Drop for Spring
The Hull Group	January 30, 2001	1 Closed Full-time Analyst Interview Schedule
Equities	February 2, 2001	3 Closed Full-time Analyst Interview Schedules
Fixed Income Research and Strategy	February 7, 2001	1 Closed Full-time Analyst Interview Schedule
Fixed Income, Currency & Commodities	February 7, 2001	1.5 Closed Full-time Analyst Interview Schedules 1.5 Open Summer Analyst Interview Schedules
Investment Banking	February 7, 2001	3 Closed Full-time Analyst Interview Schedules
Investment Management	February 8, 2001	1 Closed Full-time Analyst Interview Schedule 2 Closed Summer Analyst Interview Schedules
Equities	February 9, 2001	3 Closed Full-time Analyst Interview Schedules
Investment Research	February 13, 2001	1 Closed Full-time Analyst Interview Schedules
Investment Banking Training and Professional Development	February 21, 2001	1 Closed Full-time Analyst Interview Schedule 1 Closed Summer Analyst Interview Schedule
Firmwide	TBD	IPO Case Study in conjunction with the Office of Career Services

demonstrating the active pursuit of Harvard students: they will not fall through the cracks. As the director of Princeton's Career Services cautioned students about Wall Street recruiters: "They come after you. If you're hiding under the bed and you don't want to talk anymore, they'll come and get you" (Shapira 1998).

On the day of the recruitment presentation (and most investment banks usually have multiple campus events, as separate divisions will have their own presentations and interview timelines), a given bank's representatives descend in droves to central campus locations, usually the fanciest business hotel near campus. For Princeton, bankers will charter a bus, a few limos, and even some taxis to drive a group of thirty to fifty investment bankers, research analysts, and traders (usually alumni who will also serve as recruiters) from New York City to the Nassau Inn at Princeton. The same goes for Harvard. Elaborate recruitment presentations are held at the Charles Hotel in Cambridge or the Faculty Club; dozens of recent Harvard graduates and seasoned alumni currently working on Wall Street fill the rooms. Including recent hires from Harvard and Princeton allows potential recruits to witness former classmates as smart and successful, as having made the transition from undergraduate life onto the Wall Street fast track.

The very first Wall Street recruitment event I ever attended, in 1995 as a graduate student still contemplating research on Wall Street, was a session presented by Goldman Sachs, widely known among potential employees as the most prestigious and exclusive investment bank on Wall Street. Arriving a little late at Princeton township's hallowed Nassau Inn, I was greeted by a sea of charcoal gray, navy, and black business suits. There must have been over 150 well-coiffed and starched, professionally driven undergraduates crowding the hotel's ballroom to hear a panel of sixteen Goldman Sachs executives, mostly Princeton grads. Apprehension and eagerness pervaded the room: this was not a time for socializing but rather for competitive vying for "face time" and searing first impressions with the recruiters. Instead of saying hello to friends, juniors and seniors surveyed the room and sought to get on their marks. As the only graduate student in the room, (as far as I could tell), awkwardly attempting to both observe and participate in the recruiting process, not to mention the fact that I was dressed in an old pair of slightly wrinkled gray slacks and a denim vest (of all things), I felt completely out of place.

The lights soon darkened for an introductory slide and video presentation. It was a recorded narration with sweeping views of Manhattan and fast-moving visuals of the globe, suit-clad workers traveling or walking briskly to corporate towers, and sharp-dressed bankers videoconferencing or huddled up in teams with their sleeves rolled up. The narrator explained that a Wall Street career was all about "dealing with change." "The world is going to continue to change faster and faster, so we need people like you." When the lights came on, we turned our attention to the panel. I counted eight white men, five white women, one Latino man, one South Asian woman, and one black man. A relatively older white man, a managing director (Princeton class of '82), began to speak in a tone of pride: "We are a Princeton family. I met my wife here. Princeton students make the best analysts, which is why we recruit heavily here." The other speakers who were recent graduates introduced themselves by naming the schools they had attended: Harvard, Williams, Harvard, Princeton, Wharton, Princeton, Princeton, Princeton. "I'm from the University of Chicago," said the South Asian woman wryly. "I'm not quite as bright as everyone else." The Princetonian managing director then got down to business. "The two-year program will go by in a flash. Your learning and growth curve will be exponential. You will get actual interaction with clients. You are part of the team at our firm; the last thing you should be doing is photocopying. We hire ten people to do that, and that's all they do. We need your intelligence." It quickly became apparent that this was the evening's guiding theme. "So why should you work here?" asked the recent white male alumnus from Harvard. "Because if you hang out with dumb people, you'll learn dumb things. In investment banking, the people are very smart; that's why they got the job. It's very fast, very challenging, and they'll teach as quickly as you can learn." Some speakers emphasized the access to power offered by a Goldman Sachs position. "Our analysts can go anywhere in the world," said one of the white male vice presidents who is an alumnus from Wharton. "We've got Hong Kong, we've got Sydney, we've got London." He returned, inevitably, to the presentation's central motif; with an admiring gaze at the audience, he exclaimed, "You are all so smart!" Finally, the Princetonian managing director got up and announced, "Let's break up, go to the Nassau Inn Tap Room; drinks are on us!" The swarm of undergraduates then bee-lined toward the panelists, eager for face time with actual Goldman Sachs executives while I was still lingering in my seat. Determined to join the fray, I surveyed the scene and realized that every investment banker was already surrounded by two to three semi-circle layers of undergraduates: as the first layer moved to impress and receive the business card of the banker holding court, the second layer would quickly move into "face-time" posi-tion. The only room in the crowd for me was actually behind the speaker's back where there was no waiting line! In that position, I mainly observed throughout the night, and the only person who turned around to talk to me was the young South Asian American analyst from the University of Chicago, and I held on dearly to her business card as a sign of my initiation into this grueling process.

During subsequent recruitment presentations, I experienced much of the same: well-suited alumni declaring, "We only hire superstars," "We are only hiring from five different schools," "You are the cream of the crop." In these sessions, I was struck by how proclamations of elitism (through "world-class" universities, the discourses of smartness and globalization) seemed foundational to the very core of how investment bankers see themselves, the world, and their place in it. Representing a world of "collective smartness" and exclusivity seemed fundamentally connected not only to the criteria for becoming an investment banker but also to the very nature of what they do. What precisely were the links between elitism and the enactments of their financial expertise and global dreams, between Wall Street's claims to smartness and their promises of global prowess? Motivated in large part by these compelling presentations, I decided that to understand these grandiose, even mystifying, pronouncements, I had to get a job on Wall Street. I took a leave of absence from graduate school to participate "for real" in this process.

The "vigorous college recruiting season" is usually capped off with elaborate "sell days" to encourage seniors to accept the job. Such perks include "ski trips to Utah and dinners at Lahiere's" (Princeton's four-star restaurant) (Easton 2006; Shapira 1998). Every junior and senior that I interviewed spoke about the allure of recruiting, the constant wining and dining, the fancy spreads at upscale hotels and clubs. According to the *Daily Princetonian* staff writer Alice Easton:

> After months of dressing up in suits and ties, making their way to New York or the Nassau Inn and trying to impress panels of interviewers with their technical and social skills, juniors applying for summer internships in finance and consulting can now reap the benefits of their work: elaborate "sell days" to convince them to accept the job. . . . "They paid for two nights at a fancy hotel in New York. . . . They rented out a museum and had a cocktail party, and then rented out the VIP room in a nightclub in Soho." . . . The company later sent him chocolates in the mail. . . . [They showed recruits] a whole lifestyle. (Easton 2006)

The obvious implication is that if Harvard and Princeton students join these firms, then in a few years, they too can have it all.

During one of my visits to Harvard University to see my sister in 2000, I sat down with Kendra Lin, a premed student who was not planning to go into investment banking but wanted to understand "what the hype was all about" and possessed a genuine curiosity about why her classmates were so obsessed with Wall Street. In addition to attending the various career forums and participating formally in the recruiting process by signing up with the Office of Career Services (OCS), many Harvard students also participate in immersion programs to educate them about Wall Street and management consulting. Therefore, at the time, at the onset of recruiting season, Harvard Student Agencies, in collaboration with Harvard Business School and leading investment banks and management consulting firms, sponsored the Harvard Business Leadership Program (BLP), a week of recruitment, training, socializing, and general orientation to Wall Street financial institutions, management consulting, and general business practices. Being chosen to participate in BLP was itself a competitive process to search for "business leaders," and as the president of various student associations, Lin made the cut.

Describing her impressions of the BLP events, Lin said that the speakers who made the greatest impression were the representatives of Goldman Sachs. "They're this really elite investment bank that advises many leaders in corporate America on their mergers and acquisitions and securities offerings. They talked about how they managed the privatizations of the largest corporations in China and Spain, to name a few." While some of the non-investment-banking financial firms and smaller start-up corporations (who were in the minority) appeared "homely" to Lin, firms like J. P. Morgan and Goldman Sachs and management consulting groups like Boston Consulting Group "looked very accomplished" and "thought very highly of themselves." As a result, all the Harvard students flocked to talk to them. During the cocktail and dinner hour after the presentations, investment banks proclaimed that Harvard produced the most stellar recruits. Lin talked at length about her favorable impression of Goldman Sachs:

> I really enjoyed Goldman—as a side note, all of these firms are really talented in recruiting students. They make Harvard students feel like they are the cream of the crop. We have the best minds. This image of the Harvard student runs thick through recruiters and through people at the business school. I have heard this many times over the course of the week: that Harvard students are the best business people because you can give them any problem and they will be the ones to come up with the solution most quickly. . . . I left his speech believing that Goldman is the Harvard of all investment banks, but they all sure know how to sell themselves well.

Goldman Sachs, as Lin described, worked very hard to position itself as an extension of Harvard and, in doing so, confirmed Harvard as the progenitor of the best.

According to Lin, investment bankers emphasized how they "had the perfect life." One executive talked about how "he lives in the burbs, has a minivan, a dog, and two kids. Seriously! His wife graduated from Pritzker [the University of Chicago's business school] and is now a Harvard Medical School professor, and he is a rich VP." After hearing Lin's initial impressions on Wall Street recruiting presentations, I asked her what she thought about her week-long experience with BLP—the dinners, the socials, the business school case studies. What did she like and dislike?

> KL: It's all a schmooze fest. You have to schmooze your recruiters. You have to master rounds of interviews followed by more schmoozing, and then once you get there, you have to "live the lifestyle" of a business person. Be social, drink, go to parties, and schmooze some more. Also . . . there is no commitment really to social change.
>
> KH: Interesting observations. How did you realize just from this week, so early on, that people have to "live the lifestyle"? How were you clued into this point?
>
> KL: I think it was the set up of the whole BLP that first clued me in to that: I mean, they cater *all* of our meals, our dinners are all at the Charles hotel, and they are quite extravagant for a bunch of college kids. Hey, I love duck and sushi! Before we go into the hotel for dinner, there is a social hour where they serve juice and soda, and that's where it hit me. Basically you see all these students huddled around the bankers and consultants and kissing their ass. Everyone's all dressed up—it's a different culture. Put that together with stereotypes of businessmen from movies, you see that it really is pretty much like that.

This conflation of elite universities with investment banking and "the perfect lifestyle" is crucial to the recruitment process, reproducing as it does the ambience of Wall Street cocktail parties, where investment bankers "schmooze clients" in lavish, impeccably catered settings. These norms are enacted for and demonstrated to students, and like Lin, they immediately pick up on the importance of performing "smartness," not to mention how Wall Street business success is premised on pedigree, competitive consumption, and heteronormativity.

Not surprisingly, Wall Street's intense focus and persistence at Princeton, Harvard, and a few other campuses have repercussions for student culture. Newspapers and dorms overflow with debates about the pros and

cons of investment banking work life, excited discussions of what investment bankers "actually do," and romanticized tales of high-roller life in
Manhattan. Students begin to see "i-banking" as a "mysterious, glam-
orous and relatively undefined world" (Hall 2005). A glance at the campus
publications at Princeton and Harvard demonstrates what amounts to a
communal obsession, with constant news and opinion articles on "recruiting insanity," "avoiding the i-banking shadow," "schmoozing at Nassau
Inn," "defending the indefensible career," "the dangerous allure of recruiting," "aspiring Gordon Gekkos," "new recruits," "future financiers flock to
a Darwinian fete," "banking on pain," "i-banking ire," "how investment
banking consumed my life," and "is there more to life than investment
banking?" Heated campus panel discussions debate the relative merits of
banking and consulting, as panelists (firm representatives, usually former
students) face off with a cost-benefit analysis of the two career choices and
use the platform to further recruit students to their side. It is hardly
surprising, then, that the much-mythologized field of investment banking
often presents itself as the solution to anxieties about postgraduation life.

Although most of my recruitment participation was with undergraduates (as I myself went through the college analyst recruitment program),
the process for elite business schools for the recruitment of MBAs for
associate positions (one level higher than analyst) has similar components. For the most part, many graduate students at prestigious business
schools, such as Harvard Business School (HBS), Wharton, Sloan (MIT
Business School), Columbia Business School, and so forth, have had finan
cial experience. Most have worked as analysts at investment banks or in
management consulting firms; those who do not have a financial background have plenty of opportunity to study finance as a "concentration"
in business schools. All MBAs are literally bombarded by recruitment presentations and information sessions sponsored by their school's own student finance clubs and associations as well as Wall Street investment
banks themselves.

Starting the first year, MBA students realize that to work on Wall Street
after graduating from the two-year masters program, they must intern on
Wall Street their first summer and receive a job offer thirteen weeks into
the internship. As Bill Hayes, a recent MIT Sloan alumnus and an associate
at Goldman Sachs, described the process in 2001:

> Within a month of school starting, everyone starts coming. Hotel presenta-
> tions; meet and greets. They invite you out for drinks in the effort to get the
> best and brightest to apply. The bulge bracket firms don't have to sell them-

selves (the smaller banks do) since all the students gravitate toward them. I guess only they can afford it. They'll have a reception, and you have to meet people and hope you make some sort of connection. For Merrill, I went to a presentation, sent in my resume, and they called. Goldman came in with a whole crew of Wharton alumni, and then went to HBS afterwards. At the same time this is all happening, we have smaller events where the school Finance Club has receptions with bankers from top firms, where half of the MBA class shows up, or these clubs have information "learning" sessions like "Investment Banking 101" and "Day on the Job," which is a smaller setting, and you hope to make a contact with a recent grad to give you an "in." You have to send follow-up e-mails and thank-you's to every contact. Our Finance Club also organized mock interviews, resume workshops, and "trips to Wall Street" where anyone can go and visit all the banks. I met with Morgan and Goldman and Lehman. You go to their offices and try to distinguish yourself. . . . They only hire from these elite schools because they are already prefiltered. It makes you feel good; you've already been nominated. Bankers will say, "You might ask why we ask about GPA and test scores. Because we've done the correlation between top GPA and test scores from top schools and performance in the organization, and we know you will succeed."

Wall Street saturation of business school life is certainly equal to that of the general university population. The difference is that elite MBA programs explicitly represent themselves as channels to and of Wall Street; they are not emphasizing a general liberal arts education. Students often enter these institutions precisely to get a job in finance, and just a few months into the scramble for a job at top Wall Street investment banks, the first-round interview slots are full.

For MBAs, the selling of "the perfect lifestyle" is, on the one hand, expected and taken for granted, and on the other, understood as ironic, as most MBAs, having worked on Wall Street as college graduates, have experienced their "lifestyle" as simultaneously grueling and exploitative. What is more seductive is the forecasting of elite social networking and Wall Street influence over corporate America. Such an anointing was unmistakable at the Harvard Business School Women's Panel, an event catered for young professional women to network and apply to business schools, sponsored by Harvard Business School and held at Citigroup's Headquarters in New York City in 1999. Although designed as an open career forum, the HBS alumnae panelists talked almost exclusively about finance and management consulting: "For HBS women, 30 percent go into consulting and about 40 percent go into finance and investment banking."

"Banking internships come pretty quickly into the process. You receive one-on-one counseling before your internship decision. Recruiters are there pretty early." What struck me the most was panelist Jordan Thompson's parallel between Harvard and Wall Street: "I've never been to so many black tie parties. I was invited to so many parties and you see that people bring their intensity, enthusiasm, and ambitions as much in their work as in their social lives. I organized pub nights and cross-section mixes. When you are social chair at HBS, you have a certain carte blanche to talk to and call up the CEOs of companies." What Thompson experienced as social chair of her class mirrored the Wall Street's relationship with corporate America. Wall Street, armed with HBS graduates, has "carte blanche" to advise CEOs on the latest deals and expectations.

The Cross-Pollination of Elitism

They are declared to be "the best and the brightest." They quickly become used to the respect, status, and impressive nods from peers, parental figures, job prospectors, and society at large. Those most enamored of, or dependent on, their putative membership in "the cream of the crop" seek ways to maintain and continue the high status to which they have become accustomed, especially as graduation looms near. As Devon Peterson, an undergraduate writer for the *Daily Princetonian*, observed about the "the allures and drawbacks of elite jobs": "For four years we have enjoyed being the most elite college-aged kids in one of the most elite, unilaterally powerful nations ever to exist. . . . These banking firms provide us with a way to maintain our elite status in society by providing avenues to wealth and power that other professions do not" (Peterson 2002). Peterson's reference to himself as being at the pinnacle of power is a crucial window into the identity formation of bankers-to-be. Dafna Hochman, an undergraduate writer for the *Harvard Crimson*, similarly recognizes, not only the central importance of being the best, as defined by prestige, status, and smartness, to Harvard students, but also that what gives Wall Street crucial competitive advantage in recruiting is its acute understanding of this phenomena. Wall Streeters are able to sell themselves so effectively because they know what attracts these students: it is also precisely what investment banks themselves seek. Hochman (1999) observes, "The business world is obviously desperate to milk our minds, youth, creativity and work ethic. And they have correctly assessed what it takes to attract us: appear competitive, prestigious, and upwardly mobile. . . . They know that four years ago, we wanted the absolute best. We did not settle for number three or four on the college rankings. They prey on our desire to find the 'Harvard' of everything: activities, summer jobs, relationships and now careers."

Elite Students and Life after Graduation

Implicit in this transformation from undergraduate to investment banker is Wall Street's notion that if students do not choose Wall Street post-graduation, they are somehow "less smart," as smartness is defined by continued aggressive striving to perpetuate elite status. The cultivation of a particular kind of banker and the privileging of an elite norm, insidiously racialized, are nowhere better illustrated than with this event in Kate Miller's work life. In 1997, Miller, former analyst at Morgan Stanley, was one of its first recruits from a historically black college. In the following narrative describing her experience with a senior manager, Miller further demonstrates that what constitutes "smartness" is explicitly dependent on school pedigree as well as race.

> Well, there were a couple of officers that were known for being really good guys and being fair to people of color. And it was very interesting because I was in Word Processing [an actual floor of the bank where all the documents investment banks use to pitch deals are professionally printed]. I was trying to work on a document with some of the assistants there, and a principal [equivalent to senior vice president] came into Word Processing and was talking about his experiences recruiting that year. And he turned to me, well, he was saying to another analyst, "Well, you know, I just really have problems with the idea of us recruiting at historically black colleges. I mean, I know people say that the students that attend those schools are smart enough to attend Harvard and Stanford and get into these great institutions, but actually choose to attend the black college. Well, I have a problem with that. If they're that smart, and they're turning down one of the top institutions in the country, then I think that shows poor judgment, and we should really rethink whether or not these are the type of people that we want working at our company." He said this so that I overheard, and I guess he had assumed that I had gone to an Ivy League school because he then sort of turned to me and said, "Well, what do you think, Kate?" And I said, "Well, I went to a black college; I went to Spelman." And he just sort of looked at me and realized he made an incredible mistake and just said, "Well, I guess I lost my case. I guess you proved your point against me." So I just sort of shrugged my shoulders. Well, what do you say? You've been there for five months. You never really worked with the guy. It's

not like you two have a rapport. But it was awkward, especially to think that this was one of the cool guys who really thought that it was important to increase diversity within the company.

By virtue of "choosing" Spelman College, Miller demonstrated a lack of judgment; she was not only quantitatively "less smart" because she chose not to attend Harvard or Stanford, but she was also more provincial, less global. The complete equating of smartness with these institutions, the identification of historically white colleges as global, universal institutions, as well as the wholesale erasure of the white upper-class male privilege embedded in these universities are part and parcel of how excellence is understood. Central to Wall Street's construction of its own superiority is the corollary assumption that other corporations and industries are "less than"—less smart, less efficient, less competitive, less global, less hardworking—and thus less likely to survive the demands of global capitalism unless they restructure their cultural values and practices according to the standards of Wall Street. In a meritocratic feedback loop, their growing influence itself becomes further evidence that they are, in fact, "the smartest."

It is important to pause here to acknowledge that many of these students are of course quite aware of how the culture of smartness, as coproduced by elite universities, students, and Wall Street, capitalizes on, monopolizes, and narrows students' interests. Katherine Reilly, an undergraduate *Daily Princetonian* columnist, asked her fellow students to find "the courage to buck a system that has served us so well": "We should not let our type-A drive for success, money, or power or our fear of ending up outside the realm of 'acceptable' Princeton accomplishment dictate what we do with our lives" (Reilly 2003). Similarly, Dafna Hochman indicted Harvard for portraying the Wall Street recruiting process as every student's career process: this conflation "reflects Harvard's subtle and not so subtle attempts to challenge our values, delude our personal goals and to generally morph our diverse interests and talents into its ideal type of a respectable alum" (Hochman 1999). Fellow undergraduate *Harvard Crimson* writer Matthew Siegel wondered, "Could it be at all possible that the culture of success at Harvard drives people to skip right over the most important part of cognition—getting to know themselves and what they want and need—and instead, sends them straight into the outstretched arms of J. P. Morgan's H.R. department?" (Siegel 2003). Interestingly enough, his answer to why investment banking has so seduced Harvard undergraduates does not centrally implicate investment banking as the culprit: "It's not about investment banking. It is about the possibility that with all our running around trying to impress everyone all the time, it becomes hard to know what we really want" (Siegel 2003). Many students recognize the monopolistic hold that banking and consulting have on their future aspirations and that the very act of participating in recruiting precludes the questioning of "our place and privilege in the world" because the desire to hold on to privilege is naturalized vis à vis recruiting (Suleiman 1998). It is one thing if one's goal in life is to make "multi-million-dollar corporations even richer" or if one "cannot be happy unless you work for Goldman," but the crux of the problem is that students hardly question or ponder what they might truly be passionate about, much less the contradictions of their own privilege (Graham-Felsen 2003). Instead, these students more than likely continue with "the absurd impression that there is only one thing to do next year," that is, resort to the already-laid-out "typical Princeton job," the next step toward continued upward mobility, the sure-fire sign that one truly is the best and the brightest (Suleiman 1998).

Certainly, the pinnacle of meritocracy is necessarily precarious: it is shot through with class, race, and gender hierarchies; with the constant and anxious performance of smartness; and with a prestigious branding so dependent on the singularity of the apex that it cannot help but degrade. The fact that American culture, as Katherine Newman presciently pointed out long ago, has virtually no cultural repertoire that helps make sense of downward mobility for the middle class is perhaps doubly true for the elite, for whom expanding or diverging from the narrow path of status maintenance is understood and experienced as slippage or corrosion (Newman 1999). Where to find Harvard after Harvard? The push to replicate is excruciatingly intense. As Devon Peterson (2002) observed: "Perhaps most difficult to overcome is the naturally difficult task of giving up social status and an elite way of life."

"Wall Street University": Kinship Networks and Elite Extension

Wall Street and elite universities work together to foster and exploit this need to "find the next Harvard," in the process creating a symbiotic relationship that furthers each institution's dreams, goals, and practices. Wall Street has enjoyed long-standing historical ties with status-heavy Ivy League universities, ties that have produced generations of financiers and advisors to American industry. Since the 1980s, at precisely the time that Wall Street worked to solidify its expert influence over most U.S. corporations, these historical ties have been transformed into massive feeder relationships. Investment banks have naturalized themselves as the primary destinations for elite graduates as part of a program to consolidate and justify Wall Street's domination of corporate America, regardless of the "quality" of advice. In addition, over the past twenty-five years, student anxieties over preserving their elite status have increased, making Wall Street, at least until mid-2008, a much more attractive possibility than before. These developments, I argue, have converged to create a culture of "survival of the smartest."

Wall Street did not begin to recruit in droves at elite East Coast schools until the early 1980s. Throughout the mid-twentieth century, elite university graduates interested in business careers looked to management training programs with industrial, aerospace, or chemical corporations, rather than Wall Street firms (*Harvard Crimson* 1963; Wilentz 1975). For decades, general, "open" recruiting was not a standard practice for most businesses: Ivy League graduates relied on family wealth and networks, entered graduate school, or were approached via the "old boys' network" for financial or industrial fast-track grooming; and most Ivy League faculty, determined to perpetuate the ivory tower model, were "outraged by recruiting" (Beniger 1967). At Harvard in the 1950s, Wall Street financiers recruited a relatively small number of men directly from the well-established residential houses at Harvard College by holding small panels and conferences in intimate settings such as the Lowell House common room and the Eliot House dining hall (*Harvard Crimson* 1953, 1957). These efforts were small-scale as interest in the securities markets had plummeted after the Great Depression, and Wall Street was not necessarily the first choice for dynamic, ambitious college graduates. Furthermore, Wall Street and many other businesses searched for managers from business schools, not undergraduate programs (Masters 1986). In general, because of economic stability in the postwar era for the upper-middle and upper classes, the postgraduation job search lacked the anxiety so often associated with it later. Most elite graduates had "job futures so well established that they never have to go seek" recruiting (Wilentz 1975). Remarking on a "trend" toward "working right after college," *Harvard Crimson* writer Jeffrey Senger (1984) reported that it was not until 1984 that a majority of Harvard, Yale, and Princeton graduates sought jobs after graduation; in 1974, only one-third, and in 1959, only one-tenth. For example, with surprisingly little angst, the *Harvard Crimson*, in an article headlined "The Jobless Class of '72," said that "by choice or by chance, over half of the Class of 1972 found themselves with nowhere to go and nothing to do after graduation." The culprit was not so much economic hard times as the fact that "students who were planning on business careers were unwilling to make long-term commitments" and that those going to graduate schools "also wanted to take a breather from the academic regimen" (Bennett 1972). It is also important to remember that campus culture in the Vietnam Era was much more hostile to big business in general than in subsequent years, as evidenced (for example) by student protests against napalm manufacturer Dow Chemical Corporation's attempt to recruit at Harvard in 1967 (Beniger 1967).

As Wall Street investment banks profited exorbitantly from their increasing influence over corporate America in the 1980s, they began to recruit at elite universities on a grand scale, creating the two-year analyst programs for the express purpose of targeting undergraduates directly out of college. This new cadre of workers, no longer handpicked through small-scale networks of family, friends, and close business associates, was legitimated by placing even greater cachet on the universities where they were recruited. In place of the elite, individualized family of men came the elite "Princeton" or "Harvard" family, which relied on a new variant of kinship based on alumni rather than "old boys'" networks. Recall my own initiation into "the Princeton family" in my very first recruitment presentation in 1995 when a Goldman Sachs managing director and Princeton alumnus addressed the audience as "the Princeton family" to establish both connection with "us" and to delineate an elite selectivity—just as not everyone can be a student at Princeton, investment banking is not a profession in which all can participate. "Princeton alumnae make the best analysts." That women and minorities were not explicitly excluded in this process was a crucial part of this new ideology of meritocracy.

What made this central glue of elite-institution-alumni stick to Wall Street despite the possible dilution of elitism caused by this extension of exclusivity to all alumni, ostensibly, was the formation of a generic culture of "the best" which pervaded and extended from, say, Wharton to Wall Street. By attracting masses of elite university alumni to Wall Street, investment banks and universities coproduce an extension and transferal of elitism via what I call a human kinship bridge. For example, in 2004, when Goldman Sachs CEO Hank Paulson gave a keynote speech to Wharton MBA students, the first point he made "after stating Goldman Sachs's $23 billion in revenue in 2004" was "the importance his firm places on 'hiring and retaining the best people' in order to maintain a 'culture of excellence'." Paulson then emphasized the strong, intimate relationship his firm has with Wharton, "saying that more people were hired from the University to work at Goldman Sachs in 2004 than from any other school in the country" (Siegal 2005).

When a Harvard or Princeton education is seen as the normative "baseline" pedigree it becomes ordinary as well as collective, encompassing, even universal. Wall Street smartness is, in a sense, "generic," and it is precisely this notion of elitism so pervasive as to be commonplace, smartness so sweeping as to become generic, that reinforces Wall Street's claims of extraordinariness. Specifically, the assumption is that everyone on Wall Street is smart and comes from Princeton or Harvard; as such, this smartness generically applies to *all members of this class* or kind in a way that is naturalized and comprehensively descriptive of this entire group of workers. The notion of Wall Street smartness is so ingrained that it does not have to be emphasized as "special" or qualified; as such, smartness is not a "brand name" or external label, but a blanket, sweeping generalization about all investment bankers. Wall Street's generic smartness is so comprehensive as to connote a global application to all members. Of course, while Princeton and Harvard are pinnacle "brand names," their generic status on Wall Street further attests to how special the accumulation of merit is at investment banks.

The kinship of generically smart investment bankers guarantees the extension and reinforcement of all the social particularities of those universities' positions in American culture, while simultaneously rendering invisible its normative, unmarked privilege. Marked investment bankers, who usually strive to be generically kin (and generically smart), feel the brunt of these contradictions daily. Kate Miller observed that she "never felt like more of a black woman with all of the negative stereotypes attached than I did when I was working at Morgan Stanley." She chose not to pursue a career in investment banking (or was discouraged from doing so), so her narratives illustrate a certain level of what might be called alienation from Wall Street culture and values. She described her initial experiences this way:

> I felt like the first thing people saw when they looked at me was not a bright person who had been admitted to the analyst class but a black woman. And most of the people that I worked with really had very little exposure to other races. I'm sure some of the men had very little exposure to women on a professional basis. Even though the industry has made a lot of strides to be more inclusive of women, I still think that white male officers prefer to work with white male analysts.

This pattern of exclusion, where white male vice presidents pick white male analysts to be on their team, where Yale graduates seek to work with other Yale graduates, greatly influenced Miller's opportunity to work on "higher profile" deals and to make connections with potential mentors. Many first-year analysts get to know senior-level bankers through various formal and informal alma mater networking events. Miller poignantly observed, "If you're an analyst from Dartmouth and there are fifteen managing directors who also went to Dartmouth, then you get to know those fifteen managing directors. Well, Spelman College grad, guess what? There are no MDs, VPs, even associates that graduated from Spelman." Given that smartness and membership in a financial kin network that drives business and social opportunities are intimately dependent on both elite institutions and one's closeness to the unmarked, generic norm, Miller's various identities as a black woman from Spelman renders her less smart, less kin, and by extension, less of an investment banker.

Creating Pinnacle Status and Generic Smartness

Solidifying Wall Street as "the" extension of hyperelite universities requires the convergence of student aspirations, cultural pressures of elite upward mobility, Wall Street reframing of alumni kinship, and its marketing and monopoly of the recruitment process. In this section, I demonstrate one concrete way in which these entanglements of elitism are "operationalized" by even further narrowing the space at the top such that the most coveted investment banks and the "most" prestigious universities are not only associated singularly with each other but also distinguished from (and desired more than) the "regularly" prestigious ones. I argue that by painstakingly differentiating and creating hierarchies between and within elite universities through the recruitment process, investment bankers further intertwine their identities with the most elite universities, create demand for their jobs and institutions, and solidify their association with smartness.

As I have described, the two universities from which the prestigious Wall Street investment banks most actively recruit all students without restriction to major or department are Harvard and Princeton. It turns out that recruitment at other elite universities is not approached in a similar manner. For example, although investment banks also widely recruit at Yale, often included with Harvard and Princeton as one of the "top three" schools for banking or consulting, Yale, however, lags behind the other two in its reputation on Wall Street. According to one Yale alumnus who works on Wall Street, "because investment bankers perceive hostility" from many students at Yale, "they concentrate their recruitment energies at Princeton and Harvard. . . . They're looking to hire a larger portion of students from Harvard and Princeton, despite the fact that the number of applicants from each school is relatively similar" (Tanenbaum 2005). Yale is perceived by many of my investment banker informants to be more "liberal and 'artsy'," less free-market oriented in a sense, and perhaps even tainted by New Haven, a largely working-class, majority African American city. Instead of recruiting universally at Yale, as happens at Harvard and Princeton, banks might require Yale students to demonstrate their quantitative ability, by, say, majoring in economics or undergoing a financial internship (Engler 2006).[3]

A similar phenomenon occurs at the University of Pennsylvania. There, again, investment banks do not recruit as actively from the general undergraduate population as a whole, although undergraduates and graduates from Penn's renowned Wharton School of Business are among the most highly sought-after recruits. "Some college seniors said it was difficult to find investment banking and consulting opportunities without a Wharton pedigree. It's harder to [secure financial jobs] if you are in the College" (Miley 2000). "Wharton may be the reason big-name investment banks are attracted to . . . Penn." In 2005, over half of Wharton graduates went into investment banking (Steinbery 2006). Similar to Yale, non-Wharton undergraduates at Penn report that they need to demonstrate technical or financial expertise in order to attract Wall Street investment banks.

By contrast, investment banking recruiters at Princeton and Harvard explicitly express how they *do not care* if undergraduates are trained in finance because a skilled background or already-acquired technical expertise is *not* really what they are looking for. As Gia Moron, a media and recruiting spokesperson at Goldman Sachs, told *The Harvard Crimson*, "We have found that financial know-how is easy to teach—in fact, training is an important part of a new hire's orientation—but the skills that the most successful candidates possess are beyond teaching: Energy, a history of excellence and achievement, leadership and interpersonal skills are some of the stand-outs" (Ho 2003). According to a Princeton undergraduate, Kate Daviau ('06), "They understand that interns come in knowing basically nothing—but if you're smart and personable, it's worth it to them to hire you." The *Daily Princetonian* writer Catherine Rampell observed that from all her interactions with potential Wall Street employees during her years at Princeton, most do not even know what "financial services" is. "Most are going into finance because they haven't figured out what else they could do," yet "finance employers are seeking them out, telling them they're qualified for finance" no matter what their training, major, or department—as long as they are from Princeton. "They bombard us with food, mail, Princeton alumni connection, and they keep telling us we're qualified, we're perfectly qualified even though we've never 'held a real job'" (Rampell 2006).

This open-ended, "generic" recruitment at Princeton and Harvard not only naturalizes the students there as "the best," the elite among the elite, but also sheds light on what actually constitutes smartness for Wall Street. Being the best and the brightest, especially for college graduates, does not mean possessing actual technical skills, a background in finance, or even a specific aptitude for banking. Instead, Princeton and Harvard recruits bring to the table just the right mix of general qualities and associations: they are not too technical or geeky (MIT), not too liberal (Yale), not too far away (Stanford), and their universities carry more historical prestige than the remaining Ivies (Brown, Columbia, Cornell, Dartmouth, University of Pennsylvania). Possessed of a combination of traditional cachet, class standing, and pedigree, they can show prima facie evidence of their "excellence" by virtue of their schools' (presumably) exclusive selection processes; and they demonstrate a constant striving for further "excellence" by virtue of their participation in the intense process of recruiting and their evident desire for a high-status, upper-crust lifestyle.

Finally, Wall Street maintains pinnacle status and differentiates between elite schools by utilizing quota systems and other divisive mechanisms that reproduce Wall Street/university hierarchies. I share the experiences of a recent MIT Business School (Sloan) alumnus who is an associate at Merrill Lynch. He recounted in anonymity his experiences with Wall Street's interview process during his very first year at business school. To receive a job offer from an investment bank after graduation, an MBA student must enter recruitment during the first month of his or her first year in business school as part of the summer associate program, or else risk being excluded entirely, as full-time job offers after graduation are usually made only to those who have "survived" their summer internship, what is known as the fourteen-week interview process. During the fall, all MBA students must be "invited to interview" at a particular investment bank for a set number of job openings allocated to each university. This means that these interviews are "closed," and students have already completed the necessary "resume stuffing," interview training, general Wall Street education, and socializing to obtain an initial interview slot. My informant recounted in detail:

This is how Merrill Lynch recruited at Sloan. They let thirty people come to the first-round interview at Career Services at Sloan or at a hotel nearby. You are interviewed by two people, one associate (usually Sloanie), and one higher up. The night before, you are invited to drinks with everyone in an informal setting at a bar at the Charles Hotel [at Harvard Square]. You divide into the particular group [based on industry, such as telecom or energy] that you are interviewing for; that group has a set number they are going to fill. You meet the interviewers. There is a quota system. They want to get a decent number of people from Wharton, Harvard. The next day is the all-day interview for all of Merrill's offices and positions at once—New York, Hong Kong, London. . . . Then there's a dinner afterwards, but not everyone is invited. They will call you to let you know if you're coming to dinner. If you get the dinner phone call—dinner was at Maison Robert—that means you made it to the second round. The second round is the next day with a different group of people. That's it, and they tell you within a day or two. If you get accepted and you accept them, you get an "exploding offer," which means there's a time limit, by [the] end of January, for you to accept. Then, you have a summer-long job interview. There are lots of Sloan alumni at Merrill. For Morgan Stanley, the first round was at Sloan with thirty people; ten people got invited to the second round and then Morgan said, we only have a slot for one person from Sloan, and only one will get it. No dinner. Met with executive director and he interviewed each one at an office in the Boston, Dean Witter office. They are more selective and may have more slots for other schools. And, with Goldman, I didn't get invited to a first-round interview. With Citigroup, I got invited and didn't go to the second round, and I canceled on Bank of America.

What struck me were the quotas. Though I had known that Morgan Stanley and Goldman Sachs were considered to be the most prestigious investment banks, I did not realize that they had quota systems for particular universities. This means that the interviews are "closed" and based on a quota system for each school to make sure there's a balance (or imbalance) of Harvard, Wharton, Sloan, Columbia people. For example, whereas Morgan Stanley only allowed one slot for Sloan, which is itself a "top" business program, they allotted more slots for Wharton and Harvard Business School graduates. In parallel, although Citigroup and Bank of America were eager to hire Sloan students, many of my informants had no interest in them, as "hybrid" commercial and investment banks are considered less prestigious. Of course, with the purchase of Merrill Lynch by Bank of America (which demonstrates the continued desire and lingering ambition of commercial banks to strengthen their investment banking identities and capabilities) and the apparent transformation of all investment banks into these hybrid institutions, it remains to be seen how the hierarchies of prestige are restructured.

Investment banks seek their analysts and associates from an "exclusive diversity" of universities. As I have argued, while they seek front-office employees from Harvard, Princeton, Yale, Wharton, Stanford, MIT, Duke, Columbia, and so forth, they allot more employee slots to certain schools within this "club." Although investment banks encourage applications from most of these schools, only at Princeton, Harvard, and Wharton do they maintain the most active recruitment presence. And then there are schools that are deemed worthy, but do not quite make the cut. For example, many informants have commented matter-of-factly that investment banks recruit at New York University not so much because of its prestige, but because of its physical proximity to Wall Street. Sarah McLanahan reported that at NYU's Stern School of Business, 250 seniors attended a presentation by Goldman Sachs for eighty-eight interview slots, from which the bank intended to hire only eight to ten Stern graduates. The jobs were in credit risk analysis and global securities lending, which are mainly considered middle- or back-office jobs, rather than the more prestigious and better-compensated front-office positions in investment banking, sales and trading, and investment management that graduates from Harvard and Princeton are destined for (McLanahan 2003).

Princeton and Harvard stand apart from other elite universities for the sheer ubiquity, verging on ordinariness, of the Wall Street presence in undergraduate life. As one Princeton senior, Cleburne Wolford, class of 2005, reflected on the uniqueness (or strangeness) of his experience: "The network here is already in place to help you. A lot of my friends who went to state schools back home unfortunately have no real 'in' to the profession. State schools are not the only ones left out. While most alums interviewed said that they work with a diverse group of people from different schools and backgrounds, the banks only actively recruit at a handful of campuses —namely Harvard, Yale, Princeton, and Wharton" (Hall 2005).

It is precisely these differentiations between "always already smart" and "smart with qualifications," between unquestioned, generic, naturalized smartness and smartness that must be proved, that enact and solidify the hierarchies upon which elitism is necessarily based. With schools jockeying for the position of most elite, investment banks, engaged in a similar struggle for status, feed and exploit students' desires for a singular exclusivity. In this dance, elitism and "smartness" are coproduced and naturalized.

Justifying Dominance in Global Financial Markets:
The Culture of Smartness Writ Large

The making and legitimization of Wall Street global experts begins with the brightest people in the world. Investment banks' foundational smartness is the innate precondition and platform upon which investment bankers produce "the best" global workforce (and obscure the potentially adverse effects of their financial advice), which in turn justifies global market dominance. Wall Street's identity and its very approach to business strategy is absolutely dependent upon its kinship with elite universities, which underwrites its financial market know-how, status, and influence. Its global authority depends on attracting "top talent." At investment banks, smartness as pinnacle status, "the global," and market dominance are intimately linked in the discourse and practice of the everyday. When it comes to recruitment, "no one else in the world can do what you guys [Wall Street banks] do" and few have more at stake, as investment banks recruit much more than a few young employees; they are recruiting their status as experts in the global financial markets (Rubalcava 2001).

Investment banks' sheer reliance on the "aura" of Princeton itself—the name, the prestige, the evocation of ability and intelligence, the global cultural capital—is brought into starkest relief during socioeconomic recession. When faced with economic hard times, Wall Street downsizes immediately, relentlessly, and constantly. However, Wall Street's dependence on elite universities means that even during downturns, when they unabashedly downsize to preserve the bonus pool for their executives, they do *not* stop actively recruiting at the usual campuses. When I asked Ahmed Jamal, a vice president of telecommunications and technology at J. P. Morgan who was educated in Canada, what struck him the most about Wall Street and its cultural practices, his response struck a familiar chord:

> First of all, what you notice on Wall Street for me initially was the quality of the people. . . . Of course there are exceptions, but the quality of the people when you compare to other industries—they definitely do recruit the best. There is so much emphasis on getting in the best. *Even in times of change and reengineering, you know, the effort of recruiting never stops.* They are very active in terms of sending people to top schools and recruiting the best.

Just as downsizing occurs even during bull markets, so recruitment continues on elite campuses during recessions and market crashes.[4] Jimenez Lee, an MBA student at MIT's Sloan School of Business, said that from the point of view of students at elite schools and the university recruitment or career placement office, one of the cardinal mistakes of investment banks regarding their reputation is to mismanage the recruitment process with these institutions—hiring too few, loosening ties, or reneging on initial offers. During the market crash of 2001 and the aftermath, Alex Rubalcava, in a prescient article for the *Harvard Crimson*, taunted investment banks for even thinking of "cutting back" on Harvard recruitment in 2001. He observed, for example, that "the core competency of . . . an investment bank . . . the real value these companies bring to the world and to their shareholders is their unmatched skill at recruiting fresh-faced young students from the Ivy League." He continued, "Remember that companies that do nothing of value must obscure that fact by hiring the best people to appear dynamic and innovative while doing such meaningless work." So he urged them to "bring lots of toys," take him out to the Capital Grille, and show up in nothing "less than a $2,000 Zegna suit"; he expected "only the best from a potential employer." It was precisely "those lavish dinners with the managing directors, those Morgan Stanley-emblazoned squeeze balls and those endless series of first round, second round, supplemental, on-site, off-site, group, case, informational and informal interviews" that convinced "the best minds of my generation to follow your madness, becoming well-fed and Hermes-clad, dragging themselves through midtown streets at dawn, looking for the car service home after a rough night with a pitchbook" (Rubalcava 2001). In a piece entitled "Senior Class Consciousness," *Harvard Crimson* writer Alan Wirzbicki, like Rubalcava, warned his classmates that "most firms want you far more than you want them." It's the "dirty secret of recruiting." As a "native" participant observer so to speak, Wirzbicki hit the nail on the head: "Consulting firms and investment banks are in heavy competition with one another and depend on attracting name-brand college graduates to bolster their reputations" (Wirzbicki 2000).[5]

Smartness is strategically utilized to bolster Wall Street legitimacy as well as the everyday practices and influence of investment bankers as an elite cohort of global agents. Investment banks certainly have much at stake capitalizing on Harvard and Princeton's "halo effect," for part of what enables the acceptance and spread of Wall Street's particular, financial approach to corporate America is its association with, and strategic use of, this elitism. My informants emphasized that when investment banks attempt to win financial business or pitch deals to clients, having Ivy Leaguers doing the talking is very helpful, regardless of their inexperience.[6] Corporations are often more willing to do business when they know that a "Princeton or Harvard guy" is on the deal.[7] For example, during the initial meeting between a Wall Street investment bank and a potential client, the managing director (MD) on the deal usually begins the meeting by introducing "the deal team" (the vice presidents, associates, and analysts on the pitch) with the explicit purpose of awing the client with their smartness, and thus, expertise. The presentation (contained in the "pitch book") not only includes the proposal for the deal, the market overview and competitor profiles, and the financial rationale for, and impact of, the deal, but also the relevant biographies and posed pictures of the team members, which painstakingly details their prestigious pedigrees and affiliations as well as profiles their deal experience and industry knowledge in the corporate client's area of business. In recounting this performance, my informants describe how the MD begins the meeting by "introducing the rocket scientists" to stake Wall Street's claim that the client will have "the smartest guys in the world advising you": "At Morgan, we only have the best"; "At Goldman, we have the deepest pool of talent assembled here"; "This guy went to all the best institutions in the world." Positioning themselves as smarter, savvier, and more cutting-edge than corporate America by capitalizing on the aura of elite institutions, investment banks construct a mutually reinforcing connection between the market and the Ivy League: because we have "the best of the brightest" working for us, then what we say about the market must be believed and the deals we envision should be executed. By the same token, their naturalized smartness elides the ways in which their financial practices and advice often lead to shareholder value implosions, corporate decline, and financial crises. Smartness can also act as a cover for expedient (and detrimental) short-term decision-making.

Smartness leads to market dominance, not only because of explicit assumptions about talent and credibility, but also through the premise that smartness is spatial, that it should rightly spread, colonize, and necessarily manifest as the natural determinant and arbiter of global market leadership. For example, in 2000, during both Merrill Lynch and Morgan Stanley recruitment presentations at Princeton University, the recruiters touted the interconnection of elite institution, singular smartness, and global access, just as the Goldman Sachs representatives had during my first recruitment event (see figure 1). The main speaker, David Pyle, a managing director of Fixed Income (and Princeton class of '71), expounded on Morgan Stanley's desire "to be at the top of everything":

Figure 1. This Morgan Stanley Dean Witter ad and recruitment invitation in the
Daily Princetonian on 14 September 2000 is among the many that bombard Princeton undergraduates throughout the school year. Its use of "the global" invokes the
bank's "real-time" market prowess, speed, connection, insight, and know-how.

Our goal is to be the preeminent global firm, to be what we already are, the top. We want people coming into work every morning knowing that we're at the top and always striving to be at the top. We are global; if you're not global, you can't win. . . . People are our single most important asset. . . . Our people are the smartest in the world. . . . There is no one in the world that we can't reach and that's powerful. We're in the middle of everything. We have huge reserves of capital and human assets, and we want to recruit the type of person that always wants more, who is not happy being second. . . . Our theme is "network the world."

Similarly, Merrill Lynch's lead recruiter, a white male managing director, declared that two of the key reasons to work at Merrill are its "global footprint: it's so global, you can go where they want," and its "culture," which is centrally characterized by immersion with and amongst "the smartest people on Wall Street." This session ended with another white male director asking rhetorically, "What does 'global' mean for Merrill Lynch? Is it simply that you have an office in Frankfurt and Tokyo? No, it doesn't mean just 'global'; it means that you are *dominant*." He continued, "Merrill is equal to or better than everyone else in all product areas; we have the A-team mentality."

In these views of the world, smartness and elite pinnacle status create Wall Street's cultural superiority and its position as a "model" for meritocratic excellence, which in turn serve as a catalyst and justification for spreading its culture and dominance. These speakers, via the mantra of how "the smartest people in the world work on Wall Street," endlessly emphasized collective meritocracy as the organizational rationale for investment banking elitism. Simultaneously, recall the senior banker at Morgan Stanley who doubted Kate Miller's "smartness" by virtue of her "choice" to attend Spelman rather than the "best" universities in the world. The implicit assumption is that graduates of particular Ivy League universities are not only bearers of pedigree but also of a global, cosmopolitan outlook and market savvy that are key prerequisites of financial market influence. Through this inundation and identification with institutions and individuals whose brand of smartness is universal, Wall Street investment banks construct "the best culture," which leads to global leadership in the market and the naturalized right, not only to expand, but also to largely influence the direction of corporate America and financial markets. From this foundation of smartness and elitism, they proclaim their place in the global social order, both how their firms are working to reshape the global business landscape and the global opportunities their firm makes available to its employees. A global kinship of powerful actors based on smartness is the building block of global financial networks, which, when closely tied with resource-filled institutions, spur financial deals and financial capitalist accumulation. The culture of smartness begets global spread, justifies global financial influence, naturalizes imperialist practices, and produces financial dominance.

2

Wall Street's Orientation:

Exploitation, Empowerment,

and the Politics of Hard Work

In the late 1990s, after graduating from Harvard Law School and working for two years at a prestigious New York–based law firm, Joseph Tsai decided to enter into investment banking at Donaldson, Lufkin and Jenrette (DLJ). Having admired investment bankers throughout his time at the law firm, after being told that on Wall Street "you tell the corporate lawyers what to do and make much more money," he felt that he had finally arrived. Entering DLJ along with a cohort of recent MBAs, Joseph Tsai went shopping to spruce up his wardrobe from the somber corporate law attire to what he had imagined that a mid-level associate investment banker (one rank above analyst, and one below vice president) would wear. Inspired by Gordon Gekko, Tsai showed up the first day in suspenders. As he recounted to me,

> I think I wore suspenders my first couple of weeks and people would give me a look and then I would think, "Okay, so what's going on?" And then I noticed that junior people don't wear suspenders. It's like managing directors who wear suspenders and things like that. The way it was explained to me was that you shouldn't wear suspenders because it looks like you spent too much time on your appearance, and you are supposed to just work hard. You shouldn't be wasting time putting on suspenders in the morning. Otherwise, you are supposed to look professional at all times and especially if you are meeting with clients. . . . You are supposed to look good but not overly so.

Like Tsai, Anthony Johnson, an analyst promoted to associate in mergers and acquisitions at J. P. Morgan, described how many young analysts arrive on Wall Street "too big for their britches . . . you would think they were managing directors," yet by the first week, they realize that "there is absolutely no reason analysts should be wearing Rolexes." As former Morgan Stanley analyst Kate Miller told me, "Analysts think they are going to work on Wall Street and be this hotshot investment banker. They are seduced into thinking they get to live the high life in Manhattan, but come on, they are the lowest on the totem pole, get totally exploited for two years, hate it, go to business school, and then come back in two more years to make a quarter of a million dollars."[1]

The jet-setting, high-rolling lifestyle my informants often expected after graduating from elite undergraduate and professional schools was immediately reframed by a world of hard work intense enough to reconstitute and transform what it meant to be successful subjects in the world of finance capital. Most of my informants experienced an initial sense of shock at the extraordinary demands of work on Wall Street, though over time, they began to claim hard work as a badge of honor and distinction. Crucially, hard work came to be understood as the resolution for the unequal segregations and representations of marked investment bankers who also sought to become unmarked global experts in a money meritocracy. Unlike most workers in the neoliberal economy, elite Wall Streeters still experience a link between hard work and monetary rewards and upward mobility—although that link is importantly enabled by prestigious schooling, networking, and a culture of smartness. An analysis of "smartness" and "hard work" as key Wall Street values, combined with an in-depth examination of investment banking's organizational culture, can yield in-depth ethnographic insight into how Wall Street has reshaped corporate America, financial markets, and the very nature of work in the United States.

Orientation

Almost every investment bank has an elaborate training and orientation program for all first-year college graduates and first-year MBAs. Before officially starting work in the fall, the analyst cohort is initiated into Wall Street life through a month-long financial training course intended for nonfinancial majors to acclimate to the intensity of financial calculations. (First-year MBAs do not usually participate in this training, as they are expected to be investment banking insiders already.) They are quizzed, given homework, and ranked by performance. Since some investment banks hire first-year analysts without identifying the exact department in which they will be housed, during these first few weeks they must scramble vigorously for placement. In some cases, the analysts who excel in the financial training class are those most sought after by prestigious departments. Throughout the first month, analysts are reinterviewed and retested. Some of my informants joke that even before they officially started the job, they were staying up until 2 a.m. in the training office studying for placement interviews and exams. From the beginning, analysts are oriented into a culture of instability and competition where they must hit the ground running.

The culmination of the month-long training period is orientation, usually a three- to four-day off-site conference and team-building extravaganza which initiates new analysts and MBAs into the "culture" of the firm: the people, the work environment, the history, the internal organizational structure, the vision and mind-set of the bank. Whereas the atmosphere around training is both brutal and giddy, during orientation, the new hires are officially welcomed and given the royal treatment. CEOs (chief executive officers), CFOs (chief financial officers), CTOs (chief technology officers), heads of divisions, and managing directors all "take time out of their busy schedules" to congregate and give orientation speeches and unveil their business goals and themes for the new year. Senior management bombards the eager audience with the firm's "core values," strategies, and self-representations. When I attended the Bankers Trust orientation in Fall 1996, the themes of smartness, globalization, money, hard work, relationships, and technological prowess pervaded almost every presentation. The new hires, repeatedly lauded as the cream of the crop, were told how lucky they were to be initiated into a global firm where money, ingenuity, and opportunity flowed freely. Huge maps showing the firm's global reach were displayed. Featured speakers included both the head of BT's Latin American private bank and the head of the Asia Operations division. New recruits then spent most of the day engaged in team-building exercises, playing sports, and socializing with top executives; at night, open bars, full catering spreads, and bands were set up in various locations to further hobnobbing.

The first day of orientation began with a decadent sit-down breakfast. Then a white male managing director in his late thirties (who many considered to be in line for the chairmanship of the bank) took the podium and shouted across the room, "Show me the money!" "You will be making more money than you ever dreamed possible," he told the incoming MBAs, whereupon the audience stood up, pumped its fists, and cheered. "Well, come to think of it," he continued, "some of you guys will probably get paid more flipping burgers at McDonald's. If you make fifty thousand a year, not including bonuses, and work over 100 hours a week, that amounts to below minimum wage." His listeners snickered though they understood the joke. It would all pay off. Reflecting on Wall Street in the 1980s and early 1990s, he recalled how "we were making more money than you can shake sticks at," and assured the newly minted bankers that the money was primed to flow into their firm once again.[2]

I was initially surprised at how candid Wall Streeters were in recognizing and laughing about the exploitation of analysts (and many associates), until I realized that regularly working over 100 hours per week for two years was not only normative, but widely accepted, even touted as a positive attraction of the investment banking workplace. When I began at BT in July 1996 (and throughout my fieldwork), I was initiated firsthand into how the cultures of hard work and smartness work hand in hand with the politics of elitism and segregation. For example, during my participation in a six-week training period, the "Global Financial Management Training Program" (GFMTP), with thirty or so recent college graduates, after the first day, the tension in the room was palpably obvious, as the process of sorting and tracking had already begun. Almost instantly, I and the three other internal management consultants, all from Princeton or Harvard, were labeled "the smart ones" by the rest of the trainees, who had graduated from state schools and "second tier" private schools such as Lehigh University, SUNY Binghamton, New York University, Colgate University, and Rutgers University. Somewhat embarrassed, I kept reminding my coworkers that my knowledge of finance paled in comparison to theirs, and that they could very well be my teachers. The fact that graduates of less elite institutions predominated in our training program briefly led me to think that perhaps BT was eliminating the old distinctions. I was mistaken.

What none of us realized at first was that a parallel training class, the "Global Corporate Finance Training Program" (GCFTP), was taking place on a different floor. In this program, *all* the trainees hailed from what one of my GFMTP friends called "*your* type of school": Wharton, Princeton, Harvard, Duke, Stanford, MIT. Moreover, whereas everyone in the GMFTP group, except for the four internal management consultants, was slated to become a back-office worker (though in management positions), everyone in the "elite" Corporate Finance group was tracked to become a front-office investment banker. They had fancier food, better supplies, and a professional "facebook" which detailed their pedigrees and biographies, along with excellent head-shots. It was precisely at the moment when the GMFTP group realized the existence, not only of myself, but also of the "elite group," and uncovered the unequal positions and directions that we were tracked into, that their hope and excitement—that first job in New York City at a global investment bank, for goodness' sake—became shot through with sarcasm. Though I constantly disparaged myself and demonstrated much ineptitude, my fellow trainees assumed that I was the real Wall Streeter. When it came time for my cotrainees to be placed in less prestigious and (much) less well-paid divisions of the bank, the full weight of unequal branding and classification bore down on them. It was also during this time that my GMFTP friends began to go home early, recognizing the fact that no matter how long past 6 p.m. they stayed at work or how much initiative they showed, they were excluded from the front-office positions: for them, hard work was already severed from advancement and reward. With a mixture of both regret and resistance, they began to tell tales of how GCFTP folks and myself would have to pull all-nighters for the firm, while they could work "regular" hours. After training, except for preplanned get-togethers, I hardly ever ran into my fellow trainees. This was no accident, as it spoke to the cultural geography of segregation that was built into the very structure and spirit of Wall Street.

Tiered Elevators: Investment Banks at a Glance

Understanding the importance of spatial segregation is central to unpacking the intertwining striations that construct Wall Street's culture of work and "smartness" and upon which their pinnacle notions of meritocracy depend. The many overlays and separations of elite institutions, job placement, race, gender, and class are nowhere better illustrated than in the placement and destination of elevators at investment banks. While working at BT, I continually underestimated the amount of time it would take for me to travel from one floor to another. In order to get from the twenty-second floor to the forty-fifth, for example, it was necessary to return all the way to the lobby first and walk to its furthest end for another elevator. Sets or banks of elevators, each serving a different part of the building, were located in separate sections of the ground floor; that is, the elevators that connected only to the lower floors were the closest and most accessible from the lobby, while elevators to the higher floors were furthest away from the lobby. At BT, three elevator banks served (in order of increasing prestige) the lower, middle, and upper floors—which roughly corresponded to, respectively, the bank's "back office," "middle office," and "front office." At first I presumed that such hierarchies were particular to this building. Later, while doing fieldwork at other banks, I found every investment bank in New York City organized its elevators in a similar way, with the lower floors occupied by less prestigious departments, the upper floors by the most elite workers. These domains are rigidly segregated by race, gender, and class, as well as work schedule and style of dress. In many buildings, the CEO uses his own private elevator.

"Front-office" workers—referred to as the bank's "officers"—are the most valued employees because they are understood to generate revenue for the company. Only they are extravagantly recruited, required to participate in the various training and orientation events, and invited to various off-site retreats, conferences, and social events. The front office comprises three major departments or business units: corporate finance (also called simply "investment banking"), sales and trading, and asset management. The fact that workers in corporate finance are also called investment bankers, thus synonymously equating one part of the front office with the institution itself, signals the importance and prestige of this department relative even to other front-office units (not to mention the back office). Historically the research department, which houses the research analysts, had been considered a mere "support function" for investment bankers and traders; they helped investment bankers and traders make deals by researching Fortune 500 companies, "covering" particular industry sectors such as food and beverage, telecom, or energy, analyzing corporate strategies and stock and bond markets, rather than generating deals themselves. In the 1990s bull market, the supposedly separate functions of research and corporate finance were increasingly conflated such that research analysts began to issue mainly "buy" recommendations to prop up clients' stocks with an eye to sourcing and maintaining deals in the bank's interest. Since research units were now directly generating revenue, rather than providing "objective" analysis, they were catapulted into full-fledged front-office status, where they quickly became mired in scandal, as analysts pushed stocks despite knowledge of balance-sheet fraud and bubble marketing. Mergers and acquisitions (M&A), also part of the front office, sometimes exists as its own department, or, alternatively, is considered part of corporate finance.

At BT, my group MCG was part of the "middle office," which includes departments such as risk management and internal consulting. While technically, these groups can "bill clients," their clients are other divisions within the bank; as such, middle-office personnel occupy an in-between position, and they are not as lucratively compensated or as highly valued as front-office workers, as they do not actively generate revenue. Middle-office personnel, however, are still considered "officers" of the bank, and as such, are recruited from the same elite universities as their front-office colleagues.

Almost everyone else in the bank is considered "back-office" support staff (which includes operations, account services, trade reconciliation, technical support, word processing) and treated as a "cost center," which is understood as a division that depletes money because of the refusal of investment banks to recognize or compute their contributions as part of revenue generation. Most workers in the back office are not considered "officers" of the bank (except for a few senior executives), and thus do not participate in elaborate orientations and training sessions, cocktails and presentations, fancy dinners and retreats. They are often from middle- and working-class backgrounds, with an overrepresentation of people of color and women, and tend to receive their jobs through employment agencies, vocational and technical training networks, job postings, and word of mouth. Oftentimes, back-office workers are found not in the bank's "headquarters" building at all, but rather in less expensive locations in Brooklyn, other parts of Manhattan, or across the river in Jersey City. The back office does recruit its managers among recent college graduates and MBAs from well-established though less prestigious schools such as Pace University, Lehigh University, and occasionally Boston University and New York University (which also supplies workers for the front and middle offices).

This powerfully hierarchical deployment of space implodes the notion of a singular, homogeneous Wall Street employee. The boundaries between front, middle, and back offices reinscribe social hierarchies. Richard Pan, an Asian American technology and operations manager in Merrill Lynch's back office and graduate from Pace University, described the differences in opportunities of entry and in compensation between the offices:

> Most people on Wall Street would like to work in the front office . . . because that is primarily where all the money is—in the front office. If you want to make money, and when I say make money, I mean over half a million dollars, in the front office you can pull in more than a million dollars. You don't see people in the back office make any more than a million dollars. You have to be either a trader or an investment banker, things like that . . . but to get those jobs is very difficult. If you take a survey of the middle- or back-office people and say how many of you guys would like to work in the front office, I am sure more than half of the respondents would probably say, "Yes, I would." But there is no opportunity for them. . . . Look at investment banking—they don't

necessarily hire—you can't go to headhunters and say you want to work in investment banking, and they will get you a job. You are hired from an Ivy League school. Whether it is undergraduate hiring for the analyst program or hiring MBAs to be associates, they would go to the same school. Or it is done through word of mouth. Rarely is it done through what we have here, like we have job postings here. They do not job-post those kinds of positions.

Opportunities to enter front-office work are highly exclusionary and open only to particular class and educational backgrounds. Most front-office workers are white, upper-middle-class men and are highly compensated, although at the analyst level, there are almost equal numbers of white women and a sizeable minority of Asian Americans. Including bonuses, even the lowest-level investment bankers make six-figure compensation. "In terms of area affects, employees in corporate finance earn approximately 173% more than peers in male-dominated support functions, and professionals in sales or trading earn approximately 210% as much as those in support functions. These areas were also the most male dominated" (Roth 2003, 792). Moreover, front-office and back-office workers do not socialize with each other even during work hours (the tiered elevators making this rather difficult). The one time in the year that front- and back-office workers are meant to interact is during the department Christmas party, though front-office workers have multiple other party invitations.

Front- and back-office workers, however, do have a few things in common, namely job insecurity and a sparse work environment. In fact, front offices, as I will detail in later chapters, endure much more job turnover than other bank divisions due to more frequent rounds of layoffs and job-hopping in search of higher compensation. While the back office is constantly subjected to cost-cutting measures due to new technology and relocation to sites of cheaper labor, at the same time most investment banks generate so much information to process that back-office work is comparatively stable. For example, Howard Morimoto, an Asian American management consultant from McKinsey Consulting, was hired to do a cost-reduction project for an investment bank's Client Processing Services (CPS) division, a back-office department that handles bureaucratic and accounting details for clients' accounts (processing papers after a trade, aligning and verifying records of clients' transactions, and so on). Morimoto and his team analyzed CPS operations and interviewed workers, looking for ways to streamline their processes. He even conducted an investigative study of potential savings if the bank relocated its processing site to Tennessee.[3] In the end, not much was actually done at the time other than a few layoffs and some minor changes in policy. The assumption was that technological upgrades would eventually allow the bank to cut a good number of the department's jobs, yet the bank was unwilling to spend the money right away, so the CPS workers were safe for the time being.[4] These are Morimoto's observations of the back office:

> In the back office of an investment bank, the people there seem very different from, let's say, the people on the trading floor. In one sense they're still proud of being in an investment bank; they still feel like, "Yeah, I'm part of the bank," but in another sense I have a feeling that, well . . . you're not in the revenue-generation side, you're providing support, so back-office people feel a little neglected. They're expected to perform perfectly because that's their job, and as soon as anything goes wrong, immediately someone is pissed off at them. So you know that they're functioning well when you don't notice them at all, so that's how they're expected to be, anonymous. You can see that people who follow that career maybe want to find their own niche or even get into the revenue-generation side or make sure that they have built up enough "equity" in the firm so that they are promoted because they can't judge their performance through revenue. They can maybe do it through cost savings, but that's very limited. They have that kind of stigma and that's attached to almost all back-office people.

Given that one of the primary ways in which workers in investment banks are measured is by the amount of money they generate (or claim to generate) for the firm, back-office workers, limited by their structural role as a cost center and continually understood to be "unworthy," can only be recognized as "contributing" to the firm's profitability through cost savings or "stop losses"—which are mainly achieved via the drastic reduction of wages or the elimination of jobs.

Surprisingly, the workplace surroundings of the front office are also analogous to that of the back office. As a fieldworker who imagined Wall Street investment banks to be lined with marble halls and full of mahogany executive suites, I was shocked by the often run-down work spaces of many investment bankers in the front office. Front-office analysts and associates at most investment banks, from Merrill Lynch to Salomon Brothers, recounted to me their own initial surprise at the chipped paint, worn carpets, outdated computers, and cramped cubicles. Trading and technology floors do have the latest technologies with fast networks and multiple levels of data storage (especially in the wake of 9/11), but contrary to popular belief, the rest of the bank often lags behind. Similarly, analysts and associates at J. P. Morgan and Goldman Sachs were often embarrassed to show me their desks, as the only professional spaces that matched images of Wall Street grandeur were their lobbies, conference floors, and senior executive dining rooms and offices.

When I worked at BT, most of the front-office floors and departments had been recently renovated, so my experience was not exactly the same as that of many of my informants. However, at the time, since BT was mired in a scandal and faced a crisis of representation and loss of status in the investment banking community, the higher floors of the front office was one site where those insecurities were, quite literally, painted over. Gillian Summer, an African American investment banking analyst at BT, observed:

> It's funny because if you walk on the floors, you can tell the money-making floors from the non-money-making floors. That is just the way they have it all set up. . . . If you walk off the elevator on one of the back-office floors, the carpet is green or purple and you walk up to where they sit, and everything just looks old and torn down. You go to the finance floors and they are just remodeling it; it looks great. You get to our floor, and it looks good. You go to the fourth floor, and it is like all shabby. You go to the tenth floor and you have bugs crawling all over. You go to the ninth floor and it looks like a hospital ward; it looks very bad. The money-making floors have two men standing over there, like security-looking guard people.

It is worth noting that when BT was at the height of its prowess in the early 1990s, it did not bother to renovate its front offices. At the height of the bull market, many banks did engage in massive remodeling projects or move into newer buildings, and after 9/11, many investment banks left Wall Street for midtown Manhattan, where many of the buildings are newer and grander in scale and décor. Nevertheless, it is a crucial point to realize that throughout the late 1990s, most front-office floors were not renovated or well decorated, and office décor was not always neatly dichotomized between front and back offices. What might poorly maintained front offices say about the culture of work at an investment bank?

Generally speaking, investment banking clients, such as the CEOs of large corporations, do not visit investment banks; the banker often goes to meet them. They pitch and make deals in luxurious hotel conference rooms and ballrooms, fancy restaurants, clients' offices—but hardly ever at the bank. It is true that sometimes the geographic locations and the outside building structures of investment banks can be important representations of banking prestige and influence, as was witnessed in the late twentieth century when some firms began to install huge flat screens streaming "real-time" quotations of stock market prices on the exterior of their New York City headquarters. But by and large, most investment banks do not have prominent signs or placards marking their offices, a practice which extends back to the nineteenth century when J. P. Morgan built his bank across from the New York Stock Exchange and deliberately refused to label it as an unmarked sign of exclusivity. Much of what goes on in investment banks is closely guarded and kept private. Most casual observers I have talked to about Wall Street comment on the secrecy and mystique that surround investment banks; this experience is deliberately constructed, as investment banks are not "showroom" spaces; they do not have individual customers who come to their headquarters, nor do they have many visitors in general.

If banks are not showroom spaces for their clients or for high-powered meetings, then how are these spaces used? What goes on inside investment banks, and what might they not want "others" to see? I would argue that for many front-office investment bankers, the experience of work is akin to what Jill Andresky Fraser calls the "white-collar sweatshop." The fact that many investment bankers work, off and on, 110-hour weeks, is often disguised (and alleviated) by their business-class airplane seats and five-star hotel stays (although for a period of years after major crashes, even Wall Street bankers sit in coach and book tickets ahead of time). As such, the daily environment of the investment banking workplace looks more like an austere white-collar factory than the popularly imagined series of luxurious (but intense) power meetings and lunches in gleaming, high-tech surroundings. It is a place where highly compensated workers, in often bare and impersonal surroundings, crank out myriad versions of financial analyses and projections, where they wait for the word-processing centers to finish printing their work so they can edit it yet again before presenting their recommendations to corporate clients.

The White-Collar Sweatshop

Louis Walters, a white vice president of Facilities and Building Services at Salomon Smith Barney, vividly describes these work environments. As the spatial planner of an investment bank, Walters helped me to understand the geography of workspace and its relationship to how investment banks view their employees and the work they do.

About five years or so ago, we densified the operation. We went from every employee had nothing less than a six-by-eight position, which was our work module; then we went to a six-by-six to get more people in less space—part of the cost-control thing. I remember walking down this long row of seats that we had crammed together. Six-by-six is not a lot of room, and low partitioned. Some of them were higher, but basically, there was this long row of low gray work positions. I saw this Princeton mug, class of whatever. And, I was thinking about the sort of psychological process of going through what it takes to get into Princeton today, and the work just to get there, and then, having graduated from there, the sense of accomplishment, being part of the one percent, or whatever the words are now, the best of the best, and here he wound up with a six-by-six module, with only room for your little mug. The mug is a sort of a residual reminder that you are someone special.

Of course, the white-collar sweatshop is hierarchical in itself, which further demonstrates the heterogeneity of investment banking experiences; the division among elevator banks, between the front, middle, and back offices, is just one of the multiple axes of power relationships. Despite investment banks' self-representations as flat and flexible workplaces where anyone with the best ideas and the largest contribution to deal-making profits can be successful, the daily realities are quite different. Gillian Summers, a first-year analyst at BT, described the hierarchy in a general sense.

KH: Do you feel that the VPs and MDs are always calling the shots, or are things more flexible? Does the team all mesh in or is the hierarchy pretty much set?

GS: The hierarchy is pretty much set. Associates don't get involved with telling their VPs what to do. The VPs might say, "I want to get this deal done—however you want to get it done, get it done." Or, the VP tells the associates, "This is what I want done." Then, the associate comes to you [the analyst] and tells you, "Okay, this is what I want done." Plus, he [the associate] will make something else up to add, just to put his two cents' worth in. I mean, you [the analyst] are stuck with everything. Some of the stuff you really feel is unnecessary, and you might go back to the associate and say, "I don't think we need to do this." But he will get mad and will say we have to. So you sit there at your desk and sulk because you know it is a waste of time, and at the end of the day, it was a waste of time. It would be good if you could go back to an associate and then have him say, "Okay, this is what we really need to focus on." But, it doesn't do any good to say anything. Also, the associates, they are fresh out of business school, and they think they are hot shit. They come in there, and they don't care about processing. They know how to make the analyst do it.

Within the front office, the job positions and "deal teams" are usually composed of one or two analysts, an associate, a vice president, at times a senior vice president or director, and a managing director. The lowest rung in the front-office hierarchy is the analyst, the college graduate hired from a few elite universities in the United States.[5] Many former analysts refer to the program as "two years in boot camp." The primary job of the analyst is to "do the financials," to gather and process corporations' financial numbers for the purposes of attracting new clients and maintaining the deal. At the beginning stage of the deal, after crunching numbers in spreadsheets, analysts transfer these models into Word or PowerPoint templates, which eventually become highly polished "books" (called "pitch books") to present to potential corporate clients. Analysts are expected to leave the bank voluntarily after two years, either to find a new job or to enter an MBA program; in fact, most analysts sign only a two-year "contract," although they can be terminated at any time. In especially lucrative times, some second-year analysts can be asked to stay for a third, and occasionally analysts are "internally" promoted to the level of associate (even without an MBA). Along with associates, analysts work the longest hours. If analysts work 110+ hours a week (with four to five all-nighters a month), then a typical analyst's salary of $50,000 amounts to little more than minimum wage. Only the variable bonus of $20,000 to $50,000 (for first-year analysts) pulls analysts significantly above a living wage in New York City.[6]

An associate is usually an MBA graduate from a few elite MBA programs. In addition to sharing much of the "number-crunching" work of the analyst, the associate is the liaison between the analyst and the vice president. He or she supervises the analyst's work and makes the numbers "tell a story," meaning that the financial calculations are interpreted to justify a particular strategy or deal the investment bank is advocating. He or she then brings the analyses to the vice president for comments, makes the necessary revisions, and then edits and sends the final drafts to the word-processing department to transform into slick presentation pitch books. This continual back and forth between analysts and associates on the one hand, and vice presidents, directors, and managing directors on the other, is one of the key reasons why associates and analysts work such long hours. As one associate clarified when I asked him why, even on "light" work days, he *always* had to stay until 10 p.m. (except an occasional Friday or weekend evening), he responded, "Because MDs and other senior people never get their comments back to us until 6 or 7 p.m., when some of them leave for the day." An investment bank engaged in constant deal-generation, immediately and efficiently responding to client and market demands, must maintain a twenty-four-hour shop. If senior bankers have the privilege of occupying the normative workday and they demand something "on their desk the next morning when they arrive," then the analyst and associate are the ones working from 7 p.m. to the wee hours of the morning.

First-year associates, like analysts, are in a support role, and as such, do not normally speak at presentations and meetings with clients. Those who stay in the investment banking business—dependent of course on a multitude of factors—can be promoted after three years or so to vice president. Associates fresh out of business school usually command a base salary of $90,000 with a variable bonus of $90,000 to $180,000. Vice presidents (VPs) serve as links between the corporate client, the managing director, and the team of associates and analysts. They are in charge of supervising deals on a day-to-day basis. Vice presidents and above enjoy total compensation packages that range above $300,000 to well over half a million. Although the hierarchy varies in investment banks, it is usually true that between vice president and managing director (MD), the top of the pyramid, there exist several "in-between" layers such as senior vice president (SVP), "principal," or "director." Part of the rationale for these "mini" layers is to stall or prevent the promotion of VPs to managing director. The majority of investment bankers, no matter their tenure, never make it to MD, for multiple reasons. First, managing directors, who usually claim the lion's share of the bonus pool, hierarchically guard against its "dilution." The most commonly uttered criterion for promotion is "deal origination," meaning that the managing director is usually the one who generates and brings in new deals to the bank (or is at least credited with such), often due to personal contacts with CEOs and CFOs of Fortune 500 companies, not to mention government officials. Credit for deal generation usually means that MDs, although their salaries are under a quarter of a million, average around $2 to $4 million a year, with virtually no ceiling. Occasionally, of course, there are spaces where compensation hierarchies and boundaries are gray, where a second-year associate may be more highly compensated than a vice president, or where a vice president generates a deal instead of a managing director. For the most part, managing directors are chosen for their perceived ability and network of contacts for deal generation, not for any particular skill at "managing" others. In fact, senior managers on Wall Street are renowned for their exceptionally poor management skills, as Wall Street emphasizes short-term, competitive individualism, not teamwork or the cultivation of long-standing mentorship, or collegiality.

When investment bankers reach vice president, they are expected not to rest on their mid-level laurels but to "ratchet up" their hours and commitment, to demonstrate both up-to-date product expertise and a desire for the much-coveted position of MD. Simultaneously, beyond being "star performers," they are expected to constantly network throughout their industry and cultivate deal relationships from the boardrooms and bars to the golf course. Of course, such a dual ratcheting depends on an abundance of resources for everything from dependent care to food procurement, and a particular dominant embodiment of what constitutes financial authority, which on Wall Street continues to be mapped onto pedigreed white males. Specifically, although Wall Street banks are "hesitant to reveal any data related to their recruitment and retention of women" and minorities due to their "treacherous history" of "flagrantly discriminatory behavior and compensation practices untethered from the notion of equal pay for equal work," nine top investment banks did so after "the *New York Times* agreed to aggregate the data and not break it out on a firm-by-firm basis." The data showed that while women make up 33 percent of the analyst class, they represent "only 25 percent of incoming full-time associates" and just "14 percent of managing directors." The percentages for minorities, especially at senior levels, are less than half of the number for white women (Anderson 2006).

Hard Work

The white-collar sweatshop on Wall Street can shock the system of even the hardiest analysts and associates. The intensity of work life is especially unfathomable to twenty-one-year-olds who assume that they have "made it." Many investment bankers-to-be get a taste of Wall Street through summer internships, which, while demanding, are also limited in time, as interns return back to campus to enjoy their senior year. As Jonathan Right, a summer intern at Morgan Stanley in 1999, reflected on his summer in a *Daily Princetonian* opinion piece, he detailed both the hypermasculine seduction as well as the "price" he paid for "getting the sought-after offer" from Morgan Stanley for a full-time job after senior year. "During my last five weeks, I averaged 90-to-100-hour weeks. I did not sleep my final three days with the firm. I had two days off the entire summer. One of them was July 4. The other was a Sunday." Although he worked "all day; all night; every day; every night," he relished investment bankers' "secret love affair with Gordon Gekko," their financial power (while management consultants suggest courses of action, bankers, like Gekko, make things happen), and the "testosterone factor" of working with "awesome" guys who took him to gentlemen's clubs such as Scores (Right 2000).

Once the euphoria of winning the prized job and becoming the Manhattan investment banker has subsided, and summer abruptly ends with constant 100-hour weeks stretching into the foreseeable two-year future, analysts shift their analogies from Gordon Gekko to fairly brutal imagery. In times of heavy deal flow, analysts and associates regularly stay at work until two or three in the morning, pull all-nighters, and work both Saturdays and Sundays. The disciplinary joke that analysts and associates often share among themselves is, "You'll be lucky if you get a day off besides your wedding day." Roy Allen, now a managing director at Fidelity Investments, recounts his days as an analyst at Salomon Brothers in the 1980s: "The culture was very cutthroat . . . and it was very much geared toward survival of the fittest, period. You could just do your job, and if you were very good you were fine, but if you were just mediocre, you would be chewed up and churned out, and somebody else would be put in the seat. . . . We worked an average day of 16 hours. Many nights we were there until eleven o'clock, getting a cab home just to turn around. I mean you worked like a dog; many Saturdays, many Sundays, no regard for . . . you were the lowest of the low." The pages of the *Harvard Crimson* and the *Daily Princetonian* are filled with recent alumni reflecting on their first two years in investment banking, recounting how for spans of many months at a time, they never made it home before midnight. Keith Hahn (Harvard '03), an analyst at J. P. Morgan, described his workload this way: "I had seen documentaries on the Patan [sic] death march and the Holocaust, so I feel that I was prepared for the day-to-day i-banking life" (Widman 2004). Tom J. Hsieh (Harvard '97), an analyst at DLJ, remarked that "the job is a great springboard to do other things in finance. It's grueling though. It is akin to slavery and it will break you" (N. L. Schwartz 1999). Another Harvard alumnus, a Goldman Sachs analyst who requested anonymity, declared, "For a year you have no personal life. It's hard enough to do my laundry." His worst work week lasted 155 hours, leaving him with just 13 hours to sleep. Steve Sceery (Harvard '03), an analyst at Morgan Stanley in London, claimed that the London work environment is much more relaxed, yet even so, he said, "I'm at a period in my life where I have the most enthusiasm for adventure, no responsibilities or attachments, but instead I decided to spend 17 hours a day in an office seven days a week. It makes you start to wonder" (Widman 2004). "You have the role of being a total gimp," complains one, and as *Harvard Crimson* writer Nathan Strauss news-flashed in the article "'Extreme Jobs' Threaten Sex Lives": "Listen up, potential investment bankers: all work and no play makes for a lousy sex life, according to new Harvard Business Review study" (Strauss 2006). My informant Phillip Young, an associate in M&A at Merrill Lynch, echoed:

> The biggest downer, working 100-hour weeks, breaking dates with your friends becomes routine. It becomes so routine, that people stop calling you up. Every time they call you up and make dates with you, you call and say, "I can't make it right now. I will be there in an hour—I can't make it right now, let's extend it another hour." By the time it is midnight or 1 a.m., it's "I'm sorry, I just can't go." They are upset and they basically come to the point of, "Listen, you are always breaking dates with us, so why don't you call us when you are free." So, when you are finally free, you can't get in touch with anybody because everyone is already out. You can't plan ahead.

Many investment bankers candidly informed me that Wall Street deliberately recruits college graduates straight out of the gate (not those who have taken time off) in order to pick the most eager, fresh-faced, driven, young, unattached analysts, so they can be worked to the breaking point. As Sarah Kittery, a vice president at Salomon Smith Barney, casually remarked in passing, "If you're single, and your family lives far away, like California, the better analyst you will be." She described that although most analysts begin the year with a significant other, "all of a sudden" after a few months, everyone starts finding out that they are all single. Symbolic of how skewed investment banking calibrations of work hours become, she then commented that "investment banking would be a great job if you could find a balance where you work 12 hour days and that's it." Similarly, Chris Logan, an analyst at BT, remarked on the one hand that he "knows what Wall Street does to the young": "One of my pretty good friends from Princeton . . . worked for Morgan Stanley merchant banking, which has a reputation for virtually being one of the hardest places on their young people, and I saw what it did to him. Instead of the usual happy guy in college, they turned him basically into a snappy . . . really uncomfortable guy to be around. He gained like thirty pounds and never smiled." Yet, of course, Logan himself works "100-hour weeks, till 3 a.m. every night" but thinks of it as a "compromise," an improvement over

Morgan Stanley. The point is to create a postcollege atmosphere where, within days of beginning work, analysts and associates begin to "live" there, comparing notes about who is staying the latest and "getting slammed" the most, not to mention participating in the makeshift Nerf football game at 1 a.m.

The "office space" of investment banking analysts is literally called "the bullpen." The bullpen that I observed at DLJ was a long hallway about 150 feet long and 20 feet wide, demarcated by the high desks of administrative staff, who sat in the center of the floor, and the associates' small offices. The entrance to the bullpen was an actual plastic gate, meant as both a joke and a commentary on life at the bank. Inside the gate, cramped desks, shelves, and floors overflowed with pitch books, PowerPoint presentations, and old binders of previous deal books, not to mention soda cans, footballs, gym bags, weights, change of clothes, deodorant, and an extra suit hanging just in case. The bullpen on one of Merrill Lynch's corporate finance floors was a U-shaped area with a similar lived-in feel, peppered with the detritus of work and work distractions: suction basketball hoops, paper airplanes, a pile of take-out containers.

Two organizational "perks" are central to instituting the culture of hard work: dinner and a drive home. The first day of work, investment bankers are told that if they stay after a certain cutoff time, usually 7 p.m., they can order dinner on the firm. Without fail, every single analyst and associate partakes in this ritual: an analyst is usually in charge of the phone ordering; another analyst picks up the food from the delivery person downstairs. Some investment banks have accounts already set up with restaurants located near their buildings, and analysts simply order up to their twenty-five dollars per person dinner limit. As Malinda Fan, senior vice president at Lehman Brothers, joked, "By the end of their first year, our analysts and associates have tried everything on the menu of every restaurant that delivers within a five-block radius of Lehman." With no time to shop for groceries or cook, they soon become dependent on this service and even on the occasional day when they can leave before 7 p.m., they stay in order to have dinner.

The next hourly milestone to reach is 9 p.m., after which investment bankers can call a company car service to take them home directly. When I first worked at BT, it had a notoriously liberal car service policy: we could call a car to take us home if we stayed after 8 p.m. Investment banking friends going home "early" from the World Financial Center would walk across the street to our BT headquarters explicitly to hitch a ride with one of us. Within two months, when senior management realized that nearly everyone was staying late enough for car service, they moved the cutoff time back to 9 p.m. Hoon-Jung Kim, a senior at Harvard who had spent a summer internship on Wall Street, warned her fellow classmates not to "get sucked in" to Wall Street simply because of these mundane, but seductive perks: "They get used to being driven home in sleek black cars with leather seats and expensing dinners to the firm every day" (Kim 2000). Of course, dinners and limos home, though first understood as "perks" of the job, become not only taken for granted, but also expected and "owed" given the time spent. The following narrative by Phillip Sherrill, yet another Harvard senior who spent the summer in lockdown at an investment bank, satirizes the experience of analysts as a carrot-and-stick process of reward and punishment:

> I was so hardcore, in fact, that I didn't have time for basic maintenance or hygiene. I went three days without changing my shirt. I kept a toothbrush in my desk. I had Q-tips hidden behind my monitor. I once sat on my cloth swivel chair, hyped on free Coke and stuffed with the dinner I bought with my green corporate card, for the amount of time it took one of the senior guys in my office to fly back from his golf outing in Iceland. I'll bet your employer didn't even like you enough to pay for your brown bag lunch, but my firm bought me seared ahi lunch and fire-grilled dinner. (Sherrill 2004)

While dinner and a ride home keeps analysts and associates at their desks until the wee hours of the morning, the BlackBerry, which became widespread on Wall Street in 1999, keeps them constantly "on call" and chained to the office while at home or "on vacation." It is the key mechanism for work communication during the weekends, traveling, lunch hours, and the few hours between the end of the work morning and the start of the work day. Much more sophisticated than a pager or beeper, BlackBerrys allow for global e-mail reception (not to mention cell phone use), buzzing each time a new e-mail is received. Many of my informants admitted that they were "addicted" to their BlackBerrys within a few weeks and had acquired the ability to type as quickly on a two-inch keyboard using their thumbs as on their desktop computers. When I asked the fiancée of an associate at Lazard, a boutique investment bank, where they were going for their honeymoon, she replied wryly, "Anywhere the BlackBerry doesn't work."

Such long hours invite the question: What do junior investment bankers do all day? While most analysts and associates tout the financial and business exposure they receive as investment bankers in a global financial services firm—attending meetings with Fortune 500 CEOs and CFOs, learning the art of the deal from senior bankers, and developing expertise in financial analysis and valuation—they also freely admit that their day-to-day lives are characterized by painstaking grunt work with financial spreadsheets, then waiting for MDs to respond. As an analyst at J. P. Morgan, Anthony Johnson poignantly depicts the duality of the analyst's role, in particular the contradiction between aspiration and ambition on the one hand and mundane reality on the other. Describing how analysts often exaggerate their importance, Johnson recounted, "I met this guy [an analyst] when I first started . . . and he was like, 'Yeah, well, you know, I worked at this investment bank and day-to-day I am responsible for valuing these businesses and coming up with how much they are worth and then trying to position that with where other competitors are in the industry and what they could do to maximize their value, blah, blah, blah'. And so it sounded really great, I mean, this guy puts value on businesses." After his initiation into J. P. Morgan, Johnson reframed his initial impression: "What this guy probably did [was] a set of trading multiples and a set of transaction comparables which are among the most unsexiest, like unpopular, things to do. Everyone avoids trying to do comps, and he probably did a whole bunch of comps and then broke them up into different groups, applied like the mean and medium number that he got out of all of these comps to his business and came up with a value." Although Johnson never wavered on the importance and influence of Wall Street investment bankers' reshaping of the economy, he also felt that analysts' performance often needed a "reality check" and "for the amount of work that we do, it really doesn't pay diddly-squat."

In the white-collar sweatshop, the analysts' and associates' roles are to provide all the financial information and analysis for the two main activities of every investment banker: trying to win business, and once you win, to service the deal. For the pitch stage of the deal, the investment banking analyst, working closely with the associate, must collect, assemble, and analyze all the information for the sales presentation, not to mention prepare everyone up the hierarchy, from associates to managing director, for the initial sales meeting with senior corporate management. The pitch is when bankers "say how great the company is, how much I want to work for you, and why you want to hire us."[7] To create this pitch, the analyst must dig up, as one associate from Merrill Lynch puts it, "everything there is to know about the client" (usually a Fortune 500 company), the client's industry, how the industry is performing in the capital markets, the financial markets in general. If, for example, the client is Ford Motor Company, then the analyst (using specialty financial databases and web sites such as Capital IQ from Standard and Poor's) is in charge of accessing and charting market information on Ford's stock, such as how it is trading relative to that of Daimler and other comparable companies; any stock buy-backs, offerings, and debt issuances coming out soon; whether Ford has been recently upgraded or downgraded by Standard and Poor's, and so on. During the sales pitch, the investment banking team may propose any of the following scenarios for deals:

1. Ford should buy x, y, or z company.
2. Ford should sell itself entirely to x, y, or z company.
3. Ford can sell particular divisions or assets to x, y, or z companies.
4. If Ford is distressed, we will help raise your stock price and get more value and strategy.
5. Ford should issue debt or equity.
6. Ford should manage its pension plans through x, y, or z institutions.

Usually, the team will present one or two of these scenarios. If they present the first one, then the analyst must "run full analyses" on ten or so companies that the investment bank is proposing Ford purchase. For these ten companies, the analyst will present a descriptive overview of each, find out how their stock prices trade over time, their largest shareholders, and their latest strategic initiatives, so that the team can make the case for purchase of any of them. If there is a need to raise money for a purchase, the team runs a "debt analysis" on "what the capital markets are saying about debt today, how are the credit markets doing, what would a billion-dollar debt issuance for Ford look like, including different permutations and kinds of debt such as convertible bonds or derivatives to differentiate your bank from someone else." For the second scenario, the analyst would need to demonstrate an expertise on the internal workings of Ford by combing through all SEC documents, industry-specific news, and general business newsreels for the past year, all the while absorbing the lingo of the automotive industry. The analyst would be in charge of compiling all potential buyers, such as finding out whether or not private equity groups are acquiring companies in this area. The group must also research any secondary networks of manufacturers, suppliers, dealerships, and distributors.

Upon coalescing all of this material, usually in just a few days, analysts and associates organize the information, creating spreadsheets, graphs, flow charts, descriptive summaries, and strategic recommendations, all of which eventually make up "the pitch book," the professionally produced document used for the sales meeting. One of the key items included in the pitch is the preliminary valuation, which uses the company earnings, cash flow, price and earnings (PE) ratios, and other metrics to calculate the total stock values of what is being sold or purchased. For many M&A deals, as in this scenario, the investment bank calculates a variety of other valuations such as the "public comp," "the M&A comp," the "LBO analysis," and "the creation and dilution analysis," among others. The public comp is the public company comparison where Ford's PE ratios (its stock price per share divided by its earnings per share) are measured in light of other public companies in the same industry to figure out what "multiple" investors are willing to pay for Ford. In other words, if Ford's PE ratio is fifteen, whereas those of other automotive companies are twenty, then the investment bank will have a rationale to recast Ford's narrative to sell it at a "higher multiple," or as one informant says, "bullshit the multiple." The M&A comp surveys "recent mergers and acquisitions that have taken place in the industry" to figure the value of selling the firm and what the price points are. The leveraged buyout analysis is for the "strictly financial buyer" who is usually not interested in building the business per se. Because "they only want to do it for financial reasons," this model projects a minimum purchase price by putting "as much debt on the company as you possibly can," given the cash flow and income projections of the company, and forecasts how exponential a return can be generated for the financial investor "solely buying it for investment purposes." A "creation and dilution analysis" models how a potential acquisition scenario can have an additive or dilutive effect on share price.

While being expected to do "the bulk of analysis," analysts and associates are also expected to produce perfect copy. "You have to work on copy editing, formatting, and if you get a single mistake, this is grounds for firing." As an associate from Morgan Stanley explained, "Take bullet points. Every bullet point throughout the entire presentation needs to have a period after every line, and you better make sure there's not one missing. VPs and MDs will go ballistic, and you *will* get slammed. Every formatted table needs to say the same throughout: dollars in thousands not millions. It's all about standardization and parallel. If there is one digit after the decimal point, it must be the same throughout." Analysts and associates are vociferously berated for the slightest missteps in professional presentation and immediately disciplined. They are charged with proofing every document from the printing center at all hours of the night, and once a mistake is found, "no one trusts you, and your life can be hell for the next few months." In relaying his not-so-fond memories of life as an analyst at Merrill Lynch, Phillip Young, now an associate, remembers:

It is a very high pressure job. Your clients want it tomorrow. People are very [*pause*] if you make minor mistakes. I think that in other [work] places it could be overlooked, and they just say, "Just get it fixed." Here, every mistake—the way it is explained to me is when you are working on such a high level of clients, if they find typos, mistyped numbers, a valuation that is not done correctly—every little mistake, you get questioned like, "If this is wrong, maybe the other thing is wrong. If that is wrong, then the whole analysis is wrong." So, you want to be as accurate as possible. Everyone is under a lot of pressure, working long hours, stressing out. So, when senior people see little mistakes, they make a big deal out of it. They want everything to be perfect. . . . It's very short tempered. People are [*pause*] it is high pressure work.

Even during my brief stint as a management consulting analyst at BT, I experienced the full onslaught of a senior banker gone postal over professional representation. I will never forget the relentless tirade of my vice president over my subpar ability to manage "version control." Tasked with tracking all changes to a PowerPoint presentation made by multiple vice presidents and associates, I had trouble keeping up.[8] When I was unable to produce the latest version for my vice president the moment he asked for it, his surprise turned livid: "Kaaaren," he yelled, "this is very bad. There is NO VERSION CONTROL! All I ask for is version control! This is not good, Karen. Not good. You won't last here very long without mastering version control. Badly done." As I wrote in my field notes: "It all came down to version control. It also came down to a certain level of discipline and the exacting rigor of following strict professional detail that I had not mastered. I still can't believe he shouted at me in such a patronizing way!" While the analyst often bears the brunt of the harangue, it is important to remember that associates are the designated quality managers: they are in charge of quality control, and they are the ones who usually get "thrown under the bus" if there is one dot out of place.

If the bank "wins" the deal, it is said to go "live," and the analysts and associates gear up for 24-hour client management. Interestingly enough, as one associate recounts, "Most of our clients have people who used to work at investment banks, so clients expect bankers to work 24 hours because clients remember this is what happened when they were on Wall Street." Certainly, the trend, since the 1990s, of most large corporations hiring financially trained MBAs and ex-investment bankers instead of promoting industry managers from within the organization goes hand in hand with the financialization of corporate America and its alignment with the values, practices, and expectations of Wall Street. To return to the Ford example, if the deal is to advise and execute the selling of Ford Motor Company to company x, y, or z, then the next steps for the analysts and associates are to conduct due diligence research, write the Confidential Information Memorandum (CIM), and assemble "the data room." The CIM is what the investment bank sends out to the potential buyers, and the data room is a "data dump" of everything about the company (in this case, Ford) onto a secure web site. The typical CIM contains "a section on the company, its management, the industry, the customers, the creditors, suppliers, and then a special part for the financials of the company, the financial section." To write the CIM, the team usually visits the company being sold to get a sense of the management team, customers, and suppliers, and to begin the gathering and compiling of large amounts of data. Usually, this process is fairly top-down: investment bankers rarely "interview" individual executives, middle managers, or the rank and file; they mainly deal with the company's industry profiles, financial statements, SEC documents, Wall Street research reports, and data from the CEO and CFO. Included with this memo is "the buyers list," where the associate, in consultation with senior bankers, makes a long list of prospective buyers, which typically includes competitors, suppliers, and customers, as well as what investment bankers call "financial buyers," such as private equity firms, investment banks, and financial institutions that are not in the automotive industry but have a "strictly financial" incentive to buy. Financial buyers, not surprisingly, are frequently the top candidates and have intimate, often revolving-door relationships with the representative investment bank. Also, since mergers and acquisitions are private, not public, offerings, the prospective buyers sign a confidentiality agreement not to divulge the contents of the CIM. From here until the buy bids come in, analysts and associates serve as customer service agents, fielding questions from potential buyers as well as senior bankers, while constantly updating the data room. Once the list of buyers is narrowed down, acquirers will come up with due diligence lists, and the analyst has to go into the data room to answer pages of questions. (While this example is being told from the perspective of the analysts and associates on "the sell side," those on "the buy side" of this transaction—as part of the investment bank representing the potential buyer of Ford—access the data room to create multiple models to ascertain if the company is worth buying.) The final steps are to negotiate with the top bidders, establish the terms of the contract, bring in all the attorneys to draft the sales agreements, deal with liabilities and indemnities, and close the deal with an extravagant dinner or celebration, usually on the client's dime.

Perhaps the most frustrating aspect of work for analysts and associates, and one of the central reasons they must stay at the office until the wee hours of the morning, is that they are catering to the schedules of the senior bankers. For example, sometime during the day, an MD might ask for changes to "the deck" (which refers to the latest presentation, whether pitch or CIM) on his desk by the next morning. The next day, instead of making changes that morning, "what most often happens is the MD finishes in the afternoon, then wants something to take home by 6 p.m., then calls at 9 p.m. to make further changes and wants these incorporated into the deck by the following morning." To do so, the analysts stay until 2 a.m. to have the work done by the morning, and the cycle begins again: they never know when the MD will review it, 9 a.m. or 6 p.m., but "whenever the MD changes it, the analyst must immediately make changes." When I asked Joseph Tsai, an investment banking associate at DLJ, what he disliked most about working there, he described his hours, the paper pushing, and the waiting.

KH: Your hours are pretty bad?

JT: They are actually not so bad lately, but when I am busy on a deal, it gets crazy.

KH: What are those crazy hours?

JT: It really depends on the deal or deals—but, I mean, easily until midnight or 1 a.m. every night, including weekends, full-day weekends, and then probably pulling an all-nighter every week or every other week.

KH: Wow, that's pretty brutal.

JT: Yeah. And you kind of need a break after that. As long as there is a break, that's fine. It is hard to work until you get a break. And the problem is probably just doing a lot of things that are insignificant—like you spend a lot of time working on paper pushing so you kind of wonder at the end of the day what value added that was. You spend a lot of time doing that; you have to be very detail oriented, make sure everything is perfect, and also, just coordinating with so many people sometimes is just a pain in the ass. Trying to get the MD from capital markets to focus on something. Call down ten times, and they don't answer your call. You have to go down and grab them and that's a pain. That's probably it for dislikes. The likes—is just being able to be on this [revenue generation] side. Having come from the law, I kind of appreciate more being in the position where we are controlling the deal. We are kind of driving it, always pressing to get it done, so we can get our fee. And the financial rewards are definitely better in banking.

Phillip Young said that he was compelled to think about why bankers work such long hours after a friend was genuinely confused as to "what exactly" kept him at work so long, all the time. He explained:

> Usually during the daytime, you have a lot of meetings with your senior people. They are talking to their clients, and when you need to get things done, you don't—sort of taking orders from them. They will call you up and say, "I need this, I need that. Can you bring me this information." So you know you have to do a whole series of analytical work, but you never really get to it until much later in the day when you are free and you can sit back and say, "Okay, now, let me clear my desk and look at the numbers." And then you start crunching and understanding reading materials. You don't really get to that until 8 or 9 p.m.

I added in, "After everybody else's business is done." He continued:

> Right. You have to take care of everyone else because you are usually . . . working on six, seven, eight projects [deals] at a time. So, out of those . . . projects, maybe four . . . are really quiet, nothing is really going on, but there are three or four that's really happening, lot of stuff going on. Clients are calling. Your senior people want to know what's going on. They need this information, that information. They will call up and say the client asked for this and they need it by tomorrow. That is why you are so busy all the time. . . . I think in a typical corporate world, you may say, "I have a month to do this work." But in banking it's like you need it tomorrow, or the day after. So everything seems to be much more time sensitive, so you are now working late hours.

In addition to spending the day fielding questions from senior bankers, for analysts and associates, "face time"—time seen working hard or at least simply being at the bank—is crucial. Will Howard, a vice president of high yield at Merrill Lynch, remembered how much he disliked "face time" in the morning since he had been up most of the night, not to mention "unnecessary work" that people "mislead" you into thinking is more "important and pressing than it really is": "We work ungodly hours a lot of times when it is so unnecessary, but that is part of the culture as well." He continued, "Work is obviously their life . . . there is no question. Face time is huge. . . . And they are so quick to hang you if you are not 'a hard worker'. It is like, 'oh, yeah, work is your life, and if it is not, you are going to get hung by somebody whose life it is'." Benjamin Hong, an associate at CSFB who left the industry fifteen years ago, recounted that he was not very popular at his workplace even though he was "working crazy hours."

One of the reasons is that he avoided face time in order to get all the work done he was supposed to: "I felt I was more productive when no one else was around—I would literally go in at twelve in the afternoon. Well, it depends what I was doing; if I was on a project, I would go in at twelve noon and stay until seven in the morning. . . . Maybe six to seven in the morning. I would then go home and sleep a few hours and go back to work around twelve or one o'clock and then do it all over again for a month or two at a time until the project was done."

Most analysts are under no illusions about the extreme hierarchies of work and the vast, almost unfathomable expanse of intense, repetitive "shit work" that they are called upon to do with great speed and meticulousness. Casey Woo, an analyst at Morgan Stanley, crystallized his role in investment banking in an interview with the *Harvard Crimson* on how "sizzling hot Wall Street jobs net Harvard grads grief, greenbacks": "Essentially, my boss schmoozes with CEOs on the golf course to convince them to do something to make money in the big picture. I'm in the small picture. I do all the grunt work, crunching numbers and creating presentations." Woo said he could walk away from his experience knowing he was not only well prepared but also on the inside track for most financial jobs in the future, but he would only recommend the experience for specific personalities. "You have to like finance and you have to like pain," he said. "[People are] attracted to the name and the glamour, but there really is no glamour" (Widman 2004). Similarly, Hoon-Jung Kim, a *Harvard Crimson* columnist and former summer intern at an investment bank, writes that contrary to the "clever full-page ads put out by investment banks, promising 'dynamic and rewarding' careers," what Wall Street really wants is to harness "your tolerance for grunt work . . . lots and lots and lots of grunt work." It's precisely because of "this very energy" that "banks are so eager to recruit people like you," not "your exceptional intelligence or your creativity" (Kim 2000).

Forging Superior Workers

On Wall Street, overwork is a normative practice. One is not initiated into investment banking life until one has experienced its rigorous hours. In fact, I often heard bankers simultaneously complain and brag about how long they worked: "I pulled three all-nighters this week"; "I've been working 110-hour weeks for the past two weeks"; "I slept in my car at 3 a.m. because I had to be back to work at 6 a.m." Through this hard work, however, comes, for those analysts who come back and associates who stay, the understanding that they have become a part of the business elite, influential advisors to the top brass of corporate America. As Phillip Young put it:

> I don't think there is any other job . . . where you have only been out of undergrad for six months, yet you are meeting CEOs and CFOs and COOs and talking to them about—maybe you're not talking to them, but at least you are getting to sit in on the conversation—and talk about why they think their business is so good or bad. What do they think they should strategically do to go forward. What needs to be done, the dynamic of the industry. So, I think you get to be on a very senior level—the things that they are concerned about, the issues that they are always thinking about. You are exposed to that.

Paul Archer, now a senior vice president of corporate strategy at Deutsche Bank, started out in the 1980s at Goldman Sachs. He reminisced:

> I joined in '86 when things were very busy on the Street and that Goldman experience was a great one. It was my first professional experience, but it was all consuming. I worked probably 90 percent of my weekends over those two years. I just lived there. I was young, so I could do incredible—there were occasions when I stayed up for 72 hours and those, unfortunately, were not that infrequent. So it was very intense. But, it does tell you something if you are able to work after having not slept for 72 hours, it sort of tells you about the content of work. Granted, a lot of it was mechanical, and at that time, you don't have the framework for . . . assessing what are the skills I am really building. At the time, you are so young and you just think, "Oh, this is the place to be. There seems to be a lot of excitement, and we're doing these deals that have numbers attached to them that are bigger than anything I've ever seen before, so, i.e., therefore, it must be important."

Andrew Wong, an associate in investment banking at Goldman Sachs, explained that since Goldman is the most prestigious firm on Wall Street, its analysts are treated like associates and are groomed—through hard work, immersion with the smartest and most motivated people, and exposure to the "highest level" business deals—to become the financial elite. Wong claimed that because of Goldman's stature, it often does not have to "pitch for deals as much" because clients come to them; the result is that analysts do not spend as much of their time "building huge pitch books" to earn new business. Moreover, analysts not only get the same kinds of laptops, travel rules, car accounts, and word-processing assistance as senior bankers, but also "they bring you to every meeting" with big corporate clients; they "don't put your title on a business card because they look at you as a permanent part of the team and want you to feel a step up in front of clients [to] position you to be as senior as possible." Wong described the cumulative effects:

> Goldman has a lot of business because of who they are and their clients. It all adds up to just an amazing difference at the analyst level . . . nothing like that of my friends. It is really amazing. I have traveled so much; I have platinum on American . . . I went to plenty of meetings where I was the only person from Goldman Sachs there. I have been in many meetings where I was really the only English-speaking person from Goldman Sachs, getting yelled at by really senior people from some of our best clients like Bain Capital, basically saying, "I am not going to fucking do another deal with fucking Goldman Sachs anymore because you people are fucking screwing me." That is just something that other banks would not put their analysts in, but at Goldman, they just kind of start you like that from day one. In fact, my first month on the job, we went to California, and the morning before the presentation, we are sitting at breakfast in the hotel and the VP is like, "Why don't you present this section because you are doing all of the work?" You know, that just does not happen at other places. My first two weeks on the job having to present to Fortune 500 companies' executive management team.

Wong adds that junior people at Goldman get much more responsibility and interesting work sooner because the firm's senior banker mentors are the smartest, most hard-working on the Street, its hiring practices are the most rigorous, not to mention the fact that analysts can rely on excellent business support staff, "24/7 people" who are "willing to fly books over to you personally if that is the only way to get it to you." Given that Goldman has staff that deals with the "b.s." and "spends time checking books, just dealing with the hassles of doing deals in short time frames that cross borders," analysts have the opportunity to "go to all of these [Goldman] partners who are very senior people, very respected people, some real top people in Wall Street in what they do and get their opinions and consolidate it all, and they will give you the time." As a result, analysts and the team "look really smart to our clients because we were able to go to the smartest and best people running the different divisions at Goldman Sachs and just sit down with them and say, 'Here is the situation with our client. . . . [W]hat is your opinion as head of capital markets, as head of high yields, as head of equity research of this or that'. . . . [Y]ou can go back to the client and present all of this stuff that is the opinion from, in reality . . . the partner in leverage finance who would tell you about how he feels about looking over the finance of that company in a leveraged buyout." Given that "senior people at Goldman work harder in general, on average across the board," it not only makes "your life as a junior person much better" but you can also focus on the bigger picture. Wong argued:

> We hire the people with the most potential . . . When we look for an analyst, we always look for the people with the best grades, the people with the most eloquent . . . , the most confident people in an interview, not necessarily the people . . . you think are going to be the best analysts, but people . . . [who] will be good senior bankers. That is the way the firm has always hired everywhere. There is a culture of people stepping out to do more interesting things and to be less focused on being sure all of the numbers are perfectly correct and the "i's" dotted and "t's" crossed. It is much more focused on what is the real big picture situation. Let's advise them on what we think rather than running another five hundred worksheets, spreadsheets. Anyone can do that . . . [What] it is really about is trying to make sure the people do the deals and you get your fee.

Of course, contrary to Wong's implication that Goldman analysts do not do as much grunt work, it was oftentimes analysts from Goldman and Morgan Stanley, the two most prestigious banks, who regaled me with stories of virtually "living" at the bank. Nevertheless, Wong's interpretation dramatizes the cultural grooming undergone by budding "masters of the universe."

Moreover, investment bankers often use the culture of overwork as a site to reinvigorate workplace hierarchies, to use the infamous American work ethic to judge and segregate not only among themselves but between front and back office, as well as between investment bankers and the rest of corporate America. When I asked Julie Cooper, a vice president of High-Yield Bonds at BT, to describe the difference between the work environments at investment banks and at her previous job in corporate America, she replied:

> It's definitely a lot different. You're surrounded by very, very intelligent people for the most part, which I think automatically makes it different. I mean, not that the people that I worked with before weren't [smart], they were just a very different sort of people. I was a manager in operations. People worked hard at, but it wasn't, it was really just much more of we're here to do a job and then we're going to go home. People cared about their jobs, but had different backgrounds. They had different aspirations of where they were going. Most

of the people had college educations, but not all of them did, and you were just kind of there, and some people wanted to get ahead and some people didn't. On Wall Street everybody wants to get ahead. That's what the difference is. You're surrounded by smart people; everyone is extremely competitive. You've got a bunch of people who are a type A or at least trying to pretend that they're a type A. It's a very stimulating environment, but I also think it's a very exhausting one. I think the burnout rate is huge.

Cooper articulated what many of my informants thought—that somehow investment bankers are a qualitatively "different" kind of people than "nine to five" workers. They possess a particular combination of intelligence, ambition, and hard work, which they view as the driving and legitimating forces behind their dominant position in the financial markets. Later, Cooper concretized her views during a whisper to me in a tone conveying shock and admonishment: "I was coming down the elevator at around six o'clock one evening to grab a coffee, and my elevator bank was already completely empty because they all pretty much run out of here at five." To contextualize, Cooper worked on the twenty-fifth floor, and although the twenty-fifth floor was technically a front-office stop, she shared the elevator bank with back-office workers from the fifteenth to twenty-fourth floors. "They have a different work ethic or culture," she continued, and remarked that she almost never ran into "them" because she usually did not come down the elevator until midnight.

Andrew Wong was more explicit: he used his notion of the investment banking work ethic to frame the industry as the cutting edge of efficiency, slicing through the mediocre wastes of "the real world."

If you go to the outside world and you start working with people, people just are not motivated in the same way. It is just a pain in the ass to get anything done in the real world. People leave work at five, six p.m. People take one-hour lunch breaks, and people do this and that and whatever. Believe me, it makes a big deal, because if you are working with people who all work real hard and do whatever it takes to get things done, it just makes things so much easier. And doing things is what makes people feel good about their life and makes them feel important. This is the whole self-worth thing—to complete and do things. In a big corporation or in the academy, it is hard to get things done. [On Wall Street], you work with so many people where anyone you talk to is so responsive and pretty bright and really motivated, it just makes for a pretty good working environment. I think in the old days, back in the fifties or the sixties, people kind of just had a set pattern of life. They went to work, climbed up the ladder slowly, and did whatever they were told. I think now that people are so seduced by the capabilities that you can jump ahead and how much of a difference you can make, how important you can feel or whatever it is that gets you off. . . . It feels like now, you can get a lot done, be really productive, and it is seductive. And that is why people who have more than enough money . . . more than enough respect, still are involved in this at the expense of their families because they need to feel needed. And, there is nothing better than to complete things on a regular basis.

Many investment bankers I interviewed remarked, occasionally with envy but usually with an edge of moral superiority, how inefficient corporate America is because people move so "slowly." As Wong suggested, it is extremely common for investment bankers to interpret their own experience of overwork as a sign that they know how to "get things done," as proof of their "smartness," in contradistinction to the masses of complacent, less capable workers out in "the real world" who therefore need to be restructured to more efficient use. On a grander scale, when I asked Alex Baker, an associate in investment banking at Salomon Smith Barney, about Wall Street's impact on corporate America, he told me, "We've made everyone smarter. We know much more about how global competition works, about how to create efficiency. Before, in the 1970s, corporations were so sloppy; now they are advanced. We're the grease that makes things turn more efficiently; we understood shareholder value and strategy before anyone else."

Taken together, Wong and Baker demonstrate a core sentiment of most of my informants: that the efficient "smartness" of a corporate America restructured according to Wall Street ideologies and expectations mirrors the "internal" smartness of investment bankers, which is itself modeled and justified on a daily basis by the intense hard work, motivation, exposure to greatness, risk-taking, and entrepreneurial resourcefulness bankers are encouraged to demonstrate in their own work environments. My informants conflated the characteristics of brightness and motivation with work ethic to frame their own industry as the cutting edge of efficiency, radically transforming the mediocrity of regular corporations. Wall Street beliefs about "complacent" workplaces in "the outside world" certainly help to justify programs of downsizing and narratives of doing more work with less people and suggest how corporate America should reframe its very approach to work and employment. Of course, it is crucial to remember that with the rise of underpaid service, temporary work, massive corporate downsizings, not to mention sweatshop and informal economy labor, the dominant condition for most lower-middle-class workers is overwork; investment bankers' representation of the complacent nine-to-five "bureaucrat" is thus a straw man.[9]

The particular combination of pinnacle status and market superiority founded on smartness and arduous work begs the question of what *kind* of work is being privileged. I began to realize that my informants' definition of hard work was multilayered (and quite different from my own notions) when Jason Kedd, an investment banking associate from DLJ, after expounding on the importance of Wall Street in reengineering corporate America's productivity, declared, "Yeah, we spend so much time on the pitch books, making them look good; they're full of bullshit. After we win the deal, we just toss 'em." Soon after this exchange, I came across what I thought to be a spectacularly damning chart prominently displayed in the office of one of my associate informants. I asked him if I could copy the chart, and he laughingly said, "Sure, it's an inside joke," though he did ask me not to name the high-profile investment bank (see table 2).

When I first saw this chart, my reaction was to view it as evidence of Wall Street's slick, exploitative relationship to their corporate clients—as, in a sense, the *opposite* of "truly" productive hard work. After completing fieldwork and reflecting on banker inconsistencies, I realized it would be ethnographically inaccurate and too easily dichotomizing to read bullshitting, hype, and outright taking advantage of both corporate clients and investors as proof that Wall Street does not, in fact, work hard, or as antithetical to its understandings of what constitutes important work. While investment bankers certainly recognize that they do, in fact, bullshit their clients, they usually view such practices as justified by the hard work they genuinely put in, their superior knowledge of the market, and the financial good they are sure their interventions ultimately accomplish. (At the same time, such conscious manipulation foreshadows my later discussion of how investment banking corporate culture, in its privileging of "the deal" above all other considerations, contradicts Wall Street's own professed ideals.)

Wall Street investment bankers, by virtue of their smartness, believe that they cannot help but outwit, outmaneuver, and in short, run circles around most corporations. These kinds of charts and jokes work to perform and produce this sense of superiority and entitlement. In American culture at large, hard work is often associated with "an honest day's work," but Wall Street instead heralds a constant "24/7" engagement and what might be dubbed "value-added" work. For investment bankers, the labor of most nine-to-five workers, the honest (but plodding) day's work from which my informants regularly distinguished themselves, is understood as complacent and stagnantly routine. Most corporate work, from Wall

Table 2. "Process for a High Yield Deal" (From the desk of an investment banking associate).

INVESTMENT BANKING PROCESS	THE REAL DEAL
1. Pitch Prospective Client. Tell them how great we are at raising junk	1. Lie, cheat, steal, and bad mouth your competitors to win the business
2. Build financial model: historical performance and projected earnings and leverage ratios	2. Manipulate projection so credit ratings are reasonable
3. Analyze comparable high-yield issues to understand market rates and returns	3. Select the most aggressive companies to show the client
4. Due Diligence: Analyze the company and understand why it exists and will it exist tomorrow	4. Boondoggle: Build up your frequent flyer miles
5. Drafting Sessions: Craft the perfect marketing document to bring to market	5. Eat M&M's, ice cream bars, and cookies. Get fat!!!
6. Prepare Rating Agency Presentation	6. Mask the company's weaknesses by concentrating on 1 or 2 strengths
7. Prepare Road Show Presentation	7. Same as above – Goal: To fool the investor
8. Road Show: Grueling 8 days on the road	8. Expense account – go crazy with the client's money!!!

Street's perspective, is neither change oriented, financially innovative, nor directed toward spiking stock prices; it is not forward-thinking nor in lockstep with the market, and as such is inherently *unproductive*. It does not "add value" according to the financial parameters by which investment bankers measure success.

Simultaneously, on Wall Street, hard work is always overwork—long, grinding hours spent staring at spreadsheets, perfecting pitch books, and managing clients. Investment banks' assumptions about their cultural and technical superiority are "proved" to their elite workers every day via the internalization of overwork, their work lives providing a kind of ideological discipline that keeps them focused on market position, profit making, and shareholder value. My informants often legitimated their work and its effects on corporations by appealing to their own work ethic: the mergers and acquisitions they manage must be good because, well, they work so hard at them. The very qualities assumed to make investment bankers the world's most elite workforce also justify the power of Wall Street investment banks and the dominance of their ideologies, especially shareholder value. The fetish for working hard and working constantly bolsters claims of hyperefficiency and extreme responsiveness to the demands and rhythms of the market. Not surprisingly, then, the culture of hard work legitimates Wall Street investment bankers' roles as spokespeople for, and embodiments of, the financial markets.

Marked and Unmarked Investment Bankers and the Politics of Hard Work

Hard work is also a site where investment bankers not only demonstrate and internalize their rightful position as avatars of the market, but also negotiate the contradictions and hierarchies which differentiate some "marked" investment bankers as less worthy of the generic status of smartness that is normatively associated with Wall Street. Specifically, these investment bankers look toward hard(er) work to erase their marked status and ease their entry into the money meritocracy.

One central way in which smartness gets constituted as normative and nondiscriminatory is through Wall Street's notion of a "money meritocracy," which is its dominant (though contested) narrative justifying its social order and employee composition. The money meritocracy posits that the only color Wall Street sees is green, and because its lust for money is even greater than that of most institutions, it is inadvertently "less racist and sexist" than society at large. The logic resembles seventeenth-century political arguments for the triumph of capitalism as described by Albert O. Hirschman, where the passion for moneymaking came to be seen as a "benign proclivity," the calm and constant "interest" of "doux commerce" that would serve to overtake and countervail against more "malignant" vices (Hirschman 1997, 66). Wall Street argues that its greed for money is a "counteracting" interest against other more evil passions such as racism and sexism. Because investment banks are *so* greedy, so singularly focused on money, they become money meritocracies: whoever makes them money will be rewarded regardless of background or identity. Of course, instead of understanding desire for money as itself a constructed "passion," most Wall Streeters see it as a naturalized state. Similarly, the Wall Street mantra that "money does not discriminate" resonates powerfully with the assumption of neoliberal economic theory that racism and other prejudices form "an impediment to efficient market transactions and [are] therefore likely to be overridden in the long run by the exigency to generate profit" (Browne and Misra 2003, 495). On Wall Street, "economic outcome" is seen as constituted through skill, merit, and education, not such "externalities" as race, class, and gender.[10]

Using money meritocracy as a dominant discourse of exceptionalism, investment banks differentiate themselves from corporate America, which they imagine to be caught up in the traditional "ol' boys' network." Unlike the bureaucratic, out-of-touch managers of most corporations, Wall Street bankers are a modern, renegade breed whose singular focus on money makes possible color-blind innocence and objectivity. Peter Lucas, a white associate in equities research at Merrill Lynch, commented, "It's a place where people don't worry a lot about niceties, and since they are obviously there to make money, it's a meritocracy, and we don't have much time for much else." Throughout my fieldwork, many informants emphasized that Wall Street firms were no longer "old line" bureaucratic institutions; they were for the most part performance-based in their promotion and talent-driven in their recruitment. In order to attract the most talent, Wall Street firms claimed to have adopted diverse and inclusive approaches to hiring: investment bankers did not have to be aristocrats, but could be "geeky quant-jocks" or amazing "chess players off the street." The singular pursuit of the bottom line serves as a deterrent against any residual flare-ups of institutionalized racism, sexism, and classism, sweeping the specter of bias onto the terrain of other institutions.

In February 1998, I attended an evening panel discussion, "History of People of Color on Wall Street: A Look at Strategies and Challenges in the Twenty-first Century," presented by the National Association of Securities Professionals (NASP) and Salomon Smith Barney.[11] It was my first introduction to the interrelatedness of hard work, money meritocracy, divisions of labor within investment banks, and the invidious distinctions of race, class, and gender. The panelists were African American senior executives (both women and men) in the securities industry. All were introduced to the audience as "historical figures," for they were either the first or among the first African Americans to reach their positions in their respective investment banks. Charlene Jackson was (in the mid-1990s) the first African American woman to become a managing director at Salomon Smith Barney; Obie McKenzie was the second African American to join Morgan Stanley "in a professional capacity"; Carla Harris was one of the first African American women senior vice presidents (or "principals") at Morgan Stanley; Jide Zeitlin was one of the few African American partners at Goldman Sachs; and Fred Terrell was one of the first African American managing directors at CSFB.[12] The evening was widely attended by young analysts and associates of color across multiple investment banks, especially the analysts from the SEO program.[13] The evening generated a lively dialogue, not only between the audience and the panelists, but also among the panelists themselves, with most of the discussion centered on imparting advice to the new generation of color on Wall Street and navigating the complex racial terrain of investment banks.

The evening began with general questions about the panelists' experiences on Wall Street and how they motivated themselves to "keep climbing the ladder" despite endemic racism, the unstated but understood subtext. The panelists' responses sounded a common note of success in the face of adversity: "Wall Street is a meat grinder." "I had to work harder than anyone else." "You have to have fun and like what you do, or they will beat you down very quickly." "There's always going to be someone waiting to take your place, so you have to look within yourself to see if you really want it, and you can do it." Jide Zeitlin, a partner and managing director at Goldman Sachs and a specialist in M&A, said that in order to succeed in his career, he focused so intensely on the complexities and techniques of deals that his clients and the other bankers on his team "didn't have to talk about what country club they went to." He made up his mind to "work very hard" to make sure he was not "vulnerable," and over time, once he began to develop deeper relationships with clients, the bank "couldn't very well slight" him. Zeitlin's strategy was to use his hard work and expertise about the product (M&A) to eliminate race from consideration.

His specialty, M&A, demands rigorous hours and technical product expertise,[14] and was oftentimes considered by my informants of color to be a better fit than other departments.[15] According to many of my informants, the jobs and departments that were understood to require less socializing and "schmoozing with the elite" were also perceived as less racist and sexist, and therefore "better" places for women and people of color. This same idea also manifests in the differentiation and separation of departments within investment banks into "product side" and "relationship side," with the product side imagined to be more meritocratic and less dependent on social connections. Most Wall Street investment banks organize their departments and bankers into 1) corporate finance groups that originate the deals, advise corporations in their industry to do transactions by keeping in constant contact with various CEOs, CFOs, and COOs, and 2) "product expertise" groups, such as M&A, high-yield bonds, derivatives, and structured finance, that are known for their focus on the technical skills necessary to analyze and execute the transactions. Of course, these distinctions are blurry, for just as many deal-making bankers need to understand the trends occurring in their respective industries as well as the transactions they are selling, many "product-oriented" bankers also need to "schmooze" with clients, especially in M&A.

Zeitlin's statements echoed the narratives of the majority of women and people of color that I interviewed. Many Asian American men and women pointed out that they often did well in technology or product-focused areas because, first, it was assumed that "Asians would be 'quant jocks' anyway," and conforming to the stereotype was the path of least resistance; and second, these departments actually were more likely to function according to their representation, focusing more on hard work and profits, less on explicitly raced and gendered networks. Monica Choi, an Asian American vice president of M&A at Merrill Lynch, gave a very compelling explanation of such a strategy. I asked her, "How is the work environment, the pace, the people, or the culture of M&A different from other divisions in the investment bank?" Her reply is worth quoting at length:

> I think M&A tends to bring out people who are less social because it is much more intellectual, probably the most intellectual area within an investment bank. . . . From the simple issue of how am I going to make this [merger] work from a financial point of view, or what about the taxes, what about accounting, what about the integration of these two businesses because you walk through these factories and you see one company is doing it one way and the other company is set up in a totally different way. How do you integrate all of this? So, you have to understand every element about a business. . . . I think the nature of the M&A business is such that it is much less social. I think it does attract people who are, or people become, less polished in some respect because the firm is not hiring you and paying what they are paying you so that you are dressed really well and you say all of the right things. Other sides of this business [are] much more like that, so the environment is much different. My counterparts in corporate finance are what I call the relationship people. They basically maintain the relationship with the client. Now, they don't give advice to these clients. Their sole job is to basically maintain the relationship. So, Company X's CEO will have only one contact within Merrill Lynch, and it will be this one individual. It's his responsibility to—like if the CEO says I need XYZ—it is his job to go get the specialist within the firm. . . . Everybody is set up on Wall Street so you basically have this relationship manager. By nature, you need to be very different on that side of the business . . . because they are

not hiring you for your brainpower. If you are smart, if you happen to be smart, that is great . . . but on that side of the business, it is much more important that you are more connected from a social standpoint, to be able to connect with the CEO. . . . So it should not be surprising that I picked M&A after being a double minority, as a woman and as an Asian woman. I am a product specialist. When I get hired, I am getting hired for my understanding and my expertise, and so when they take advice from me, they don't really have to like me. They can say, "Oh, she is a bitch!" Whereas on the relationship side, they really do have to like you. And so you see little things like their social manners are much more refined. Their talents are just amazing. Just to give you an example, I mean, they always laugh about this, but this Saturday, I had to set up a conference call. I have not done this in a really long time, so I did not really even know how to do it. We had to get the relationship manager! Because it is their job to make sure that the client is really comfortable and always has everything that they need, so the things that they have to be good at and the skills that they learn are different. So they are a lot better golfers— seriously. It is totally, completely, absolutely true. Because they are invited to socialize when the CEO has a benefit. I couldn't really do that partly because I don't really know how to suck up that well. But you really do need to push away your pride and serve your clients with whatever they need. Because that environment is about who likes who, it is a lot more political. It is not as defined as my side of the business. Either you know it or you don't on my side of the business. There are some gray areas . . . [but they are] extremely few relative to the other side of the business. Because *there*, it is very, very important that people like you. It could be they just think you are a really cool guy or you are a really cool girl or woman—or the fact that your father is X, Y, and Z; that helps. Those things are very, very important: your background and how connected you are. For example, there was an analyst straight out of college who was an amateur golf guy, whatever, he was a really, really good golf player, kind of one level below pro, but could have gone pro. He played with Tiger Woods, and he knows Tiger Woods really well. I couldn't believe it because this guy spent the entire first year doing zero work! All he did was play golf because the clients loved him. They thought he was fabulous. He was giving them tips on how to hit the ball. It was actually very comical because he had to do something for me, and he didn't know how to do it! I was like, "How is it that you are a second-year analyst and you don't know how to do this?" And I had no idea what his background was and whatever. So, I basically told his boss, "He is useless. I need somebody else. I cannot use this guy." Then his boss was like, "Oh, now come on, be nice. Maybe he just needs to learn this stuff." So I said, "Well, I don't have time to teach him. You teach him." It kind of bothered me—like, why is this guy so stupid? This is such basic stuff. He should have learned this stuff. He has already spent a year here, and he doesn't even know what investment banking is all about. This is what I found out. I was so upset because I haven't even been *invited* to golf outings. That is what I call them. And here was this first-year analyst, twenty-two years old, going to Pebble Beach on behalf of Merrill Lynch.

Zeitlin and Choi had similar strategies and interpretations of their career paths: both focused on being experts in M&A, a "product area," and both realized early in their careers that they were not particularly well connected and were not being invited to the country clubs and golf courses. (It is important to mention that these spaces of whiteness enact white male privilege and set the stage for the hypermobility of young white men by allowing them uninhibited access to powerful, older white men.) As such, both understood that highlighting their product expertise was one of the few accepted ways to distinguish themselves. Besides challenging the money meritocracy myth, Choi's detailed explanation helped me to understand how some product areas can provide shelter and an opportunity to carve out expertise that is not immediately measured or solely privileged by its closeness and access to white male space and networks.

At the panel discussion, Zeitlin's comments prompted Obie McKenzie of Morgan Stanley to ask, "Can African Americans succeed on the basis of their relationships, not product knowledge? Can you forget that you are black?" Fred Terrell, like Zeitlin, replied to this exchange by reframing the narrative of separation between skill and hard work "versus" relationships in terms of career stages: "Very early in the career, focus on your core competencies, work as hard as you can to be as good as you can. Wall Street does reward the good idea. Without that foundation, you won't get to the second stage. . . . The second part of your career has to do with relationships, to sell the deal. Can you get the business just based on knowing the answer?" Rather than chart a possible career progression that led to true insider status, Terrell turned to the notion of merit as an alternative to relationship building: "Wall Street is greedy enough that they are willing to overlook to some extent those who are not white. So, you may not be vacationing in the same place or get invited to the house in the Hamptons, but who cares?" In the end, Terrell could not conceive of people of color being able to enter the relationship side of the business without technical competence as their main asset. He did not argue that African Americans on Wall Street could simply "get the business just based on knowing the answer," but rather articulated a strategy of mapping the racial terrain in stages so as to stave off or avoid direct confrontation with racism, that sought to focus on hard work and ideas before, or instead of, invitations to the Hamptons.

Terrell's explanations clearly reflect aspects of the division of labor on Wall Street. At the analyst and associate levels, one's job requirements are more focused on creating presentations and compiling spreadsheets, yet as one moves to the vice president level and upward, one is promoted only when one begins to sell and generate deals to various corporations and institutions. As such, privileged social networks are more obviously required for the "second stage." At the more junior levels, especially on the product side because of these departments' own narrative of themselves as caring mainly about money, skill, and hard work, there do seem to be comparatively fewer obstacles for people of color and women.[16] Charlene Jackson, however, after listening to Zeitlin and Terrell's comments, began to show some exasperation at their continued adherence to the dichotomy of hard work versus relationships. She stated emphatically:

> Working 110 percent to 125 percent capacity is only one part of it. There's hard work, but there are also the political and social realms. People of color and women don't know how to be a part of the political and social realms. We're still not getting where we need to be, so we work harder and harder, but we end up *behind!* So, we need to find a mentor, get a guide; we need to be invited to that country club and get access to powerful men. . . . We need to know the land mines. The onus is on the people on this panel. It's not just about hard work: I learned how to play golf.

Jackson's intervention here was important, for she demonstrated that concentrating on hard work and skill development or finding the "right" department does not negate the existence and the importance of "the social and political realms." In fact, focusing only on hard work can be detrimental to the extent that one "postpones" or attempts to ignore differential power relationships and the conflation of success and "access to powerful men." This does not mean, however, that Jackson disagreed with Zeitlin and Terrell's strategies; rather she added nuance to their arguments.

Focusing on Jackson's comment about needing a mentor, a young black woman in the audience, an associate at Barclay's Bank who had just received her MBA, asked the panelists at what point in her career would having a mentor be the most crucial. Carla Harris answered her question, arguing for the necessity of mentors for at least the first ten years on Wall Street. Within the first couple of years, you "need to broaden [your] skills

set" and "find someone to help you navigate through the land mines."
Harris described a promotion scenario: "They might be in a meeting
saying 'We're gonna screw that one this week, but not him'. Someone
needs to be in there carrying your side. So, stop working so hard and go
find one [a mentor] because otherwise you're wasting your time. Who's
going to be *in the room* fighting for you?" Following Carla Harris, Charlene
Jackson revealed a strategy similar to that of Zeitlin, Terrell, and Choi,
demonstrating how tightly guarded Wall Street boundaries are and how
remarkably bleak prospects for advancement continue to be for some: "If
you're African American, you need a five-year exit strategy because the
chances are really slim to advance. You have to make certain choices. You
know if you're African American, you're gonna be in 'public finance.' On
the issue of should you spend your time being in a relationship business or
product business, in a relationship business, you would have to talk about
the country club; in product, you wouldn't have to, just show expertise.
Had I stayed in corporate finance [a relationships business], I would not
have become an MD [managing director]." In this dialogue, both Harris
and Jackson demonstrated that regardless of one's department, devotion
to hard work, or technical expertise, working on Wall Street is social and
political. The segregations based on invidious distinctions cut across departments such that in order to be promoted, one must have connections,
a mentor, someone in power "in the room" fighting for you.[17] One might
also have to learn how to play golf.

Since socializing in exclusive contexts is an inescapable part of the job,
many of my "marked" informants found that this narrative of separation
(hard work from relationships) was not only hierarchically segregationist
but also misleadingly detrimental to future promotion because it disguised the extent to which "professional space" is constructed beyond the
confines of the workplace. Still others did not engage as much with this
separation because they experienced the site of their exclusion "outside"
of the workplace; for them, it was not so much about which departments
of the bank were less discriminatory, as marking was even more heightened in spaces physically outside the workplace but still within the bank's
general social milieu, in social settings counted as important for "professional development" and "networking." (It is important to note, however,
that departments on the "relationship side" are more likely to emphasize employee interaction outside the workplace.) For example, Christine
Chang, an Asian American vice president in the High-Yield Division of BT,
gave a common yet pivotal example of her exclusion from such spaces of
"professional development."

I am not particularly interested in sports, so when all of my colleagues are discussing that, I don't have anything in particular to add to that conversation. A lot of Wall Street entertainment involves going to strip bars. It is not something that I am particularly interested in, so I get left out of that realm of entertainment. So, it is stuff like that. It is having to do with not fitting into the culture. It has never really had much to do with people not giving me a chance or not having a lot of responsibility. That has not been tough at all. I feel lucky in that way. It is more not having a lot of commonality with everybody else who works in the industry. That makes it tougher.

For those who have historically (and presently) *not* been excluded from the Street's "walls," one's "social" life and "work" life intersect and overlap such that both spaces aid in strengthening the density of one's professional network. Because the boundaries are often unseen, there exists little differentiation between the two spaces and very little consciousness about the fact that what counts as "professional" space is not confined to the office cubicle. More importantly, the particular places that often do count as after-work social spaces (from the strip club to the country club) have been long-term perpetuators of exclusion. As such, those experiencing blatant ostracism from the spaces of after-work socializing have often welcomed the limiting of the boundaries of what constitutes "the job." Segregations and boundaries, even those delineating certain departments as less concerned with background, relationships, and by extension, after-work socializing, can sometimes serve as a form of protection, albeit one that often interferes with career goals and mystifies power structures. What constitutes the space of work, then, is a highly contested political as well as personal struggle.

Carla Harris's and Charlene Jackson's call to "stop working so hard" alerted me to the dangers of being perceived as working *too* hard in the context of racial and gender discrimination. In addition to only certain workers being disciplined and pressured to work even harder within this discourse of color-erasing meritocracy, these same workers can be taken advantage of and perceived as unstrategic precisely *because* they are working so hard. Read as being too willing to "give away" their time, their time is understood to be less valuable. To concretely demonstrate this phenomenon, I turn briefly to my informant Julie Cooper's interpretation of how her 100-plus-hour weeks for six months on a massive project affected her career. A white woman who recently became a vice president in the High Yield Department at BT, she described her new job as "incredibly intense, and the hours were sick and insane. I mean, I worked on average from

8 a.m. to 2 a.m., five days a week and Saturday and Sunday usually about 10 hours a day. . . . [I]t was brutal." Cooper evoked an image of work she will never forget: the night before her wedding she worked until 3 a.m., and when she was leaving, the escalators had already been turned the other direction in preparation for morning traffic. But, assuming that hard work was usually a positive thing on Wall Street, I asked, "Well, at least do you feel like it was good for your career?"

JC: No, I actually don't think it was good for my career. Because I think on Wall Street, in particular, if you show that you're willing to kill yourself, you would think that would be a good thing, but I don't really think it is. I think that a lot of it is based on perception. . . . If you are willing to say, "Oh fine, you want me to do analyst's work, even though I'm a VP, no problem. You want me to do whatever, I'll do it." And so what they do is they end up giving you more and more of the stuff you shouldn't have to do because you'll do it. And so I don't think it was helpful. I think that people look at it and say, "Well, she did it, but we could have gotten someone else to do it." Not, "Wow, here's someone who basically gave up her life for six months."

KH: And did it all.

JC: Did it all. They don't think, "We usually have four people do this, we did it with one person." I think that they were happy the deal got done . . . but I don't think that from my perspective it was a good thing for me. . . . In terms of how you're treated here, there is that hierarchy, you know? I was an associate, I have my MBA; *you* [referring to me] were an analyst. I never really believed in that, but I think that a lot of people do. You come in, you pay your dues, you do your work, and if you show that you're willing to do grunt work when you're supposed to be beyond that, then I think that's a bad thing.

KH: I also always hear stories about people who didn't do anything—the analysts and the associates do it all—but they get credit for the deal.

JC: Right, exactly . . . in terms of the way a lot of other people perceived it, it's like, "Well, you're doing all this, but you're stupid to be doing it because you're not going to get paid and you're not going to be appreciated." For example, my husband. . . . He is not as hard of a worker as I am, he is probably not as smart as I am, but he will do much better on Wall Street than I will because he has confidence in himself.

Julie Cooper's insights into how her contribution was interpreted by her peers and bosses are crucial to situating the politics of hard work. Many women on Wall Street are often pressured to "tackle assignments others shunned as losers or even take brief career detours to get tough jobs done for their bosses, who are almost always male" (White and Hymowitz 1997). As Cooper's story alerts us, such efforts are often not highly valued and go unrewarded as many investment banks see them as both defining women's "limited" capabilities (what they can do) and their "natural" abilities (what they are supposed to do). Furthermore, after having accomplished such mammoth tasks, which are often not the high-profile deals given to men, women are often interpreted or represented not as "leaders" of the deal but rather as being overwhelmed and reduced by the work. Women are imagined, as well as structurally positioned, as stupidly "not beyond" the grunt work (and correspondingly unworthy of high-profile work) by virtue of having done it.

How most women, especially women of color, navigate not only hard work but grunt work takes on the added dimension of what I call "class slippage." The "socks over hose" phenomenon is a case in point. Raina Bennett, an African American analyst in emerging markets at Lehman Brothers, and Malinda Fan, an Asian American senior vice president in structured finance at Lehman Brothers, were discussing one afternoon how many women who work on Wall Street wear sneakers during the commute and then change into their heels once they arrive at the office. Because many women wear skirt suits to work, they already have on pantyhose underneath the white athletic socks. The end result, Bennett and Fan agreed, is "tacky." The entire "look," which pairs the suit with hose and socks and sneakers, is distinctly "unprofessional." I was surprised by their observations, as I assumed that most women who worked on Wall Street (and corporate environments in general), especially in the commuting frenzy of New York City, practiced this change-of-shoe routine. "Don't you two do that?" I asked. They look at me with feigned horror and replied that they did not: they wore the same leather pumps, with a solid, medium-high heel, throughout the day. Later, one confessed that she used to do the "shoe-change-thing," but only for the first couple of months at her job; she quickly learned the ropes. Upon further rumination, the significance of this change of shoe practice became clear: the socks and sneakers over hose is a marker, albeit imprecise, of a lower-class status. First, most front-office "professional" women live in or close to Manhattan, or have access to car transportation into Manhattan, but back-office workers and administrative assistants tend to live farther away—in Brooklyn, Queens, Bronx, or Staten Island, or in remoter neighborhoods in New Jersey or even Pennsylvania. They face much longer commutes than higher-ranking women, and therefore need to change into sneakers for the long haul home. Second, many of the younger administrative staff who work in the front office (and who are usually support staff for male investment bankers) wear higher heels than the professional women, and thus need to change into sneakers for more comfortable commuting.[18] Front-office women, then, make sure to distinguish their dress from that of administrative staff: they wear body contouring suits that are not too tight, heels that are not too low or too high, hair that is coiffed but not too high or too hair sprayed. Because women in general are often treated similarly as a class and are "feminized" as support staff, female investment bankers must constantly guard against class slippage: being mistaken for assistants or "admins." Thus, they must police themselves and each other for such class infractions as wearing socks over hose. This concern is even more pronounced among women of color, as racial hierarchies threaten to "deprofessionalize" them even further.

Gillian Summers, an African American analyst at BT, who had been working on Wall Street for only a year, illustrates this point with her story about a tray of muffins. In investment banking, especially during highly profitable years, meetings are usually accompanied by overloaded trays of food. I have heard many stories of women who have avoided standing near coffee spouts for fear that men will mistake them for administrative assistants and ask them to help with the food and pour coffee. After one meeting, Summers was astonished at the amount of food left over and appalled when no one helped the administrative assistant, also an African American woman, carry the trays out of the meeting room. Summers struggled through an internal debate. Although she knew that she was "not supposed to," she did not want the administrative assistant to think that she thought herself "above" carrying the tray and also wished to compensate in some way for her colleagues' lack of consideration. In an attempt to maintain rapport, she checked to make sure no one else could observe her, quickly carried out one tray, then disappeared back to her cubicle.

> GS: Yes, it's like if you are at a meeting and there is a tray of bread or whatever, and you know that people in your department want it, you can't take it because they would say, "What are you doing?" You can't do that.
>
> KH: Oh, you mean when you see a tray you can't . . .
>
> GS: Yeah, when you are in a meeting and you know your group wants it, but you can't take it to your group. You have to let the secretary do it because if you take it in, it's like you are not supposed to do that.

When I asked her why not, she replied that it was not professional, that if your peers or bosses witness you performing a "support" role, they will believe that you do not take your own time seriously and might assume that you are willing to be taken advantage of and do "scut work." They will lose respect for your professionalism via your association with administrative work (work that is beneath the front office), and they might begin to exclude you from certain high-profile projects. It is much better to waste the food than to be associated with its assemblage (meant for food service and administrative staff), its transfer (meant for administrative staff), or its leftover consumption (meant for those more "in need"). I then asked Summers, "Can you associate too much with administrative staff? I mean, do they [her bosses and peers] start looking at you funny if . . ." She answered:

> That's the thing about that—you really can't, even though I will go over and talk with them sometimes because there is one that I was really good friends with. But, on the whole, if we are working and see each other, I will say "Hi," nothing to indicate you speak to them. You can't ask an admin to go to lunch or breakfast. If they see you with them too much, they are like—you know. I just don't. . . . And for me, don't let a black person, like a computer person, come up on the floor and come over to fix my computer, because they will think there is something going on. It is just like little stuff like that.

Summers believed she had to be careful about social relationships with other African Americans of any rank: "Like one of the guys from finance, he just happened to be a friend, but anytime that we are in word processing at the same time and people see us, they are like, 'What's going on with you two?' And, I am just standing there talking about work, but people just make more out of it—it's ridiculous." Bankers of color must be careful about contact between two people of the same (nonwhite) racial identity, as any such interaction can be interpreted as class slippage, sexual innuendo, or a kind of racial solidarity that white colleagues find threatening.

Kim Chung, an Asian American research analyst at Salomon Smith Barney, had the same issue with a "tech guy"—also Asian American—who was sent to troubleshoot her computer. Feeling guilty that the technician was doing all the work while she was just standing there, she got down on the floor with him and helped him. Then a peer walked by and pulled her aside, admonishing, "Kim, you just can't do that. What if the VP sees you?" Because Chung thought that she was simply trying to be helpful, she did not realize at first that she was crossing a boundary in a way that could shape representations and perceptions of her status and professionalism. The boundary transgressed was perhaps made even more dangerous because Asian Americans are often stereotyped as "computer nerds" and being seen helping an Asian American IT worker might associate her with that kind of support work.

Herein lies the rub: there continually exists the danger that professional women get mistaken for administrative staff, where hard work, instead of being associated with upward mobility, is reduced to, as well as conflated with, grunt work. This danger is even more heightened for women of color. Much of the scholarship on race, gender, and work in the United States has demonstrated that groups at the intersections of marginalized identities of race and gender are simultaneously stratified by class (Jones 1998). In other words, because jobs, pay, and work are often segregated based on race and gender, and most of these jobs are devalued as "unprofessional," then those who straddle class lines in their professional identities are often in danger of slipping, via gender and race, downward in perceived rank. As junior-ranking women of color, both Summers and Chung were, in a sense, always already in precarious positions; their class performances were still too fragile to withstand the weight of racial and gender lumping. Their experiences therefore often center on maintaining front-office distinctions in order to avoid the conflation and the collapse of class distinctions—practices deemed necessary for career promotion. Since the front office recruits only from the most elite universities in the country, most of these marked bankers are not from poor, working-class families, and as such, most Wall Street minorities usually experience class slippage in terms of race and gender.[19]

In an investment bank the presentation of self is crucial. Not surprisingly, the range of possibilities for self-representation is extremely narrow, and while restrictions certainly affect normative investment bankers, the limitations and boundaries on one's image repertoire are more onerous and the consequences of straying over them are much more dire for women and people of color. Kate Miller, a former analyst at Morgan Stanley, in describing the culture of investment banks, stated that "image is everything," affecting even how one eats lunch.

> KM: Image is everything from the way you dress, the way you talk, the way you respond to situations, the way you approach a problem. Even something as ludicrous as the way you eat or—these are such little things. If you ate in the lunchroom too often, there was a perception that, you know, it just wasn't something that was done. Everybody brought their food back to their desk. And you could be sitting around joking and talking in your office, but you were at your desk.

KH: Could you bring your own lunch?

KM: That was an indication of being maybe frugal or being concerned about [money], you know. Yeah.

I never knew anyone who worked in Wall Street's front offices who brought their own lunch, whereas many in the back office and the administrative staff certainly did. Front-office workers always purchased lunch at the bank's cafeteria or at quick-eat shops within walking distance. Bringing one's lunch was not a sign of upward mobility—it connoted a lower-class concern with overspending, a relationship with money that was not nonchalant. It sent messages of asocial behavior, as frugality took precedent over going out and buying lunch with colleagues. What's for lunch, therefore, is a profound sign of class differentiation. At the same time, going out to lunch or eating in the cafeteria were activities one had to control strictly. Being seen eating and talking in the cafeteria too often or for too long was not considered professional, except on occasion, because it connoted time away from hard work. Cardboard take-out trays and boxes, then, were the primary tools of food transport and were more fully stocked in the cafeteria than dining room trays meant for eating in the dining room. In fact, many of the front-office floors featured their own "express cafés," where only the brown cardboard boxes were available, as everyone was expected to buy lunch *and* bring it back to their desks to continue work. Certainly, these express cafes were double-edged swords: they functioned both as amenities for money-making floors and as constant reminders to quickly get back to the white-collar sweatshop.

The hard work needed to forge the smart "men of mettle" who serve as a disciplinary exemplar of the new prototype of worker under short-term financial capitalism is itself calibrated on the bodies of unmarked investment bankers. Given this broader culture of hard work and achieving generic smartness, nonnormative racial and gender status only make the marked work harder to look generic. While such strivings include working even harder and focusing on building "technical" skills and product knowledge, ironically, for the marked, such practices often backfire as hard work slips into grunt work, and professional class slips into support staff, ultimately threatening not only their upwardly mobile performance and compensation, but also their ability to represent the successful subject (and model) of finance capital.

3

Wall Street Historiographies and

the Shareholder Value Revolution

As I worked at a Wall Street investment bank in 1996–97 and then began intensive ethnographic fieldwork in 1998, shareholder value was just on the cusp of inundating American culture as the central explanation and rationale for corporate restructuring, changing concepts of wealth and inequality, and the state of the American economy. Although this strand of shareholder-centric thinking had at that point been dominant in investment banking for at least fifteen years, it was still relatively uncommon in popular media representations and even academic discourse outside business schools and economic departments. In the post-millenary, post-Enron era, however, "shareholder value" has become a part of mainstream, everyday discourse, and it certainly seems as if cultural critics and social scientists all "know" what shareholder value means and what is at stake in the social economy of stock-price dominance. I recall my initial surprise during my time at Bankers Trust (BT), when senior bankers and colleagues all assumed that I knew what BT's "true" (though unstated) mission statement was. I had assumed that a corporate mission statement, albeit a public relations device in line with the agribusiness claim to "feed the world," would be individualized to particular corporate purposes, visions, and strategic initiatives, addressing such questions as "why are we here," "what do we stand for," and "what does our business seek to accomplish." Instead, I was told that regardless of what engravings or plaques decorate our offices, "the mission (of all of Wall Street and all corporations) is *always* to create shareholder value."

Contextualizing Shareholder Value

Shareholder value was the most important concept with which my informants made sense of the world and their place in it: it shaped how they used their "smartness" and explained the purpose of their hard work. However, just as smartness and hard work are represented as unmarked, meritocratic ideals embodied by Wall Street despite their groundedness in hierarchy, shareholder value itself is an all-encompassing objective, which implodes and contradicts in practice. Although shareholder value and "the shareholder revolution" of the 1980s and 1990s are precisely what allowed for Wall Street to solidify its influence over corporate America, they also outline a cultural ideal that eludes full realization. Yet it is only through analyzing the particularities, intricacies, and contradictions of Wall Street's shareholder value ideologies, and how they historically came to be the predominant measure of U.S. corporations since the 1980s, that the ethnographic present will make sense.[1]

I would argue that despite its ubiquity and dominance in American capitalism, "shareholder value" continues to be a black box, an uninterrogated concept that desperately needs to be contextualized within particular power relationships, institutional configurations, and a specific interpretation of financial history. When discussing with other academics the ascendancy of shareholder value and the often radical effect it has had on American business culture, I am often asked, "What's so new about that? Hasn't capitalism always been about making as much money as possible?" These questions project an ahistorical capitalism across time and space; conflate profit with stock price; flatten the complexity and multiplicity of capitalist institutions, values, and motivations; and reinforce dominant approaches to capitalist histories. Apprehending shareholder value, then, necessitates delineating its meanings, uses, and effects in the present, as well as how historiographies of shareholder value and a particular capitalist past are used to justify Wall Street interests. This chapter unpacks the ethnographic present, which I argue begins with the 1980s takeover movement. In the next chapter, I demonstrate how the key concepts that allowed for this shareholder revolution in the ideology and practice of how corporations should behave were in play long ago.

To briefly illustrate the massive shift in cultural understandings of the corporation from the 1950s to the present time, consider the following juxtaposition. In *The Concept of the Corporation* (originally published in 1946), a classic study of industrial capitalist organization, Peter Drucker describes the mission and the character of the corporation, using General

Motors as his prototype: "If the big-business corporation is America's representative social institution it must realize these basic beliefs of American society. . . . It must give status and function to the individual, and it must give him the justice of equal opportunities. . . . [T]he corporation in addition to being an economic tool is a political and social body; its social function as a community is as important as its economic function as an efficient producer" (Drucker 1972, 140). Drucker rebukes neoclassical economic arguments that the corporation is simply "the sum of the property rights of the individual shareholders." The notion of shareholder ownership of the corporation is an "old" and "crude" but "linger[ing]" fiction (Drucker 1972, 20). Writing in the heyday of manager-dominated bureaucratic firms, Drucker emphasizes: "In the social reality of today . . . shareholders are but one of several groups of people who stand in a special relationship to the corporation. *The corporation is permanent, the shareholder is transitory*. It might even be said without much exaggeration that the corporation is really socially and politically a priori whereas the shareholder's position is derivative and exists only in contemplation of law" (Drucker 1972, 20–21, my emphasis). In the immediate postwar period, then, the corporation was dominantly understood as a social institution, an organization with constituents and responsibilities well beyond the individuals and institutions that owned stock in the corporation. The primary concern of the corporation was the maintenance of the integrity of the organization over and beyond what was dubbed as the "derivative" claims of the shareholder—which might have to be sacrificed for the good of the corporation itself.

Consider, then, an article in *Fortune* magazine published on 20 March 2000 detailing the values and ethics of the new "dot-com" economy. In the article, Randy Komisar, a former "virtual" CEO of such Silicon Valley corporations as WebTV, makes a telling observation about the values and expectations of today's corporate entrepreneurs. Describing how entrepreneurs "pitch ideas" to venture capitalists (the Silicon Valley parallels of New York City investment bankers and private equity firms), Komisar states: "People walk into a VC [venture capitalist] presentation and their first line is about *exit strategy*. They're not talking about the investors—they're talking about themselves. How will they cash out? And this raises a subtle point: These founders don't think of themselves as CEOs of operating companies. They think of themselves as *investors*" (J. Useem 2000, 85, my emphasis). What are the social implications of the CEO as investor rather than long-term employee committed to building a permanent social institution? If the CEO sees the company as a stock and himself or herself as simply another investor, it is not surprising that the notion of the company as an ongoing social organization, an institution with multiple stakeholders and roots in particular communities, falls by the wayside. As *Fortune* writer Jerry Useem observes, modern entrepreneurs eschew "building sustainable companies with long-term economic value," instead "pumping a concept, 'flipping' it to an acquirer, then hopping to the next hot opportunity like a day trader riding momentum stocks." Such ventures are known as "burgers—built to be flipped" (J. Useem 2000, 84). Despite the tendency to conflate Wall Street and corporate America at large, for most of the twentieth century, the two sectors have used competing (and changing) approaches to profits and corporate governance. In fact, the dominance of welfare capitalism from the New Deal to the 1980s depended, not only on paternalistic corporate practices and state policies and regulation, but also on the insulation of American business from the stock market.

How did we get to this point where corporations have shifted from complex, bureaucratic, social firms into liquid networks of shareholders? What are the implications for "traditional" constituents of the corporations such as "the worker" if corporations are now conceptualized as components of individual and institutional stock portfolios governed by an ideology of instant liquidity and convertibility into cash? Although a large corpus of critical academic literature has emerged about the demise of welfare capitalism, most of these accounts—focusing on neoliberal governmental policies, postindustrialism, changes in the means of production, flexible accumulation, globalization—have ignored the importance of Wall Street financial institutions and capital markets in constructing this new world (dis)order. And few have focused on the crucial concept of shareholder value.[2]

During fieldwork, there was no phrase I heard more than "shareholder value." This concept pervaded almost every discussion I had with investment bankers, stock portfolio managers and traders, research analysts, even management consultants—virtually anyone who had anything to do with Wall Street. For my informants and friends, "shareholder value" meant more than raising the stock price of a corporation: it also signified a mission statement, a declaration of purpose, even a call to action. Creating or reclaiming shareholder value was morally and economically the right thing to do; it was the yardstick to measure individual as well as corporate practices, values, and achievements. Because shareholder value is the standard by which corporate behaviors and debates are constructed and measured, I approach it as a vital thread connecting American corporate and Wall Street culture.

In my initial discussions with informants, one of my primary concerns was to understand how Wall Street investment bankers negotiated the linkage between their celebration of shareholder value, and massive corporate downsizing and socioeconomic inequality. Nearly every financial professional I encountered on Wall Street, nearly every business school student (MBA) in finance, took it for granted that shareholder value is and should be the main goal for all corporations. When I asked Edward Randolph, a vice president of risk management at Merrill Lynch, what the goals of an investment bank were and how they affected corporate America, he replied that investment banks existed to improve shareholder value, to increase the stock prices of the corporations they served. "The goal of the firm itself," he told me, "should be to create shareholder value," adding that "there's no illusion that they're looking to enhance the community in any way."[3] Kate Miller, a former analyst at Morgan Stanley, gave a similar reply. "What banks try to do is improve shareholder value for the companies that they're representing. And that, financially, is a good thing for the market." Anthony Johnson, an associate in M&A at J. P. Morgan, added that investment banks, while helping their corporate clients raise shareholder value, also generate revenue for themselves, in turn causing their own stock prices to rise.

What struck me initially was that in most Wall Street investment bankers' articulations of shareholder value as the primary goal of all corporations (including their own banks), there was hardly an acknowledgment of how their strict adherence to shareholder value might undermine the productivity and health of the corporate clients they advise. While my informants would recognize the "consequences" of shareholder value primacy such as restructuring and downsizing, these undersides were often uttered as a matter of fact, as if there were no tensions to be resolved. This is not to say that my informants were not sympathetic to downsized workers; in fact, most had thought about rampant job insecurity and acknowledged that massive job loss, including their own, was a typical result of shareholder-value-led corporate restructuring.[4] Yet did they not see or acknowledge how corporations they were purporting to grow and help via streamlining for shareholder value were in fact hurt by their very advice and influence? What was I missing?

Given my assumption that a strict focus on stock price both justified corporate restructuring *and* detracted from the broader work of the corporation, not to mention long-term corporate health, I jumped at the opportunity to talk to Stan Clark, who had been downsized with me at BT and who I had hoped would help me clear my confusion. Clark, though initially shaken, quickly landed a highly coveted position as a portfolio manager in the investment management department of Merrill Lynch. I had been eager to talk to Clark because of his multiple positionality: he was laid off from a company because of the dictates of shareholder value only to become part of a company where he now determined which corporate stocks to buy based on the companies' adherence to shareholder value. How did he negotiate being called upon to uphold the values that had rendered him jobless? Located at these crossroads, Clark seemed "the perfect" informant. Perhaps he could capture what Wall Streeters truly felt about the relationship between shareholder value and corporate downsizing and the seeming divergence between what was good for the corporation and what was good for the stock market. I asked Clark (whom I assumed would be alert to the downsides of shareholder value), "Do you think there is a contradiction between the company and the share price—I mean, the whole debate about does a CEO do what's good for the company or what's good for the share price. Is there a conflict?" He answered:

> *What you said doesn't make sense* because in theory, what is good for the share price is good for the company because the company is the shareholder. As long as the share price goes up, that is all [the company] cares about. What you are thinking is: Is [corporate management] doing what is good for themselves instead of what is good for the company? There is a lot of conflict there. They are doing a lot of things to try to work on [the problem of management self-serving]. Stock options, for example. A lot of CEOs have it so they are tied to options. Then, obviously, with the stock options, they would have the very best interest to get the stock price up, which means the shareholder interest . . . (my emphasis)

I was floored. Clark helped me to grasp the building blocks of Wall Street's shareholder value worldview by exclaiming, "What you said doesn't make sense," and filling in the blanks. Resolutely contradicting me, he brought me outside of my own categories for a pivotal moment: by presuming a conflict between a company's health and its stock price (because for me, employment is an important measure of corporate health), I had completely missed the point.[5] Whereas I had assumed that the corporation included multiple constituents, the most important being employees, Clark understood the company to be synonymous with its shareholders. Whereas I had thought that corporate purpose was about growth, productivity, and the welfare of its workforce, and that the central struggle in modern capitalism was between capital and labor, Clark said that the former was about ownership and shareholder value (not productivity or employment) and the latter was about the struggle between the owners of capital versus managers, where managers had squandered the fruits of capital by sharing them with other constituents. He spoke passionately about the poor stewardship and excesses of managers and how it was Wall Street investment bankers who realigned managers to their true purpose of increasing shareholder value. If a CEO did not do what was good for the stock price, then he or she was being self-serving and the only way to guard against management self-interest was to tie compensation (via stock options) to the stock market. In this worldview, corporations exist for the sole benefit of shareholders, and any attempt to separate shareholder interests from those of the corporation was selfish and nonsensical. Although in the modern history of capitalism in the United States, the desire for profit accumulation is not new, what is clearly unique about Wall Street's shareholder value perspective is that employment is thought to be outside the concern of public corporations. Job loss was certainly a sad event, but beyond the responsibility of corporate America. Thus, for Clark, there could be no conflict in his experiences.

What I also observed during my first year of fieldwork was that simultaneous with the celebration of shareholder value among investment bankers was the specter of Wall Street–led or advised deals in corporate America, such as mergers, acquisitions, and IPOs, failing according to multiple parameters, from a decline in shareholder value itself to massive losses in profits, corporate morale, productivity, and jobs. In other words, the corporate restructuring done in the name of shareholder value often led to a destruction of the very ideals investment bankers claim to champion. In the face of this "evidence," investment bankers continued to maintain a faith in shareholder value, and although some of my informants began to question whether or not shareholder value was actually being achieved, especially in the long term or when the deals imploded shortly after the fact, such a doubt did not seem to destabilize their belief in the righteousness of their particular mission, nor their belief in "the market."

Their approach to, and understanding of, shareholder value was contradictory in two ways. In one sense, most investment bankers simultaneously celebrated an ideal of shareholder value while rationalizing its possible failures. More seasoned investment bankers, who have experienced multiple financial crises and failed mergers, could discern the problematic nature of much of their deal making. Yet the particular neoclassical logic of their shareholder value worldview gave investment bankers the tools to negotiate this tension, even translate ideals and actions into a social good. In another sense, a contradiction existed between their "model" of shareholder value and its actual effects. In chapters 5 and 6, I demon-

strate how an ethnographic investigation of Wall Street institutional culture helps to explain this gap, not to mention sheds light on the particular
workings of finance capital. But for now, to understand my informants'
narratives of shareholder value triumph, it is crucial to analyze the ideological and material catalysts for the shareholder revolution—how shareholder value came to be dominant in the first place.

The Takeover Movement of the 1980s and
Wall Street's Collective Memory

The takeover movement of the 1980s was perhaps the single most important set of events to stimulate the "liquidation" of corporate America.
Wielding the threat of corporate takeover, Wall Street investment banks
forced corporations to choose between shareholder value and other alter-
natives of corporate governance, and thus "actualized" the shareholder
value worldview by instigating fundamental structural changes in U.S.
corporations in line with Wall Street's particular vision of what corporations are and whose interests they should serve. (How Wall Street
historically came to this particular vision and movement requires a fuller
genealogy of the neoclassical assumptions and the politics of the rise of
the modern corporation and shareholding, which I turn to in the following chapter.) Galvanized by invoking a "freedom" restoration narrative
grounded in entrepreneurial private property rights for the purpose of
enacting a particular social mission, the very cultural act of buying or
selling a corporation constructed a fixation on its stock price and dramatically narrowed the community of constituents that matter. By putting
corporations "in play," proponents of shareholder value created a historically unprecedented environment where all the largest corporations were
up for grabs to the highest stock-price bidder, thus forcing them to be
immediately responsive to the exigencies of the stock market.

Essentially, the takeover movement helped to create not only a market
in corporations but also a market for the *control of corporations*, where Wall
Street financiers, wealthy individuals, and institutional shareholders who
bought enough stock could claim ownership and through this property
right demand, revive, and enact what had become the largely moribund
fiduciary rights of shareholders in corporate governance. The takeover
movement culturally commoditized and transformed the very definition
and purpose of a public corporation: the corporation *became* its quickly
exchangeable stock in the financial markets, and its primary mission was

to increase its stock price. As part of everyday practice, corporate managers were made to loathe low stock prices, as such a status signaled corporate vulnerability to cheap acquisitions, symbolizing inefficiency and the shackling of true capitalist expression via the shareholder. "These takeovers created a 'zero-sum game', between shareholders who stood to gain and other stakeholders, such as employees, managers, suppliers, communities, and, often, creditors, who were generally losers in such transactions" (Whitman 1999, 94).

But, the question at present and the reason why it is crucial to understand the takeover movement is: given that even into the early 1980s, corporations were not yet understood to be simply their stocks, how did shareholder value become so taken-for-granted by the 1990s? How did corporations come to be understood as pieces in a financial game, so easily bought, sold, and dismantled?[6]

When I asked my informants about the most important financial development in recent times, the majority of them pointed to Wall Street's role in the takeover movement of the 1980s. This, in their view, was the pivotal event that aligned corporations to shareholder value. They spun a compelling narrative of how in the postwar era an elite, complacent, and self-serving managerial class squandered corporate resources extravagantly on themselves or on ill-advised expansions, and allowed foreign competitors to overtake the United States in productivity, innovation, and strategy. As a result, corporate stock prices no longer reflected companies' "true worth," the economy suffered, and stockholders—the rightful owners of corporations—were betrayed. According to this vision, one of the main goals of the takeover movement was "unlocking" the value of "underperforming" stock prices, which were depressing the entire economy.

My informants used the takeover movement as a historical-cultural device, an ideological and temporal marker that enabled them to position themselves and their articulations of shareholder value in opposition to the "bad old days" of managerial decadence and incompetence. "If you look back to the old days," Stan Clark told me, "all the companies were basically just fat, dumb, and stupid. [T]hey didn't change. They were making [enough] money. The [managers] didn't care. Now, you have Wall Street with all these shareholders. . . . You can't just be dumb, fat, and happy. You have to change. Shareholders are looking at . . . your excess expenses. . . . Back in the old days, wide town employment was a big thing. They didn't ever hardly lay off. Nowadays, they have to lay off because shareholders say, 'Look, you have all this excess overhead. . . . You have to cut out the fat. We want a lean, mean operation'. So . . . Wall Street is definitely making a much more efficient corporate America." Andrew Wong, an M&A associate at Goldman Sachs, echoed Clark's understanding. "Basically . . . you [had] fat American corporations" that were blindsided by Japanese competition in the early 1980s, particularly in the auto industry. "Corporations were huge conglomerates that served the whims of executives to some extent. And there was not a focus on stock market performance." Clark, Wong, and others contrasted the "dumb" habits of American business before the 1980s with the "smart" meritocracies of Wall Street bankers, suggesting an almost eugenic blueprint for a society where only "the smartest" survive.[7]

As commonly understood on Wall Street, in the 1980s it was investment bankers who realigned managers to their true purpose of increasing shareholder value by wielding the full force and discipline of the stock market. To many, such as Jason Kedd, a specialist in M&A at DLJ, the key figure of the 1980s was Michael Milken, inventor of junk bonds, a type of financial instrument that enabled corporate raiders to launch hostile takeovers of corporations, lay off workers, then strip their assets, and extract as much immediate value as possible. Because the value of a company sold off in bits and pieces was collectively greater than its intact value on the stock market, my informants deemed shareholders to have been well served by the takeover and demolition of corporations. "By creating a market for junk bonds, you allow some corporate raider to go in, buy up a company, break it up, and if it turns out that the company has a lot more people than necessary, then laying off people to pay debt." Michael Williams, a vice president of sales and trading at Lehman Brothers, explained that when a company's stock price was lower than the total value of its separate assets, "there was either something wrong with the stock market, which may be true, or there was something wrong with the guys who were running that company. Because if they [the managers] were smarter, they would have been generating more value for the shareholders. They would have been using the assets more productively and making more things . . . that would have added to the stock price." That all the corporation's stock could be bought for $50 million and its "parts" could be sold for $75 million was evidence enough of the stock market divining shareholder betrayal, which in turn justified the takeovers. The effect of the takeover binge of the 1980s, Williams concluded, was that "corporate America became a lot more concerned with their stock prices and earnings and . . . became more efficient." Williams called the wave of mergers and layoffs "kind of a pruning process." The money saved by shareholders, he said, "was put to better use" and "made everyone sharper." As Jason Kedd

further explains, shareholders could then invest in other productive operations, which would in turn create jobs. The stakes in his view couldn't be
higher. This sort of market discipline is a "necessary evil." Without it,
"you end up like the Soviet Union," with low output and long waits for
basic services—"if you get those at all."

Thus Wall Street, according to its own collective memory as expressed
by my informants, rescued American business in the 1980s—"the glory
days of Wall Street," in Andrew Wong's words, a period when "everything
awakened," there was a new focus on the stock market, and "companies
were living in fear" of hostile takeovers. Wong argued that going into the
new century, "American companies are the strongest because we have
gone through this whole period of shareholder value focus, management
reorganization, restructuring of companies. American companies have cut
the fat everywhere, [have] refocused strategies, and are basically ready to
kick ass." By refocusing corporate priorities on creating shareholder value,
Wall Street of the 1980s brought into being lean, "kick-ass" corporations
and a rising stock market, which in turn enabled a booming economy
while at the same time returned capital to its proper hands. Although the
global financial meltdown of 2008 has fundamentally destabilized some of
these dominant narratives of advancement, laying bare their contradictions and consequences, in my informants' worldview (however ironic it
may appear now), the takeover movement marked a new horizon, a watershed moment that framed their understanding of progress.

Wall Street's particular understanding of history is disseminated through
investment banks' institutional memory, business schools, colleagues, the
financial media, and pop culture. A number of my informants, trying to
convey their understanding of the era, cited Oliver Stone's movie *Wall
Street* (1986), starring Michael Douglas as ruthless financier Gordon
Gekko, who put "the deal" above all else, uttered the famous line, "Greed is
good," and was brought down on insider trading and stock manipulation
charges by his young protégé, son of a union worker.[8] Much ink has been
spilled recounting, critiquing, and celebrating the Deal Decade (also known
as the "ga-ga eighties" or the decade of greed).[9] Since the 1980s, scores of
memoirs, movies, exposés, journalistic reports, and thrillers have been
written about Wall Street investment banks, junk bonds, leveraged buyouts, insider trading, and the takeover movement.[10] Succeeding generations of investment bankers have imbibed Wall Street's self-justifications,
generating a remarkably coherent Wall Street historiography based on the
rightness and inevitability of the strategies adopted by corporate raiders,
junk-bond traders, and other major players in the 1980s.

However, the socioeconomic crises of the 1970s did not automatically necessitate a dismantling of corporate and governmental safety nets and regulations nor an overhaul of the financial and social structure of corporate America; other responses were possible.[11] Advocates of shareholder value urged American business down one of many potential paths. But while the assumptions that shareholders are the "true owners" of corporations, that corporations are solely private property, and that shareholder betrayal caused a post–Second World War corporate decline are all problematic and contestable assertions, they must also be understood as strategic and political claims to truth and power that have had very real consequences. I argue that Wall Street in the 1980s capitalized on the socioeconomic downturn of the previous decade to launch a campaign that aligned corporate values and priorities to the interests of the stock market and Wall Street firms.[12] Business economist Marina Whitman declares that "more than any other single factor," "the restructuring-takeover phenomenon of the 1980s" ushered in the changes in capitalist values that demanded the goal of increasing stock price for the gain of corporate shareholders. This wave of mergers, acquisitions, and downsizings "tore asunder . . . the fragile reconciliation between the property and social-entity views of the corporation and its obligations" (Whitman 1999, 93–94).[13] This restructuring movement gained so much momentum that it left virtually no company untouched: "Fully one-third of the Fortune 500 in 1980 no longer existed as independent entities in 1990. One-third of the 1990 Fortune 500 had been targets of hostile takeover bids; and two-thirds, fearing such overtures, had established antitakeover defenses" (Whitman 1999, 9). Perhaps even more telling is that one decade after the watershed 1980s, by year-end 1999, the dollar volumes of mergers and acquisition deals in corporate America were up by almost 400 percent from the height of the takeover movement in 1988.

Historicizing the Takeover Movement

My informants consistently pointed to the conglomerate wave of the 1960s as the preeminent example of managerial self-interest and waste and the primary reason for the ensuing "underperformance" of corporate America as it entered a more competitive world stage in the 1970s and 1980s. Conglomeration was the expansion of corporations through external acquisitions, most often in "unrelated lines of business" (O'Sullivan 2000, 109). The unwieldy creations that resulted became one of the main targets of the takeover movement, the poster child for what was wrong with corporate America and how Wall Street could fix it. According to George Baker and George Smith, business school professors and proponents of Wall Street shareholder value, the conglomerate wave was "grossly manifest" of "managerial opportunism" (Baker and Smith 1998, 15). Baker's and Smith's account exemplifies a very familiar (and dominant) narrative of self-interested and incompetent managers reacting to heavy-handed antimonopoly regulation. Restrained from "anticompetitive mergers," "expansion-hungry managers" found "new outlets for their surplus cash" by "cobbling together companies in *unrelated* industries" (Baker and Smith 1998, 15). My Wall Street informants understood conglomeration in the 1960s as a ridiculous and unstrategic business fad. As Anthony Johnson, an M&A associate at J. P. Morgan, put it, "They combined defense companies that manufactured nuclear weapons with makers of kitty litter." Such poor managerial decisions, in their view, rendered the corporate America of the 1970s inefficient and unprepared for global competition.

This narrative must be troubled. While most shareholder value advocates rest the blame for conglomeration solely on corporate America, in fact Wall Street also played an important role in devising the strategy in the first place. Though financiers elide such histories from their worldviews, investment bankers encouraged and influenced senior executives to use their profits to buy unrelated companies. In the 1960s, before Reaganomic deregulation, or rather "reregulation," antitrust laws prevented large corporations from buying or merging with similar corporations to prevent monopolies.[14] Therefore, although conglomeration was certainly in keeping with their own organizational structures premised on nonintegrated, hierarchical segmentation between divisions and between workers and managers, which in turn hampered innovation, corporate America was pressured by Wall Street (even then) to find new ways of increasing stock prices.[15] In fact, the term "go-go sixties" was used to describe Wall Street's preoccupation with conglomerates and hot growth stocks (Brooks 1987). Conglomeration was heralded by Wall Street and managers alike as an effective expansion tool, promoting diversification, growth, and what would later be dubbed "one-stop shopping." They were understood to be "a group of several companies in different businesses making up one corporation . . . to enable an older corporation to move into a fast-growing business by buying a company already in that business instead of starting from scratch, sometimes representing an effort to give a company a shot in the arm" (Low 1968, 201). Certainly, this "shot in the arm" caused the stock market—after decades of dormancy or stability from the Great Depression into the 1950s—to "finally" reach and surpass the heights of 1929. In 1968, the Dow Jones Industrial Average surpassed 1000 points after hovering around 500 for decades, and over 20 million shares were traded (compared to only 2 million shares in the mid-1950s) (Low 1968, 168). Shortly afterward, the stock market crashed and many individual investors and speculators were burned.[16]

In the stock market boom of the 1960s (like the bull market of the 1990s), one of the major practices of investment banks was to encourage corporations to buy other companies because the acquisition became "cheap and easy" as the corporation used its highly priced shares as currency to buy up other companies. Investment banks in turn made hefty advisory and commission fees as well as a percentage cut of any other fundraising needed to enable the deal. Acquisitions and conglomerations skyrocketed: "The number of announcements to merge with or acquire another company grew from an annual average of 1,951 in 1963–67 to 3,736 in 1968–72, reaching a record peak of 5,306 in 1969" (O'Sullivan 2000, 109).

In *Mergers, Sell-Offs, and Economic Efficiency*, a study of the consequences of M&A activity in the 1960s and 1970s, Ravenscraft and Scherer demonstrate that the proclaimed profitability and efficiency benefits of conglomerates were predominantly false, as companies actually declined in productivity and the "synergies anticipated from acquisition frequently did not materialize" (Ravenscraft and Scherer 1987, 212). Although Ravenscraft and Scherer state that conglomerates failed "to manage acquired companies as well as they were managed before acquisition," they point out that there were no major downsizings of acquired (or acquiring) companies, as there were in the 1980s and 1990s (Ravenscraft and Scherer 1987, 213). Shareholder value had not yet overtaken the concept of corporations as social institutions with commitments to their employees. Although since the 1980s, M&A have become virtually synonymous with mass layoffs, in the conglomerate wave of the 1960s, the employees of the acquired companies were typically retained.[17]

Similarly, the takeover movement failed to solve the many organizational and productivity problems that conglomerates and U.S. corporations faced in the 1970s. Because most of the corporations targeted for takeover in the 1980s were identified precisely because they generated plentiful and constant cash flows, it remains questionable how "underperforming" these corporations actually were. Rather, the takeover movement transferred corporate wealth into the hands of large shareholders and their advisors, and downsized multiple constituents from corporate participation and profit sharing. Shareholder value advocates wove a narrative of historical birthright, managerial incompetence and betrayal, and corporate decline, capped by the restoration of shareholder rights and the consequent revival of U.S. capitalism, while ignoring their own participation (like invisible hands) in the failures of conglomeration.[18]

In addition to the galvanizing cry of anticonglomeration, the takeover movement was also made possible by governmental deregulation and the privileging of privatized market control, as well as the growth of institutional investors and their increasing stake in the stock market, all of which Wall Street investment banks actively advocated for, working to incorporate these transitions into their shareholder value rationales. The Reagan-led dismantling of antitrust enforcement, along with changes in capital investment rules, enabled Wall Street to combine and recombine companies in multiple configurations with little oversight, all the while supported by new flows of investment money which were previously protected from a variety of risky investments. Until the 1970s, pension funds and insurance companies as well as savings and loans institutions faced legal restrictions on the amount and proportion of their portfolios they could invest into the stock market—a legacy born out of the Great Depression, when banks and investment trusts were barred from gambling depositors' savings on the securities market. In the 1970s, however, oil-induced inflation created pressure for investment funds and banks to generate higher returns in riskier endeavors such as the stock market, not to mention third-world debt. Geographer Gordon Clark, in his comprehensive study of the pension management industry, describes how institutional investors, in the 1950s only minor players on the stock market, have come to dominate shareholding, now controlling "the majority of the stock of the largest 1,000 US corporations" (Clark 2000, 62–63). It was the "transfer of stockholding from individual households to institutions such as mutual funds, pension funds and life insurance companies" that "made possible the takeovers" as this development empowered Wall Street, created an institutional buyers market to fund takeovers, and "gave shareholders much more collective power to influence . . . the corporate stocks they held" (Lazonick and O'Sullivan 2002, 14). Investment banks sold so many stocks and bonds of companies that had been taken over to these growing institutional investors (financial products that for a time appreciated astronomically because of the massive transfers of wealth involved in the dismantling of corporations) that these investors became permanent clients and supporters of Wall Street. Keeping "a laser-bright beam trained continuously on firms' quarter-to-quarter financial results," investment banks were not only strengthened by the growing "shareholder activism" of institutional investors, but also used these institutions as evidence of their mass investor constituency (Whitman 1999, 11).

Importantly, in the 1970s, Wall Street itself was experiencing a crisis in profitability as well; many of its staple revenue-generating tools, such as underwriting, had been saturated, many (if not most) of its conglomerate deals had gone sour, and investment banks were "induced to search for new sources of profits" (O'Sullivan 2000, 163). According to Thomas Douglass, managing director in strategy at BT, who has worked as an investment banker and as a management consultant, breaking up the conglomerates that Wall Street had helped assemble in the first place created a whole new source of profits.[19] In the 1980s, the M&A business looked increasingly attractive to investment bankers because they did not have to put their own money at risk to compete in the business, yet the fees were enormous. It is hardly surprising, therefore, that they worked hard to construct, in the first place, the very market for corporate control.

Takeover Players, Mechanisms, and Worldviews

What made the 1980s so revolutionary was the primary focus on shareholder value *as well as* the sheer enormity and hostility of the transactions. With dramatic share price increase being the main purpose of the takeover (as well as the protection against being taken over), corporate downsizings were rampant. "As a result, employment by Fortune 500 companies dropped substantially in both absolute and relative terms. Their employment rolls fell from over 16 million in 1979 to 11.5 million in 1993. During the early 1970s, these firms had employed one of every five Americans in the nonagriculture workforce; by the early 1990s, that fraction had dropped to one in ten" (Whitman 1999, 9). In previous merger waves in the twentieth century, companies were not bought and sold only to be liquidated; one of the purposes of conglomerates, albeit illusory, was to build on existing capabilities of the corporate organization to increase profits. The crucial difference between the speculative booms of the go-go sixties and the ga-ga eighties was, in the words of Wall Street historian John Brooks, that whereas "the acquirers of companies in the sixties usually intended to operate them or let them operate themselves, those of the eighties . . . seemed . . . to be for the purpose of dismantling them in whole or in part for a quick-cash profit" (Brooks 1987, 29).

It is important to take a moment to understand the differences between takeovers and M&A.[20] Although both takeovers and M&A occurred in the 1980s, the 1980s were characterized more by the takeover, while M&A became dominant in the 1990s. Whereas a merger connotes the coming together of *two companies*, a takeover usually refers to the acquiring of a company by wealthy individuals (occasionally top corporate executives) or a group of "takeover specialists/investors" from a variety of Wall Street investment firms, both aided by financial innovations such as junk bonds and large investments from pension and mutual fund capital. The distinction is subtle but important: in the context of the early 1980s, it was not yet part of American corporate habitus for corporations to take over, restructure, and downsize other corporations; they conglomerated instead. For takeovers and massive restructurings to take place, they had to be initiated, in a sense, from "outsider" corporate raiders and, initially, rogue (then mainstream) investment banks and financial firms, by those who were entrenched in the opposing worldview that corporations needed to come under financial market control. By the 1990s, Wall Street, though offering more of the same practices, began to distance itself from the excesses and predatory image of the 1980s by reframing its goals and financial products. This reinvention was necessitated by the crash of 1987, scandals, and the obvious failures and implosions of companies that had been taken over. Wall Street and the financial media no longer used the terms "hostile takeover" or "corporate raiding," resorting instead to the general, traditional, and more respectable term, "mergers and acquisitions." Junk bonds became "high-yield" bonds. Corporate buyouts and breakups were remarketed as restructurings, synergies, and economies of scale. Takeovers were thus repackaged and made socially acceptable, and most major investment banks in the United States began to sell such services like any other product offering. Moreover, by the 1990s corporate America was so successfully aligned with shareholder value worldviews that corporations, with the advice and instigation of Wall Street investment banks, began to initiate M&A with other companies. Most acquisitions did not have to come from Wall Street takeover groups but from corporations themselves working in close advisory relationships with investment bankers, allowing for record volumes throughout the past decade. Although the rationale for M&A transactions continued to be shareholder value, the discursive style of its promoters and storytellers emphasized market populism and shareholder democracy rather than the derring-do of robber-baron corporate raiders and their hostile takeovers. Whereas in the 1980s, the rhetoric of shareholder value was largely confined to the takeover movement, in the 1990s its values seeped into most corporate discourse, shaping corporate governance as a whole. Both takeovers and M&A involved, however, a variety of similar rationales, techniques, and mechanisms.

In the 1980s, the key actors in the takeover movement were individual corporate raiders, groups of investors (from small Wall Street investment firms, also called "private equity shops," as well as large investment banks), and senior, incumbent management of the company (Brooks 1987, 30). Corporate raiders were mainly wealthy white men from the United States and England, independent financiers or owners of their own corporations; the best known in mainstream and financial literature included T. Boone Pickens, Sir James Goldsmith, and Carl Icahn. Private equity firms were usually founded by a small group of investment bankers or investors who, not only gathered large amounts of funds to invest in the buying and breaking up of corporations, but were also involved in the finance-led control and running of corporations until they were "ready" for reselling. They popularized a particular technique of takeover called a "leveraged buyout" (LBO), which I explain in detail below. The example par excellence of the private equity firm was Kohlberg, Kravis, and Roberts (KKR), the name representing the three white men who founded this firm, alternatively known as "an LBO shop." They controlled a large investment fund (generated from rich individuals, pension and mutual funds, banks, insurance companies), which they used to take over companies by buying up their stock. Major investment banks and bankers, such as Morgan Stanley, Goldman Sachs, First Boston (now CSFB), and Drexel Burnham Lambert, worked with private equity firms to raise additional funds for takeovers, but played no subsequent role in controlling or operating the corporations they invested in. That was left to private equity firms.

Although Wall Street private equity firms usually initiated the actual takeover of a corporation, larger and more established Wall Street investment banks and bankers (along with their lawyers) played a crucial role in the process, especially in raising capital. Like corporations who were initially wary of taking over other corporations, the most established investment banks (as opposed to more renegade ones such as Drexel Burnham Lambert) at first avoided directly spearheading takeovers of corporations that had formerly been their clients and their fiduciary responsibility, although they certainly participated in and helped to instigate the process. Among the more conservative, blue-blood investment banks, takeovers were initially not considered "gentlemanly." For example, Drexel Burnham

Lambert was an investment bank, yet because it specialized in raising funds for takeovers through the selling of junk bonds, it was not considered (especially in the early 1980s) as reputable as many of the most established, "white-shoe" investment banks such as Morgan Stanley. But, by the mid-1980s, most investment banks on Wall Street had full-fledged junk bond departments *and* M&A departments, and by the 1990s, they had become the primary instigators of corporate mergers. Instead of "just representing" corporate America, "investment banks have gotten into the business of buying companies for themselves," as part of the larger process of turning "corporate America into a board game" (M. Lewis 1991, 76).

Highly ranked corporate executives (particularly CEOs and presidents) were also important players in the takeover movement. Because of the historical antagonism between "social-entity" managerial capitalism and the ideology of shareholder value, it is crucial to unpack the roles and representations of these senior managers who became shareholder-owners. According to Wall Street's dominant logic, salaried managers, since they are motivated by either nonowner self-interest or the interests of multiple stakeholders, are unable to fulfill their singular fiduciary duty to the shareholder. The only way, then, for managers to get out of this quagmire is to become owners themselves. Through an LBO, a few senior managers, often with the help of Wall Street private equity firms and highly leveraged junk bonds, participated in the buying up of the stock of a corporation, and through this process, became owners. Wall Street supported such a conflation, for "in a theoretical sense, it represents a kind of change generally thought to be healthy: a partial reuniting of corporate ownership with corporate management, reversing the broad twentieth-century trend toward [the] separation" of ownership from control (Brooks 1987, 205). Ironically, the managers who completed this transition were often lauded by the financial media as "brave risk-takers," when in fact they put very little down of their own capital, used borrowed money to buy the company, put the corporation in debt, sold off pieces to service the debt, took the company public again, and cashed out to make millions. In essence, these managers were participating in a transfer of wealth from the multiple corporate stakeholders to themselves as shareholders and thus set a precedent for the primacy of shareholder value as the goal and measure of good corporate governance.

Michael Lewis, Salomon Brothers bond trader turned author of *Liar's Poker*, called this an attempt to "turn the managers into entrepreneurs," noting sarcastically that, unlike the "poor and indolent managers" who supposedly created the conglomerate mess in the first place, these newly minted entrepreneurs "are never lazy or dumb" (Lewis 1991, 66). In a larger sense, the takeover movement of the 1980s helped to radically reshift the interests of senior executives from the workings and constituents of the corporation as a social institution to those of Wall Street and large shareholders. For example, before the 1980s, CEOs made about forty-four times the salary of the average worker—already indicative of a fairly steep hierarchy—yet after the 1980s, CEO salaries rose to over four hundred times that of the average worker. Whereas past CEO salaries were in a sense "tied" to the salaries of other employees in the organization and were held, albeit amorphously, to be proportional to the profits of the organization as a whole, today, CEO compensations are linked instead to bonuses and the stock market, with the largest boost coming from stocks and stock options, which can be immediately sold or "vested" after a short-term waiting period. From 1980 to 1994, "the mean value of stock option grants to CEOs increased . . . by a massive 682.5 per cent" (O'Sullivan 2000, 196). The deal decade "transformed the notion of what was legitimate for . . . a small group of people to *extract* from US corporate enterprises to the extent that they were willing to become the ostensible servants of financial interests" (O'Sullivan 2000, 196). And, even in the context of volatile corporate earnings, strategic failures, and economic downturns, CEOs, via their golden parachutes and stocks, are both shielded from responsibility as well as incentivized to create short-term stock price spikes in order to cash out.

Wall Street investment banks also made takeovers possible by constructing and popularizing new financial products and techniques for takeover specialists. These were techniques for "financing transfers of corporate control," which "depended on the development of a network of relationships that could harness the growing pressures for financial liquidity" (O'Sullivan 2000, 163). The most notable of the new tools were the junk bond and the leveraged buyout. LBOs were a long-standing financial technique, resurrected by private equity firms such as KKR for this new context of stripping conglomerates; this technique was then picked up and commercialized on a global scale by Wall Street investment banks through the vehicle of junk bonds.[21] The LBO, dubbed the paramount Wall Street scam, the "leveraged rip-off," was the quintessential and most highly symbolic takeover of the 1980s; they were "the Reagan era's most distinctive contribution to the culture of finance" (M. Lewis 1991, 65). In an LBO, purchasers use borrowed money to buy the stocks of the company (using the company itself as collateral) and then strip the assets and cash flow of the company to pay down the debt.[22]

My informants pointed to the junk bond as the central financial innovation in the takeover arsenal. Junk bonds are, in essence, risky bonds: they offer the holder of the bond (the lender of money) the enticement of extremely high returns, but the flipside is that they are very risky and could be become worthless at any time. Prospective corporate raiders only needed to put down a minuscule down payment because they were able to raise the rest of the capital by issuing junk bonds. With the help of junk bonds, a $10 million stake could buy a $200 million company—thus the term "leveraged buyouts," as one dollar was "leveraged" to act as twenty. This narrative, of course, begs the question: who would buy such risky junk? Who would lend money knowing that the buyer only invested a meager five percent or less of the total price? Leveraged buyouts became possible only in the context of a mass market for junk bonds, with large institutions investing heavily in them. This is where the legendary Michael Milken, a Wharton business school graduate and former head of junk bonds at (now bankrupt and defunct) Drexel Burnham Lambert, came into the picture.[23] "Pumped into buyouts, Milken's junk bonds became a high-octane fuel that transformed the LBO industry from a Volkswagen Beetle into a monstrous drag racer belching smoke and fire" (Burrough and Helyar 1990, 140). Milken created the market for junk. He made junk bonds "liquid" so that people could sell if they so chose, but this meant there had to be a ready supply of willing buyers, which Milken found among institutional investors, not to mention that to maintain junk bond solvency, companies were necessarily liquidated to service these debts. Although the act of liquidating a corporation to pay off private debt was viewed as destructive and even revolting by critics and the mainstream corporate community alike, dissent was often muted because raiders and bankers were able to link their activities to the necessary pains of shareholder revolution.

Will Howard, a high-yield bond specialist (the sanitized term for junk bonds in the 1990s after the scandals of the late 1980s and the crash of 1987) at Merrill Lynch, explained the process by which takeover specialists ensure huge returns:

> What they [private equity firms] do is they will use the high yield we raise [the junk bonds that Merrill Lynch helps them to issue], put in a little bit of money themselves, buy a company, use the company's cash flow to pay down the debt. . . . So that their pie, which was really small, just keeps growing as the company pays down the debt. So that when they sell the company—three or five years later . . . by that time the debt is a much lower

percentage of the overall value of the company and the value of their equity is much higher, and those guys will make a fortune, an absolute fortune.

After a few years of "turnaround time," KKR, for example, takes the company public again by going to the stock market to cash out on their "investment." What does this mean? As Howard explained, KKR's initial investment to own the public company—that is, take it "private"—might be only a small percentage of the total stock market capitalization of the company (say, 3 percent of a $500 million company, thus $15 million); the rest is bought through a network of leverage, that is, via debt, most of it junk. Once KKR starts to pay off the debt to the various lenders and bondholders, the value of their equity in the company, according to the rules of corporate accounting and Wall Street interpretations, begins to rise correspondingly. The junk bondholders, for example, do not get any stock (equity); they just get paid back at a high interest rate, so the more debt KKR pays off, the greater the value of its equity stake in the company. Then, KKR, with the help of an investment bank, can resell "their own" company to the public by issuing new stock in an Initial Public Offering (IPO). When the company goes public again, it can issue, depending on the calculations of an investment bank, 50 million shares at $15 each for a windfall $750 million. Considering that in this hypothetical transaction, KKR only spent $15 million of its capital to own the entire company, it will have made profits of $735 million (minus expenses), which is then parceled out among the equity investors of the investment fund.

The 1986 leveraged buyout of Safeway is a quintessential example of the social beneficiaries and consequences of a "successful" takeover. According to Susan Faludi's Pulitzer Prize–winning investigation, Peter Magowan, then Safeway's CEO, teamed up with KKR to buy the company from its shareholders at $67.50 a share, "82 percent more than the stock was trading at three months before" (Faludi 1992, 289). He rationalized the LBO as a way to fend off corporate raiders Herbert and Robert Haft. Although Magowan had assured his employees that "no one will get hurt" or lose their job, Safeway downsized sixty-three thousand workers and managers, "put whole divisions in Kansas, Oklahoma, Arkansas and Utah . . . on the auction block," severely reduced wages and benefits while increasing hours and performance standards, and slashed capital improvements by more than 50 percent (Faludi 1992, 287, 296). The investment banks who advised the takeover received $65 million in fees; the lawyers and accountants $25 million. Peter Magowan and other top Safeway executives "received $28 million for their shares" as well as "options to buy a total of 10 percent of the new Safeway at only $2 a share." These shares at the time of resale "to the public" four years later were valued at $12.125 a share and totaled more than $100 million. The five KKR partners, who invested only $2 million of their own capital, "received a 20 percent share of the eventual profits from any sale of Safeway" estimated to be over $200 million. Finally, KKR and its investor group, on top of its deal fees of $60 million, took the rest, estimated around $700 million (Faludi 1992, 285, 289–90).

A year before the takeover, Safeway posted record profits of $235 million; five years earlier, they had instigated a corporate strategy that remodeled stores, "experiment[ed] with employee productivity teams," and slowly phased out less profitable division through attrition and limited layoffs. In this case as in many others, there was no evidence of global uncompetitiveness, technological distress, or lack of profitability, but "all that wasn't enough for takeover-crazed Wall Street, where virtually no company was invulnerable to cash-rich corporate raiders" (Faludi 1992, 288–89). Mired in a colossal debt of $3.1 billion with interest payments a crippling $400 million a year, KKR and Magowan not only dismantled Safeway's infrastructure (which caused a rippling effect for its "dependent industries") but its way of life, values, and priorities. Not insignificantly, George Roberts, the "R" of KKR, claimed that since the Oregon public-employee pension fund invested in the KKR fund which bought Safeway, "the masses" benefited. He justified the LBO by stating that Safeway employees were finally being held accountable to global competition. Such a scenario demonstrates in no uncertain terms a hierarchical clash of values and the strategic purpose of shareholder value, designed to create a huge transfer in wealth and a drastic change in corporate America. The company whose "first store had been opened by a clergyman who wanted to help his parishioners save money" and whose longtime corporate motto had been "Safeway Offers Security" was redefined. Now, "the new corporate statement, displayed on a plaque in the lobby at corporate headquarters, reads in part: 'Targeted Returns on Current Investment'" (Faludi 1992, 287–88).

Leveraged buyouts were also frequently used to acquire companies formerly assumed to be "too big" (or too stable) for takeovers. Today, no corporation, regardless of size or history, is safe. In the previous merger wave of the 1960s, many corporations were considered too large to be bought or sold. Because most individuals and even institutions were unable and unwilling to use millions of their own capital to buy up the shares, multibillion-dollar companies were not (and could hardly be imagined as) targets of takeovers. Corporations such as RJR Nabisco, whose takeover by KKR in 1989 was one of the largest buyouts in history with a price tag of $31.4 billion, were once considered immune to such tactics (Burrough and Helyar 1990). Even if buyers were willing to take a loan, the loan would be too risky and the collateral too high. Such takeovers were not only virtually impossible to transact without the junk bond phenomenon, but also *culturally unthinkable* given the ingrained understanding of corporations as permanent social institutions.

LBOs generated such an environment of fear that corporations restructured themselves *in anticipation* of takeover attempts, hoping to raise their stock prices and render themselves less vulnerable to the restructuring rationales of corporate raiders. Shareholder value advocates applauded this avalanche effect of LBOs as a salutary spread of market discipline. By the mid-1980s, we see an illustration of Foucault's notion of capillaries of power: corporations across the United States were restructuring as if doing so out of individual choice and efficient self- and shareholder betterment. While Wall Street's stock market surveillance was constantly in the background, the actual threat of an LBO was no longer necessary (Foucault 1980).

Although the main rationale for takeovers is to increase the stock price, other related justifications include the replacing of complacent managers, the reuniting of management and ownership, and perhaps most characteristic of the 1980s, the "trimming of fat," the disciplining of labor, and the efficiency of spending that comes with the burden of paying off debt. According to Wall Street, such a process readied corporate America, finally, for global competition. As one of my informants stated, "junk bonds and leveraged buyouts make companies work—mean and lean. Since they have to pay the interest expense, they trim out all of the fat. It is harsh. But in the long run, it's great." When I asked Christine Chang, also a high-yield bond vice president at BT, what she thought of the efficiency-through-debt argument for takeovers, she replied that she thought LBOs have "created efficiency":

> Because a company which becomes leveraged has this big additional expense they might not have had before, interest expense and all the debt, it does force you to cut out a lot of excess staff. . . . There are a lot of companies out there with the corporate jet, the golf club memberships and huge expense accounts and a lot of other nonsense that you have to get rid of once you are trying to serve this large debt load. Sometimes it just forces you to be a little leaner and meaner than you were before. . . . I think one of the reasons why the economy

is very strong and vibrant today is that a lot of the excess fat was cut out of American corporations.

The concept of "disciplining through debt" was popularized and widely accepted by the business community in the 1980s. What was rendered invisible by this discourse was that this debt was a mechanism through which corporate wealth was transferred from the multiple stakeholders of a corporation to a small number of owners. Despite Wang's reference to frivolous golf club memberships, the bulk of the cuts were actually in people's jobs, research and development, and infrastructure. Not surprisingly, since the selling off of assets inevitably cuts into productivity and profitability, countless LBOs imploded under the weight of their own debts. Owners were only able to cash out spectacularly (if done quickly), not by newly redesigning productive corporations, but by dismantling previously accumulated wealth and infrastructure and instituting new, hyperexploitive labor practices. The share prices of companies that have been taken over often decline sharply in the medium-term; thus timing is crucial for takeover artists who want to cash out.

The takeover movement did not occur without resistance, although corporate patriarchs, hampered by their own hierarchical practices, were unable to convincingly argue an alternative to shareholder value or an effective moral stance. There is perhaps no better illustration of Wall Street's values and its clash with those of corporate America than a simulation of a corporate takeover at Columbia Law School in 1987 as part of an "Ethics in America" documentary series. Discussing the scenario of taking over company X, dubbed "Peachtree," were actual key figures in the takeover movement, divided (rather neatly but effectively) into corporate raiders and investment bankers who "championed" shareholder value versus corporate CEOs and governmental officials who sought to protect multiple stakeholders. It is interesting to note that corporate raiders and investment bankers were willing to take part in such a public-minded event and a striking indication that arguments for the moral and social good of the takeover movement are in an important sense deeply held beliefs, not always mere rhetorical window dressing.

Not so ironically, two of the central actors in this forum, Sir James Goldsmith, a British corporate raider, playing himself in this simulation, and Robert E. Mercer, real-life CEO of Goodyear Tire and Rubber, playing the CEO of Peachtree, had just a year before engaged in a protracted struggle when Goldsmith had attempted a takeover of Goodyear. This harrowing experience led a top Goodyear executive, who "saw the mounting power of LBO buyers as the next plague to be unleashed by Wall Street" onto Main Street, labeled the LBO "'an idea that was created in hell by the Devil himself'" (Burrough and Helyar 1990, 141). Mercer, arguing that Goldsmith's track record meant that this takeover would dismantle the fictional Peachtree and destroy jobs, had resisted the attack on Goodyear in the name of the company's long-term survival and the interests of multiple stakeholders—but not without taking defensive measures that similarly restructured the corporation, put it in debt, and reduced research and development.

In this simulation, Mercer and Goldsmith faced off again along with James Bare, chairman and CEO of Borg-Warner, who also played a senior executive of Peachtree, and T. Boone Pickens, a corporate raider, who, like Goldsmith, played himself. The specific context was that Pickens and Goldsmith had already begun to accumulate the stock of Peachtree, were interested in taking over the company, and had just announced their intentions: they would pay $30 a share for the company. Peachtree's stock was currently selling at $20. In the negotiations, the starkly different values of each side were cast in bold relief.

First, Goldsmith justified the takeover by pointing to the "ossified" structures and "inefficient" conglomerates created by the "entrenched" managers of the 1960s. "Let the market free, and . . . cleanse through market action a structure which was wrong," he proclaimed. "Liberate the pieces so that they can become valid companies, and of course make a profit at the same time." Takeovers "cleanse" decades of managerial inefficiency to give corporations a fresh start and a fighting chance. "The demagogue," he said, "will tell you that he is in business for all these constituencies, of suppliers, communities, employees, and everybody else. That's not true, and if it's true, it's a mistake." He denounced the claims of "do-gooder" managers who hide their self-interest and complacency behind altruism as dangerous "nonsense" that makes for bloated, uncompetitive businesses. Goldsmith had never heard of "a well-managed company that had been taken over by force," though some companies "have gotten better because of the fear of being taken over . . . but you take away that fear, they'll go down the drain." His main purpose was to "marry management and capitalism," for such a union is the "greatest life-giving thing an economy can have."

Mercer tried to respond by interrogating the corporate raiders about their "plans" for the corporation: what were their intentions, how would they strategically run and build the corporation, what were their long-term goals? Pickens answered simply: "The plan is that we want to give your stockholders $30 a share and the stock is selling at $20. . . . *Just know* that we're going to run the company, and we're going to pay a big price for it. You haven't been able to get the price . . . up to $30 dollars a share." After explicitly asking Pickens again what his plans were, and having Pickens again answer that the plan was an increased stock price, Mercer pointed out that such an answer was *still* not a plan: "It's a one-time hit, where we get a spike in the share price, and we cash out a corporation instead of operating it as a viable operation sometime in the future." In response, many in the simulation argued that because the primary duty of a corporation is to maximize shareholder value, simply paying the $30 fulfills that obligation. Mercer, characteristic of how managers have historically negotiated shareholder value with multiple stakeholders, challenges these "champions" of shareholder value:

> We keep talking about shareholder value, when really what these gentleman are talking about is price because the value is price and quality, and quality has some enduring time period to it, whereas we are talking short-term here. If you're sitting in front of a CRT here and that spike comes up and you have a fiduciary responsibility to that firm you're managing, that stock is gone. . . . The rules currently are that the directors have to look after the interests of the shareholders. And, with that interest, I say that we have to have a plan that means that the corporation will survive, will become more competitive, will increase jobs and enhance its value over a period of time and not just in one-shot price.

Although Mercer cogently pointed out the contradictions in their logics—that shareholder value is unsustainable without a corporation that is productive, and that stock price should measure long-term, "quality" corporate performance—his arguments were ignored in favor of a discourse of immediate shareholder rights. Even though these shareholders are mainly professional investors who "will take very big positions for what they hope will be a very short period of time, and they hope to profit from the present market price and the deal price" (as Warren Buffet, also playing himself in his simulation, pointed out), they are to be credited for pushing up the share price of Peachtree, which its current management was "unable" to do. In the final statement of the simulation, James Bare first summarized the superseded managerial point of view: "I think you have presented an enormous dilemma for the CEO of Peachtree. . . . I was trained that a corporation was a guest in this society to present quality goods at a reasonable cost. We were not trained to react to the financial markets and such. We were trying to find a balance between long-term and short-term; we were trying to be sensitive to our communities because we genuinely believed that that would optimize our profits by reacting to those particular needs." But, he defeatedly concluded, "the fact is, we must change," because "the Street is telling us that the trader or the short-term investor prevails, and therefore it's my duty to react to that."

Because of the traumatic socioeconomic dislocations caused by the takeover movement of the 1980s, there was an extended social and political resistance. Even the mainstream media was very critical of the myriad insider trading scandals, stock market manipulations, and the "human cost" of corporate takeovers, and many writers explicitly identified Wall Street practices and elite privilege as the causes of human suffering. Government officials and lawyers helped to bring down the largest insider-trading ring in financial history: Michael Milken, Ivan Boesky, Martin Siegel, and Dennis Levine. Wall Street investment banks such as Drexel Burnham Lambert and Kidder Peabody, leaders in the junk bond scandals, were bankrupted or severely crippled. James Stewart, Pulitzer Prize–winning author of *Den of Thieves*, wrote that the criminal "conspiracy" that characterized Wall Street in the 1980s cannot be simplified as "the ill-gotten gains of individuals" (Stewart 1992, 21). The bigger picture of criminality must include the nation's financial markets, completely "corrupted from within" (Stewart 1992, 22).

Individual shareholders also resisted. In 1990, Bryan Burrough and John Helyar told the tale of KKR's LBO of, what was at the time, the largest company ever to be taken over. This deal was heralded as a victory for RJR Nabisco shareholders because in order to take over such a large corporation, KKR had to outbid two other raiders such that the share price of RJR more than doubled in a year. "Yet in the world's greatest concentration of RJR shareholders—Winston-Salem, North Carolina—few were thanking Johnson [the CEO] even as the money gushed into town. Nearly $2 billion of checks arrived in the late-February mail. Now, more than ever, Winston-Salem was 'the city of reluctant millionaires.' Local brokers and bankers got calls from distraught clients. 'I won't sell my stock,' one sobbed. 'Daddy said don't *ever* sell the RJR stock.' They were patiently told they had to. They were told the world had changed. . . . 'You have to understand,' said Nabby Armfield [a local resident], 'Reynolds wasn't a stock. It was a religion'" (Burrough and Helyar 1990, 507). Individual shareholders engage in multiple practices not foretold or accounted for by Wall Street's treatment and understanding of stocks. Moreover, while these former "owners" of RJR were getting checks in the mail, they were also losing their jobs. But as the backlash raged from 1988 to 1993, Wall Street had already begun a counter movement to redefine and insert M&A into the mainstream of corporate practices.

The "Reclaiming" of Shareholder Value

Alfred Rappaport, business school professor and author of *Creating Shareholder Value: The New Standard for Business Performance*, a classic "how-to" book in financial business literature, gives a telling description of Wall Street worldviews of the takeover movement and the ways in which shareholder value was historically maximized. Considering corporate raiders, private equity firms, and investment banks to be "champions of the shareholders," Rappaport applauds them for their "attacks on two fronts. First, they are constantly searching for poorly managed companies, where aggressive changes in strategic directions could dramatically improve the value of the stock. Second, they identify undervalued assets that can be redeployed to boost the stock price. As a result, many executives recognize a new and compelling reason to be concerned with the performance of their company's stock" (Rappaport 1986, 3–5). And, what exactly are these changes in strategic direction which increase the value of the stock? The first is simply to give a tender offer (an offer to buy at a certain price) for a company's stock as a way of generating fear and transferring corporate control from those who are not *as* concerned with stock price to those who *primarily* are. In the purchase of a company, the investor-raiders usually buy the stock from the shareholders at a premium —meaning above the current market price—and according to shareholder value worldviews, this act of giving the shareholders a premium at a single point in time "adds value," that is, is worthwhile in and of itself. Allocating resources to other constituencies besides the shareholder constitutes "overfunding," and as such, these companies are "undermanaged." In this sense, it does not matter if *after* the company is sold, it is broken up, downsized, and suffers from a long-term decline in performance. Given the array of practices that are possible to increase the share price, Rappaport shows how the sole concern for the stock price creates an environment and understanding of total fungibility: that is, the point is not that there exists a definite set of "practices" that a corporation must adopt in order to raise its stock's value, but that the entire corporation (from pension funds to jobs) becomes a site for transferring, exchanging, and selling in order to quickly increase the stock's value. The entire organization becomes a site for potential liquidations, and not surprisingly, the corporation as a liquid transfer site for stock-price appreciation is usually unsustainable. The productive capabilities of corporations can only be reallocated to shareholders and depleted without replenishment for so long.

Rappaport identifies "excess cash" and "overfunded pension funds" among company assets most ripe for liquidation (Rappaport 1986, 10). This concept of being "overfunded" is worth unpacking. Companies present themselves as attractive takeover targets precisely at the point when their assets sold separately will collectively command a higher price than the current stock market value. In fact, one of the main goals of an LBO is "to buy the company from the shareholders for less than it was worth, auction it in pieces at fair market values, and pocket the difference" (M. Lewis 1991, 77). That the sale of its assets can be lucrative certainly does not identify a given company as unprofitable or poorly performing; it only signifies that the stock was "undervalued." In other words, the "ideal" target company for takeover is oftentimes a very well-performing company that enjoys an abundant cash flow, a rich company with well-funded pensions and "excess" cash! Does this not signify that these takeover candidates are "healthy" by a variety of other measures, and that these measures are precisely those that fly in the face of Wall Street worldviews? The justification of such devastating and seemingly bizarre practices lies in the financial world's particular interpretation of shareholder value, narratives of shareholder oppression, and as I will demonstrate, the institutional culture of investment banks. *Not* finding ways of "creating" more value for shareholders would result in what Rappaport calls "significant *exploitation* of shareholders" (Rappaport 1986, 8). Similarly, Baker and Smith, business school professors and shareholder value activists, praise the takeover wave of the 1980s as a movement to strategically use the market to "contest managerial control," take back capitalism, dismantle the managerial regime, and "rebirth" financial capitalism to its rightful dominance in American business (Baker and Smith 1998, 20).[24] Rappaport notes triumphantly that by the 1990s, "maximizing shareholder value" came to be "embraced as the 'politically correct' stance by corporate board members and top management. . . . As is the case with good ideas, shareholder value has moved from being ignored to being rejected to becoming self-evident" (Rappaport 1998, 2–3).

A certain model of shareholder value thus becomes apparent. Shareholder value is a mission-driven cause that overcomes the wrongful allocation of capital and embodies the sacred identity between profits and private property. Any attempt to interpret the corporation as a long-term social institution whose profits and responsibilities are allocated to multiple "stakeholders," from employees to communities, constitutes an attack on the inviolable rights of the shareholder. Shareholders *are* the company, and there is no space for employees to challenge downsizing or stock price primacy because all other constituents are written out of this narrow definition of the company. This definition presupposes that an exclusive focus on the stock price for the purpose of enriching the "owners" is necessarily righteous regardless of who may be adversely affected.

Delving into the cultural meaning of shareholder value allowed me to see ethnographically that financial worlds are as vividly characterized by specific values, morals, and cultures as any of the communities with which they clash. Theorizing the dominance of finance-led capitalism as a subsuming of local and complex cultural values by an external, abstract market process and logics needs to be reframed. Rather than accept "the market" as shorthand for such assumptions, it is crucial to unpack the particular and contingent cultural meanings and ideologies represented as "the market" to understand that moments of "financial market takeover" are perhaps better analyzed as power struggles over diverging and hierarchical cultural values and practices. As Giovanni Arrighi writes in *The Long Twentieth Century*, "Finance capital is not a particular state of world capitalism, let alone its latest and highest stage. Rather, it is a recurrent phenomenon which has marked the capitalist era from its earliest beginnings in late medieval and early modern Europe. Throughout the capitalist era financial expansions have signaled the transition from one regime of accumulation on a world scale to another. They are integral aspects of the recurrent destruction of the 'old' regimes and the simultaneous creation of 'new' ones" (Arrighi 1996, ix–x). Although I would argue that Arrighi's assumptions of the cyclical recurrence of finance capital expansions need to be historically and locally contextualized, I take his point that the accelerating financialization of capitalist practices must be understood as a condition and sign for a new regime of cultural values and norms. It is perhaps during such moments of flux that anthropologists gain heightened access to both the new values which are emergent and the old values which are being dismantled. To theorize the shift that began in the 1970s—a time when, as scholars from multiple disciplines concur, dramatic changes were occurring in the social economy of the United States—I routinely referenced work by anthropologists and many social scientists that pointed toward globalization, changes in technology and information processing, and shifts in the regimes of production from Fordism to flexible accumulation. What I did not envision was that Wall

Street and many economists told quite a different story to explain these large-scale transformations, namely the narrative of the shareholder value revolution.

Shareholder value has been, on the one hand, largely ignored by anthropologists as a powerful explanatory tool, and on the other, decontextualized, naturalized, and globalized by institutional financial interests and many economists. Thus, a historical and localized understanding of shareholder value is crucial to understanding drastic transitions in capitalism and the extent to which corporate values and mainstream economic assumptions have changed since the mid-twentieth century. For example, in the postwar era, there existed the socioeconomic assumption that a rising tide lifts all boats, albeit unequally (Dudley 1994). During boom times, the understanding was that most Americans would fare well, and during busts, most Americans would fare less well, but corporations and governmental and bureaucratic support structures were there to cushion the blow. In the 1990s, as I have described, during a historic economic boom time, workers in the United States suffered massive downsizings; in fact, the better "the economy" did (in terms of leading economic indicators such as stock prices), the worse many people fared (in terms of wages, downsizings, living standards, benefits). Social scientists have pondered the seeming contradiction of the "jobless recovery," but I argue, however, that the notion of a jobless recovery is only a quandary if social scientists are still trying to explain today's social economy using the terms and assumptions of the post–Second World War era (Aronowitz and DiFazio 1994). In other words, if shareholder value, not welfare capitalism, is the ideal, then the jobless recovery makes perfect sense, for stock prices (which spike because of downsizing), not jobs, are the focus and the measure of corporate health and success.

Implosions of Shareholder Value

Whether or not shareholder value was achieved, however, was not unequivocal. Despite my informants' homage to the takeover movement and their embrace of the mission of shareholder value, not only were their cultural practices contradictory, but they also struggled deeply with the gaps or disconnects between their faith in shareholder value and its actual enactments. Although it is clear that they did not simply follow shareholder value as an ideological imperative (other cultural and structural forces influenced them), I would not go so far as to say that my informants as a whole were perfectly aware that shareholder value contradictions existed, that they simply and deliberately misled their corporate clients to destroy shareholder value while superficially paying it lip service. In this section, I depict a diversity of contradictory events I encountered regarding shareholder value during my fieldwork and beyond.

Throughout my research, on the one hand, I heard almost unflinching allegiance to shareholder value, and on the other, I continually learned of instances where the share prices of companies that Wall Street constantly "touched" (for example, through M&A and divestitures) declined in the long term.[25] For example, in May and June 1998, during my first year of fieldwork after being downsized from BT, Wall Street was abuzz with the initial announcement of the merger of Daimler-Benz with Chrysler Corporation. My informants were literally beside themselves with excitement: it was not only a "global," cross-border megamerger between a storied German car company and an American "big three" auto maker, but it was also heralded as one of the most complicated transactions (due to transatlantic legal, corporate, and labor regulations and frameworks) ever completed. They exuberantly predicted many more cross-border deals and an unprecedented wave of innovative M&A deals for the coming years. In particular, my informants marveled (and envied) at the potential windfall that Goldman Sachs, who advised Daimler-Benz, and Credit Suisse First Boston, who advised Chrysler, would reap with the closing of this deal. Together, both investment banks were estimated to reap a combined windfall fee of $80–100 million on this $43 billion deal (Haar 1998; Holson 1998). The financial press heralded the deal as a "marriage in heaven" that would result in "annual savings and revenue gains of at least $3 billion" and allow the new "synergistic" entity DaimlerChrysler to achieve economies of scale to enter new markets and achieve massive cost savings. As CEO of Daimler, Juergen Schrempp, who would take over as lead CEO, claimed, " 'We'll have the size, the profitability and the reach to take on everyone. . . . Our efficiency and our bottom-line focus will make us the most profitable automotive company in the world'" (Lipin and Mitchener 1998). Daimler-Benz, with its share price not only above $100 but also multiple times its earnings, was easily able to purchase Chrysler, whose stock price was around $50, with a lower price to earnings ratio. To cap off the year, 1998 was Wall Street's best year yet in M&A transactions. *Institutional Dealers' Digest*, a central trade magazine for investment banks, awarded the Daimler-Chrysler merger the much coveted investment banking "Deal of the Year" Award, and Goldman Sachs won "Bank of the Year," with a "hand in almost 40% of all mergers and acquisitions" globally and having "advised on announced deals worth $960 billion" (*PR Newswire* 1998; *Business Wire* 1999; W. Lewis 1999).

Less than two years later, the megamerger was proclaimed a "nightmare" (Ball, White, and Miller 2000). I myself was perplexed by the extent of the disaster and wondered how to make sense of it, given my informants' utter confidence in the much heralded deal's achievement of shareholder value. (Interestingly, financial journalists, having seen many a merger implode, were not surprised: they quickly dubbed the Daimler-Chrysler merger a "celebrity wedding" indicating their expectation that like most megamergers, shareholders would be left "heartbroken" [Leach 2001].) The merger turned out to be a "megaflop" by multiple measures: by the third quarter of 2000, DaimlerChrysler's income plummeted 92 percent, with its Chrysler division losing $512 million, and its market capitalization (its stock price times the number of shares outstanding) was $43 billion, *lower* than that of Daimler-Benz *alone* before the merger (Ball, White, and Miller 2000). The following year its share price had plummeted from $108 to $45, and the Chrysler division was hemorrhaging more than $1 billion a quarter (Ball 2001). But, beyond these shareholder value measures (which began to decline even before the deal was officially closed in November 1998), DaimlerChrysler began to downsize workers and executives almost immediately after the merger was finalized, failed to integrate German and American management, and by 2001, announced that it would lay off over twenty-six thousand workers, "idle six plants," and sell off "non-core" assets (Ball 2001; Eldridge and Valdmanis 2001). For the first six years of the millennium, DaimlerChrysler experienced losses, volatility, downsizings, spinoffs, plant closings, and continual crises, and by 2007, its largest shareholders urged the company to eliminate "Chrysler" from its name, returning to Daimler-Benz AG, and to sell off Chrysler, which it did with the assistance of J. P. Morgan (Bloomberg, and AP and Staff Reports 2007; Cimilluca and Walker 2007; Milne 2007). Ironically, in 2007, Goldman Sachs, the original lead advisor to Daimler-Benz's purchase of Chrysler, advised Cerberus Capital Management, a private equity firm, in its buying of Chrysler from DaimlerChrysler for $7.4 billion (the price Daimler originally paid for Chrysler was $33 billion). According to the *Wall Street Journal*, the DaimlerChrysler split amounted to a "second payday" for Wall Street investment banks that reap "fees at both ends" by bringing together and soon after "dismantle[ing]" companies (Cimilluca and Walker 2007). As for my informants, though they acknowledged the failures of DaimlerChrysler, which became something of a joke (whose punch line was that high-end and low-end companies do not mix well), they continued to pursue, advise, and herald M&A and massive corporate restructuring as a strategy for shareholder value.

According to both short-term and long-term measures, investment banks actually *fail* to practice shareholder value in many deals. Proponents of the economic benefits of shareholder value constantly face not only declining stock prices in the long term but also declining corporate performance on multiple other fronts. As for the aftermath of the 1980s, the discipline of debt turned into the punishment of default, as many companies not only failed to keep up their junk bond payments, but also the debt that financed these buyouts did not fund investments in new productive assets nor improve "efficiency," but were merely "transfers of value away from other claimants on enterprises' existing cash flows" (O'Sullivan 2000, 169). With a decade of data to analyze, O'Sullivan reaches stark conclusions about the consequences of the takeover movement of the 1980s: there is a "striking dearth of unambiguous evidence to support" the shareholder value theory; shareholder value is not beneficial for corporate efficiency or employee productivity; and the central assumption that shareholder wealth is an adequate measure or "proxy for corporate performance" is wrong (O'Sullivan 2000, 167,169). "Since [proponents of shareholder value] tend to begin from the premise that the appropriate way to measure the 'creation of value' is to focus on stockholder wealth," they do not address the problem of innovation, for example, or the consequence of such a narrow vision of value (O'Sullivan 2000, 174). Many scholars in business and management have themselves shown that the earnings and profitability of takeover targets often decline in the post-acquisition period (Ravenscraft and Scherer 1987; O'Sullivan 2000). Poignantly, appeals to the efficiency and eventual social good of shareholder value collapse on their own terms. The conclusion in the aftermath of the M&A boom and bust in the 1990s is the same. Shareholder value must be read as a political strategy to monopolize corporate control and advocate for "the demands of financial interests to reap high returns" in a very short amount of time. This logic of shareholder value imposed certain practices that "victimized the poorly protected parties such as workers, suppliers, and host communities" (O'Sullivan 2000, 172).[26]

"We Can Wing It Like That": The Problem of Efficiency in Shareholder Value Narratives

The question then becomes, how did my informants explain the real-world failures of the strategies that were supposed to achieve shareholder value? When asked, some were able to produce textbook neoclassical responses that neatly linked corporate restructuring, shareholder value, and efficiency, though I soon began to realize that such circular logic was believed by only a minority of bankers. Jason Kedd, an associate investment banker in the M&A Department at DLJ, responded this way:

JK: Say you have a large conglomerate. If the value of the pieces separately is greater than the whole, then arguably, it is better to break the company up because if I am a shareholder, that means I get more economic value out of my investment, which I can then reinvest in something else to create jobs. If I am an employee, then there may be some temporary dislocations in the economy, but long-term, with a higher employment rate because at the end of the day, the most efficient, the most imperative industry should survive. The best operation should survive.

KH: So, you are saying that the way it works is even though with corporate restructuring, there is going to be an initial downsizing of jobs and dislocation, this will create more value for shareholders and ultimately because you are creating more shareholder value, then in the long term, things are better for the economy?

JK: Exactly.

Kedd made sense of shareholder value-led downsizings by using rationales of efficiency, long-term economic value, and the prospect of a "better" overall economy. By justifying restructuring and the breakup of companies with discourses of future excellence, Kedd not only excised worker trauma from his account of downsizing but also deflected into a vague future concerns and critiques that corporate restructurings might subvert the professed result of the (supposedly) "best," "most efficient," and "most imperative" companies. He not only assumed shareholder value was ample justification for corporate dismemberment, but also that share-price-led downsizing would necessarily produce profits, jobs, productivity, and efficiency. Asset stripping, then, gets read as a social good, as a sign of "fixing" previously inefficient corporations.

Similarly, Christine Chang and Julie Cooper, both high-yield bond vice presidents at BT, also explicitly rationalized and equated corporate restructuring and downsizing with efficiency. When I asked Chang about

Wall Street's role in corporate restructuring, she replied, "Well, that is just a matter of making the economy more efficient. In the end that is good because you take people out of dead-end jobs anyway and sort of force them to find something in an industry that is growing. But, I am sure, if you are on the other side of that equation, it is a lot harder." Julie Cooper, assessing Wall Street's impact on U.S. corporations, said, "Obviously, Wall Street has helped corporate America make money, and Wall Street has made a lot of money off corporate America." In her view, the dominance of shareholder value "forces companies to be much more cognizant of what they do and how what they do is perceived." "Corporate restructuring," she asserted, "is driven by efficiency needs . . . because you're rewarded for being efficient. And if you're more efficient, your stock is trading at a higher multiple, so you can get your money out at a cheaper price." For both Chang and Cooper, "efficiency" was simply a taken-for-granted translation phrase automatically used to explain why restructuring led to higher stock prices: whenever shareholder value and restructuring got mentioned, so did efficiency.

The majority of my conversations, however, hovered between Kedd's textbook confidence and more hesitant accounts that admitted some hints of doubt, though certainly not enough to support a robust challenge to the narrative of shareholder value, downsizing, and efficiency. Joseph Tsai, an associate investment banker at DLJ, began our conversation on efficiency making the typical argument that investment banks have made corporate America more efficient, while admitting that investment bankers sometimes "pitch" ideas and actions that hurt the company:

> I do recognize the ills of investment banking. There was the whole junk bond phase where we pull leverage up in order to juice up the returns of these leverage buyout companies and funds. There is some cost to that, but the idea behind that deal is . . . efficiency, efficiency with regard to the investors. You are basically trying to get the highest return to the investors, but there are social costs involved. If you are leveraging up a big company, and the company can't meet its obligations, it is going to fail and lay off dozens of workers, so there are social costs. But you would like to think at least that you do the efficient capital structure thing and the firms that should survive, would, and those that are muddling along—they should die anyway eventually.

While Tsai briefly acknowledged that the "costs" of investment banking's practices of shareholder value could damage the company itself, as well as society, he soon deflected attention away from Wall Street and on market-based "survival of the fittest," sparking me to inquire further:

KH: So, what do you think is Wall Street's social impact?

JT: Including economic or are we talking moral here?

KH: Both.

JT: Economic impact, I would hope that Wall Street is creating more efficiencies, and I must sound like an economist with all this efficiency B.S.

KH: Do you feel like it is B.S. when you are saying it, or do you think it is true?

JT: No, I think it is true. But, I've been reading my finance textbook too much, fills me with doctrine. I would *hope* that it is creating efficiencies and that is leading to raising everybody's standard of living.

KH: And have you found evidence to the contrary, like when you were saying to some extent, there has been evidence of costs and dislocations?

JT: There are short-term dislocations, but *hopefully* they are short-term.

KH: Okay, so when you said moral, how about moral [costs]?

JT: I wasn't ready to answer that question. I mean, it is the drive for profitability now; everything now is about shareholder value, and *then* you wonder about social responsibility and whether that has any role to play.

KH: Do you think shareholder value in general is a good thing or do you feel . . .

JT: I think it is a good thing in terms of allocation of capital. I mean, *hopefully* you are using the capital to the best use, allocating it to the best use. . . . But in terms of society or community, I am sure there are other considerations. Procter and Gamble donated a lot of money to charities. I am sure this doesn't really enhance shareholder value, but it is something that they should do.

KH: Do you think focus on shareholder value detracts from the side of community?

JT: I think it detracts from it. It is probably different if your goal is to be a responsible member of [the] community, if your goal is to make sure your plant is operating so that you create jobs. . . . It's a different way of thinking than shareholder value.

KH: Do you think, then, that companies should move more toward that direction, that different way of thinking?

JT: I would like to think that everything—maybe I'm an optimist—that everything will work itself out so that if you do have the emphasis of shareholder value, that everybody is made better off and there will be more money to be devoted to civic works or charity, that it can be a win/win situation.

KH: Oh, right, this focus will lead to other things?

JT: Right, everybody being better off, this trickle-down theory that my hero, Reagan, espoused. (my emphasis)

Not ready to recognize how shareholder value practices collapse even on their own terms, my informants instead focused on a conflict between shareholder value and the interests of "the community" at large. Yet, often seemingly on the verge of acknowledging that shareholder value creates social dislocation, they recoup shareholder value, not in terms of its actual effects, but in terms of "financial textbooks" and neoclassical economic theories, or in terms of hope, optimism, and faith. My exchange with Tsai illustrates that shareholder value is not always unproblematically naturalized as a social good; even those who profess to hold this view often sense ruptures and fractures in it. At the same time, this conversation also demonstrates shareholder value's annexation and renaming of the conflict and separation between shareholder value and "community" such that they become one and the same.

Edward Randolph, a vice president of Risk Management at Merrill Lynch, has an understanding of social cost similar to Tsai's yet is more critical of efficiency. When I prompted him with a question about the relationship between corporate restructuring and shareholder value, he readily acknowledged that Wall Street–driven layoffs are "obviously, from a social point of view . . . a bad thing":

> ER: When you have people who are out work, and I often think about people who are in their forties or fifties with children. . . . It's gonna be very hard for them to find a new job, a job that is probably as well paying as they've had. I think it's a real issue. I think it's been fortunate that . . . there's been a booming economy, and so it seems that people are picking up work, or unemployment seems to be under control in many respects. However, if the market, if the economy does slow down, I don't know. It is somewhat scary. Chase is going to lay off 4,500 people, what happens to them? I don't know what happens to those people. I often wonder about it. I think there are some fairly significant social—but I think they're being hidden for the time being [by] the fact that the economy is kind of rolling along.
>
> KH: Do you feel like the restructuring, the downsizing, helps to increase efficiency?
>
> ER: I think it probably does in most firms. But at the same [time], I think a lot of firms found, and I think they're getting better at it, but when they first, when this whole fad started in the eighties, they often did cut stuff to the bone and started to cut what they called muscle rather than just fat. And so they did overdo it in many respects. I think one of the things that they did was they cut a lot of middle management out, and they found that middle management actually played a valuable role in terms of

connecting senior management to the product or to the more junior people. That caused some problems.

Randolph talked about downsized workers without incorporating or justifying their predicaments into the discourse of efficiency. In fact, in addition to articulating his concern for downsized workers, he gave important examples of corporations being *inefficient*, of "overdoing it" and "cutting muscle rather than fat" for short-lived results in the rush to shareholder value. At the same time, while he engages with, and goes beyond, "social costs," he does not question the cornerstone concept: that restructuring does add shareholder value.

Finally, to my surprise, some informants were simply dismissive of the discourse of efficiency. Below is a conversation with Anthony Johnson, an investment banking associate in M&A at J. P. Morgan, on the relevance of efficiency explanations for justifying corporate restructuring:

> KH: Given that employment is affected by corporate restructuring, in the cases where people lose their jobs, what is the rationale? Is it like, "Well, we're becoming more efficient, we're hoping the company grows, so in the long term, people will have more jobs?" Is that—I don't know if that is even a rationale.
>
> AJ: *Well, we can wing it like that. For me, it is all about getting the share price up.* Take Morgan, for example. We have long been accused of having too much fat. We have gone through a process of kind of trimming people out. And the day it was announced we would be trimming our workforce, our stock price jumped three bucks because people recognized that we were finally getting down to trying to become a lean, mean investment bank. So, when you do an M&A transaction, people are expecting a rationale for it. And in that rationale, management is going to talk about where there might be synergies or opportunities that have good value. The market is looking for you to act. It is going to mean laying off workforce and taking a big restructuring charge to become the entity you said you were going to become. (my emphasis)

This discussion with Johnson demonstrated that efficiency might not be the dominant justification for corporate restructuring done in the name of increasing shareholder value. "We can wing it like that": efficiency, here, simply serves as a marketing strategy, one of many claims that investment bankers can use to legitimize restructuring after the fact. Julie Cooper similarly pointed out that "from a shareholder-investor perspective, it's all about playing the game. It's about meeting analysts' expectations. It's about managing your balance sheet so you look good at the end of the quarter."[27] The crucial issue is to "get the share price up"—this is enough of a goal.

When I asked Bob Gibson, a managing director of Sales and Trading at Nomura Securities' New York office (though he is a veteran of Wall Street and used to work at Kidder Peabody), about Wall Street's impact on corporate restructuring, he responded, "Well, let's just think that it's probably toward efficiency."

> KH: When you say probably, does that mean that there are mergers that don't work?
>
> BG: Sure, you'll find plenty of examples of mergers that didn't have the payoff that was once projected, for example, the highly touted merger between Smith Kline Beecham and Glaxo which just recently became unraveled. Seems to me that in the investment community, shareholders, the big shareholders, the institutional shareholders thought this made a lot of sense, but when it came down to the final, putting the finishing touch on it, the two CEOs were wrangling about little things like who was going to be the most powerful, [and] the deal came unraveled. So sometimes it's not a good idea.

Although Gibson followed by saying that "shareholders are ultimately the beneficiaries, and there are all kinds of things that do get done for that purpose," his halfhearted invocation of efficiency and his example of a disappointing merger are indicative of the unstable and contested discourse of efficiency. Significantly, Gibson blames, not the dictates of shareholder value, but rather the personal failings of ego-driven CEOs for the merger's failure.

Taken together, my informants' contradictory and inconsistent use and understandings of efficiency taught me a few things. First, efficiency was not as central to explaining "native" Wall Street worldviews of the relationship between corporate restructuring and shareholder value as I had assumed. Second, efficiency rationales did not clarify how Wall Street's shareholder value ideal could not fully make sense of corporate restructurings' (seemingly inefficient) failures to produce corporate "health" or shareholder value. I then began to realize that part of my surprise stemmed from the spell of efficiency that entrances many academic interlocutors.

For example, let us return to this notion of the "jobless recovery." Sociologists Stanley Aronowitz and William DiFazio, perplexed by how exponential economic and stock market booms could bear seemingly no relationship to employment cycles, described the late twentieth-century economic "boom" as the "puzzlement" of a "jobless recovery." They explained this reversal of American economic sensibilities by pointing out that efficiency and technological productivity were pursued at the expense of people and jobs; they rationalized that massive job cuts were the result of the industrial restructuring necessary to make the economy more "efficient" in a highly competitive global market (Aronowitz and DiFazio 1994). Efficiency continued to mean a high ratio of output to input, and as such restructuring and downsizing led to lower labor inputs, cost savings, and therefore greater productivity. To make sense of this conundrum, they accepted, not only the "fact" of, and movement toward, efficiency, but a particular interpretation of efficiency that directly explained, translated, and bridged corporate restructuring and downsizing with productivity, profits, and stock price.[28] I had begun to learn from my informants about some serious challenges to social scientific interpretations of both efficiency and textbook finance.

First, I argue that it is crucial for social critics to rethink their notions of efficiency, as their understandings of efficiency grounded in labor and industrial productivity linked to sustained corporate growth are no longer appropriate to new financial concepts of efficiency, which are measured by the number and size of deals and transactions that create short-term stock price increases. Certainly, financial transactions still necessitate a particular kind of labor from Wall Street, which in turn depends on the accumulated surplus value from labor in corporate assets, as opposed to being delinked from productive labor. As David Harvey warns, even in a context where stock market and financial values are the dominant influence over corporate actions, "if all corporations seek to survive by purely financial maneuvers without enhancing or restructuring production, then capitalism is not too long for this world" (Harvey 1999, 320). My point is, however, that although the productive process continues to be crucial for the extraction of surplus value and a necessary precondition for financial maneuvers, the rules and priorities structuring what corporations are and who can lay claim to them have radically changed. For many investment bankers, efficiency referred to the set of practices which most quickly and cheaply translates corporate actions into rising stock prices; that is, the ideal corporation is one where all corporate practices lead directly to increasing stock prices. In some cases, they fully recognized how "inefficient" their practices were when measured by fairly standard metrics, that is, in terms of counterproductive layoffs followed by immediate rehirings, and the lack of success of mergers and acquisitions. Of course, the ironies do not stop here: it follows that inefficiencies and failures in major corporate practices done in the name of shareholder value will boomerang against shareholder value itself. It is thus also crucial for academics to recognize that *not only has the definition of efficiency changed, but also that efficiency is simply not being produced* in that investment bankers oftentimes do not create shareholder value, the very measure of the "new" efficiency. Although my informants did not fully question the mission of shareholder value, I saw their contradictory and uncertain uses of efficiency and their resorting to desperate "hopes" of efficient results as evidence of fissures between the ideal of shareholder value and its practice.

Shareholder Value Temporalities

In my interviews, I found that seasoned Wall Street investment bankers who have been through multiple financial crises have often formulated a subtle critique of shareholder value's short-term foci and its corresponding long-term failures, though stopping short of a rejection of shareholder value. In explaining what he disliked about Wall Street, Corey Fisher, a managing director at Vanguard Investments, critiqued its obsession with immediate results.[29] "Wall Street has an extremely short-term focus," he said. "I think that the world does not, that businesses operate in cycles that don't necessarily conform to [Wall Street's] calendar dates. . . . The problem is that we still try to get these corporations and institutions to try to adhere to artificial constraints that we set, and the cycle is going to play out the way it is going to play out. There is nothing you can do to it. So, when you artificially impose a structure that is really not meaningful, what you wind up doing is creating some tough times for people." Fisher then pointed to the example of publicly held companies, which are required to make quarterly reports to Wall Street, and how this cycle might be wholly irrelevant to some businesses. He called such short-term emphases "the key driver . . . of behavior for a lot of these companies" and said that they "wind up making decisions that may not necessarily be in the *best interests of shareholders over the long term*, but help them to meet short-term expectations of the Street" (my emphasis). I asked him how the Street got that way.

> KH: Has it always been short-term? How did [the Street] get its values and start making all of the corporations believe it? How did that translation happen?

CF: I think that over time, it has actually compressed. Now, we are just so time-conscious. I don't really have a solution to it, but I'm just observing that this is a reality. So, you've got basically a timeframe that does not necessarily conform to the business cycle of an enterprise, and you have demands being made, let's say from the buy side [institutional investors]. On our side of the business, which has become a major driver of corporate behavior, [are] institutional investors . . . under a lot of pressure to perform. So, the money managers in a place like this, every quarter they have to report to their clients, on which stocks and which bonds they have bought and sold and how they did versus a given benchmark that they have agreed to when they take on the assignment. And because of the ninety-day timeframe they are operating within, they place that same requirement on the managers of these enterprises. That's really how it starts.[30]

His remarks illustrate how Wall Street investment banks use stock-market temporalities to frame and discipline the timeframes of corporations. Quarterly deadlines are ill-suited, not to mention detrimental, to long-range plans (such as research and development) that may not post rising profits each and every quarter, yet businesses are punished for not continually meeting these expectations.

Three other senior bankers also evinced unease with the temporal strictures of stock-based business strategies. I asked Thomas Douglass, a managing director in strategy at BT, "Is shareholder value about the long term or about the short-term boosts? Is there a contradiction?" "It depends on what the shareholders are looking for," he answered, then described the "really active" shareholders, "who are very short-term focused. . . . People get so excited about being able to make money quickly":

The way the stock market has been going, everybody's happy, everybody's thinking, "Hey, I can get rich; this Christmas I'm gonna buy something even bigger." And so that focus on quarter by quarter, seeing the stock price go up, seeing big dividends and everything else. What does that translate into? Well, individual stocks then turn into big pools of money, big pools of securities, and you want to see big returns on those. So, what does *that* mean? That means the people at the individual companies have to focus on what do we do by next quarter to show a really big gain, right? And then the people that are buying the securities of those individual companies are gonna look and favor the companies that are showing that big gain, so that they can show a big gain by the following quarter. And the people [usually institutional investors] that are buying the pools of securities are looking for the one that made the big move quarter to quarter, so [they] can move along with them and grow quickly. So, it's this huge thing that feeds on itself. . . . That's what's driving all of this, in my opinion. You've got both the shareholders that are being very short-term-focused and then driving everyone else to remain short-term-focused.

Douglass also pointed out that executives are "incentivized" to work for the short term, and spoke of "lots of examples of CEOs that tried to take that five- to ten-year view who got nailed because their one- to two-year production level was not what Wall Street thought it should be."

John Carlton, also a managing director at BT in the high-yield department, admitted that, "Yes, short-term orientation is negative," but then pointed out how difficult it is structurally to emphasize the long term: "The flip side is if you do not want to do that, what do you do?" If you "want to emphasize long term . . . how do you do it? Well, you have to figure out incentives that work for longer terms and that is sometimes hard to do." Carlton pointed out that shareholders are not "by nature" short-term in that they could certainly invest in a stock for twenty years; it is instead the compression of temporality on Wall Street itself *and* the linking of senior management to the stock market during the shareholder revolution that have engendered the short-term focus. When I asked Justin Graham, a managing director of emerging markets at Lehman Brothers, about Wall Street's impact on American corporations, he answered that "it has had a tendency to make them very short-term." According to Graham, there exists a discrepancy "between what Wall Street *pretends* the objectives or the criteria ought to be and what they actually are." Investment bankers claim that they want corporations to create shareholder value, but from the standpoint of the corporations, one of the main and only feasible ways to actually live up to the (unstated) short-term and immediate demands of shareholder value is to, as Graham critiques, "ring the cash register" as many times today as possible, which in turn detracts from shareholder value.

As all of these informants were among the most senior investment bankers on Wall Street (though not representative heads or executive committee members of investment banks, and as such, did not have explicit "spokespeople" roles, which might have compromised their candor), all had experienced gaps between ideal and practice. However, the dominant ideology among informants who were younger and less senior was best exemplified by my former colleague Stan Clark, who made little or no distinction between profits now and profits later. Clark recognized Wall Street's short-termism: "Wall Street likes to call itself long-term. The reality is that your funds performance is graded on a quarterly basis, not an annual basis, so you care about the short term." Yet such observations were quickly rationalized with the understanding that, as Clark concludes, "what you are assuming is that a company that performs well on the short term is going to perform well on the long term."

My analysis of Wall Street's shareholder value worldviews has shown that the values and practices that have historically governed the stock market have been translated and utilized to govern corporations themselves. It is precisely this conflation, this "coming together" of financial and shareholder values with those of corporate America, that has legitimated the dismantling of welfare capitalism. Corporate organizations are today measured and treated according to how Wall Street values and evaluates financial assets. The precarious balance that corporate America had wrought between catering to stock prices and administering to the multiple and conflicting participants of the corporation has been tipped decisively in favor of financial values and interests. I suggest in this chapter that part of the reason and impetus for the success of this conflation (of stock-market values with that of corporate America) in the late twentieth century is that in Wall Street worldviews and narratives, corporate America should always have been accountable only to shareholders. To hear Wall Street tell the narrative of stock market and shareholder ascendancy in the late twentieth century is to hear a narrative of justice prevailing after a prolonged hijacking of the modern corporation by a "fat, dumb, and happy" bureaucracy.

Despite the insights these narratives of shareholder value gave me, they also led me astray. I had assumed that apprehending the underlying complexities and rationales of Wall Street's notions of shareholder value and efficiency would lead me to an understanding, not only of Wall Street's ideologies, but also how it enacted and actualized its worldview. I had assumed mistakenly that shareholder value would bridge the rationales of financial markets to its restructuring of larger social relations. Attributing so much explanatory power to these discourses more often than not confused me. While bankers reconcile these contradictions by arguing that what they do in the short term *should* lead to long-term shareholder value creation, this rationalization came across as self-serving. How can I account for the fact that even when my informants realized that a particular corporate restructuring they advised was not a "solid deal"—that it could result in shareholder value decline (and be detrimental according to other socioeconomic parameters)—they still pushed the deal through and continued to use shareholder value as justification? How are they called upon to *both* downsize corporate America (and themselves) *and* detract from shareholder value?

When I saw that corporate restructurings conducted in the name of shareholder value often led, not only to massive insecurity and a loss of knowledge that hampered morale and productivity, but also to a decline in the very measure Wall Street holds dear, I realized that the model of shareholder value, despite its role as Wall Street's moral blueprint, could not fully explain how investment bankers were propelled to seemingly contradict their own value system. As such, I realized that my central question had to be reframed to ask what else was mediating shareholder value such that the presumed correlation between constantly rising stock prices and downsizings often broke down under the weight of bad deals and poor strategies, leading more to financial booms, busts, and fiascos than "actual" shareholder value. How did investment bankers practice in the name of shareholder value at the level of the everyday, on the ground? It is to this question that I turn in chapters 5 and 6. Shareholder value cannot be understood as discourses divorced from the everyday institutional culture of Wall Street investment banks. In other words, there is no pure, unmediated shareholder value, and Wall Street investment bankers are not freestanding individuals in the market; rather, they are strongly influenced by their financially oriented corporate culture, which they imbibe and enact through their employment experiences in these particular organizations. It also follows that both shareholder value's short-termism and its exclusion of all other stakeholders are not inevitable; its meaning and constitution change over time, are dependent on power relations, and are enacted through particular cultural and institutional contexts. Shareholder value, for example, could just as easily be used to justify long-term corporate growth and employee stability (as it is currently used to defend short-term deal making and downsizing) by making the case that such practices enact sustained stock price appreciation. Moreover, the values and practices of Wall Street investment bankers, which can be well apprehended through a study of their organizational culture, are not only interior to the financial markets. Their actions and their particular corporate culture, not only influence the purpose and behaviors of corporations, employees, and the very nature of work in America, but serve as a model of how employees throughout the United States should behave.

4

The Neoclassical Roots and Origin Narratives

of Shareholder Value

My examination of Wall Street's pivotal role in reshaping corporate America and constructing financial and corporate crisis would not make sense without first analyzing how investment banking legitimacy was won. The rise of shareholder value and the ensuing investor "revolution," which in turn made possible the influence and dominance of Wall Street worldviews, practices, and cultural norms, were the outcomes of long-standing struggles over historical interpretation and neoclassical demands and assumptions. The concept of shareholder value, as Wall Street currently understands it, rests not only on a crude reinterpretation of the historical relationships between corporate America, the stock market, and investors, but also on decontextualized extrapolations (and new adaptations) from neoclassical and classical economic thought.[1] Much like myths of "family values," which derive their moral authority and disciplinary agenda from invoking an idyllic past of the nuclear family, the narrative of "shareholder value" generates much of its authenticity and persuasive force by claiming itself as the original state of economic life, and by extension, entrepreneurial, free-market capitalism as the true nature of human society. It is on nostalgia for a *perfect* capitalism that shareholder value thrives.

To problematize and historicize the logics of shareholder value, it is crucial to examine both the very specific relationships between the assumptions of private property, ownership, self-interest, profits, and efficiency that underscore the conceptual foundations of shareholder value in neoclassical economic thought and how these relationships have changed over time. For example, the coming of the modern corporation—with its complex organizational structure, multiple constituencies, and burgeoning sense of paternalistic "responsibility"—problematized and contradicted traditional neoclassical concepts such as individualism, private property, and self-interest which came to serve as the basis for shareholder value ideology. A protracted struggle thus ensued. On the one hand, fearing the subsuming of entrepreneurial proprietorships into complex corporate firms, neoclassical advocates sought to reduce the multidimensional corporation to the one-dimensional framework of the individual owner/entrepreneur/shareholder. This imposition of particular neoclassical paradigms onto a complex social organization has had the long-standing reverberating effect of providing a justification for the denial of modern corporations' multiple constituents.

On the other hand, managers and many constituents of the corporation both resisted and accommodated these developments: they defended "welfare," managerial capitalism while simultaneously constructing apologies for their "violations" of neoclassical terms and conditions. Although many managers and employees (as well as scholars and observers of the corporation) worked to create new concepts and practices rooted in twentieth-century understandings of corporations as societal institutions, shareholder value still lurked in the background, championed by Wall Street and the discipline of economics and finance as the default basis for the modern corporation. While the managerial challenge was quite dominant throughout the mid-twentieth century (even seeping into Wall Street values and practices, ensuring that neoclassical assumptions themselves did not remain static), shareholder advocates nevertheless worked to translate the modern corporation into the individualistic terms, values, and structures of neoclassical economics despite its irrelevance, indeed hostility, to such an organization.

Of course, the ahistorical imposition of neoclassical values onto the modern corporation was only possible with the help of a powerful historical narrative that retold corporate and stock market history with shareholders at the center as owners and originators of corporate America. I thus analyze the rationales and goals undergirding the formation and growth of the stock market *and* of "public" shareholding in order to contextualize and confront the neoclassical fable that the shareholder was the original funder and controller of U.S. corporations. Neoclassicism and its many advocates did not simply influence the structures, values, and priorities of modern corporations; they also helped to construct a version of corporate history and of shareholding that has gone relatively unchallenged and that has been readily accepted by most mainstream observers of the corporation. The problematic social ramifications of this narrative of the modern corporation lie not so much in its constructed-ness, its blurring of historical "fact," as in its posing as "The History" of corporate America, which denies the complexity of corporate histories and the multiple constituents involved in the making of the corporation. In a sense, one particular, interested narrative, a single point of view, has fashioned itself as present-day reality and historical background, content and context, and it has become nearly impossible to dislodge this narra-tive from its privileged position, so intricately embedded is it in main-stream economic theory and American culture at large. Even critics of shareholder value find themselves using neoclassical rationales and origin myths in their attempts to reimagine corporate priorities, often uninten-tionally translating new priorities back into neoclassical terms.

One answer to this conundrum is to counter the erasures of both Ameri-can corporate *and* Wall Street history, in particular the usually ignored *separation between them.* One of the most egregious mistakes in neoclassi-cal narratives of corporate history is their refusal to understand the his-tory of stocks, shareholders, and the stock market as a phenomenon different from (though related to) the history of corporations, and thus constructed on a diverging set of values and historical trajectories. Con-flating the values and the history of the stock market with those of corpo-rate America has, in effect, imposed the demands of shareholders and the primary importance of liquidity and volatility (that is, stock market val-ues) onto corporations. By delving into the narratives of capitalist myth-making and their concurrent shaping of capitalist practices, I denaturalize the building blocks of shareholder value, investigate the dominant refram-ing of mainstream financial history, and call renewed attention to a cap-italist struggle between corporations and the stock market that spanned over half a century.[2]

It is important to emphasize that I undertake this genealogy of share-holder value and corporate America as a "retelling" of history neither to produce a cardboard past against which to measure the present, nor to deduce a simple, linear cause of current conditions. My foray into the historical vastness of capitalist thought and change in the United States during the twentieth century is shaped by my knowledge of, and concern with, Wall Street practices and narratives today. As Foucault argues, "the past" is continually recreated by the concerns of the present; thus I do not assume a simple, one-way relationship of causality between past and pres-ent. It is precisely a concern with the present-day discourse of shareholder value and its uses that precipitates and frames my investigation into its past linkages and collaborations.

Neoclassical Assumptions and the
Problem of the Modern Corporation

The dominant theoretical perspective on the goals and values of corporations has arisen out of the discipline of economics, which in turn has been dominated by the neoclassical tradition (Schrader 1993). To understand the history and persuasiveness of shareholder value, it is crucial to understand the ideological assumptions which render it natural and legitimate. The most obvious problem with neoclassical economic theory is simply that its core premises are significantly different from, and clash with, any understanding of the firm as a social organization. Neoclassical theories are derived from the "classical" worldviews of Adam Smith in the eighteenth century, built upon and reconfigured by the "neoclassicists" of the nineteenth and early twentieth centuries—all before the modern corporation was established as the major organizational form through which business in the United States is conducted. Even contemporary iterations of neoclassical theory bear the marks of their precorporate origins, having never attempted to take into account the corporation as a social institution and refusing to acknowledge how its multiplicity could change the very foundations of economic theory and business norms. David Schrader (1993, 2) has characterized neoclassical theory as "woefully inadequate to the task of providing a sound understanding of the managerial corporation." Instead, corporations have been continually made to operate according to neoclassical values, however ill the fit.

At the center of Adam Smith's *The Wealth of Nations*, the founding text of classical economics, is the notion that individual acts of economic self-interest combine, through the "invisible hand" of market forces, to further the best interests of society at large. Smith, like many classical economists who followed, centered his theories on the single individual, the notion of an entrepreneur who both owned a small, private enterprise *and* managed it. The dominant neoclassical assumptions in economics and mainstream business today are certainly grounded in these worldviews, though many pivotal additions and reworkings were necessary. Even after the modern corporation came to be the dominant form of economic organization in the early twentieth century and the "visible hands" of multiple constituents and managers became apparent, neoclassical theories maintained the centrality of the individual entrepreneur. In fact, throughout the twentieth century, in the face of a completely new socioeconomic phenomenon, entire schools of economists, notably from the University of Chicago, "steadfastly maintained that all important work in eco-

nomic theory could be carried on from the perspective of an individualistic analysis with an assumption of perfectly competitive markets"
(Schrader 1993, 67). The resurgence of shareholder value in the 1980s,
then, can be read as part of a long line of neoclassically inspired worldviews attempting to collapse and treat the corporation as a single profit-
maximizing individual in the market. Championed by Wall Street financial
institutions and brought to prominence during the leveraged buyout
movement, the shareholder value movement became, arguably, the culmination and most effective demonstration of neoclassical values in the
history of American business.

Specifically, neoclassical capitalist worldviews recognize the presence of
two entities: the individual owner and private property, understood as an
exclusive unit. The individual and his private property are the only two
inputs into the equation;[3] other actors or claimants cannot wedge themselves into this limited space. Moreover, Adam Smith imagined that the
individual owner-entrepreneur would necessarily manage his own enterprise, and as such, he would be solely entitled to all the fruits of his
property, the profits. It is precisely because the owner controls the enterprise *and* gets to "own" the profit that he, driven by self-interest, is compelled to use his industrial property and labor "efficiently" and grow for
the strict purpose of accumulating more profit. This pivotal sequence—
ownership, control, full access to profits, efficiency—constitutes the neoclassical, logical order of the relationship between individuals and private
property. The glue stringing this causal chain together is the concept of
self-interest as motive and the invisible hand as automatic market mechanism. For the capitalist world to be aligned properly, capitalist owners
must have full access to the profits through complete control over their
private property (Berle and Means 1991).

There is perhaps no better example of the historical and practical inapplicability of neoclassical economics to the analysis of corporations as
social institutions than Adam Smith himself, who believed that the managerial corporation would inevitably fail because its very structure ne-
gated his assumptions about the interests and motivations of owners and
managers:

> The directors of [joint-stock] companies, however, being the managers rather
> of other people's money than of their own, it cannot well be expected, that
> they should watch over it with the same anxious vigilance with which the
> partners in a private copartnery frequently watch over their own. Like the
> stewards of a rich man, they are apt to consider attention to small matters as

not for their master's honour, and very easily give themselves a dispensation
from having it. Negligence and profusion, therefore, must always prevail . . . in
the management of the affairs of such a company. It is upon this account that
joint stock companies . . . have seldom been able to maintain the competition
against private adventurers. They have, accordingly, very seldom succeeded
without an exclusive privilege; and frequently have not succeeded with one.
(A. Smith 2000, 800)

To fit into this theoretical legacy, large, public companies had to be understood as if they were merely the creations and appendages of individual entrepreneurs. Because neoclassical values recognized only the single owner-
entrepreneur as a legitimate actor, its advocates worked to replace the
social organization of the corporation—the multiplicity of claimants and
constituents engaged in labor and production—with the singular "owned"
concern of the individual in his quest for profit. As Schrader outlines:

The neoclassical theory of the firm starts out with the claim that all firms are
created and *owned* by individuals. While it is . . . obvious . . . that all firms are
created by individuals, with the help of a legal structure that makes incorporation possible, it is . . . much more controversial . . . to claim that corporations
are owned at all. Nevertheless, it is precisely *this claim that corporations are
owned by individuals*, whether one individual, as in the case of the small owner-
operated firm, or a vast number of individuals, as the theory claims to be the
case with large managerial corporations of highly dispersed stock ownership,
that allows for the *assimilation of the notion of the firm to the notion of the
entrepreneur*. (Schrader 1993, 93, my emphasis)

In keeping with this logic, the shareholder was (and still is) *the perfect
device to reconcile the structure of the modern corporation with the expectations of neoclassical values*. To elide the complexity of the organization and
to avoid treating it as such, the totality of such concerns (that is, the
corporation) was parceled into stocks and "sold" to the shareholder as
proxy for the owner-entrepreneur. In the nineteenth century, this translation, sleight of hand even, was solidified in corporate law: the de jure
purpose of corporations was to generate profits for their shareholders,
who in the eyes of the law owned the modern corporation.

Historically, in the financial market system of U.S. capitalism, the
founders/owners could "cash out" of their business *while keeping the enterprise intact* by assigning a stock value to it, translating their stake into
cash by selling the stock and leaving the enterprise *and control* in the
hands of managers and other employees. In a sense, shareholders have

exchanged cash for shares of stock, not control, but according to neo-classical values, this transaction legitimizes the shareholder as the new owner *and* controller of the corporation, and thus the only recipient of all corporate largesse—an equation I problematize in later sections. With this symbolic as well as monetary transfer, the *shareholder now symbolized and "stood in" for the whole of the corporation and became the sole locus of concern and analysis.* The neoclassical theory of the modern corporation, then, combined the notions of private property, ownership, self-interest, and profit maximization in the body of the shareholder. The reimaging of the shareholder as embodiment of the corporation enabled neoclassical advocates to rationalize that the corporate interest was identical with the *self-interest* of the shareholder. As such, in the transition from owner/entrepreneur/family firms to large corporations, neoclassicism under-stands the shareholder to be the only "natural" successor to the original owner-entrepreneur of the firm, the only legitimate recipient of property transfer because of the assumption that property should be kept "private" and passed on from owner to owner.

Moreover, neoclassicism imagines shareholders to have been once upon a time closely tied to the corporation's activities, managing and oversee-ing the firm's operations. This model of shareholder ownership and con-trol is based on, and only makes sense in, a context where enterprises are small and shareholders, as part of an initial circle of investors, are deeply involved in the business. The problem, however, is that neoclassicism equates shareholder "ownership" with ownership by private business fam-ilies and entrepreneurs when in fact most modern shareholders have never run corporations. Although there were certainly instances where shareholders, as close family or friends, were operationally part of the business, for the most part, shareholders in general have been historically removed from corporations as providers of capital to owners (not neces-sarily to the enterprise itself), *not* managers of corporations. What is forgotten is that historically shareholders have had a distant relationship to the corporation, as they have looked toward the stock market to realize their gains. What neoclassical advocates ignore (and obscure) is that the politics of shareholder value, which insists that corporations should be run only for shareholders, has the effect of *concentrating* control over corporations in those institutions that claim to speak for, and in the name of, shareholders: Wall Street and the stock market.[4]

The modern corporation could have revolutionized the dominant eco-nomic and business ideologies of the time. Schrader (1993, 7) describes it as "a genuine collective entity that features a very conscious 'visible hand' type of coordination of economic activity," and argues that "a recognition of the collective and consciously coordinating character of modern business must sooner or later force a modification in economic theory." What occurred instead was itself revolutionary, for economic theorists and advocates of shareholder value were able to adapt the modern corporation into an ideology that had been "designed to talk about individual agents" (Schrader 1993, 20). In the neoclassical imagination, the goal of all economic enterprise is to be able to narrowly pinpoint and quantify "ownership" of private property, yet the very structures of modern corporations —given their negotiations of multiple constituencies from workers to managers to community—resisted this framework. Faced with this stark conflict of values and organizational form, a choice had to be made— whether to reject neoclassical values as incapable of explaining this new socioeconomic phenomenon, or rather to force these values onto the corporation in an attempt to change its very structure into one governed by the terms of neoclassicism. Instead of abandoning the "laws discovered by previous generations of economic theorists," which "failed to be operative in a world in which a significant number of economic agents were corporate in nature," advocates of neoclassical proprietorship used the very theory which predicted the demise of the managerial corporation to explain the success of (their version of) the corporation (Schrader 1993, 19). They extended Adam Smith's legacy by forging his stamp of approval on a form of organization he believed was destined to fail. This silent revolution for shareholder value came at a great price, sowing the seeds for the dismantling of the corporation in the name of the shareholder. Although this translation, finally accomplished in the late twentieth century, was nominally in favor of the individualized masses of shareholders, ultimately it benefited Wall Street dealmakers and advisors, and, to some extent, large-scale investors in the stock market. This discursive and practical reorganization laid the foundations for a form of social violence tantamount to the institutional erasure of the interests of all groups concerned besides shareholders—or rather, their proxies.[5]

Shareholding, the Stock Market, and the Rise of the Modern Corporation

The shareholder value narrative depends on dual mythologies about the origin and rise of both the stock market and the corporation. These myths both characterize shareholders as the original owners *and* controllers of corporate America, and weave the story that it was through the mechanism of the stock market that Wall Street inventively channeled capital from masses of shareholders large and small to fund the growth and expansion of corporations. Wall Street brought together investors with entrepreneurs, creating a link between ownership and control similar to that of an individual proprietorship. According to this narrative, throughout the twentieth century, as corporations expanded, managers and government regulators usurped shareholder control over corporate resources, inevitably squandering or misdirecting them. It was precisely this mismanagement that spurred shareholder champions such as Wall Street investment banks to campaign for their rights in the 1980s. By crediting shareholders with the birth of corporate America, these discourses also locate them prior in time, as a necessary precondition for corporations' very existence.[6] Directly addressing these long-standing, foundational myths necessitates a brief return to the beginning of the twentieth century. I approach the formations of the stock market, shareholding, and the rise of the modern corporation to depict the social contexts in which mass shareholding and the stock market were constructed as separate from the control of corporations.

The 1890s to the 1920s is a period understood by many historians as the era of the "corporate reconstruction of American capitalism," during which business in the United States moved from the recurrent depressions and crises of laissez-faire, robber-baron capitalism into a relatively more coordinated and bureaucratic period, characterized by the larger-scale form of organization that would come to be understood as the modern industrial corporation (Diner 1998; Sklar 1987). At the turn of the previous century, after "the third long depression in three successive decades" and because of the rampant instability of rapidly growing but uncoordinated and hypercompetitive markets, many entrepreneurs and industrialists turned to, and were influenced by, Wall Street financiers and investment banks (Sklar 1987). Wall Street bankers helped to orchestrate the merger movement of the 1890s, which assembled many of the nation's largest corporations such as AT&T and U.S. Steel.[7] Financiers ultimately controlled many corporations via large conglomerates (called trusts) and systems of interlocking directorates, where investment bankers not only sat on corporate boards but directed their cash flows.[8] Their central intervention was to create economies of scale, monopoly control, and to some extent, stability in these nascent industries, rather than growth or innovation.

Despite stark similarities with the present in Wall Street financiers' influence over corporate governance and investment, their dominance arose from the use of trusts, directorates, and loan financing, not from speaking as the voice of masses of shareholders or controlling the stocks of these corporations. In fact, public shareholding of industrial corporations was still quite unusual.[9] Throughout the 1880s, "not a single industrial corporation was listed on the New York Stock Exchange," the Dow Jones Industrial Average did not exist until the mid-1890s, and "the age of the publicly traded industrial corporation" did not dawn until around 1900 (S. Fraser 2004, 171). Wall Street's stated purpose was to promote corporate stability and coordinate capital flows into American industry, differing in this respect from the mission (and the volatility) of investment banking since the 1980s. Through this process, dubbed "Morganization," financier J. P. Morgan and "his confederates erected a kind of private economic command center" which "prohibited self-destructive competition, rationed out investment capital, and centralized the management of the economy in ways repugnant to the devotees of laissez-faire" (S. Fraser 2004, 158).

Simultaneously, throughout the early twentieth century, owner-entrepreneurs chartered private businesses into industrial corporations that began to expand beyond Wall Street's control, a development that accelerated after the Great Depression. To grow, most corporations relied primarily on retained and accumulated earnings from the enterprise itself, family wealth, and the occasional commercial loan to fund the business, rather than Wall Street financing or stock offerings. Many corporations, in fact, explicitly resisted the power of Wall Street financial capital to dictate to industry, and the "Street was never able to exercise the degree of control it wished to" (S. Fraser 2004, 305). Ford Motor Company, Standard Oil, Wanamaker, and many other corporations chose to rely directly on retained earnings as a way to establish independence from bankers. Wall Street's sphere of influence was limited to certain industries such as railroads; "new regional centers of economic influence emerged independent of the Street's dominant institutions"; and many new corporations "relied on internal financing or on local or regional banking resources in the Midwest and West" (S. Fraser 2004, 305).

Yet, in the face of these developments, a New York Stock Exchange spokesman in 1913 proclaimed that "no industrial progress" could ever occur without the Exchange's role in the issuing and distribution of securities—when in fact the Exchange mainly dealt in the buying and selling of shares in the secondary market, *after* productive capital had already been raised (Ott 2007, 124). Historian Julia Ott (2007, 126) argues that in the New York Stock Exchange's "imagined economy," it "claimed responsibility for raising the capital that funded all new firms and innovations" to construct and recast its role in the economy as "productive and contributory (rather than parasitic or predatory)." Such commentary, even at the nascent stages of stock market development, demonstrates the importance of self-representations of finance as productive and akin to "real" property ownership in shaping Wall Street's identity as a progenitor of corporations via finance capital. Historically, the stock market has mainly enabled owners of private enterprises to "cash out," not to raise capital for future productive investments. Of course, with the explosion of financial innovation in the late twentieth century (that is, junk bonds, derivatives, securitization of myriad kinds of payments such as mortgages), Wall Street has certainly "raised" capital for a variety of financial transactions such as corporate takeovers and mergers and for buying sophisticated trading products, but they have not been the primary source of operational business investment for most major corporations.[10]

The notion that public shareholders invest in productive assets "actually has little basis in the history of successful industrial development in the U.S." (O'Sullivan 2000, 49). For most of the twentieth century, most corporations raised capital through the issuance of bonds, meaning that the stock market did not have to skyrocket for corporations to have access to more capital. O'Sullivan argues that "corporate retentions and corporate debt, not equity issues, have been the main sources of funds for business investment" (O'Sullivan 2000, 78). These corporations relied on the stock market, not for original funding, but for founders and entrepreneurs to cash out of their enterprise and to find "a convenient way to transfer ownership between limited circles of business associates" (Baskin and Miranti 1997, 177–78, quoted in Ott 2007, 75). It allowed owner-entrepreneurs of successful private enterprises in the late nineteenth and early twentieth century to cash out while maintaining the management and organizational structure of the enterprise that had helped to make the business a success.

Today, my informants, following much of the financial and business literature, assume that the stock market collected and funneled the capital necessary for corporate America to grow, when in fact it was the other way around: the rise and growth of modern corporations helped to generate the stock market.[11] To illustrate, consider the following statements from investment bankers, who, being recently trained at business schools, have been educated in this worldview that corporations are historically indebted and beholden to the stock market. Jason Kedd, an investment banking associate at DLJ, first described capital raising as an investment bank's "sole function": "The kind of sole function—a primary function of an investment bank is capital raising, which is very important. You want to build a new plant. You want to acquire another company. Or, if you just want to raise debt, raise less expensive debt and pay off more expensive debt. The whole reason is you need to raise capital, which is fundamental to the function of . . . any market place, private and public." Christine Chang, a vice president of high-yield at BT, based her argument that Wall Street's impact on society is "positive" on its capital-raising abilities:

> Companies need access to capital to grow. Wall Street is one of these places where your company has to prove itself. . . . In the U.S., strong companies have a chance to access capital and grow in a way that companies in other countries without strong capital markets don't. For all of the criticism of Wall Street for being so concerned with quarterly earnings, etc., which is a valid criticism by the way, what that stems from is this basic philosophy that a company has to be making money and churning a profit in order for investors to be interested in it. [T]hat can be taken to the extreme, but the basic point is to make sure that successful companies get more money so they can continue their operations while companies which are bleeding are not attractive to investors and therefore, are closed down and stop using the resources of society.

Similarly, Julio Muñoz, an associate in investment banking at DLJ, called Wall Street "a necessary evil," because "companies just need capital, and Wall Street has been able to provide them with capital to grow":

> Companies could never have become the huge corporations they are if they didn't have access to massive capital, and that's what Wall Street does. It really provides access to massive capital. Let us say you need to incorporate your mom and pop's capital into the economy. The way to do it is through the purchase of stock or debt instruments in the massive capital markets. You need an instrument that will consolidate all that and create a way to get it to the corporation. A corporation is not going to look for it. It doesn't have the resources to look for it.

The capital needed by corporations, he argues, "does not come from easy or accessible sources"; Wall Street's role is to find and distribute it.

Contrary to mainstream Wall Street assumptions, it was the state that "catalyzed both mass investment and investorism" during the First World War through the mass selling of Liberty war bonds to some 30 million middle-class Americans. This process linked the practice of investment with national citizenship, democracy, and the public interest, and it was precisely this sensibility (not to mention the potential political usefulness of the small investor), reframed for capitalism, that was then used to popularize corporate stocks (beyond federal bonds) as key "economic-political stake[s]" in America (Ott 2007, 3). The number of corporate stockholders, below half a million early in the century, had by 1929 increased to as many as 10 million (Ott 2007, 1, 74).

Given this historical opportunity created by the state's war economy, corporate leaders and Wall Street developed the tenets of shareholder democracy to promote their own long-sought cultural and economic legitimacy, articulate a conservative, antiregulatory, anticollective political agenda, and obscure unequal class antagonisms through an employee buy-in of the corporate capitalist agenda (S. Fraser 2004; Ott 2007).[12] Setting the foundational premise for presentist ideologies of share holding, corporations and investment banks strategically deployed neoclassical principles, such as personal economic autonomy and private property, to promote mass stock ownership as a path to economic independence. Wall Street investment trusts and brokerages argued against the necessity for labor organizations and government-administered social welfare, for the individual can "compensate for his lack of independent proprietorship in the traditional sense by assuming the mantle of corporate shareholder"; in an era of large corporations, it was through "investment, rather than production or consumption," that individual economic betterment could be pursued, that the "salaried man could preserve his political stature as an individual property-owner" (Ott 2007, 16). As Wall Street lawyer James Dill argued, the move to sell shares to the general population "would go a long way to winning the loyalty of the middle classes to a new incorporated system of private property" (J. Fraser 2001, 296). While using the rhetoric of individual entrepreneurialism and property ownership, corporations and financiers consciously did *not* promote either control in these corporations or assurance that the financial markets would treat individual investors fairly through market transparency or equitable regulation.[13] They used unregulated, indirect claims to ownership as a way to claim public support and cultural legitimacy for the modern corporation and Wall Street.

Remember that during this time, Wall Street financiers had a "commanding position over the economy" in their "dual roles as investment banker and corporate director," and executives of corporate America had begun to solidify their own dominance over the daily control and operations of the enterprise (S. Fraser 2004, 293, 298). As such, advocating for wide distribution of shareholding posed no threat to Wall Street or public corporations. In fact, they recognized not only that "the public," the common mass of shareholders, had no actual "control" of (nor sustained input into) the corporation, but also that the very shares sold to individual investors at the time were nonvoting, watered-down stock, whereupon increased distribution actually solidified legitimacy and power in the hands of management and financiers, to whom all voting shares and powers were allocated (Ott 2007, 427).

Of course, the very concept of widespread shareholding "was itself a significant cultural revolution, as until then most everyone assumed an indissoluble connection, a profound existential identity between the ownership and control of property" (S. Fraser 2004, 256). Interestingly enough, it was mainly economists, legal scholars, social critics of Wall Street, and advocates of a "New Proprietorship" who worried, not only about the separation and dilution of ownership from control and the relationship between shareholders and corporate managers, but also about the small investor as a victim of Wall Street and the trusts (Ott 2007). Because Wall Street financiers enjoyed direct influence over corporations as well as the securities market without governmental, regulatory oversight, they were able to manipulate "securities for short-term gain," opening up "a fatal divide between the average anonymous shareholder seeking regular and reasonable returns on his investment" and Wall Street "webmeisters"—a troubling foreshadowing of the present (S. Fraser 2004, 313). Economist William Z. Ripley, a champion of neoclassical notions of individual proprietorship and an outspoken critic of Wall Street, railed against the disenfranchisement of shareholders from active input and control in the enterprise. Critiquing the "'passing of ownership from Wall Street to Main Street'" as an "optical illusion," Ripley called on the federal government to help restore the potency of shareholding and individual proprietorship (S. Fraser 2004, 389). It is crucial to recognize the contradictory relationship between Wall Street and neoclassical advocates and assumptions: whereas the codification of private proprietorship via the shareholder helped to set the foundation for the recent Wall Street shareholder revolution, which in turn flaunted this legacy for legitimacy, it was precisely neoclassical advocates who harshly lambasted Wall Street for ignoring, appropriating, and taking advantage of the idealized, common shareholder.

At the same time, the very notion of returning to a time when shareholders owned and controlled their enterprises is itself a fantasy. As Ott also recognized, Ripley advanced "the fiction that previously, American firms had been run in the fashion of New England town meetings" (Ott 2007, 427). Regardless, this "restoration" narrative also framed the corporate political economy, as the modern corporation designed certain benefits of the burgeoning welfare, managerial capitalism according to this reimagined tradition, such as corporate employee stock ownership plans (Ott 2007, 15). And, it is precisely this new era of capitalist organizations' emphasis on "traditional" notions of proprietorship that allowed Wall Street in the 1980s to recast the corporation from long-term social institution into an aggregation of stocks in individual portfolios.

Wall Street and corporate executives advocated for widespread shareholding, not as a vehicle to give shareholders control (as public shareholding was understood and actualized to be a dilution of control), but as cultural rehabilitation. Their motives were to promote conservative social and political goals designed explicitly to counter state regulation of markets, foreclose contestation over the control of corporate governance by invoking the semblance of agency via investing, and resist worker unrest. "Presenting stock market investment as intrinsically democratic experience," they "solicited acquiescence to corporate capitalism and to privately administered financial securities markets" (Ott 2007, 15). This antiprogressive sensibility held true with the shareholder revolution's attack against welfare capitalism in the 1980s, in particular its assumed inefficient largesse and social programs which highlighted race, gender, and class inequities. Shareholder value's notion of democracy rested conservatively on the unmarked shareholder-entrepreneur, empowered through unfettered participation in the "trader nation."

Liquidity, Not Control

Business historians Walter Werner and Steven Smith write that for much of the past century, critics of corporations have been "looking for modifications that will correct whatever it is they see as a misdirected use of public corporations' immense power," yet because of "misreadings of corporate history," their attempts at corporate reform are distorted. Their failure to understand the history of the "development of public corporations and securities markets" dooms them to "replicating a *past that never was*" (Werner and Smith 1990, 154, my emphasis). In this section, I focus on the historical construction of the separation between ownership and control of corporations. The stock market in the United States was formed *in order to separate* stockholding from the control of corporations and its "internally generated corporate revenues," which were left in the hands of career management (Lazonick and O'Sullivan 1997, 13). Moreover, it was the rise of the modern corporation and the state's promotion of bonds during the First World War, not so much Wall Street orchestration or ingenuity, that actualized the stock market. As Werner and Smith argue, "Attempts to return control to shareholders who never had it are, therefore, misguided" (Werner and Smith 1990, 154).

The corporation and the stock market were built for, and according to, diverging understandings, purposes, and results. The corporation was understood to be an illiquid institution. It was in contrast to this permanence and fixity that the stock market was created. One purpose of the stock market was precisely to separate people's investment strategies (buying and selling at will) from the day-to-day business of corporations. The stock market locates the stockholder *outside of the corporation itself*; it is to the stock exchange where "most security holders look both for an appraisal of the expectations on their security, and by curious paradox, for their chance of realizing them" (Berle and Means 1991, 247). In other words, the stock market, not the corporation, became the site of engagement for stockholders, the place where they could buy and sell their securities, where they would turn for pricing and evaluation. *Historically, stockholders participated in the stock market, not the corporation.* Despite this alternative historical interpretation, the legitimacy of corporate managers was continually doubted and contested in the face of the persistent "ideology that public stockholders are the true owners of the enterprise" (Lazonick and O'Sullivan 1997, 15). As a result, managers themselves were also kept from fully integrating multiple constituents into the firm, not simply because of the lingering suspicion that managers were interlopers, but also because even they were often unsure of whom they were supposed to represent. In this context, managers often contributed to the shareholder value cause: yet another casualty of a past that never was.

A key rationale for creating the stock market was to make shareholding liquid—that is, to make stocks easily convertible into cash or other stocks. Adolf Berle and Gardiner Means wrote in 1932 that "one of the recognized functions of modern finance has been to make mobile the wealth otherwise locked up" (Berle and Means 1991, 248). One of the main goals is securitization, which is "the transformation of hitherto 'unliquid capital' into tradeable instruments," a process which, in light of the "massive advances in telecommunications and electronic networks," has increased the mobility and globalization of capital (Sassen 1998, xxxv). Given that fluidity of return is the primary goal of the stock market, stockholders were meant to have little responsibility for the corporation itself, for what constitutes liquidity in this particular context is impersonality and separation from responsibility for the enterprise. For corporations to exist as long-term social institutions, they demand energy, resources, responsibility, even immobility from its caretakers; they need workers, customers, managers, suppliers who are committed to the organization. Whereas owners of nonliquid property are "in a sense, married to it" since the "quality of responsibility is always present," owners of stock property necessarily "have no direct personal relation" to the corporation, for they have exchanged and translated fixed corporate property into a liquid form, stock (Berle and Means 1991, 249–50).

Stocks, however, are not simply different in form and character than corporations, but also have a separate and different mechanism for retrieving and realizing their value:

> Liquid property . . . obtains a set of values in exchange, represented by market prices, which are not immediately dependent upon, or at least only obliquely connected with, the underlying values of the properties themselves. Two forms of property appear . . . related but not the same. At the bottom is the physical property itself, still immobile . . . demanding the service of human beings, managers . . . Related to this is a set of tokens, passing from hand to hand . . . requiring little or no human attention, which attain an actual value in exchange or market price only in part dependent upon the underlying property. (Berle and Means 1991, 251)

The stock exchange has historically assigned "an acceptable value" to stocks, *not* corporations, and it was because stocks are liquid property removed from corporations that such a mechanism of exchange worked. Stocks, then, are not little pieces of corporations, mirror representations, or a faithful repository of all that a corporation does and says—as Wall Street would currently have most Americans believe. Stocks belong to a diverging social construction (the stock market), which operates not only separately from corporations but also according to different goals. For example, the price of a stock can be stratospherically high or "undervalued," yet correspondingly little has changed in the corporate organization itself. "Most striking of all, a liquid token acquires a value purely and simply because of its liquidity" (Berle and Means 1991, 251).

These differences between stocks and corporations do not mean that stocks have *become* "divorced" or abstracted from the corporation, but rather that stock prices represent a particular set of values historically divergent from corporations. Stock movements could be based on high-volume trading in the stock market, panic, speculation, various expectations about a new field or technology, or global economic trends and indicators. The shareholder's "real right of disposition is . . . over the token itself, over any returns which may be distributed to him, and over the proceeds of its sale. He has, in fact, exchanged control for liquidity" (Berle and Means 1991, 251). His "rights" begin and end with the stock, not the corporation. Importantly, Wall Street and corporations were only willing and able to sell these corporate stocks because the ownership of these securities was understood as an opportunity to profit through the future selling of the security in the stock market, *not* because it required personal commitment to the corporation. "This lack of control was a feature of public stockholding that portfolio investors not only accepted but favoured. The market in industrial securities evolved in the United States to effect the separation of stock ownership from strategic control because it offered American households liquidity but did not require commitment" (O'Sullivan 2000, 70). Stocks were a "liquid" purchase, something buyers could trade at any time—provided, of course, that the stock market was itself able to maintain the confidence of investors and the volume of transactions.

The securities market was deliberately constructed, then, to allow "investors to treat their shares as financial assets rather than as vehicles for participation in corporate affairs. . . . There has been no erosion from an earlier, more pristine era to the distortions of today" (Werner and Smith 1990, 128). Through a design based on compartmentalization, stocks were purposely "made to approximate, so far as mechanisms could do so, the advantage which money has of ready exchangeability, though not at a constant price" (Berle and Pederson 1934, 11). As philosopher of money Georg Simmel has argued, the stock market helped to create the *independence* of the stockholder from the corporation and its managers. Acting as both connector and separator, the stock market connected an individual to a stock and yet at the same time, because of the stock's transferability and mobility, allowed the separation of the individual from actual control over the corporation and its daily operations. Simmel himself heralded the joint-stock company (that is, the modern corporation) as the "pinnacle," the ultimate example of the effect of a monetary economy because it is "completely objective to, and uninfluenced by the individual shareholder, while the company has absolutely nothing to do with him personally except that he holds a sum of money in it" (Simmel 1997a, 245). In the joint-stock company, "shareholders are united solely in their interest in the dividends, to such an extent that they do not even care what the company produces" (Simmel 1990, 344). What the stockholder does have is a connection and association with *other* stockholders; as investors, they are united simply because they have "common possession of a fund of money" (Simmel 1997b, 245). Ironically, today, through a massive confluence of ideas, forces, and actions, Wall Street and advocates for shareholder value have reconfigured these assumptions such that, to quote Simmel, those who had historically "absolutely nothing to do with" the corporation now control it.

It is important to mention, however, that whereas Simmel's understanding of the relationship between shareholding and the joint-stock company is premised on his generalized analysis of the characteristics of modern money (which both generated an exhilarating individualized freedom and brought about a "vapidity of life," a loosening of human connections), I do not approach stocks as characterized by innate "properties of money," nor do I assume money itself to be governed by universal logics which naturalize and predetermine its workings and effects. Rather, I understand stocks and the stock market as particular cultural formations and social relations in which stocks are imbued with historically specific characteristics, embedded in local social domains, and governed by particular rules.[14] Moreover, whereas Simmel argues that money, "by driving a wedge between the person and the object, not only goes on to destroy the beneficial and supporting connections, but also paves the way for independence of both from each other so that each of them may find its full satisfactory development undisturbed by the other," I do not assume that finance by its very nature loosens, destroys, or abstracts from human connections (Simmel 1990, 337). On the contrary, I approach finance as measured by values that are often in conflict with many people and communities, and it is precisely this hierarchical conflict, not the innate nature of money itself, that generates such a sense of disconnection and destruction.

In this section, highlighting a competing historical perspective—the deliberate crafting of liquidity, not control—demonstrates that "public stockholders' lack of control over industrial corporations' retained earnings has *not been imposed by corporate managers* or government regulators, as some have contended"; rather, this "lack" was deliberately constructed in the very historical constitution and structure of stockholding (Lazonick and O'Sullivan 1997, 15). The use, therefore, of stock price as *the* measure of corporate value and success is certainly cause for alarm, for in addition to the ill-suited values of liquidity, the stock price is not culturally or historically connected to the practices of the corporation—not to mention that stockholders are not involved in the daily workings of the corporation. Yet, because today corporations have become liquid investments, dependent on the fluctuations of the stock market, they are also subject to a new set of expectations and governance structures. The triumph of the notion that shareholders have always controlled corporations has rendered invisible the separate histories and spatiotemporal location of shareholders and the stock market, and has allowed Wall Street (as the institutional voice of the stock market) to gain control of corporations. This means, specifically, that those whose relationship to corporations have been characterized by a complete historical separation and lack of commitment, whose values were structured through liquidity, and whose experiences have been characterized by transitory flexibility, are now the ones directing corporations. While one part of the traditional notion of property is reclaimed ("owners" controlling their property), the other, more substantive part of the tradition—that owners are attached and committed to their property—is long gone.

From Wall Street's point of view, the fact that corporations are today "reconciled with" and being evaluated by the stock market according to standards that have historically been "ignored" by managers and are separately lodged in the stock market is a positive change, a correction of the old mistake of understanding corporations as societal institutions. This conflation, however, does not actually empower dispersed, individual shareholders to have input into the corporation. Through speaking on behalf of the individual stockholders, who are portrayed as by nature unorganized and unable to look out for their interests, Wall Street has mobilized shareholders as a kind of private army. The notion of the stock market as the sole measure of corporate success and the means by which corporations allocate resources and define priorities is a creation, not of the nineteenth century, but of the 1980s. "In historical perspective, market control over the allocation of American corporate resources stands out as a recent development" (Lazonick and O'Sullivan 1997, 10). Although Wall Street, bolstered by a historical narrative of legitimacy, considers this "return" of shareholder value to be a recovery of the original, pure state of corporate America, it is in fact a new phenomenon.

The Modern Corporation and the Reimagining of Neoclassical Assumptions

What was so radical about the modern corporation, and how did it destabilize neoclassical norms? The development and growth of corporations caused a "revolution" in American socioeconomic organization by creating "the separation between ownership and control" (Berle and Means 1991). Given the normative expectation that owners and managers should be one and the same, it was precisely this separation that unraveled the sequence of events and the unity of assumptions upon which neoclassical logic depended. As Berle and Means put it, the key problem is that, "Ownership of wealth without appreciable control and control of wealth without appreciable ownership appear to be the logical outcome of corporate development" (Berle and Means 1991, 66). (Again, this evolutionary notion that shareholders were once "in control" of corporations demonstrates that even those who critique neoclassical values and consequences, such as Berle and Means, subscribe to certain neoclassical norms.)[15] In the modern corporation, managers develop strategies and oversee operations, and as employees who have expertise in the daily operations of the enterprise, they can also help themselves to a healthy share of the corporate profits. Thus, the neoclassical sequence of capitalist causality is sundered when the putative owner of property surrenders both control and automatic entitlement to its proceeds. The tight unity between ownership and control that drives the system—"the atom of property"—is dissolved (Berle and Means 1991, 8). The corporation cannot be unproblematically viewed as an extension of the capitalist individual's will, and the values of self-interest and efficiency are threatened. With the increase of managerial control, even the fiction of shareholders' rights, which had been reconciled in the legal definition and mainstream assumptions of the corporation, became increasingly undermined.

Managers were the new and unknown consequences of the modern corporation; their control threatened the foundations of business common sense, and so they came to be the key targets of shareholder value advocates. One of the main neoclassical complaints about this new class is that they own so little stock that the pivotal notion of running a company for individual profit is broken. Managers (supposedly) have little incentive to use corporate resources efficiently because there is no possible reason (social or otherwise) that an individual would be impelled to run a corporation for any cause besides his own self-interest. Following the neoclassical assumption of self-interest, the actions of managers have only two possible interpretations: either 1) they run the corporation inefficiently because they do not have access to profits and thus cannot fulfill their self-interested desire for personal gain, or 2) out of self-interest, they run the company so as to enrich themselves, essentially stealing from the owners. As Berle and Means argue, "In the operation of the corporation, the controlling group . . . can serve their own pockets better by profiting at the expense of the company than by making profits for it" (Berle and Means 1991, 114). Because self-interest is the obvious motive recognized in neoclassical logic, the only conclusion is that managers have usurped the rightful place of the true owners to run the corporation for their own self-interest. Self-interest (of managers), then, has begun to work against the system, which strikes the neoclassicist as rather perverse.

On the other hand, following neoclassical prescriptions also means that in order for managers to run the company efficiently, they *must* have access to some of the profits. If, according to the profit logic, only those who have access to the fruits of the property can manage it efficiently, then how can managers be expected to run the company well if they cannot expect a share in the result? Giving profits solely to the shareholders/owners would stay true to the logic of (private) property but would not make sense according to the logic of the profit motive because shareholders are "no longer" in control. The traditional concept of profit, then, is torn asunder as well. These neoclassical precepts create a problematic and untenable relationship between owners and managers, an antagonism that would be utilized in the future to rally for shareholder value. Application of this logic fosters the notion that only one party is entitled to the spoils: the corporation must be an extension of either its shareholders or its managers, but not both, and all other groups are, by default, excluded from corporate stakeholding. Even those in favor of managerial capitalism have little discursive space to talk about any other motives or results of managerial influence besides self-interest and the desire for total control.

The neoclassical critique of managerialism turns on a compelling narrative of the abused shareholder, rendered powerless by the dispersal of concentrated shareholdings and the rise of self-serving managers running companies in their own interests. In this drama, the owner is positioned as the victim, denied his rightful role in the modern corporation by manager-usurpers. It is partly this notion of the wronged owner reclaiming his just rewards that has fueled such righteous (and moralistic) activism for shareholder value. The movement, however, to simplistically equate or "reunite" the stockholders of the modern corporation with the owners of private enterprises is extremely problematic, for the stock price becomes a reification of the corporation as a whole, rather than merely one attribute of a social entity with many attributes. Given this neoclassical subtext, we can begin to understand why Wall Street finds corporations that are run by managers who do not own substantial amounts of stock in the corporation to be simply "unnatural"; why organizations that retain their earnings to reinvest in the organization itself, or even in employees and communities, are viewed as breaching the bonds between owner and property. By working with the demands of unions and other constituents, or even deferring profits, managers are thought to squander shareholder value because, simply put, they spend money that is not theirs to spend. The crucial point is that managers who run corporations *not* based on self-interest (because they don't own stock) *cannot* be trusted because self-interest as measured by the stock market is the primary engine of successful business. Any other action becomes *self-serving* because, unlike self-interest, which is conceptually linked with efficiency and prosperity, self-serving behavior creates lazy managers on stockholder welfare.

Berle and Means, like many economists at the time, worried that the new corporate system could undermine the very foundations of industrial enterprise in the United States, which had been founded on "the fundamental economic principle of individual initiative," but they also realized the dangers of assuming managerial selfishness and the unequivocal privileging of shareholders.[16] Given that "the surrender of control over their wealth by investors [had] effectively broken the old property relationships and . . . raised the problem of defining these relationships anew," Berle and Means recognized that the roles and positions of managers in the corporation and community were "yet to be defined" (Berle and Means 1991, 4). Whereas most economists and financiers simply took for granted that managers effectively stole from shareholders and ignored any possibility that new corporate structures transformed traditional understandings of private property, Berle and Means (1991, 7, 9) saw the importance of interrogating the core of neoclassical thought to question "the ends for which the modern corporation can be or will be run," as the very "nature of the profit-seeking enterprise" had changed. Since the historical "attributes" of ownership—investment in, and management of, enterprise— "no longer attach to the same individual" but to separate groups as "the stockholder has surrendered control over his wealth," they argued, it is crucial to question whether the "traditional logic of property" still applies, as the very relation of entitlement the shareholder-owner had to "his" wealth—that is, the corporation—has "essentially changed" (Berle and Means 1991, 297–98).

Further, Berle and Means confronted the very foundations of neoclassical logics by challenging the main principles of Adam Smith directly, demonstrating their inadequacy and inapplicability:

> Underlying the thinking of economists, lawyers and business men . . . has been
> the picture of economic life so skillfully painted by Adam Smith. Within his
> treatise on the "Wealth of Nations" are contained the fundamental concepts
> which run through most modern thought. . . . Private property, private enter-
> prise, individual initiative, the profit motive, wealth, competition,—these are
> the concepts which he employed in describing the economy of his time and by
> means of which he sought to show that the pecuniary *self-interest* of each
> individual, if given free play, would lead to the optimum satisfaction of human
> wants. Most writers of the Nineteenth Century built on these logical founda-
> tions, and the current economic literature is, in large measure, cast in such
> terms. Yet *these terms have ceased to be accurate*, and therefore tend to *mislead*
> in describing the modern enterprise as carried on by the great corporations . . .
> [and are] inapplicable to a dominant area in American economic organization.
> New terms, connoting changed relationships, become necessary. (Berle and
> Means 1991, 303, my emphasis)

They cautioned the reader that Adam Smith wrote during a time when
businesses were run by owners of small enterprises with only a few workers and apprentices. Because of the development of the modern corporation and the stock market, there now existed different kinds and notions
of property, which could not be conflated under the "old" idea of "private
property" (Berle and Means 1991, 297). The business community needed
to restructure its categories because "we must have in mind primarily
these very units which seemed to Adam Smith *not* to fit into the principles
which he was laying down for the conduct of economic activity" (Berle and
Means 1991, 304, my emphasis). Proponents of shareholder value, to the
contrary, used Smith's repudiation of the corporation to demand the opposite: that the modern corporation be retrofitted according to outdated
economic laws and precepts.

Berle and Means proposed a different way of thinking about private
property. Any understanding of the modern economy, "in so far as it deals
with the quasi-public corporation, must be in terms of the two forms
of property, active and passive, which for the most part lie in different
hands" (Berle and Means 1991, 305). They drew a distinction between
"passive property," or stocks and bonds, which "gives its possessors an
interest in an enterprise," but "practically no control over it" and "no
responsibility"; and "active property," which they defined as entities controlled "by individuals who, almost invariably, have only minor ownership
interests in it" (Berle and Means 1991, 304–5). Although this notion
of active and passive property is not a complete rejection of Smith's ver-

sion of private property, it is a start. They warned against the conflation of "token" passive property and active property (precisely what the shareholder revolution achieved!) and questioned whether active property should ever be "possessed" and "looked upon as private property" in the neoclassical sense.

Furthermore, they critiqued the neoclassical profit motive by demonstrating that even motivation has changed its character. "For Adam Smith and his followers, it was possible to *abstract one motive*, the desire for personal profit, from all the motives driving men to action and to make this the key to man's economic activity. They could conclude that, where true private enterprise existed, personal profit was an effective and socially beneficent motivating force" (Berle and Means 1991, 307, my emphasis). Yet, in the modern corporation there exist many constituencies, demands, and purposes, and Berle and Means realized that it was becoming "unclear" how corporations and society would benefit if shareholders were able to press claims of exclusive control. Although they did not propose to prescribe the new motives and dispositions of active property, their purpose was to put the issue up for rethinking. They did mention, however, that the promotion of activity and coordination across multiple groups is more beneficial to such large-scale social enterprises than the values of individualism, single-group entitlement to all profits, and cutthroat competition.

In the end, Berle and Means rejected the old notion of private property. Quoting German industrialist Walther Rathenau, they mused that because of a "depersonalization of ownership," the modern corporation "assumes an independent life," belonging to no one, like the state or church (Berle and Means 1991, 309). As such, the modern corporation should not be analyzed "in terms of business enterprise but in terms of social organization." They emphasized the importance of regulating this power for the "public benefit" and "a wide diversity of economic interests" and argued that managers must begin to "accept responsibility for the well-being of those who are subject to the organization . . . whether workers, investors, or consumers" (Berle and Means 1991, 309–10).[17] They began to assemble an alternative template for how corporations might be governed responsibly. "Neither the claims of ownership nor those of control can stand against the paramount interests of the *community*" (Berle and Means 1991, 312). They explained:

> Eliminating the sole interest of the passive owner, however, does not necessarily lay a basis for the . . . claim that the new powers should be used in the

> interest of the controlling groups. . . . No tradition supports that proposition. *The control groups have, rather, cleared the way for the claims of a group far wider than either the owners or the control.* They have placed *the community* in a position to demand that the modern corporation serve not alone the owners or the control but all of society. (Berle and Means 1991, 312, my emphasis)

The diffuseness of both ownership and control opened up a space for claims of the community to be included in a new conception of property rights. "It is conceivable . . . almost essential," they wrote, "that the 'control' of the great corporations should develop into a purely neutral technocracy, balancing a variety of claims by various groups in the community and assigning to each a portion of the income stream on the basis of public policy rather than private cupidity" (Berle and Means 1991, 312–13). No one group should benefit at the expense of others. Because corporations will be the dominant institutions of the modern world, on par with the political and governmental power of states, business practices must become similar to "economic statesmanship" (Berle and Means 1991, 313).

The Managerial Challenge

The modern corporation did not simply morph into a reflection of neoclassical dreams. In the aftermath of the stock market crash, the Great Depression, and the New Deal, when Wall Street and the investment community were stripped of much of their influence over corporations, and after the post–Second World War boom when corporations experienced unprecedented growth largely independent of Wall Street and the stock market, advocates of "stakeholder" managerial capitalism mainstreamed their version of corporate governance and values. Although historians and scholars of American capitalism often lump together corporate managers with Wall Street, it is necessary to both understand them separately (or at least delineate their divergences as well as overlaps), and to document how they change over time. I discuss how from the postwar period until the early 1980s, "managerial values" were able to reframe what constituted shareholder value by recasting such goals as stability, growth, even social responsibility as eventual creators of shareholder value. The practice of shareholding itself changed to become relatively long-term, as the shareholder was reimagined as patient and nondemanding to counter notions of shareholding as "careless" and speculative.

As early as 1914, Walter Lippmann observed that "the real news about business" was that "it is being managed by men who are not profiteers. The managers are on salary, divorced from ownership and from bargaining. . . . The motive of profit is not their motive. That is an astounding change" (Smith and Dyer 1996, 48). As Smith and Dyer (1996, 44) explain, "This view of the corporate manager's responsibilities received respectable support from intellectual bastions like the Harvard Business School, and it became *de rigueur* . . . for managers to deny . . . exclusive preoccupation with profits and to assert that [they] are really concerned with the equitable sharing of corporate gains among broader constituencies." O'Sullivan (2000, 102) describes the growing emphasis on managerial professionalism and the notion that "like all professional men [the manager] has a responsibility to society as a whole." Economists Paul Baran and Paul Sweezy (1966, 21) point out that by the 1960s, the modern corporation did *not* operate under the assumption that it was "merely an enlarged version of the classical entrepreneur." Although most "formal economic theory" continued to follow the classically-derived description of the corporation as identical to the "profit-maximizing individual entrepreneur," many in the business community argued that the modern corporation represented "a qualitative break with the older form of individual enterprise and that radically different types of behavior are to be expected from it" (Baran and Sweezy 1966, 20–21). At the annual meeting of the American Economic Association in 1956, economist Carl Kaysen spoke of exactly this "qualitative break" in corporate goals and behavior. He described "the wide-ranging scope of responsibility assumed by management" as one of the "characteristic features of behavior" of the modern corporation: "No longer the agent of proprietorship seeking to maximize return on investment, management sees itself as responsible to stockholders, employees, customers, the general public, and, perhaps most important, the firm itself as an institution. . . . From one point of view, this behavior can be termed 'responsible': there is no display of greed or graspingness; there is no attempt to push off onto the workers or the community at large part of the social costs of the enterprise" (Kaysen 1957, 314). Kaysen then declared, strikingly, that "the modern corporation is a soulful corporation." In their reading of Kaysen, Baran and Sweezy (1966) caution that, although the modern corporation is a different organism from the profit-maximizing individual, the major goals of these corporations are still profits, high managerial incomes, and growth. Of course, the extent to which the modern corporation could be understood as "soulful" is problematic, even far-fetched, given our long history of corporate exploitation, but for my purposes here, it is important to demonstrate the popularity of the belief that corporations *could* be soulful, that profit maximization for "owners" should not be the only guiding principle of business, and that corporations under the leadership of "neutral" managers accommodated the growth of multiple constituents. In these instances, the emerging capitalist practices being espoused upset, or at least destabilized, a narrower focus on profit and property. The stakes were quite high, as proclaiming the soulfulness of the modern corporation was an affront and challenge to proponents of "traditional" economic thought.

In 1957, Theodore Houser, then CEO of Sears, Roebuck and Co., delivered a series of lectures for the Graduate School of Business at Columbia University.[18] In one talk, titled "Big Business and Human Values," Houser addressed how management in large organizations could pursue growth and profits, "the ends of business," without "destroying human values in the process" (Houser 1957, xi). He addressed specifically the debate about corporate constituencies and responsibilities, speaking to the opposition between stockholders, stock prices, and Wall Street on the one hand, and the long-term stability and multiple constituents of the corporation on the other. He asked the question, "If stockholders own a corporation, does not management do their bidding?" and answered with the following:

> The answer lies in part in the fact that ownership through widely dispersed stockholding does not generally bring with it a sense of responsibility. All other aspects of ownership of material possessions entail a large degree of responsibility by the owner, and this leads to a sense of loyalty, or of pride—a feeling of continuing desirability. Such attitudes are notably lacking toward a corporation in which one has only a stock interest. . . . He is exceedingly mobile in leaving one corporation and going to another, as evidenced by the fact that transactions on the New York Stock Exchange indicate a rate of turnover of the total capitalization of listed companies every five to six years. (Houser 1957, 32)

Stockholders are fickle, mobile, and irresponsible. (That the rate of turnover hovered around five to six years compared to the few weeks it would take today for trillions of shares to change hands is itself evidence that Wall Street in the mid-twentieth century was markedly different.) Houser reframed the conflict between shareholders and managers from a perspective where managers are seen as improper agents of shareholders to one where managers counter the irresponsibility of shareholders. Managers and shareholders do not have similar interests or motives, and hence should remain separate.

In Houser's view, the interests of corporations and their stockholders are inherently incommensurable: a "basic conflict" persists between "what is most desirable and necessary, long term, to the corporation" and the implicitly short-term, private interests of shareholders. A corporation goes on "as long as the society of which it is a part goes on," and as such it does not operate according to the same timeline, viewpoints, or measurements of "any human span of life" (Houser 1957, 36). Houser also held that the new corporate economy necessitated new business structures and organizational processes. The notion of the individual worker in capitalism had changed: "There is still a premium on native capacity, skillful effort and initiative, but these must be exercised within the framework of an organization. *What actually happens to the individual is ultimately determined not by the free play of the market, but by the administrative processes of an organization*" (Houser 1957, 4, my emphasis). He stressed the importance of the modern corporation as a social organization which serves the material and cultural needs of the people, and in this vein, "those endowed with the ability to lead these great organizations should begin to conceive of their remuneration partly in terms of the satisfaction of making a real contribution to national progress" (Houser 1957, 28). He went so far as to equate business leaders with educators, scientists, and public servants, stressing the importance of employee confidence and security.

Compare this multivalent notion of remuneration to executive compensation today, which is paid through stocks based on short-term shareholder value, or through a separate bonus compensation structure based on the size and quantity, not quality, of deals made. This shift has led to the divorce of the compensation of senior management from both workers' salaries and the "health" of the organization. For much of the twentieth century, managers of the large corporation, those empowered to make strategic investment decisions, were relatively enmeshed in the social relations of the organization and in the process of "organizational learning." As such, the decisions they made about the allocation of corporate resources were based, to some extent, on knowledge of the firm, and this "organizational control" by managers, prevalent until the 1980s, ensured "committed finance to American industry" (Lazonick and O'Sullivan 1997, 9). Though plagued by shortcomings, such as the refusal to fully integrate workers into organizational learning or the compartmentalization of labor into hierarchical cultures of "the hand" versus "the mind," the committed finance and situated knowledge of the managerial regime from the 1920s onward made possible "the pursuit of innovative investment strategies" (Dudley 1994; Lazonick and O'Sullivan 1997, 15). In stark contrast, the financial proponents of "market control" in the

1980s wanted "financial liquidity, not financial commitment." One of the defining features of a "market-oriented system of corporate governance" is "the presumed though not always enacted alignment of strategic managers with public stockholders" (Lazonick and O'Sullivan 1997, 8, 10). While these strategic managers received exorbitant, personal rewards via bonuses and stock options (linked to, but also sheltered from, the stock market), most "delinked" employees experienced lower earnings and less stability.

Suffice it to say that the imagined communities and values of U.S. capitalism from the immediate postwar era until the 1980s did indeed represent a break from the self-interested, profit-maximizing individual of early twentieth-century (as well as late twentieth-century) capitalism. Despite multiple lapses and egregious failures, corporations at least *imagined* themselves to be permanent social institutions committed to productive growth and the public service. Differently positioned workers and communities came to expect that corporate America could help bring millions of Americans into the American dream; there was the understanding that corporations could be bargained with. These expectations of upward mobility and what Kathryn Marie Dudley describes as a "tradition of opportunity" would not have been possible had corporations not envisioned themselves as social and public institutions: "The plenty of the postwar years has affected the national psyche profoundly. Three decades of virtually unbroken wage growth have shaped the aspirations and expectations of several generations of Americans. During these years it was possible to believe that everyone was participating in a tradition of opportunity. There were still marked inequalities . . . but the 'rising tide,' in President Kennedy's words, really did seem to be 'lifting all boats'" (Dudley 1994, xx). It is not surprising that during the socioeconomic restructuring of the late twentieth-century, workers in the United States suffered a "crisis of expectation" (Dudley 1994), as the fantasy of the rising tide is inconceivable under the logic of shareholder value. When shareholder value became the dominant measure of corporate success and practices, much was written about the death of the good corporation.[19]

Shareholding and Wall Street Worldviews in the Postwar Era

Given the relative dominance of managerial capitalism, it would be ahistorical to assume that Wall Street values remained static during this time. Such an approach would not only privilege presentist worldviews, but also empower "market" values by rendering them impervious to change. During this period, for example, the very nature of stockholding changed—both the character and intensity of Wall Street's understanding of, and commitment toward, shareholder value as well as what kinds of practices created proper shareholder value. Such changes cannot be separated from the fractured and uneasy dominance of corporate and welfare capitalism and the competing articulations of multiple stakeholders in the corporation. Such a change also demonstrates the coproduction of "values" and institutional arrangements across domains. The spirits of capitalism, no matter how seemingly robust, are contingent and dependent.

Historian Steve Fraser, in the only cultural history of Wall Street that comprehensively chronicles the roles, representations, and symbolic life of Wall Street in American culture, describes that for at least forty years after the Great Crash of 1929, Wall Street, metaphorically and literally, was a ghost town. Catapulted by the Great Depression, Wall Street spiraled into sharp decline, followed by a pervasive and long standing stagnancy, as shareholding (which they had promoted and used mainly for cultural legitimacy) came to be seen as deceitful, unproductive, and unstable (S. Fraser 2004). To limit the power of Wall Street, Congress enacted such measures as the Glass-Steagall Act, the Securities Act of 1933, and the Securities Exchange Act of 1934. These reforms were "market and exchange reforms" to protect investors. The Glass-Steagall Act prevented commercial banks (banks that held individuals' deposits) from investing in the stock market; the Securities and Exchange Acts created the Securities and Exchange Commission, required providing sufficient securities and issuer information for potential investors, and regulated the trading of these securities on the stock exchanges.[20] The New Deal, which helped to construct a social welfare system that "saved" American capitalism but "did not change it," when combined with the serious weakening of Wall Street investment banks and the stock market, helped to set the stage for new kinds of capitalist relationships and the control of corporate management over the direction and affairs of corporate America (Williams 1966, 439).

Given this context, not only did Wall Street investment banks and the New York Stock Exchange receive much revilement and little business, but corporate America was able to act independently from the financing, not to mention ideologies, of Wall Street. The "protracted sluggishness of the market" and the diminished stature of Wall Street were evident at multiple levels from employment and technological decline to a restructuring of shareholding norms and the meanings of shareholder value (S. Fraser

2004, 478). Citing both a *Fortune* article describing Wall Street in the 1940s as a "blighted area" and a *Barron's* article identifying it as a "depressed industry," Fraser argues that Wall Street was "the only business not helped much by the general improvement in the economy," and one telling indication of this was that "good families didn't send their sons to work there" (S. Fraser 2004, 473, 480). "In the good old days in 1928, 17 percent of the graduates of the Harvard Business School started careers on the Street; in 1941, only 1.3 percent did. A near universal conviction held that "nobody in Wall Street knows what hard work means" (S. Fraser 2004, 473). During this period, brokerage firms shut down branches, and many Wall Street investment banks closed their Wall Street offices and moved uptown. Whereas in 1920, "the raucous staccato of ten thousand ticker-tape machines had provided the jazzy accompaniment to Wall Street's fandango," "only two thousand machines were left by 1941, their rhythms slowed as the Street grew quiet, almost inaudible to the American ear" (S. Fraser 2004, 473). Leon Levy, one of the founders of Oppenheimer Investment Funds, reminiscing in 2002 about how much Wall Street had changed since he joined in 1948, vividly recalled that in the 1950s, "tape watchers had to be a particularly patient breed then, as Dow Jones computed its industrial average only once every hour, and even then it was often late" (Levy 2002, 43). Even Charles Merrill, founder of Merrill Lynch, described the stock market of the 1950s moving at "a horse-and-buggy rate" (S. Fraser 2004, 480). Thus depicted, this Wall Street could not have been further from recent images of effortless technological supremacy, global reach, and seamlessly exercised power. This lackluster Wall Street constituted visceral evidence of the stock market's relative inconsequence in the growth and expansion of American business during this period.

The Dow Jones Industrial Average remained stagnant or inched up very slowly in the mid-twentieth century, as rising stock prices were not a priority for corporations—or shareholders, for that matter. "It took twenty-five years for the Dow Jones average to once again reach the heights it had achieved in 1929. More telling still, volume on the Exchange didn't surpass its 1929 highs until 1961. A place once synonymous with risk now ran from it like the plague" (S. Fraser 2004, 479). This lack of "volume" indicates that even those who did own shares did not trade them often; the dominant shareholding strategy was to hold stocks, to wait for shares to appreciate slowly as generators of steady income. As Levy (2002, 44) describes, "There were far fewer stocks than today, and they traded far less frequently. Daily volume was measured in the hundreds of thousands of shares traded, in contrast to today's hundreds of millions. (There are 100 times more shares listed today than there were in 1955.) In the early 1950s, roughly 15 to 20 percent of the shares on the New York Stock Exchange traded each year, as opposed to roughly 106 percent turnover today."

Given this context, one could certainly argue that Wall Street practices of shareholding and shareholder value imbibed, even reflected, the prevailing norms of managerial capitalism. The patient timeline of shareholding allowed corporations to follow their "internal" organizational timeframes without constant pressure from shareholders, even as individual share ownership gave way to institutional consolidation in the post–Second World War era. The motivation to convince and force corporate management to continually increase stock prices, actualized via the twin practices of accumulating large amounts of stock (to leverage claims of "ownership") *and* constantly buying and selling it (which generates the volatile up and down movement of stock prices) in order to signal approval or disapproval of corporate strategy on stock prices, was noticeably absent. "The fund manager emerged as a new Wall Street type; soberly turned out, reassuringly flashless, carrier of the Street's featureless 'institutionalization'." The vast holdings of institutional investors, $219 billion by 1971, was "parked in blue-chip, high-capitalization Dow industrials, safe-and-sound companies like GE, GM, and Procter & Gamble. These were dubbed 'one-decision stocks'—you bought them once and held on to them forever" (S. Fraser 2004, 496). Shareholders not only approached investments as income that appreciated slowly and steadily over time, but by virtue of these actions, they helped to create a reality, a generation after the great crash, in which many stocks became relatively stable and secure.

Perhaps most importantly, most individuals and institutions simply avoided becoming shareholders. In the 1950s, "only 5 percent of Americans owned stocks" (Levy 2002, 43); institutional investors refused to invest in the stock market and were in many instances prevented from doing so. Depending on particular state and legal regulations, most large funds from trust funds to mutual and pension funds could not invest more than 50 percent of their portfolios in stocks and were often limited to 25 percent. Even with these restrictions, most trustees and institutional investors did not bother to push this limit. Stocks were widely thought to be too risky, and most professional investors opted to "stash their entire portfolio in bonds" (Levy 2002, 43). Contrast such a practice with the early 2000s, when fund managers who invested in bonds could be fired for being "foolishly conservative" (Levy 2002, 5).[21]

In light of such rampant suspicion, the securities business became quite desperate to improve its image. In the 1940s, Charles Merrill, setting out to "evangelize the Stock Market to the 'thundering herd'" took a survey of public opinion that showed most Americans continued to be deeply suspicious of the securities business (S. Fraser 2004, 479). In the mid-1950s, the New York Stock Exchange (NYSE) launched an extensive public relations campaign to educate the public as well as generate more shareholders and stock-buying activity:

> The director of the New York chapter of the Public Relations Society of America told a group of investment bankers that Wall Street was a public-relations disaster area, that most of their countrymen viewed them as "paunchy, silk-hatted tycoons," a discreditable bunch of "selfish, conniving schemers." He advocated a full-bore publicity counterattack through the press, radio, and that newest mass medium, TV. But the task was a daunting one: how to get people to shed the image of the market as a casino, to reimagine it as a seaworthy vessel tacking carefully on the treacherous seas of upward mobility, manned not by drunken sailors posing as brokers, but by "professionals," sage investment counselors. (S. Fraser 2004, 479–80)

The Public Relations and Market Development Department of the NYSE worked in conjunction with Alfred Politz Research, Inc., of New York City "to provide the Exchange community with facts necessary for continued progress in the service of the investing public and the national economy" (New York Stock Exchange 1955, 5). Through consumer surveys and field interviews, the Politz researchers focused on the following issues and populations: first, they conducted a nationwide survey of three thousand people representing "a cross-section of American public" to ascertain their "knowledge and attitude" toward common stock investment, the NYSE, and Wall Street firms. Second, they focused on why upper-income investors, those who made over $7,500 a year, "do and do not invest in common stock" (New York Stock Exchange 1955, 4–7, 17). In rather disappointing findings for the NYSE, they found that over 90 percent of the surveyed adult population would not even consider the stock market as a way to "invest some extra money," and 77 percent could not describe what a stock was.[22] Even when Alfred Politz Research surveyed upper-income individuals, who typically invested in life insurance, home ownership, savings accounts, pension funds, real estate, and bonds, the majority did not invest in the stock market. They not only conceived of the stock market as too risky, irregular, and insecure; they also approached "investing" in general as being about long-term security, with a "comfortable, secure old age" and "security for family" as the most common investment goals. Even among upper-income individuals who already owned stock, only 12 percent pointed to "quick profit" as an objective (New York Stock Exchange 1955, 34–35).

Corporate America capitalized on Wall Street's decline and the public's attitude toward speculators: large corporations actively distanced themselves from the Street and articulated alternative business worldviews and priorities. As Fraser (2004, 488) describes, "The world of the giant, publicly traded corporation maintained a wary distance [from Wall Street]. As a practical matter this aloofness was facilitated by the financial independence of postwar corporate America. . . . Flush times meant plenty of internal capital resources to finance expansion and innovation. Between 1950 and 1973, nonfinancial corporations funded 93 percent of their capital expenditures out of internal resources. During the postwar era, 70 percent of corporate profits were on average reinvested in the company, as compared to 30 percent in 1929." Moreover, part of corporate America's strategy to "widen the gap" with the Street was to engage "in what might be called ethos building, crafting an ideology of cooperative-minded business, concerned about its social responsibilities to employees and local communities" (S. Fraser 2004, 486–87). The institutional arrangements of financing, in conjunction with the shift in worldviews and Wall Street's decline, allowed shareholder value in everyday practice to become secondary to the corporations' other priorities. "Compared to today, there was only muted talk about shareholder value; on the contrary, that anonymous and passive mass of stakeholders took a backseat to the corporation's livelier, more demanding constituents and clients" from unionized employees to customers (S. Fraser 2004, 491). Meanwhile, corporate executives continued their critique of financiers as short-term speculators, only interested in quick financial returns.

Although managerial capitalism was dominant, shareholder value and the various (even discrepant) ways in which this concept was utilized remained a strong undercurrent in business thought, especially since shareholder value was enshrined in corporate law. Despite the critical understanding of shareholding as an elitist and exclusionary practice, there existed also the competing claim of shareholder value as a populist vehicle through which "the people" could own America. Recall that whereas Wall Street financiers had little interest in regulating transparency in the stock market, enfranchising the masses or shareholders, or allowing for shareholder agency in corporate decisions, reviled and without a cause after the Great Depression, Wall Street came to champion shareholder value as their own. By the 1960s, Wall Street investment banks, the stock market, and shareholding began to gain momentum for multiple reasons: "blue-chip" industrial corporations grew so massive and their reputations for stability and steadiness so solid that they attracted more investors, accelerating the growth of their stock prices; memories of the Crash were fading, and Wall Street investment banks and institutional investors had launched long-standing campaigns to increase shareholding. New financial instruments such as mutual funds and techniques such as "diversified portfolios" and "risk management" helped assuage fears about shareholding; the conglomerate movement created the go-go 60s market boom, which also drew institutional investors into equity investments. By 1967, institutional investors had already grown to control an "estimated 40% of outstanding Big Board shares" (D. Browne 1967, 11).

Despite the growing linkages between the stock market and corporate America in the 1960s, the values and practices of managerial welfare capitalism remained normative even for Wall Street institutional investors. In a *Harvard Business Review* article on the conflicting viewpoints of "professional managers and professional shareholders," Gordon Donaldson concluded that although "most academic writers have been on the side of the stockholder interest in discussions of how businesses ought to be run," "every indication points to the emergence of the management (corporate entity) viewpoint as the dominant one in the long run. . . . My guess is that it will be financial theory and not management practice that will have to change if the two are to continue to have a valid relationship to each other" (Donaldson 1963, 129).

Dudley Browne, the vice president of Finance and Administration for Lockheed Aircraft Corporation, in an address before the American Management Association, pointed out that institutional investors now controlled large blocks of Lockheed shares, climbing from 17 percent in 1962 to 29 percent in 1965. Although worried at first that these investors would "turn out to be traders, constantly in and out of the market" and that the resulting instability and volatility of Lockheed's stock price would hinder the company's ability to plan long-term programs, he concluded that "on the whole, Lockheed's experience with this new phenomenon in finance has been quite satisfactory," as the corporation's institutional investors have so far not decided to sell off their stakes, *and* Lockheed feels flattered that large investors continue to be interested in its stock

(D. Browne 1967, 11). He added that "there are potential problems of varying magnitude. . . . But I am confident that most of these problems will remain theoretical rather than real" in that even if institutional investors controlled most major corporations, managers would not find themselves "at the mercy of funds" (D. Browne 1967, 34). His optimism was characteristic of the confidence and relative independence of corporate America at the time. His concluding paragraph is worth quoting in full. Citing a study by Capital Gain Research Bureau that "a fifth of the total outstanding shares of America's leading airlines are now held by funds," he states:

> Will the funds unite in a plot to take over the airlines with the battle cry, "American today, tomorrow Trans World!" I don't think so. . . . Imagine being on an airliner and hearing the speaker system come on: "This is your captain speaking. We are now circling at 10,000 feet. We'll be landing in just a few minutes—as soon as we get clearance from Merrill Lynch, Pierce, Fenner & Smith." Is this any way to run an airline? You bet it isn't! Or any other business for that matter. And I'm sure institutional investors would be the first to agree. They do not want to perform any dangerous experiments on American industry. And for good reason. They own so much of it. (D. Browne 1967, 34)

That Browne's fantastic and meant-to-be-impossible scenario actually occurred—that Wall Street's "clearance" is now, metaphorically speaking, required for most corporations—is testimony to the extent to which the largest corporations were separated from Wall Street demands (which had themselves shifted) in the postwar era.

The Persistence of Neoclassical Assumptions

Despite what is called by historians the corporate reconstruction of American society in the early twentieth century, the changeover was not so simple. Corporate capitalism accommodated many of the key assumptions of classical political economy—private property, self-interest, individualism, owner favoritism, shareholder value—during the course of its ascendancy. "Although tending toward relative decline and a permanent position of subordination," writes historian Martin Sklar, "nevertheless, market relations, forms of thought, political movements, and cultural patterns associated with small producer and proprietary enterprise remained widespread, influential," and contrary to overtaking these sentiments, managerial capitalism "lacked anything near full legitimacy in the

minds of a considerable segment of the people and their political representatives" (Sklar 1987, 15). In fact, the very acceptance of the modern
corporation in mainstream American culture was premised on its accom-
modation of neoclassical values "rooted in the past," and "corporations
were themselves impregnated with attributes of the proprietary era"
(Sklar 1987, 15). Correspondingly, the "social responsibilities [of man-
agerialism] were certainly not enshrined in corporate law" (O'Sullivan
2000, 102), and "the doctrine that business must operate first and foremost in the interests of the shareholders remained a staple in the teaching
of corporate law" (Smith and Dyer 1996, 44).

Highlighting the persistence of the neoclassical, U.S. courts in 1919 up-
held "the property concept," that is, the notion that corporations existed
for the benefit of the property-owners, the owners of stock. In *Dodge v.
Ford Motor Company*, the Dodge brothers, as shareholders of the company,
sued Ford for suspending dividend payments. The company had used
these payments to expand its businesses and lower prices. "Ford's position, as quoted by the press, was that 'the purpose of a corporation was to
produce good products cheaply and to provide increasing employment at
good wages and only incidentally to make money'" (Whitman 1999, 75).
The Michigan Supreme Court, however, ruled in favor of the Dodge brothers, holding that profit for stockholders was enshrined in corporate law
and was unequivocally the "primary purpose of the corporation and the
sole obligation of the directors" (Whitman 1999, 92). Of course, this
"lack of formal legal recognition of the legal and economic *obsolescence* of
the shareholder-designate concept of corporate management stemmed in
part from the powerful emotional attachment in the United States to
the idea that the shareholder 'owned' the corporation," despite the overwhelming evidence that corporations had fundamentally changed the assumptions of private property (O'Sullivan 2000, 102, my emphasis). The
continued bias of U.S. economists toward neoclassical theories necessitated that corporate managers and other advocates of managerial capitalism continually "defend their 'right to manage'" (O'Sullivan 2000,
100, 103).

The primary justification invoked by managers—that with the growing
importance and broad-based objectives of the corporate organization, corporate managers had become "trustee[s] for society" as a whole—never
fully dislodged the neoclassical dictate that an emphasis on self-interest
and private property always, in the final analysis, serves the public interest and that the corporation is reducible to these "market" parameters
(O'Sullivan 2000, 103). While managerialism rendered problematic and

contradictory certain suppositions of neoclassical economics, it was unable to clearly articulate an analytical framework that supported its organizational and social responsibility theses. What O'Sullivan characterizes as the "nebulosity" of managerial ideology could not compete with mainstream business, financial, and academic communities and their neatly choreographed, "carefully reasoned" neoclassical assertions about the roots of private enterprise and shareholder value in human nature (O'Sullivan 2000, 103). Thus, proponents of the managerialist theses faced the daunting task of translating "socially responsible" capitalism into neoclassical terms, generating a backlash against their authority. This strategy not only accommodated bringing managerial capitalism back into neoclassicism, but also gave critics the ammunition to assert that managerial actions and conclusions had no basis in economic theory and failed to address the "traditional" economic concerns of motivation, efficiency, and profit, which neoclassical economics easily explained. Economist Edward Mason in the 1950s argued that corporate management never figured out how to bridge the tensions and motivations between private and public, between shareholders and everyone else. Compellingly summing up this tension, Mason explained that "the modern rehabilitation" of corporate management as dispenser of "equity" not only denies "an essential part of the justification of a private-enterprise system"—profits—but also necessitates querying "why duly constituted public authority is not as good an instrument for dispensing equity as self-perpetuating corporate managements." For most business observers, claiming that corporate objectives can provide "the best of both worlds by equating long-run profit maximization with equitable treatment of all parties at issue" does not address the central issue of vagueness of purpose (Mason 1959, 11–12).

Finally, the persistence of neoclassical assumptions was further fostered by the rise of the stock market in the go-go 60s as memories of the Depression faded and Wall Street worked to reestablish its dominance. Consider that by 1960, even defenders of New Deal and managerial capitalism such as Peter Drucker and Adolph Berle had gradually begun to imagine the stock market as (again) the potential site of a "'people's capitalism', in which annual stockholder gatherings were likened to . . . 'the town meeting'"—despite the fact that "a smaller percentage of people directly owned shares in 1960 than . . . in 1929" (S. Fraser 2004, 497). By 1967, Carter Henderson and Albert Lasher lamented in *20 Million Careless Capitalists* that individual shareholders were allowing "their" corporations to become quasi-governmental public organizations. Dubbing individual shareholders "the 20 million careless capitalists," Henderson and Lasher chided them for being "monumentally unconcerned . . . about the money you've so painfully saved in order to invest in common stocks" (Henderson and Lasher 1967, 13). The consequences of individual stockholder's nonchalance are critical:

> Suppose every stockholder took his responsibilities as seriously as some . . . who have actually influenced management decisions by invoking the powers readily available today to all stockholders. A new force would certainly come into being in our economy that could be every bit as powerful as management and labor are today. . . . This could be unusually important today, when America seems to be evolving from a private enterprise to a public enterprise society, from a society where the corporations you own decide what kinds of goods and services America needs, to one in which the Government increasingly provides the guidance under which these decisions are made. A well-publicized example of this was the federal government's decision—not the automobile industry's decision—that the American consumer needs safer cars. (Henderson and Lasher 1967, 13)

Henderson and Lasher looked to shareholder control as an antidote to government regulation and chided shareholders for knowing absolutely nothing about the corporations they owned beyond "the close of yesterday's" stock prices (which is precisely what they are socialized to pay attention to and value). They labeled the separation of ownership from control a historical injustice committed by selfish managers and perpetuated by "careless capitalists" (Henderson and Lasher 1967, 19).

As institutional investors accumulated more and more corporate stock, they began to articulate shareholder value as a way to restructure the very way corporate managers approached corporate governance. In an address to the Financial Executives Institution in Chicago in 1968, Glenn Miller, an investment banker at Watson and Co., a Chicago-based investment firm, issued a warning to corporate management that they ignored shareholder value at their own peril. Building on the recent accumulation by institutional investors in the stock market (and away from bonds), he described the growing power of Wall Street and alerted corporate management to the "importance of creating a favorable image with investors" by keeping its stock price as high as possible in order to both "help them in their own growth and acquisitions, and defensively protect them from raids by others who may be seeking to gobble them up." The manager who disregards his stock price "is living in the dark ages" (G. Miller 1968, 27–28).

The Death of the Schizophrenic Corporation

These two dominant visions of capitalism (one understanding the corporation as social entity, the other viewing the corporation as financial property), with multiple variations therein, engaged in a protracted tug-of-war and coexisted at the height of managerialism. The rising influence of the social entity concept of the corporation, which reached its height in the 1950s and 1960s triggered a sort of neoclassical revival dedicated to returning the corporation to its so-called roots in private property and the laws of "the natural liberty" (O'Sullivan 2000, 104). The continual back-and-forth of these two discursive camps was so apparent that it prompted William Allen, a chancellor from the Delaware Chancery Court, a leading jurist in corporate law, to describe it as "our schizophrenic concept of the business corporation," where the social-entity side would argue that the property focus creates "short-termism," a practice of "corporate myopia" without "patient capital," and those on the property side would declare that corporations cannot be accountable to multiple parties without losing focus and creating zero accountability for corporate managers (Allen 1992; Whitman 1999, 92).

Nevertheless, for a half century, this "schizophrenia" caused no particular crisis or breaking point because managerial capitalism, aided by a series of court cases reconciling the two points of view, was able to "substantially broaden the scope of managerial discretion without abandoning the basic premise of *Dodge v. Ford Motor Company*" (Whitman 1999, 93). Managers, given the unprecedented growth of corporate America, were able to appease shareholders with healthy dividends and steady profitability, while also dealing with multiple nonshareholding constituents. Chancellor Allen explains how corporations, with the aid of the courts, negotiated the opposing demands of two worldviews:

> The law papered over the conflict in our conception of the corporation by invoking a murky distinction between long-term profit maximization and short-term profit maximization. Corporate expenditures, which at first blush did not seem to be profit maximizing, could be squared with the property conception of the corporation by recognizing that they might redound to the long-term benefit of the corporation and its shareholders. [W]ithout abandon[ing] the idea that directors ultimately owe loyalty only to stockholders and their financial interests, the law was able to approve reasonable corporate expenditures for charitable or social welfare purposes or other actions that do not maximize current profit. (Whitman 1999, 93, quoting Chancellor Allen)

Managers used the distinction between long term and short term to translate corporate priorities and practices. Social responsibility was marketed as benefiting the long-term interests of shareholders, a process of translation that lasted into the 1970s without massive fissures.

Many scholars and shareholder value advocates sought to expose what they saw as flaws in this approach. They contended that management's attempts to appeal to long-term shareholder value was misleading because the worldviews and policies of professional managers were quite different from those of professional shareholders, indeed in total opposition to them. Citing the "wastage of the stockholders' property values," business school professor Gordon Donaldson argued that managers cannot simply assume that "in the long run what is best for the corporation and for management is also best for the stockholder" (Donaldson 1963, 129). He demonstrated that the financial objectives, policies, and results of corporate actions can differ dramatically, depending on whether managers identify as agents of the shareholders or as "trustees" of multiple constituents. Equating long-term shareholder value with the well-being of the corporation as a social entity does not give priority to shareholders and allows management to act "inefficiently" and "conservatively" to preserve the corporation itself at the expense of dividends, stock prices, and profits (Donaldson 1963, 129). Although Donaldson recognized that the "absolute priority" and "full maximization of stockholder interest is a theoretical extreme which is not attained in practice" and which would not be adequately measured in light of the complexity of the corporate organization, he also argued that control by managers with no "primary allegiance to any single group" was unacceptable. Shareholder value should be a "statement of tendency" and given relative priority, and managers cannot "wishfully" assume that shareholders are either "loyal" and thus "insensitive to competing investment opportunities," or that the potential disloyalty of shareholders vindicates managers who try to keep corporations from turning into "vehicles" for short-term financial gain (Donaldson 1963, 129). Donaldson's discomfort with managerial acts of translation exemplifies the growing turn against managerial capitalism, which eventually enlisted managers in a crusade against their own influence.

The decline of managerial capitalism and concomitant rise of the shareholder value movement can be clearly traced in the changing priorities of the Business Roundtable, a committee composed of CEOs of the two hundred largest and most influential corporations in the United States, from the 1970s into 1990s. In 1978 the Business Roundtable named "social responsibility" as part of the four core functions of a corporation's board of directors, but by the 1990s, obligations and proclamations to shareholders had both subsumed and obliterated all other "functions" of the corporation (Whitman 1999, 95–96). In the 1970s, the CEO Round-table used "the distinction between short-term and long-term profitabil-ity" to reconcile socially responsible corporate practices without abandon-ing the basic premise of shareholder value (Whitman 1999, 96). To justify their vision of the corporation to Wall Street bankers, investors, and academics in business and economics fields, managers legitimated invest-ments in research and development, employee benefits, or capital im-provements instead of shareholder dividends or immediate share price appreciation as temporary deferrals (or ultimate creators) of shareholder value. The danger of this kind of discursive translation is the insertion of shareholder value as baseline measurement for all corporate practice. With some temporal flexibility, stock price was seen as having the ability to stand for and to symbolize all the positive results of corporate choices.

In 1981, just three years after declaring the integral importance of cor-porate social responsibility, the same Roundtable lamented the challenge of balancing the public interest with private profit. They stated that " 'bal-ancing the shareholders' expectation of maximum return against other priorities" is the greatest challenge of management (Whitman 1999, 96). This admission of a conflict between shareholders and "the public" inter-est signaled a disruption of the managerial regime's delicate balance, as shareholders increasingly rejected appeals to the corporation's long-term interest. By the 1990s, Whitman says, "In [the Business Roundtable's] 1990 and 1997 statements on corporate governance, 'corporate social responsibility' is no longer listed as a separate and distinct function of the board of directors. And the description of balancing shareholders' expec-tations against other priorities as problematic has been replaced by the assertion that the board's paramount responsibility is to the stockholders [and] that obligations to other stakeholders *complement* rather than con-flict with this primary responsibility" (Whitman 1999, 96, my emphasis). The crucial difference in the 1990s was the redefinition of shareholder value as the ultimate goal without temporal qualifications, without the subtext of potential conflict. What Donaldson in 1963 had assumed was strictly theoretical—an absolute focus on shareholder maximization that had never truly existed—had by the 1990s become the dominant idea in the business culture of the United States.

In the late twentieth century, the attempt at reconciling shareholder interests with managerial practices ended. The new logic was simply that shareholder rights effectively trumped, subsumed, or even incorporated all other claims. In other words, there is no need for contestation or translation, as increasing the stock price complements all other goals of the corporation and would ultimately benefit everyone. The implications are enormous and far-reaching. Under the umbrella of "long-term shareholder value," practices that benefited the long-term stability of the organization and the employees, but not the immediate profit of the shareholders, could be legitimated. The very identification and description of shareholder value as "long-term" demonstrated a concern for the corporation as an organizational entity. In the 1990s, these openings were foreclosed: a conflict could not exist or be reconciled between shareholder value and other corporate interests because by measuring shareholder value, one could measure everything.

5

Downsizers Downsized: Job Insecurity

and Investment Banking Corporate Culture

Being downsized from my potential field site threw into sharp relief the volatility of the environment I was about to study, not to mention the precariousness of the postmodern "field." It was a jolt to realize that investment banks were themselves subjected to the restructurings, the ruthless cuts, and the obsessive focus on stock price that they foisted on corporate America. When I was downsized myself, I was shaken out of my initial rubrics and assumptions that always posited Wall Street as "the downsizer" and corporate America as "the downsized." When I contemplated fieldwork, such a dichotomy was part of my conceptual apparatus: I assumed a one-way relationship wherein Wall Street demanded downsizings to boost stock prices, while corporate America for the most part had to comply. Traumatized corporate bodies contrasted sharply in the imagination with swaggering bankers, a booming stock market, and a largely invulnerable Wall Street that called the shots with little fear of consequences. Even when I started to work on Wall Street myself in 1996 and heard plenty of stories from my peers about job worries—bankers abruptly changing positions, departments, or banks; sudden, panicked applications to business school; and the peculiarly traumatic transition from working 110 hours a week to unemployment—I did not make the connection between these experiences of volatility on the Street and what the Street was demanding of corporate America in the name of "the market." I did not yet fully comprehend that Wall Street's peculiar culture of employment offers a crucial window onto investment banking's worldviews and practices.

Most bankers, it turns out, resort not to shareholder value rationales, but to extrinsic market universalisms as a way to explain their own predicaments. Such a discursive practice can obfuscate the cultural origins of their approach to downsizing. Because Wall Street's reliance on externalized market explanations reinforces dominant anthropological assumptions of market abstraction, it is easy to overlook how market discourses can describe or signal investment banking work culture, in particular bankers' understandings of market temporality and their specific relationship to market movements. Both market externalization and shareholder value, however, serve as only partial explanatory models of Wall Street's interaction with corporate America; we also need to look at investment banking corporate culture. It is investment bankers' experience as employees (which in turn reshapes the market models they learn and proclaim) that instills a specific disciplinary model of employee liquidity, insecurity, and workplace relations; motivates them to export this model to the rest of U.S. business; as well as renders their own model superior. In particular, bankers' constant preoccupation with the possibility of losing or changing their jobs—when coupled with Wall Streeters' paramount concern, compensation—frames how investment bankers understand and shape both their own lives and the grander trajectories of corporate America and the financial markets.

A brief explication of my conceptualization of investment banking corporate culture will be instructive. Mainstream business and organizational behavior literatures tend to conceive of corporate culture in terms of the firm's "personality": the customs, norms, and values of the founders or top management, as distinct from the firm's economic values and practices, and bounded by the firm's walls. I argue that it is important to understand the culture of firms in a more broadly anthropological way, as unbounded, porous, contextual, and constantly changing. Specifically, I focus on the workplace lives and organizational culture of investment bankers and banks as a crucial analytical site to demonstrate their interpermeability and spillover with the financial markets and corporate America at large.

I borrow from Erica Schoenberger's contextualized and open delineation of corporate culture, which she describes as "inherently and deeply implicated in what we do and under what social and historical circumstances, in how we think about or understand what we do, and how we think about ourselves in that context. *It embraces material practices, social relations, and ways of thinking.* Culture both produces these things and is a product of them in a complicated and highly contested historical process"

(Schoenberger 1997, 120, my emphasis). The corporate culture I focus on is based on what my informants have deemed central to understanding their organizational milieu: for example, issues of job insecurity, compensation, the pace and demands of work life, and how transactions are distributed, completed, and rewarded stood out as their central concerns. In my analysis, such issues are crucial precisely because they inform corporate strategy, how investment bankers think and act upon the world. As Schoenberger (1997, 122) contends, "The relationship between corporate culture and strategy is also more intimate than is normally conceived. Strategy embodies knowledge and interpretations about the world and the firm's position in it. It is an exercise in imagining how the world could be or how it ought to be. In this light, strategy is produced by culture. At the same time, since the past strategic trajectory of the firm embodies specific configurations of practices, relations, and ideas, culture is also produced by strategy. The two are mutually constitutive categories." Given the influential position of investment banks, the "strategic trajectories" of investment banks, which are informed by their "cultures," intersect with the trajectories of other corporations, markets, and economies. To analyze this nexus of investment banking culture and strategy, I focus on their approaches to, and practices of, employment as important lenses into the worldviews, practices, and expectations that Wall Street has of itself as well as of corporate America.[1]

The Downsized Anthropologist

I was one of two employees not actually present when the ax fell. It was around lunchtime on 11 January 1997. I was at a meeting on the eleventh floor as part of a project tracking and analyzing BT expenditures on technology over the past few years. When I got back to my cubicle at around 12:45 p.m., everyone was gone. The entire floor seemed like a ghost town, eerily silent. Something was off balance. Could the whole department have left for lunch? After sitting at my desk for about ten minutes wondering whether or not I should go eat by myself, the door to the conference room opened, and most of our group of about twenty-five workers streamed out. They all looked flushed and agitated, as if the wind had just been knocked out of them. They rushed back to their cubicles, to their phones, or hurried outside. My cubicle mate and fellow analyst Andrea spotted me, exclaiming, "Where *were* you?" and told Kristi, another fellow analyst, to explain everything to me. Kristi crouched down next to my desk and whispered that our entire group, including our boss, had been what they call "disbanded."

We were all just laid off. I was shocked and did not know what to think. What did this mean? The first-year analysts (there were four of us, including me, and all of us were women) decided to leave the building to discuss this dilemma. Donna, another analyst, said that the first thing she thought was, "I can make it in time for Harvard spring recruiting." She had graduated from Harvard only a year ago. Kristi had deferred Harvard Law School for a year to work at BT, so she had a backup plan. Andrea just kept shaking her head; she did not know what she was going to do. She was a few years older than Kristi and Donna, and as such, she did not fit the usual straight-out-of-college analyst profile, and like me (if I had chosen that route) might have had a harder time getting another Wall Street job after so little experience. In the hiring of analysts, most investment banks prefer people straight out of college, who tend to have fewer attachments and can be pushed to work extremely hard.

"Quiet, we can't talk here," Andrea said, so we all said nothing as we waited tensely for the elevator. When we got outside, they couldn't wait to describe the meeting for me. Everyone's face, they said, turned white. Our group head, the managing director, almost choked on his words, so a vice president had to step in to deliver the news. George, a first-year associate, had seemed very nervous. Julie, a second-year associate, was visibly upset, and Janice, our administrative assistant, had looked shocked and pained. My impending fieldwork was common knowledge in the office; they couldn't believe I had managed to miss this, since it was precisely what I was planning to study.

We decided to go for coffee at the Station, a usual hangout place for investment banking analysts. On the walk there, Andrea wondered if BT was in some sense breaking a contract with us, as most analysts are understood to belong to a two-year program. Unfortunately, this "contract" is only implied, merely the usual practice in the industry, not a written, legal obligation. When we came to work at BT, the contract we signed contained no stipulations about how long the firm had to keep us (or how long we had to stay).

Later we talked to Maria and Lacey, two vice presidents in our group, who told us we were "lucky" in a sense because things could be much worse. "I guarantee that you will all be fine," said Lacey. "You're all really smart people and have great backgrounds. Our group carries a lot of weight and, let's face it, you all are cheap. Departments have been laying off MBAs like crazy and in a couple of months, they're going to realize that they need more people, but are they going to hire another MBA? No, they're gonna hire a cheap analyst like yourself who doesn't complain about bonuses!" Maria told us that usually "disbanded" groups are immediately escorted out of the building by security, their belongings shipped to them later in UPS boxes. Maria and Lacey had themselves survived four layoffs each, and said that on Wall Street, everyone is rather desensitized to layoffs, unlike "old economy" companies out in the hinterland of corporate America, where executives are not prepared to take this kind of instability. They recounted the story of RJR Nabisco's huge LBO-derived layoff binge, when the company kept an ambulance waiting outside because they were not sure how the middle-aged managers would take the news. Those guys were "old school," and we should be thankful that we were so quickly being initiated into the pace and instability of work life on Wall Street.

After a while, I began to understand why they thought we were "lucky." Since downsizing happens so often in investment banks and is often conducted with such brutal speed, our situation was downright luxurious. It is important to underscore that because we were part of the internal Management Consulting Group, which was understood at BT to be a "middle office" advisory function less subject to the scrutiny and immediacy of the market, our managing director (who lost his job as well) was able to negotiate a deal for all of us: we could continue working on our current projects for the next five months until June, and we could use work time to hunt for new jobs. This was absolutely unheard of on the Street and a stark contradiction to the normative practice of forcing downsized employees to pack up and leave within as little as fifteen minutes (or at least that day). Our boss and managing director Kevin Ferguson had often talked about how he was construed as "odd" on Wall Street because he cared about managing a group of people, about building a business, and his leveraging of his senior position so that employees could use the resources of the workplace to find another job while still getting paid demonstrated this commitment. Throughout the next five months, he helped to successfully place many in the group; in addition, many of us received severance packages and outplacement services. Not surprisingly, the severance was dependent upon not suing BT (a taken-for-granted "exchange" on Wall Street since it is uncommon for downsized employees to sue their former banks) and not getting another job immediately (which most of my coworkers did). Since we served a consultative function and did not traffic in sensitive, proprietary information concerning "live" deals such as mergers or stock offerings, we were considered relatively "safe" to keep around.

The first-year associates, the ones who came straight out of business school and had student loans to worry about, were the most nervous, yet many began receiving calls from headhunters and interviewing for jobs *that very afternoon* or the next day. Because we were internal consultants who participated in advisory projects all over the bank, our department was considered a "transition" group anyway, meaning that after two years, most of the second-year associates transferred into parts of the bank that they had previously consulted for. Except for the first-year associates, then, this sudden change was understood simply as a chance to move forward more quickly. As one of our colleagues, Stan Clark, said about the vice presidents, "They all came here through headhunters anyway, and the second-years have tons of headhunters [after them], so they aren't very worried." Because most people in our group were either newly hired or were brought in from other firms by headhunters, no one considered this group their permanent home: none of us were homegrown, and no one expected to stay. As a downsized anthropologist, I was not sure how to sympathize with my colleagues, as my situation was quite different. I was an employee about to become a fieldworker, and my main source of anxiety—having to excise myself from the group relatively soon to pursue an academic career—was actually relieved by being downsized. Although I would not have been breaking any contracts or time stipulations, as investment banks do not make such long-term commitments to employees at my level, I had been privately worried about the inevitable day when I would have to quit. Although my superiors knew my stay in the group would be temporary (as was everyone else's!), the exact timing was left up to me. Since the job left me first, I was spared the agony. After seven to eight months, I had already begun feeling the effects of constant 12-hour days (considered a mild schedule by front-office standards); as my co-workers joked, "Things couldn't have worked out better for you." I was sorely embarrassed, as I had begun my fieldwork with the understanding that I would be "studying up," and here I was, for the moment grateful for the soft landing of graduate school.

Although I was open about my intentions and future plans, I still felt nervous and guilty about my ambiguous position at work and avoided giving anybody an exact description of my future project (to be sure, I had not defined it in my own mind yet, anyway). I was purposely waiting to write all of my dissertation fieldwork grants after my time at BT. When I interviewed for my job, I explained the complexity of my situation. Below is an excerpt from my personal journal, where I recounted what my interview "spiel" had been:

Coming from anthropology, I am interested in learning about how the dynamic business world works and about Wall Street culture, and I think that I bring many skills to the table such as an understanding of globalization, culture, and U.S. economic values. I am taking a leave of absence from graduate school to explore this world and to work for a while. After my position, I intend to come back to finish my Ph.D. I would like to formulate my future research out of my real world experiences and perhaps conduct a study of the culture of Wall Street and its effects on corporate America. Of course, Wall Street might seduce me from ever coming back.

When speaking to my peers, I often used the words "probably" and "most likely" when discussing my return to graduate school. Surprisingly, my vagueness turned out to be much more forthright than the strategies of many of my coworkers. On Wall Street, in addition to the everyday exaggerations of resumes (such as rounding up the size and impact of deals done), the norm was not to divulge one's intentions to the firm. In fact, analogous to the bank's own activities, the norm was to dissemble. No one *ever* alerted the bank that they were leaving for business school in a year, that they were waiting to take a promised new job in a few months—right after bonuses were paid. No one reported actively looking for other jobs, or getting an offer from a competing group. Thus, I was relieved to find out that what I had feared would be perceived as dishonesty or disloyalty to BT actually appeared benignly eccentric to many bankers. As I learned more about Wall Street, I also began to understand why many Wall Street workers protected themselves with equivocation. It became clear that my informants (and most front-office workers on Wall Street) considered their jobs to be temporary and had few qualms about hopping from one bank to the next.[2] During job interviews, they might profess their long-term "fit" and interest with a particular group, only to leave after year-end bonuses were paid. My temporary stint at BT actually fit the normative timeframe of a Wall Street job, and my planned departure appeared less threatening to the bank than the expected career path of most of my colleagues as I would not be leaving to work for a competitor.

Because job insecurity is so rampant at investment banks, whole "outplacement," "headhunting," and "executive coaching" industries have sprung up in the shadows of Wall Street in order to facilitate, cushion, and propel the job change process. Not surprisingly, headhunting agencies are most commonly associated with industries that have the highest volatilities, namely Wall Street and Silicon Valley. Whereas outplacement firms provide resources to downsized employees, headhunting agencies recruit and place employees from one company to another whether or not they have been laid off. Individual recruiters are referred to as "hawks"; they wait on the sidelines with their ears and eyes open for the slightest shifts or hints of dissatisfaction in order to grab an employee from one job and place him or her at another. Firms that specialize in senior bankers call themselves "executive placement firms" rather than headhunters and refer to their recruiters as "senior consultants." Many high-level recruiters used to be investment bankers themselves and make use of their own network of connections to drum up headhunting business. If, for instance, there is "buzz" that the chief financial officer of Salomon Smith Barney or the head investment banker of Health Care and Biotechnology at Merrill Lynch is unhappy or unsatisfied, headhunters will vie to place him or her with a different firm, in return for a lucrative fee often based on a percentage of salary. Or, alternatively, if an investment bank wants to steal a particular executive from a competitor, it might hire headhunting services to contact and lure the executive.

For downsized employees, investment banks often provide outplacement services along with such assistance as counseling, group sessions, cubicle and desk space, voicemail, and resume workshops. To retain these services for a downsized employee, investment banks pay a percentage of the employee's salary (the calculations can vary) in order to provide career transition and career management advice. These services are limited to front- and middle-office workers. Our administrator, for example, did not receive these services, and neither did those downsized from departments such as Audit or Account Services. Ironically, then, outplacement services are available for precisely those employees who have the least interest in and use for them. My informants generally scoffed at outplacement services. Instead, they used their already existing networks based on intra- and inter-Wall Street networking, elite alumni affiliations, and professional group associations among others. As many of my informants reminded me, and I experienced myself, the "actual" reason for outplacement is mainly symbolic, to limit liability and serve as a form of public relations. When one is downsized from a bank, one signs a contract (a normative practice) relinquishing the right to sue the bank and speak to the media in exchange for outplacement services and a severance package.

The majority of my coworkers and friends refused even to set foot in the outplacement agency, as that would represent a direct confrontation with the fact of being laid off. Using outplacement signified that one's skills and sociopolitical network were not strong enough. For most middle- and front-office workers, unemployment is a temporary state, and "successful" workers on Wall Street are supposed to land jobs without using such services. Many are able to line up a future job even before they are downsized. Going to the outplacement firm and using its services, then, became a sign of defeat, and did not bode well for one's Wall Street career. Some of my informants did report visiting such an agency once to check it out (while trying to avoid being seen), and said they never went again. Few of my BT colleagues actually made appointments with their assigned outplacement counselors.[3]

As for me, I did not realize that I could simply avoid the outplacement counselor who had contacted me during the last few weeks of my time at BT, so I accepted my assigned appointment. The main reason I went was to tell the counselor that I would not be needing her services as my future job plan was to return to graduate school; the other was that the ethnographer in me was curious to see what an outplacement firm was like. My understanding of Wall Street employment was in fact greatly enhanced through my experience with outplacement agencies and their counselors who, because they had observed countless waves of Wall Street layoffs, were experts on the particulars of industry restructuring. Below is an excerpt from my fieldwork journal on 11 June 1997 about my first day at Lee Hecht Harrison, the outplacement center then based in the World Trade Center.[4]

Yesterday was my first day at the outplacement center. It is a service provided for unemployed workers, usually in the financial services industry. An entire business has sprung up because of the immense volatility of this industry. A business paid for by the very bank that laid off its workers—hmmm. They provide you with a little cubicle, access to word processing and long distance phone calling. A very far cry from one's own office but nevertheless, a helpful transition. It hardly provides any networking opportunities as far as I can see. Gina Thomas, a consultant as they call them, mentioned that networking was "eavesdropping and sitting close to the people who were also making frantic calls to find jobs." What kind of networking is that? Although the outplacement center also provides career consulting, job interview skills, research facilities, strategizing for the next job, identifying personal goals, I did not see anyone partaking in these. I saw only seven people total: three white men and two Asian men, all in their late thirties and forties, and two white women, both in their twenties or early thirties. It was strange to be there. Everyone went out of their way to avoid the other people. The very spatial arrangement of the place conveyed and perpetuated the fact that no one had a home or sense of belonging there, as no one could use or "claim" the *same* cubicle-desk or phone day after day. They were all anonymous, rotating, and constantly changing. You can use or "activate" any phone at any empty desk by dialing your code. And, at the end of each visit to the agency, you pack up your stuff into a 14 x 20 bankers' box and store it in the storage room in alphabetical order. Gina gave me a tour of the storage room in case I wanted to leave stuff at the agency, and the sight of a few rows of boxes with names scrawled on them packed and tucked away in a long hallway of shelves struck me as so lonely—so nomadic and impersonal that it made me viscerally long for my nameplate and messy desk.

By summer 1997, as Maria and Lacey predicted, everyone had found a job. The bull market was in full swing, the emerging markets financial crises had not yet "officially" begun, and many investment banking departments were rapidly hiring (even as they were also firing). Replete with interviews and connections, some managed to finagle both a new job and severance pay by waiting longer to accept the new position; others just opted for the "security" of the new job. Through this particular experience of downsizing, I realized that the trauma and dislocation I was imagining was unequally distributed among the downsized. Though constant, their experiences of job insecurity were so seemingly well tolerated and expected that it hardly seemed as if it had happened. The shock of being a downsized anthropologist showed me directly that job insecurity lay at the heart of Wall Street's self-conception. Through constant layoffs, the attendant outplacement and headhunting industries, and compensation schemes (more on this in the next chapter), insecurity is built into the very structures of investment banking organizations, and used as a character-building, formative experience to recommend for other workers. What I had not anticipated was that ethnographically tracking job insecurity would eventually lead me to view and understand the social construction of financial markets quite differently, and much more concretely.

Investment Banking Approaches to Work

It is important to bear in mind that I conducted fieldwork during what was then called the longest U.S. bull market (and what is now acknowledged to be one of the greatest bubbles in U.S. history, after the subprime meltdown and, of course, the Great Crash) and that my research indicated that even during these flush times, job insecurity pervaded the Street. In 2001 after the stock market crash, many friends and colleagues asked me if I would be studying the current recession, the post-dot-com environment, and Wall Street's bloody aftermath. They worried that I might have a skewed view of the industry, as my active engagement with Wall Street occurred from 1996 to 1999. I reminded them that I was indeed on Wall Street during a recession and "mini-crash," and that my informants continually worried about job security. It was the emerging market crisis of 1997, initially marked by Wall Street currency traders' devaluation of Thailand's currency, which flowered into a full-scale financial crisis engulfing the economies of what were known as the Asian Tigers: Hong Kong, Singapore, Malaysia, and South Korea. In mid-1998, Russia's bubble burst, signaling a "global" financial market meltdown that also included the Latin America debt crisis and the collapse of the hedge fund Long-Term Capital Management. Because Wall Street is constantly engaged in unsustainable market practices in multiple kinds of markets simultaneously (sometimes at cross purposes), at any given moment, even in a dominantly "strong" economy, there are downturns and crises. That one of the biggest and most visible markets—the U.S. equity/stock market—seemed (on the surface) booming did not mean that there was not a fairly large crisis brewing within or somewhere else.

Through fieldwork, I realized that one of the main reasons why I had not noticed Wall Street's "self-downsizings" is that investment banks usually do not cut tens of thousands of jobs at once, and do not regularly publicize layoffs. Rather, they often keep downsizings quiet and away from media attention by conducting smaller, regular purges continually. Malinda Fan's story is instructive here. Fan, a senior vice president (SVP) at Lehman Brothers until its bankruptcy in 2008, worked at the firm since graduating from college in 1994. She has never worked for another firm and was promoted from analyst to associate to vice president, and finally SVP. She was one of the only people she knew (or I know) on Wall Street who managed the nearly impossible feat of building her career in one firm. To do so, however, she had to survive eight mass downsizings since 1994 (about one every year and a half) and switched skill sets, job descriptions, areas, and departments within the bank more times than she can remember. Each time I talked to her during her time at Lehman, she had different bosses *and* colleagues. Although Malinda Fan's survival at one bank is extraordinary, the context of her career is not, as investment banks, on average, conduct a significant downsizing every year and a half or so, with continual "purges" in between and along the way. As I will detail, although I interviewed many of my informants during the high-flying "new economy" year of 1999, they were preoccupied with job insecurity. Encountering the ubiquitous experiences of constant movement and anxiety allowed me to piece together the unavoidable fact that Wall Street firms freely downsize during boom times and to unravel the taken-for-granted associations between economic downturns and job insecurity on the one hand, and boom times and job security on the other.

For most Fortune 500 companies (that is, corporate America), the normative practice has been to conduct two to three large downsizings a decade. Investment banks, however, often go through at least two rounds of layoffs per year. The general strategy is to continually and quietly purge small numbers of workers, while strategically spreading rumors of empty bonuses in order to encourage unsettled workers to go ahead and leave; occasionally massive, "take-no-prisoners" layoffs also occur. Many bankers, once they detect the signals that a purge is in the offing, begin their job searches immediately, yet wait until "January or February without the markets getting any worse" to receive their bonuses before hopping to the next job (*Economist* 1998). In 2000, many business writers, reflecting back on the bull market, seemed completely unaware of the continual small layoffs made in all Wall Street firms throughout 1998. A journalist, for example, wrote that in "1998, during the Russian debt crisis, Merrill was the only firm that laid people off, and they got raked over the coals, because when the markets came back right away, Merrill was scrambling to get people and everyone else was cooking with gas" (Kirkpatrick 2000). In fact, in October 1998, when Merrill Lynch announced that it would engage in a massive round of layoffs of 3,400 jobs and 900 consultants, other investment banks from Salomon Smith Barney to DLJ began to "quietly" fire people (McGeehan 1998). In November 1998, J. P. Morgan announced that it would reduce its staff of 16,500 nearly 5 percent, though it had been making "piecemeal job cuts for weeks," not to mention the fact that it had already cut its staff by about 5 percent in the first half of 1998 (Murray 1998). Though largely unannounced, throughout 1998 most firms had been "trimming workers by the handful, avoiding disclosures of total cuts" (Murray 1998). In February 1999, when markets rebounded, small cuts continued.

Perhaps the main difference between bull and bear markets is that during boom times, investment banks hire profligately, often without strategy or limitation. It comes as no surprise that firms often follow these hiring binges with announcements of "overcapacity" and rounds of firings, a cycle indicative of a particular industry culture of intensity and excess. This culture is brutally pronounced during recessions, but it is crucial to understand that it holds during the good times as well. In the late 1990s, investment banks hired to keep up with the maddening "pace of profits" and, a few years later, found that they needed to "get back to" 1998. For example, Wall Street investment banks employed 644,000 workers in 1998 and 772,000 in early 2001, a mere two years later (Craig, Gasparino, and Sapsford 2001). By the end of 2001, in one of the largest cuts recorded on Wall Street until the recent crisis, securities firms had slashed over 116,000 jobs. From 2003 until 2006, when investment banks not only "recovered" through the subprime buildup and surges in M&A activity but also began to post record profits and bonuses, with each year surpassing the previous one, they continued to engage in round after round of layoffs. In 2004 the financial services industry announced almost 98,000 downsizings, in 2006 "only" 50,000 or so, and in 2007 over 150,000 (Challenger, Grey & Christmas 2009). And yet throughout this time, according to the New York State Comptroller's office (2006a, 2006b), investment banks were also *adding* close to ten thousand jobs each year. These drastic and sometimes simultaneous spikes of hiring and firing are an integral part of Wall Street's "yo-yo" employment strategy. Such an approach not only creates continual motion and unrest among bankers, but also ensures that investment banks profit during both booms and busts, including some of the "worst" periods in their history: "Wall Street firms have fared better in this downturn [2001–3] than they did during the one of 1987–90. Strategic layoffs and better risk management have kept most of the firms in the black" (Knox 2002). Similarly, in 2007, even on the cusp of the subprime crisis, Wall Street bonuses were at the second highest total ever, a staggering $32.9 billion, while downsizing smashed the previous record with the loss of over 150,000 jobs (Challenger, Grey & Christmas 2009; New York State Comptroller 2009). (Not surprisingly, the scale and scope of layoffs in 2008— 260,110—has demolished this record, though, as has been much heralded in the recent press, bankers still paid themselves $18.4 billion in year-end bonuses—almost as much as was paid at the height of the previous bull market in 2000 [Challenger, Grey & Christmas 2009; New York State Comptroller 2009].)

To achieve 1998 levels of employment, all investment banks engaged in one brutal round of layoffs followed by a series of smaller prunings followed by yet another devastating round of large-scale cuts. On 1 October 2001, just a few weeks after September 11, Morgan Stanley announced that it would cut "200 investment bankers, or about 10% of its banking staff," and most investment banks, according to headhunters and outplacement firms, also cut 10 to 15 percent of their workforce (R. Smith

2001; Thornton et al. 2001). In 2002, when Goldman Sachs revealed that it had already "axed 541 employees in the first quarter" and planned to keep "pruning staff 'modestly' by a percentage in the 'mid-single digits' through year-end," this announcement "quietly set in motion another round of brutal layoffs" throughout all of Wall Street. By 2002, Merrill Lynch had already "cut so many people that it is 10,500 people below its 1999 staffing level" (Thornton 2002). In 2003, with Wall Street experiencing "stirrings of recovery," layoffs continued despite the fact that pretax profits hit $15 billion, more than double 2002. "Profits are booming because firms have slashed costs, enabling them to boost earnings as the market turned around last year" (Zuckerman, Smith, and Craig 2004). According to Wall Street employment consultant Alan Johnson, "Layoffs aren't over by any means. Firms are going to be reducing their head counts by between 5% to 10% [over the rest of 2003]. . . . That means investment banks will be down 25% from their peak in 2000" (Thornton 2003). In 2004, investment bankers were back in demand and posted record earnings that began to surpass even the heights of the previous bull market. As *Business Week* noted: "Few companies have appeared as invincible as Wall Street's major investment banks in the last several years. Whether they were extracting themselves from damage, making up for moribund merger activity by behaving like casinos and trading aggressively for their own accounts, the banks inevitably racked up billions of dollars in record earnings" (Thornton 2004a). Yet, throughout 2004 and 2005, as Wall Street investment banks announced that they planned to "hire as many as 30% more [MBA] grads in 2005 than they did in 2004," they also continued the layoffs (Thornton 2004b). According to the *Economist*, in 2004–5: "Credit Suisse First Boston announced a restructuring that involved lots of layoffs and may lead to further departures. J. P. Morgan Chase quietly sacked people in New York and London. Deustche Bank did likewise in Germany and is expected to make cuts elsewhere. Firms continue to pay fines for transgressions during the last bull market. Save your tears. A strong fourth quarter (ending on November 30th) meant record earnings for almost all America's top investment banks. Since 2002, the share prices of Lehman Brothers, Merrill Lynch and J. P. Morgan Chase have doubled" (*Economist* 2005). And business schools still remember that from 2002 to 2004, a number of new associate hires were fired during the summer even *before* beginning their new jobs.

Investment banks' up-and-down employment strategy is perhaps their most consistent cultural practice. It means that whereas in 2002–3, "the securities industry . . . [had] huge stockpiles of empty office space, especially in New York City," by 2005, "Lehman Brothers, Goldman Sachs and Bank of America [were] reportedly scouting for additional New York office space" (Kelly 2003; *Economist* 2005). In 2005, Merrill Lynch, which had jettisoned over one-third of its entire workforce, was hiring again, and bonuses, like earnings, were reaching record highs. Of course, such an approach engenders contradictory results: many firms on Wall Street overcut, only to realize that they no longer have the capacity to take advantage of new opportunities. J. P. Morgan and Goldman Sachs slashed their Asia workforce in the late 1990s only to realize that, as a result, they failed to "get some big China deals." However, these deals were "only delayed" as Wall Street vigorously ramped up their Asian operations (Healey and Shameen 2001).

Conducting fieldwork during the boom gave me a unique opportunity to observe the daily mind-set and practices constitutive of the bull market, including how the gut-wrenching changes of 1998 prepared the way for an even more devastating 2001. To the extent that downsizing helps to create booms, then the "rational" correlation of high and low employment with the highs and lows of the market is explanatorily deficient: there is uneven correlation between profits, boom times, and job security. Investment banking identities are grounded in the organization of their institutions, and Wall Street makes decisions about employment in the context of specific organizational structures that are related to, but are not simply mirror reflections of, the stock market or shareholder value. Examining the culture of investment banking institutions is crucial to understanding their desire and ability to make instant shifts in their business plans and in their deployment of "human resources." As central constructors of market norms and expectations, their everyday organizational habitus becomes an exemplar of corporate "best practices."

A year after I was laid off, I contacted Gina Thomas, my outplacement counselor at Lee Hecht Harrison, for an interview to learn more about her perspective on volatility and downsizing on Wall Street. I began by asking Thomas about her job.

GT: As a broad picture, we work with companies, primarily financial services, because we are here in the Wall Street area. They are usually eliminating positions or downsizing or merging or whatever, so the outcome is that they wind up needing fewer people than they originally had. And our role is to assist those people to determine if they want to stay within the same field, to really assess the advantages and disadvantages of their choice with regard to their career. And we provide them with the tools, insight, research, and other resources that will assist them in pursuing [new jobs], whether it is the same or a different field, in as expeditious manner as possible.

KH: I did not realize before how volatile Wall Street jobs were. You always hear about how GM is doing a big cut or how AT&T is doing a big cut—and they are *big* cuts—but not here. Do you think it is the same here on Wall Street?

GT: I think it is a little *more* because I think you will find, with some exceptions, that even though there are big cuts [at the GMs and AT&Ts], if you were to ask about the longevity—how long people had been at the firms before their space was being cut—I think on average (and we haven't done that particular study) . . . you would find that people had been in those companies a lot longer. It's not unusual for us to see Wall Street people who had been in a company for only eighteen months before the ax fell. And it's also not unusual for it to have happened to the same person—the same young person—several times in just the early part of their career. . . . [I]n other fields it may have happened to them more than once, but they are a lot older. I see people who are . . . younger than thirty, and this is their *third* time. Sometimes they have been doing Latin American research or have been primarily associated with the emerging markets or something, and so they will get in with a firm where [it] starts out with a commitment, and it turns out not to be as lucrative as they thought it was going to be, or it hasn't been as well thought out, and so as a result, the whole department can be disbanded. That can happen a few times.

Because Thomas had observed multiple rounds of layoffs and had counseled individual workers who had lost their jobs, her perspective gave me a clear indication that downsizing could actually be much more frequent on Wall Street itself than in the corporations who must meet Wall Street's expectations. Many of my informants, also using corporate America as a point of contrast, alerted me to why this might be the case.

Almost unanimously, most investment bankers maintained that the "culture of employment" on Wall Street was very different from that of U.S. business as a whole. They particularly emphasized that whereas the culture of investment banks, as I will explain, is to embrace constant change *without* any future strategy or planning, most large corporations, even in light of the shareholder revolution, usually attempt whole-scale and disruptive change with some kind of short- to medium-range strategy. By comparison, investment banks are much quicker to react to the latest market movements, even to the detriment, not only of their own (and other corporations') shareholder value, but also to the sustainability of their own organizations. Consider the following two conversations.

Ahmed Jamal worked for a telecommunications company before becoming a "global telecommunications specialist" at J. P. Morgan, where he helped to supervise the firm's technology investment and architecture. Although not an investment banker per se, his observations about the general pace of change in investment banks as compared to his previous company are quite telling. During our conversation, Jamal differentiated Wall Street from corporate America by emphasizing Wall Street's heightened sense of speed.

> [Wall Street's] whole service focuses on advising people how to handle money. So, you're the first one that should understand what the bottom line is. And it shows. People are very much in tune with expenses versus profit. Constantly being compared to others, and it's a very mean industry and, you know, survival for the fittest. That's the bottom line. I can give you a quick example. . . . Working for a telecommunication firm, when they announce that they're reducing their work force, it took six to eight months for them to actually be able to do it, go through the whole process of evaluation, making sure what jobs need to be cut, reduced, and then actually executing the plan. It took almost eight months for them to do it. You don't have that luxury in a Wall Street firm. You just don't; you *do not*. I know, for us, the first phase was pretty much done in less than a month. Immediately identify what needs to be done on a global basis. If a certain office wasn't performing, staff was reduced until the office was shut down. Certain business lines were reduced, eliminated, refocusing resources on ones that [were] more profitable. It was very swift, very quick, and it was done, and most people knew about it *after* it was done. Very quickly—you just do not really have the luxury of time. So they are becoming efficient. Of course, that comes with a price.

The crucial point is not that investment banks and the telecommunications company ended up downsizing workers—that much we know to be the norm—but rather that investment banks focus on immediacy.

Paula Wiley, an associate in investment banking at then Chase Manhattan/Chemical Bank, provides a similar perspective because Chase, before it merged with J. P. Morgan, was by and large a commercial bank (although since the 1980s, it had gradually moved into investment banking). The major difference between a commercial and an investment bank is that a commercial bank is not primarily in the securities and stock market businesses, and its business—taking deposits and lending to individuals and corporations—is relatively more stable, thus more akin to corporate America.[5]

> KH: This is a very general question, but what would you say to someone who didn't work here, who had no idea what goes on, and who asks, "What is Wall Street like?"
>
> PW: I think it is difficult to say in general what Wall Street culture is, but I would say that it's—well, most of the people are very aggressive and certainly it is a tough world in a way. You have to perform. If you don't, you have nothing to look for on Wall Street. Nobody is going to have mercy for you. If you don't perform, you are out. I think commercial banks are still more lenient with people, more tolerant than real investment banks like Goldman [Sachs]. It would take longer for commercial banks to fire somebody. They would think more about it, so I would say there is more job security still in commercial banks, although I think it is changing.
>
> KH: Do you think that job insecurity is worse on Wall Street than other industries?
>
> PW: It is because it is very sensitive to the changes in the financial markets. I guess we just noticed it. Actually, it doesn't even seem like it was a major downturn just recently [1998]. But, it was big enough to force [investment] banks to fire people.

Taking both Jamal's and Wiley's observations together, *what accounts and allows for this particular temporality and culture of immediacy* (beyond the obvious assumption that because investment banks are in "the business of making money" and of "advising people how to handle money"—where money is both the product as well as the goal—their very job description demands finding the quickest paths to make money)? I address this question toward the end of this chapter and the next, but before doing so, it is crucial to first problematize the notion that job insecurity arises mainly from investment banks' proximity to and intimacy with the capital markets and market cycles. This assumption, I argue, resorts to market externalizations (that is, "the market" as the black-box rationale for job insecurity) instead of recognizing that Wall Street's corporate culture constructs investment bankers' experiences of and approaches to job insecurity, and localizes their very understanding of "market."

Narratives of Job Insecurity on Wall Street

During my fieldwork from 1997 to 1999, I asked every Wall Street invest-ment banker I talked to about the issue of job security. During these bull market years nearly all of my hundred or so informants weathered at least one restructuring, downsizing, or job change, and by 2003, only two of my former informants were still working at the bank where I had first met them. This issue was in the forefront of everyone's consciousness. I was constantly regaled by extraordinary stories of job mobility. Regardless of rank or status, the vast majority held that on Wall Street, job security does not exist and maintained that investment banking was the *most* insecure of all professions. When I asked the question, "How long do you see yourself working in this industry?" most Wall Streeters answered either "I don't know" or "Hopefully, for the foreseeable future." Even well-estab-lished managing directors gave a noncommittal "maybe" or "we'll see." Such conversations revealed the meanings and effects of such instability for highly privileged workers and pointed toward the consequences of Wall Street's peculiar employment culture for U.S. business at large.

To include a variety of narratives on Wall Street employment practices and experiences of job insecurity, I highlight a broad cross-section of Wall Streeters, paying attention to include seasoned veterans as well as ana-lysts and associates who have only worked on Wall Street for a few years (although on Wall Street two years is certainly enough time to experience multiple iterations of job insecurity).[6] Although most of my informants understood their own layoffs to have been caused by "market downturns" during times of economic crisis, after conducting fieldwork over a span of several years, I realized that my informants seemed to experience job insecurity practically *at all times*, although they often *retrospectively* asso-ciated these anxieties with times of crisis. (I, for one, was laid off with no larger industry or company crisis in the immediate foreground.) This continual resorting to "external" market factors to explain layoffs even when they occurred during "boom times" allowed me to further inter-rogate the taken-for-granted linkages and associations between down-sizings, downturns, and bear markets.

At the height of the bull market in February 1999, Raina Bennett was laid off after two years as an analyst in the emerging markets group at Lehman Brothers. She had already survived one round of restructuring and one group change: she was now on her third boss. She was part of a division that monitored Latin American companies for potential U.S. ac-quisitions, privatizations, and capital raising. A couple of months after her downsizing, I sat down with Bennett at a trendy Manhattan café, and she recounted for me her experiences leading up to her predicament. Here, she describes what her roller-coaster work environment was like during the last six months of her employment:

> The crisis in Asia just happened, but no one really thought that it would affect Latin America to the large extent that it did. The environment changed dramatically, and all of a sudden, we went from this very bullish perception of the market to all of a sudden, "Gosh, we are going to have to lay off people." And then, obviously, [it culminated] in my layoff and the layoff of my group. Let me talk about the market environment and how that changed, first of all. The market environment just changed dramatically because all of a sudden, far from it being just an Asia problem, people came to the realization that the influence of the market was truly global and that no market would be left in the dark or left out of this crisis. All of a sudden no deals were being done. People became very concerned about Brazil. The currency started falling: there [was] a lot of speculation, and all of a sudden in January, we faced a situation where the currency lost 25 percent of its value. . . . What that meant for Lehman and for financial markets was that there was absolutely no faith in the market all of a sudden. No deals were being done. Only a few countries were able to get financing. What was interesting from my perspective is that there had been so much talk about all of these privatizations that were going on. . . . People felt very positive, and all of a sudden this happened and the whole idea of privatization went down the drain. . . . And this meant that at Lehman, people were going into work every day, and there was no hope. They were just sitting there looking at empty screens. Prices keep going down, and you don't know when they are going to recover.

It was difficult to ignore Bennett's continual emphasis on her experience of whiplash turns, of euphoric highs that immediately spiraled into devastating lows. Her experience that "all of a sudden" she was out of a job certainly indicates that Wall Street's approach to downsizing is instantaneous and absolute. Bennett portrays markets as capricious forces of nature, unpredictable, unstoppable storms. All she and her group could do was brace themselves against the coming onslaught. In the context of the U.S. securities markets, I will argue later on that investment banking strategies and practices during the bull market helped to construct the 2000 crash, among others, by mortgaging long-term productivity. It would not be a far reach to surmise that in the "emerging markets," the continual short-term bond offerings, privatizations, and financial restructurings (according to the tenets of structural adjustment) that enabled "the boom" also helped to fuel the crises felt in Asia, Russia, and Latin America.

When I asked Bennett what reasons the senior managers gave to justify their job loss, she uttered one word: "Market." She went on, "It was the market; the market could not justify a group of this magnitude, and we don't feel that we are well integrated." I then asked her what reasons she herself would give for her own downsizing.

> We started hearing that Merrill Lynch had the big layoff. . . . After that, you knew it was just a matter of time before everyone [had] layoffs. It filters through. At Lehman, no one ever talked about it, but even back in December, people were like, "Oh, I can feel something has happened." . . . Bonuses came, and they were very bad bonuses. That is a big signal right there. Then, in January, they basically sat everyone down and said, "Okay, guys, we thought and thought and thought about this but now it's like, sorry, we can't support this group as it is." . . . I mean, it's the hard reality of the business. Like, it's a risk that everyone has to take being in this business, that your job security isn't really there. And even for myself, I had changed groups, and even though the new area I was working in was doing some business, because it was linked to the market, there wasn't any justification for a large group of people.

After she constructed Wall Street's market proximity as the reason for her layoff, I asked for her impression of Wall Street culture, now that she had some distance from it.

> KH: What are some of your impressions in terms of what people do there, the values, or the work environment? Do you feel distant from that place now?
>
> RB: Yes, definitely. And I intentionally have kept a lot of distance. I haven't been hanging out with . . . my finance buddies. My impression is that I didn't realize just how shortsighted they were at that point. They are literally; it is all about today, and it's whether you can make money today, and if you can't make money today, you are out of there.
>
> KH: The bank or the people?
>
> RB: The bank *and* the people. Well, the bank, definitely. And then the people, you are only going to succeed if you think that way. *You need to be thinking I'm going to get as much as I can today because you don't know what is going to happen tomorrow.* And, that brings me to the second point, and that is: I realize the kind of mentality you have to have to be in that business, and I did not have that mentality. I tried to fool myself with "oh well, people *like* me." Yeah, they like me, but that does not mean people will champion

me because the way I am is very different from what they are looking for. You have to be very hard-nosed. . . . I am a person who likes to help other people out. I am not going to steal information or hide information because I don't want to share what I have with other people. There is that little bit of stinginess about the way people operate, very self-centered. You've just got to be that way. Think about yourself and only yourself. And then also just the driving force of money. . . . It's like a few dollars mean a lot. . . . It's like now that I am out of there, gosh, I can't believe I lasted so long. They're in another environment.

KH: Do you have a concrete example that demonstrates how they have to make money today?

RB: The mentality? Well, let's say on a bad day, the market is really quiet. Something unforeseen happens, and the market tanks. It starts tanking in the morning, and in the evening it is still tanking. My view would be, "Well, good, if you are not in the market, you didn't get involved in the market, that's great. Why be in there?" And their view . . . was, "Damn! I should have shorted the market. I should have taken action. I could have made this money. I am so stupid. I've got to get involved now and make a decision." It's like the attitude of you always have to be in there doing something. You don't just sit back and let things unfold because that is very passive. You really have to be pro-active.

A few months after her layoff, Bennett surmised that her disposition and practices, her "mentality," was contrary to what investment banks demanded, and this clash of values, which she encapsulated as her refusal to think only about making money today regardless of tomorrow, contributed to the loss of her job. In addition to remarking that her group was politically "not well integrated," she observed that investment banks treat their employees and deal with their various businesses based on a short-sighted value system where "if you can't make money today, you are out of there." Bennett hinted at how the institutional culture of investment banks enables and constructs why, who, and when to downsize, and thus how downsizing might occur at the intersections of markets and organizational structures.

Yet what strikes me is that Bennett was able to separate the market-centric rationale for her downsizing from her perceptions of the cultural practices of Wall Street. Although she realized that the values and every-day practices of investment banks certainly contributed to her downsizing, she still named "the market" (as external force) as the main reason for her layoff. By naturalizing the agency of downsizing in markets and market cycles, she dispersed responsibility from particular investment banking actions. What is missing is an analysis of how the values and practices of investment banks helped to construct both "the market" in emerging markets and in the United States *and* their approach to employment and the workplace. I argue that it is the cultural understandings and organizational incentives of investment banks that help contribute to the creation of both unstable, unsustainable markets *and* jobs. (Of course, it is important to note that in Bennett's case, her downsizing was directly linked to a pronounced emerging markets crisis, and this might certainly explain her attribution of such agency to "the market.")

Similarly, Christine Chang, a vice president in high-yield bonds at BT, discussed the dependency of her job on the volatility of the market.

> KH: If everything is changing so fast, does it affect people's experience of job security?
>
> CC: It means people jump around a lot. Depending on the economic environment, people get thrown out of work a lot and have to land someplace else doing something else. For a while, the junk bond market completely fell apart after Mike Milken went to jail. People lost a lot of money on junk bonds. The companies that issued junk bonds went bankrupt. For a while there, it seemed like the market was going to die entirely. I think people started looking for other things to do. That has happened in different products on Wall Street over the years. I think in 1994, the mortgage security market went through a very tough time. A lot of people were thrown out of work then. It is not the best place to be if you want a very steady, predictable job, because the markets are volatile, which means that your life and career are going to be volatile.

The volatility of the market does not result simply from constant cyclical movement but also from the continual shifting of financial fads and products, such as the collateralized mortgage obligations that fueled the subprime debacle. Products that predominate one year, employing entire floors of people, can be decimated the next, the departments previously devoted to them shrinking to one or two desks. Interestingly enough, the rise and fall and rerise of junk bonds (renamed as high-yield bonds) is centrally indicative of Wall Street's notoriously short-term institutional culture: mired in scandal and a "dead market," their products widely considered financial toxic waste, junk bonds investment bankers (still associated with smartness) were not discredited, tainted, or assumed to lack judgment but rather were sought after to rebuild the highly profitable market after the late 1980s.

Julie Cooper, also a vice president of high-yield at BT, associated layoffs with downturns, but also said that insecurity is present on Wall Street "every single day":

KH: With things being so dynamic here, do you think there's a lot of job insecurity on Wall Street?

JC: Oh yeah, it's huge. Huge. I think that every single day you realize that your job could be gone the next day. You have a downturn in the market, and they lay off hundreds of people or you have a downturn in just your desk [your particular area's] performance; all of sudden they need to lay off people. You know, your company decides they don't want to be in that product anymore; they lay off an entire department. I just think that's part of life here.

Joseph Tsai, an investment banking associate at DLJ, echoed Cooper, arguing that job insecurity "on the Street" is perhaps the most pronounced of any industry because your business "is" the market: "Because the market is so fickle and it goes up and down so fast that the probabilities of a huge market downturn is more likely [on Wall Street] than if you are in a company and your product all of a sudden dries up. It is different." Julio Muñoz, an associate in M&A at DLJ, also linked employee downsizing solely to uncontrollable market movements: "That's probably something you will see in your study. The number of bankers and how it moves. It really moves like an accordion."[7]

Finally, Edward Randolph, a vice president of strategy and risk management at Merrill Lynch, pointed to dependence on market cycles as the major theme governing Wall Street employment. He did, however, give a broad overview of the context and experiences of job insecurity on Wall Street, worth quoting at length:

KH: So, how long do you see yourself working in this industry?

ER: I don't know. I mean, it's tough . . . I don't plan a lot for the future, though I think a lot about the future. When I think about ten years' time from now, I don't have a clue where I'll be. . . . I'm a little worried in that this is a risky business to work in. You get paid a lot of money; you're paid a hell of a lot of money, really, when you think about it because of that risk and that uncertainty. For instance, I [just started] this new job at Merrill. Now there were rumors yesterday that Chase was going to take over Merrill. Something like that comes out of the blue. Before you know it, with some of the mergers that have been going on, there are some extremely talented people who are out of jobs at the moment. . . . Like the last three or four years [1996–99], there's been so much business going on, these firms built up a lot of excess human capital, hired a lot of people, and when firms combine and the market starts to cool down a little bit as it has recently, there are a lot of people on the Street looking for work. So it is very cyclical, and if you're working in the investment banking business, you work so hard. There are people, probably friends of yours who are analysts or associates in corporate finance; they're working mega hours, sixteen or eighteen hours a day. You can only do that for so long. And you get paid very well to do that, but it's interesting, every Monday morning there is a markets meeting where all the investment banking people get together to talk about what's going on in the market. I would guess eighty to one hundred people in that room. These are the people who are the core of the corporate finance business, and I would be surprised if more than five or ten of them were over the age of forty. Maybe that's a slight exaggeration, but by the time you're forty, if you're an investment banker, [you've] made enough money and [you're] kind of burning out.

KH: What you were saying about the rumor of Chase taking over Merrill— do you think takeovers and mergers are the main contributors to the insecurity? Or is it just that people don't really value their employees that much?

ER: I think senior management does look at it like there's a lot of human capital out there, and we can just get what we want. Obviously [you] want to retain real stars. . . . You find that in a cycle like this where there's been a lot work going on, [you] build up a lot of people. So all the banks are very fully stocked at the moment. If the market collapses, or there's a big turn down or slowdown in the business, they're going to have no hesitation to lay all those people off very quickly. There will be people on the street, and . . . so that's just the way it is. . . . [T]he reason it's risky, it's not only because of consolidation, but also because it's a very cyclical business.

Randolph described the constant threat of job loss and critiqued their manner of overhiring only to get rid of this "excess human capital" in downturns or even slight "slowdowns." He pointed to the high burnout rates on Wall Street and banks' willingness to lay off employees with great speed and "no hesitation." Although it seems that he was anticipating a downturn (the matter of how banks "anticipate" market cycles will be addressed later), he did not locate much agency with the executives and banking culture actually responsible for hiring and firing workers.

Despite my informants' complex articulations of their experiences of job insecurity, their tautological answer of market causality leaves the culture of investment banks and corporate decision-making largely uninterrogated and elides the fact that market prescriptions are social actions taken by cultural institutions. Employment policies and strategies do not simply and reflexively follow autonomous, naturalized market laws. This is not to say that market volatility does not affect job insecurity (it most certainly does) the point is that market volatility is itself located and formed at the intersections of particular values, practices, and institutions. While it is understandable to mistake "the market" as an autonomous and abstract force if one does not have access to its inner workings, what does it mean that a similar apprehension of the market also characterizes the articulations of privileged bankers regarding their own employment insecurities? Although the relatively powerful and powerless both resort to market abstractions and autonomous universalisms to explain their own economic circumstances, they do so in divergent contexts, with different consequences. *The question then becomes: what else does it mean that investment bankers appeal to the explanatory force of the market to make sense of their own job insecurities?*

Insecurity, Downsizing, and Market Externalizations

I found that the dominant usage of market-centered assumptions in their cultural repertoires prevented investment bankers from understanding their own role in constructing their downsizing, not to mention market cycles and crises themselves. First, given that the majority of my informants' narratives pointed to "the market" and market volatility as *the* actor in their unstable employment experiences, I realized that if, as many investment bankers claim, their employment was directly tied to the volatility of the markets, then following this logic, they should feel greater job security during booms and less during busts. Like the spontaneous ebb and flow of ocean waves, when the stock market moves, so too does investment banking employment. Since this was certainly not the case, I realized that given the dominance of market-centered assumptions that link job insecurity with downturns in the market, not to mention the exaggerated optimism of bull market rhetoric, it was difficult for my informants to articulate that they experienced the bull market as not only as a time of booming possibility but also one fraught with insecurity—precisely because they used market naturalizations to link job losses primarily to down cycles. Downsizings, however, are a common strategy even during stock-market booms and are an integral part of what might be called "bull market" culture.

Sometimes it takes an outplacement counselor such as Doug Baird to see beyond the easy conflations of market cycles and bank employment. He has observed Wall Street from multiple standpoints and institutional locations, as before working as a senior counselor at Lee Hecht Harrison, Baird received an MBA and worked at Morgan Stanley for over a decade. He also occasionally served as a consultant to support groups for the downsized, such as The Five O'clock Club and The Forty Plus Club, both based in New York City. I met Baird through my outplacement counselor Gina Thomas and actually attended one of his downsizing seminars/support groups. A year later, in the fall of 1998, as investment banks were still reeling from the Asian and Russian financial crises and after I had begun fieldwork, I sat down with Baird and asked him when he usually received the most downsized clients and if the numbers of layoffs were in sync with the recessionary, down cycles on Wall Street.

KH: How does your role shift during the peaks and troughs? Do you have a lot of clients lined up now, as opposed to two years ago?

DB: Well, downsizings produce a lot more business for us because a lot more people are being released, and so we have a lot of people using our service. *But, you know, Wall Street releases people in good times and in bad times.* And my theory is that in the bad times Wall Street releases people because they don't want to dilute the bonus pool, and in good times Wall Street releases people because they have plenty of money, and they say, let's just replace them. We don't care what it costs because we've got plenty to go around. So generally in good times and in bad times, we see a lot of activity. The time when we are least busy is when things are just sort of moving along more evenly. But when it is robust out there, we see a lot of people.

KH: That's interesting. I didn't know.

DB: Because the firms just don't care. They say, "Get rid of them. We can easily afford to absorb the cost of a recruiting firm, and we can bring more people on board. And if we don't like them, we will get rid of them, too."

Although I realized that rampant downsizings also occurred during bull markets, it still had not completely sunk in ethnographically. Holding on to the taken-for-granted assumption that associates a good economy with relatively more stable employment, I was surprised when Baird made me aware that investment banks can "release" as many workers during mar-

ket downturns as during bull markets. Interestingly, Baird did not corre-
late these releases to shareholder value, but rather to Wall Street's cultural
strategy of constantly replacing employees and avoiding the dilution of
the bonus pool. He thus hints at the importance of investment banks'
approaches to compensation and employment in the analysis of Wall
Street downsizing—and ultimately, as I will demonstrate, in Wall Street's
construction of financial market crises.

To give three other examples, in September 1998, Roy Allen, a managing director at Fidelity Investments, conceded that investment banking
employment might *not* parallel market cycles. Even on Wall Street, what
constitutes a bull market is both highly contested and saturated with
bearishness.

KH: Do you think there is a lot of job insecurity in Wall Street?

RA: Yes, there's a lot of job insecurity. It's gotten worse. . . . I think now on
    Wall Street, it's been the best of times and the worst of times. It's been
    the best of times in terms of Wall Street firms making money, but people
    are as insecure as they have ever been, maybe worse. The consolidation:
    maybe it's right, maybe it isn't, but it is creating a great deal of disloca-
    tions for people. I think there is a whole repricing of what you're worth in
    the marketplace. . . . There will be more consolidation, and it will not be
    the cat's meow it has been the last couple of years.

In December 1998, Megan Mills, a senior management consultant for the
financial services industry at McKinsey Consulting, described the environment of job insecurity during the "bull market" years.

KH: What has the work environment and job security on Wall Street been
    like since the beginning of the bull market, say around 1995? Are there
    major differences between then and now?

MM: It is difficult to generalize, and I will tell you why. Because, although
    1995 . . . was a stellar year, there were definitely all these pockets within
    an investment bank that collapsed. So like '94 and '95, the mortgage
    market went away. And at various houses on the Street, including Gold-
    man Sachs where my husband worked on the mortgage desk, the mort-
    gage desk went away. So you had people that did experience what it is
    like to have a market go away. [But] what you did *not* have is what you
    had in late summer, like August and September [1998], when a *market*
    went away. When I am talking about a market going away, it is like
    Russia. It went away, and it so deeply impacted people. I think the
    ramifications are that it will impact people differently at different levels.

I think at the junior level, people are thinking, "You know, I went to investment banking for the money, because the life sucks and the work is
really not that interesting when it comes around to it . . . [but] maybe it
is *not* worth it." Because people my year who went to investment banking are not going to get paid . . . and they are working their asses off.[8]

Allen's point that bull markets breed layoff-inducing mergers and consolidations, and Mills's point that "pockets within an investment bank" collapsed alerted me to the fundamental instability of Wall Street employment and to the difficulty of distinguishing between periods of boom and
bust. Also, in December 1998, Phillip Young, an associate in M&A at
Merrill Lynch, described the intricacies of Merrill Lynch's approach to
downsizing during the emerging market crisis of 1997 and 1998: "I had
the impression that most of the layoffs came from emerging markets, but
they were across the board. I think every department was asked to give a
little and to cut some people. I think that especially occurred in investment banking. *I think investment banking took [this opportunity] to sort of
clean house. It is a good excuse to say we need to fire people, so they get rid of
the bottom 5 percent or something*" (my emphasis). Departments technically
not "dependent" on the emerging markets, even groups that were booming during 1998, also laid off 5 percent of their workers. That Wall Street
was taking advantage of this crisis to "clean house" signified a more
complex approach to employment than simple market dependency.

It is certainly remarkable that investment bankers, champions of short-
term shareholder value who demand practices and values from corporate
America that will immediately increase stock prices, do not in turn appeal
to shareholder value as one of the main rationales for their own job
insecurity. This is not to say that no one does, but the majority of my
informants pointed instead to the vagaries, volatilities, and cycles of the
market. On the one hand, I would argue that such rationales also fall prey
to neoclassical virtualisms, where the fetishization of theoretical models,
such as the market logics of invisible hands, obscures the actual daily
practices of Wall Street investment banks. On the other, I also realized
that I had to resist a dismissive interpretation of my informants' reified
justifications. Although abstract concepts such as "the market" are important formulations through which finance speaks, such expressions often
form a taken-for-granted shorthand, a simplifying or encapsulating language, and as such cannot be taken at face value. Perhaps these market-
centered explanations, even in their opaqueness, are culturally significant and needed to be taken seriously, interrogated, unpacked. Does not

Bennett's experience of her downsizing as "all of a sudden" reflect Wall Street's cultural approach to downsizing as instantaneous and unforgiving? Why not read her representations of the market as also a local description and expression of the normative practices of investment banking work culture, indicative of Wall Streeters' conflation of their own cultural identity and practices with that of the market? Rejecting investment bankers' dominant representations of the market does not take seriously the fact that market abstractions are not a transparent reflection of reality.

Investment bankers' appeals to naturalized market cycles must also be understood as particular cultural self-representations borne out of everyday Wall Street work life, not reifications of market dominance or abstraction. Reading market externalization *as* market cultural identification, I argue that investment bankers' "marketspeak" actually dramatizes their self-understanding that banks "are" the market (or embody it). Their local understandings of temporality, what one might call "Wall Street time" or "hypercapitalist time," are constituted through Wall Street's institutional culture. Taken together, rampant job insecurity and an emphasis on instant action and performance, not only truncate and tighten bankers' temporal register, but also demand a total, "real-time" identification with financial markets. It is not surprising, then, that given the extent to which investment banking culture and its identities and strategies are informed by a particular understanding of time, my informants represent themselves as highly market responsive. Because the construction of market trends, the management and analysis of market data, and the processing of market transactions—the "pulse" of the market—pass through or originate on Wall Street, it should come as no surprise that investment banks see themselves as adapting more closely to the rhythm of the market than the rest of corporate America. Simultaneously, the quickness of investment banks' reactions signifies their absolute identity with the market, that their sense of who they are, their cultural distinction, is the ability to channel the market, to have the market act through and with them immediately.

Of course, while investment bankers construct and drive the market, they are in turn shaped and constrained by it; their approach to the market thus becomes one of simultaneity with, and anticipation of, the market. Ironically, this temporal identification with the market does *not* lead investment bankers to be "future-oriented"; their anticipation of potential market failures has little effect on restraining or shifting their practices. To the contrary, planning and strategy are frequently discounted as bankers work almost solely in the moment. In the next chapter, I demonstrate that Wall Street's strong sense of temporal simultaneity with the market, coupled with their anticipation and understanding of constantly impending crisis, causes them to intensify the very unsustainable financial practices which instigate crisis and lead to failure in the first place. Investment bankers' approach to corporate America collapses the latter's corporate temporalities into their own particular Wall Street timeframe with unfortunate consequences.

The Brave New Workplace

Although I would argue that job insecurity and "no long term" are endemic to *both* investment banks *and* major corporations, certainly there are different valences and degrees of insecurity and market adherence. Not all institutions are alike, and the workplace is not everywhere homogeneous. I suggest that given the dominance of Wall Street in influencing corporate America, the workplace practices and approaches to employment that have been cultivated on Wall Street have certainly helped to constitute the brave new workplace in general. For example, Kate Miller, an investment banking analyst at Morgan Stanley in 1998, who eventually left to work for Pepsi Corporation (and thus has perspectives from both kinds of institutions), used compelling imagery that sheds light on how Wall Street investment banks cast judgment on the rest of corporate America:

KH: So, do you think the investment banking industry is more dynamic and constantly changing as opposed to other corporations?

KM: Investment bankers and banking in general respond very quickly to changes in the market. 'Cause that is their business. That's what they advise their clients on, that's how they make their money. So, I think yes, they're very in-tune. Pepsi is a very slow corporation. It's slow because it needs to be. You look at something like a Morgan Stanley, you might liken it to a fighter plane that can change course very quickly. Because generally speaking, the teams [in investment banking] and the industry groups are so isolated and work within their own little industry so well that they can see a trend or a change, and they can go off in a different direction. So I see them as little fighter pilots. Whereas something like Pepsi is this huge, big, mammoth conglomerate that has offices and companies and restaurants all over the world. If it were able to turn that quickly, the lives that would be shaken and affected would be just incredi-

> bly great. So they're almost like an aircraft carrier that has to turn four
> degrees an hour in order to change its course smoothly.

Though Miller's description of investment banks as nimble fighter pilots leading change and corporations as large, slow-moving aircraft car-
riers certainly makes the important point that banks and corporations
have very different organizational structures, it is crucial to situate the
political implications of such representations. Given the privileging in late
capitalism of the representations and marketing of flexibility and constant change, the very notion that corporations are extremely slow compared to investment banks implies a hierarchy where Wall Street has
adapted while corporations are still plodding along (Martin 1994).

Crucially, this analogy is personalized to compare the superior skills of
investment bankers versus those of "the average" worker. For Wall Street
bankers, one of their key imagined social roles as "market-doers" is to
create liquidity, to speedily unlock and allocate money (as in the takeover
movement) to its "best" use. Through their own immersion in the market,
especially the anxious, difficult experiences of constant downsizing and
reinvention, their skills and lives—embodying the market and their roles
in it—have also become "more liquid." As such, it comes as no surprise
that Michael Williams, vice president of Emerging Market Sales and Trading at Lehman Brothers, used his market identity to construct a moral
lesson where investment bankers' experiences and understandings of
"hard-hitting" change and restructuring can be used to as a "solution" to a
better economy and workforce. Unlike Wall Streeters, most average people are not like "cash," and crucially, their "skill set" is illiquid. Williams
explained:

> If you have a skill set, you can't just trade that skill set in for another skill set.
> It's lumpy. In the same way that a house has less liquidity than cash does. And
> a skill set has even less liquidity than a house does. A person's family, home,
> and life have even less liquidity. . . . When we see that some people, because
> they have no liquidity in their lives, either in their skill set or whatever, say in
> their ability to move, they suffer and can't do anything about it; we empathize
> with the person. Now, if there were a way that we could somehow give that
> person a new skill set right away or add liquidity to their lives so that they
> could make a switch, then the world would really, really be better off. But, I
> think where morality meets economics is in that analysis, is in thinking about
> the liquidity in a person's life. . . . So, "What's the solution" to make their lives
> better? If you are going to unemploy 50,000 people, or 2,000 people . . . what
> are they going to do? Well, it really depends on their skill set and what is out

there. The problem is that there is just going to be a lot of people all with the same skill set looking for very few jobs, so they are going to have to find new places. I don't think that there is anything wrong with that. I think that it is probably better than any other way of doing it because you could keep things going with a sort of a slow bleed for a very, very long time, where everyone is slowly getting poor, or you could do it . . . where a specific group of people takes a very hard hit, but then they can find ways to move on. From there, another specific set of people takes a very hard hit and that way the whole is moving forward in a better way than it would be if you tried to protect everybody and then slowly, slowly went downhill. It is definitely a tradeoff. And, it could be a convenient morality because, presumably, on Wall Street you have better chances to remake your life. You have a better safety net if you have been working for a while and you saved enough money. I don't know if that makes sense.

Unclear about whether or not Williams was framing himself or his role on Wall Street as exemplar, I inquired further, "Interesting liquidity metaphor. So, relating what you said back to what Wall Street does, is it Wall Street's function to help make people more liquid?" Williams answered: "Well, it is the process—it can include the process of creative destruction where you need to get rid of things that don't work or focus on things that do work, and it's very much bound up in that. The interesting thing is that you could have people like the LBO takeover artists who are very selfish and evil and immoral and who succeed very much in a system that still, paradoxically, is beneficial to the whole." In addition to being more liquid than the rest (having acquired the ability to move and transfer jobs and skills), Wall Street's larger social—and market—purpose is also the necessary evil of forcing the average worker to become more liquid. Investment banks thus position their own approach to change as *the* reference point for corporate America, and investment bankers, the least "lumpy" of workers, function as the ideal (currency) standard—that is, the most cashlike—of employment.

It is important to underscore that the liquidity of investment bankers' skills set is dependent upon the corresponding "financialization" of corporate America, the high demand for their financial advice, and the dominance of Wall Street worldviews. Even in the wake of the Lehman Brothers bankruptcy and Merrill Lynch's sale to Bank of America in September 2008, executive headhunters pointed out that investment bankers at both Merrill Lynch and Lehman Brothers "who have been key to putting together banking deals can expect good job prospects": "Bank of America . . .

will likely hire on Merrill's top bankers" and "small investment banks and growing foreign banks . . . will also take an interest" (Gomstyn 2008). That being said, as the current economic downturn transforms the pinnacle status upon which investment bankers' marketability depends, and Wall Street continues to hemorrhage jobs, even the most cashlike of workers might find themselves becoming less hireable, less liquid.

A brief examination of the world of work and the very concept of career in general demonstrates just how dominant Wall Street practices have become in the age of flexible accumulation and shareholder value. In *The Corrosion of Character: The Personal Consequences of Work in the New Capitalism* and *The Culture of the New Capitalism*, Richard Sennett argues that today, jobs and corporations are evaluated via the multiple demands of Wall Street and the stock market, which are "too dynamic to permit doing things the same way year after year, or doing the same thing" (Sennett 1998, 22). In this Wall Street–modeled new economy, given that organizations continually "swell and contract" to meet its latest demands, and employees are "added and discarded as the firm moves from one task to another," the very values of loyalty, trust, and commitment that were mutually constitutive of the worker and the firm have been discarded (Sennett 2006, 48–49). In this context, both the firm and the worker lose: not only is the long-term institutional knowledge of the firm continually destroyed, but workers are denied "the gift of organized time" to engage in the long-term and stable planning of one's work and life, to survive social upheavals and establish some kind of command over one's life narrative (Sennett 2006, 36). In this fragmenting and casualization of the workplace, "a young American with at least two years of college" is expected to "change jobs at least eleven times in the course of working," but perhaps even more importantly, such an environment contributes to the "corrosion of character" (Sennett 1998, 22).[9] The stable bureaucratic structures of the corporation have not simply been dismantled but also replaced by a new institutional structure that values disloyalty, irresponsibility, and immediacy. Gone are the institutions with "lifetime longevity" that allowed "social relationships [the] time to develop" and individuals to "matter" to others in the workplace (Sennett 2006, 36). After all, when one is downsized on Wall Street, an investment banker has less than fifteen minutes to physically leave the premises, much less participate in a ritual to sustain connection. In this economy, "to make it you really have to plunge into much more superficial social relations. It is *dysfunctional* to feel loyalty to an organisation" (Benn 2001, my emphasis). It comes as no surprise that the hypercasualization of employment found on Wall Street has become the dominant trend for all workplaces.[10]

Sennett attributes the workplace instability of corporate America to the dominance of short-term shareholder value, which has radically changed the institutional structure of corporations and, by extension, the individual workplace experience. He writes:

> Enormous pressure was put on companies to look beautiful in the eyes of the passing voyeur [the short-term investor]; institutional beauty consisted in demonstrating signs of internal change and flexibility, appearing to be a dynamic company, even if the once-stable company had worked perfectly well. Firms like . . . Enron became dysfunctional or corrupt in responding to this investor parade, but even in periods of market downturn the pressure on firms remained the same: institutional solidity became an investment negative rather than a positive. Stability seemed a sign of weakness, suggesting to the market that the firm could not innovate or find new opportunities or otherwise manage change. (Sennett 2006, 40–41)

Such practices thrive precisely because "the stock prices of institutions in the course of reorganization thereby often rise, as though any change is better than continuing on as before." As Sennett explains, in today's markets dominated by "impatient" financial capital, rapid "disruption of organizations has become profitable. While disruption may not be justifiable in terms of productivity, the short-term returns to stockholders provide a strong incentive to the powers of chaos disguised by that seemingly reassuring word 'reengineering'" (Sennett 1998, 22–23, 51).

As I have also demonstrated, however, shareholder value demands often do not result in a rise in stock prices; these disruptions are frequently not profitable. As such, going beyond Sennett's analysis, it is important to question "the effects" of the shareholder value worldview espoused by Wall Street investment banks and backed by large amounts of institutional investment capital. Given the implosions and contradictions of shareholder value, we should ask what was working in conjunction with this worldview such that constant change, which can lessen productivity, became the dominant and necessary practice? I have argued in this chapter that rampant job insecurity, constant change, and downsizing on Wall Street—given the particular culture of smartness and its punitive work ethic—serve precisely this catalyzing role of forging the cultural and institutional environment necessary to impel Wall Street downsizing as "the model" of workplace relations in general. The power of these daily institutional norms to explain the brave new workplace cannot be ignored in favor of a top-down discursive implementation of shareholder value. This constant state of employment insecurity, as I demonstrate in the following chapter, when coupled with investment banks' approach to compensation and what I call their "strategy of no strategy," not only works to transfer a particular disciplinary model of employee liquidity, insecurity, and workplace relations to corporate America, but also serves as a key window into understanding Wall Street investment banks' role in the construction of financial market crises.

6

Liquid Lives, Compensation Schemes, and the

Making of (Unsustainable) Financial Markets

Investment bankers' approaches to downsizing and the financial markets are inseparable from the structures and strategies of their own workplaces. Their generalized understandings and daily practices that shape the financial markets are framed through their own experiences of compensation, job insecurity, corporate restructuring, market identification, hard work, and pinnacle status, and this employment habitus in turn shapes (and is shaped by) how they approach corporate America and how they influence the capital markets and financial crises. In this chapter, I bring together and allow the various threads of investment banking's financial culture that were introduced in previous chapters to intersect and converge in order to unearth the relationships between the values and actions of investment banks, the corresponding restructuring of U.S. corporations, and the construction of financial market booms and busts. Through linking the culture of smartness (chapter 1), the galvanizing ethic of hard work (chapter 2), and rampant job insecurity and market identification (chapter 5), with the politics of compensation and the strategy of no strategy, I will not only demonstrate the contradictions and implosions of shareholder value that I introduced in chapters 3 and 4, but also how downsizing and financial crisis get enacted. My central purpose is to not only analyze Wall Street's role in the reshaping of U.S. corporations but also to shed light on how Wall Street helped to concretely *instantiate* these changes. By exploring the mutual constitution and interconnections between investment bankers, Wall Street firms, corporations, and the stock market through the mundane access point of Wall Street's corporate culture, I attempt to re-envision the market as a site of human values, emotions, and institutional norms.

Two developments in the social studies of finance provide important toolkits for this approach to understanding broader assemblages, processes, or change (such as financial markets, crises, and massive corporate restructuring) through the workings of a powerful, influential institution (Wall Street investment banks and their corporate culture). First, to culturalize markets and counter the dominant representation of Wall Street as detached and abstracted from the lives and concerns of most people, this chapter focuses on Wall Street's everyday institutional culture and demonstrates the interconnection between the biographies and actions of individual bankers and broader financial change. This approach, located at the intersections of individual, institutional, national, and global practices, builds on Hirokazu Miyazaki's analytical work in his exploration of Japanese proprietary traders' "temporal incongruity . . . in the global financial markets," their sense of "being behind" the global changes spurred by financial markets (Miyazaki 2003, 256, 261). To unpack this "lagging" temporality, Miyazaki analyzes their engagement with the market in multiple registers: their particular trading strategies, individual life trajectories, Japanese corporate culture, and a national temporal location and identity of needing to "catch up" with the United States (Miyazaki 2003, 257). In contrast to Miyazaki's informants, who understood their market models and identities to be "behind" the financial markets as symbolized by investment banks in the United States, my informants often conceive of themselves "as" the market and strive to become one with its rhythms and movements. I will argue, however, that while Wall Street's strong sense of temporal simultaneity with the market allows investment bankers an anticipation and understanding of constantly impending crisis, such access (when coupled with the particular exigencies of their workplace culture) causes them to intensify the very unsustainable financial practices which instigate crisis and lead to failure in the first place. Their institutional values and cultural practices incentivize both the spread of risk (onto corporate America, the larger economy, and even themselves) and its intensification (using leverage for complex transactions, selling hedging instruments that turn out to be bets themselves). What cushions Wall Street's hard landing is not the bankers' much-touted future orientation and risk-management skills, but the deliberate tethering of their fortunes to those of the global economy so that they can command state support and bailouts.

Second, investigating the relationship between dominant financial representations and models and their effects reveals how Wall Street's worldviews and cultural models get implemented in corporate America and financial markets. As such, my approach draws from another fruitful development in social studies of finance that queries the relationship between financial models and market practices, in particular, how financial theories get performed (Callon 1998; MacKenzie 2006). Donald MacKenzie has demonstrated that the financial model itself and its attending assumptions have played a constitutive role in actively shaping market practices: these theories have legitimated and been incorporated into the very infrastructure of market action. Drawing from this work, Bill Maurer called for more research on "money's pragmatics," where finance's performative effects enacted by and through multiple interlocutors are tracked and examined (Maurer 2006, 16). By analyzing how models and markets are mutually constitutive, by studying financial "feedback loops between the worlds modeled and instantiated by finance theory," research on finance can stress interconnection, demonstrate the work of actualization, and challenge abstraction, as well as allow, importantly, for unpredictability and gaps between the model and the effects (Maurer 2006, 26).

Investment bankers' key cultural justification for their reshaping of corporate purpose is the notion of shareholder value, which distills their ideology and serves as an ideal "model" of how corporations, including their own, should behave. I have demonstrated that the results predicted by shareholder value often do not materialize in corporate America, as Wall Street's demands of corporations often lead to stock-price volatility, decline, and corporate crisis. Despite being Wall Street's blueprint for change, shareholder value has not simply remade the world in its own image. As such, models cannot assume "in advance what those effects might be" (Maurer 2006, 26); and there are other models of Wall Street's operations on the economy with perhaps even more explanatory power.

Examining investment banking's exemplary culture of downsizing, smartness, and hard work offers a crucial window onto the ways in which banks make markets in general. My own downsizing at BT highlighted the job insecurity of investment bankers and established that shareholder value could not fully explain how and why Wall Street was continually motivated to inflict such a model of employment on itself. Moreover, I realized that these "self-downsizings" could yield insight into Wall Street's restructuring of corporate America and workers at large, as both were enactments of the same habitus of downsizing. Through the examination of key discourses and practices "here" on Wall Street and how they are deployed in specific contexts of corporate restructuring within investment houses, I could test their model of shareholder value as well as think through how downsizing was effected both within and without.

Contrary to my expectation, I found that investment bankers' job experiences, especially their own downsizings and job insecurities, do not afford them much (nondisciplinary) empathy or understanding for the plight of the average worker in today's economy. How are investment bankers motivated to recommend downsizing for others despite their own vulnerability to the same process? Some pieces of this puzzle have been laid out in previous chapters: empowered by their prestige and elite educational pedigrees, their experiences of hard work, the moral high ground and historical purchase of shareholder value, and their role as mouthpiece of investor capital, investment bankers learn to thrive in a corporate culture that is characterized by slash-and-burn expediency. Recall my informants' self-characterizations of smartness, speed, hard work, flexibility, and global prowess in explicit contradistinction to "nine to five" corporate workers whose steady, clock-watching routinization produces "stagnant," "fat," "lazy" "dead wood" that needs to be "pruned."

In this chapter, I introduce investment banking compensation schemes as a central component of its institutional culture. Wall Street approaches to compensation not only solidify job insecurity but also engender a relentless deal-making frenzy with no future orientation, which in turn sets in motion not only financial booms and busts but also the *transfer* and imposition of investment banking models of employee liquidity onto corporate America. Far more than shareholder value, the model being actualized is the bankers' *cultural model of themselves as coeval and identified with the market*. In other words, investment banks' organizational culture produces (and is produced by) their self-understanding as embodiments of the market, as the ultimate "liquid" employee. It is precisely this cultural model, often obscured and misinterpreted as abstract, naturalized market process, which not only describes and analyzes, but also performs the financial markets. Given the influential reach of investment bankers, their personal crises and institutional culture are dramatized in the production of financial crises.

A Moment's Notice

I begin this discussion by recounting at length a conversation I had with Thomas Douglass, a high-ranking veteran of Wall Street investment banks whom I met at BT. He was a wealth of information about the cultural politics and organizational intricacies of investment banks. As leader of his own group, where he had some maneuverability to build his own organization within the bank, he acquired a considerable knowledge of the bank's employment practices, particularly as his own inclinations ran quite counter to them. In this conversation, we discussed why and how Wall Street seemed to be able to react much more quickly to "the market" than other corporations and industries. Douglass described how certain organizational and strategic practices of investment banks enable them to create these conditions:

TD: Wall Street has a way, [more so than] other industries, [of] being willing or being eager to react quickly to market changes and market dynamics and being willing to include how they treat their human resources as part of that reaction. So, for example, a contract that Wall Street works out with [a new hire] when he comes: it says number one, you get paid for performance. So if you make billions for us, then you'll get a cut of it. Number two, on your side, you have to accept this Darwinian proposition. So what does that mean? That means you need to fight. Because if you make billions for us, we'll give you what we think is fair, but that might only be a million, not five million. You might feel bad, [but] pay for performance means you've got to fight for what you get, what you think you deserve. Now, that all translates in Wall Street's mind into you having an opportunity to make a lot of money very quickly. On the flip side of that is the fact that if we suddenly don't need you, we will ditch you because we are doing what makes good business sense for us and that could mean getting out of a business, and if that's your specialty, then that means we divest ourselves and you along with that business. And we will build in certain cushions to the equation that will at least relieve us of our legal obligations to you. And we probably do not feel any moral obligation to you.

KH: So, why has Wall Street led other industries to react quickly to market dynamics?

TD: Because Wall Street *prides* itself [in reacting quickly] and also because it has a lot of the technology, the M&A capabilities, just the drive, the staff to make course corrections, quickly, right? Because the business that it's in is really information processing . . . as opposed to building widgets, right? It leads the rest of the industries out there in its ability to make a change—*to suddenly decide, hey, I'm out of this business, cut the people, escort them out of the building, now I'm in this other business. Right? Let's find the people that can do that one for me.* If it's Procter and Gamble or somebody like that and they manufacture something; if you have a mold for something, if you decide to discontinue a line, you got to shift to another line, you got to build molds, engineers have to come in and work on it. Wall Street, gone, business out. You come downstairs, twenty-fourth floor, there's nobody there. So it's very different. That's why it's faster.

KH: So, you mean that Wall Street is this leader because it can shift course so quickly, and so other corporations say, "Oh look, Wall Street is always responding to the market, and they're totally making this profit," and so we need to do the same thing but don't realize that we're a completely different creature. We can't just upsize and downsize like this because it will cause major problems in the long run.[1]

TD: I think it also causes major problems for Wall Street, but why? Some of the cultural aspects that you're talking about. . . . . There is no stability whatsoever. You always have to worry. For example, [when] I was first on Wall Street, when I was trading, I was single, no kids. I had responsibilities, but I lived a very cheap life. I didn't move to Manhattan and get the expensive apartment. I lived way up in the Bronx, almost up in Westchester. I had a two-bedroom apartment. It cost me $700 a month, with a garage, and I spent almost no money. So, if I got fired from that job—I mean, when I got a bonus, I put it in the bank, you know, I'm buying CDs for myself. It was very boring, very stable. And so, if there was a big course correction and my firm decided to get rid of me, I can survive for quite a few months and still have a home and a roof over my head. But imagine suddenly . . . you've got some three- or four-bedroom place on Park Avenue here in New York and a spouse. The spouse isn't working because we have four kids, and she's watching them, and we got people helping her watch them, and we've got whatever we do on the weekends and a couple of cars and a townhouse someplace else or someplace out in the country. All of a sudden you've got this thing that's built up and hopefully by then you're making a hell of a lot of money to pay for all of that, but there aren't a lot of other jobs that will pay that same amount of money and allow you to keep all of those things the same way. *And you're working for this firm that at a moment's notice decides, that prides itself on being able to pull out of the business that you're in and cut you and escort you out of the building* (my emphasis).

Douglass's detailed narrative gave me an excellent depiction of the cultural environment of investment banks—the worldviews and ethical structures they nurture, as well as the multiple consequences of these values and practices. The corporate identities of investment banks, founded on swift and creative responses to the marketplace, are both constitutive of, and constructed by, their approach to employment and compensation, the very practices that allow banks the license to restructure at a moment's notice.[2] As Douglass hints, there exists an intimate relationship between "pay for performance," job insecurity, banks' ability and desire to shift gears "at a moment's notice," and their larger business strategies.

Strikingly, Douglass depicts the primary assets of investment banks— employees—as the most essential as well as the most expendable. Investment banks, like many corporations, continually proclaim that their primary assets are their people. The best thing about working on Wall Street is supposed to be the "raw intellectual ability" and intensity of the bankers; it is the "quality of our people," my informants say, that underpins Wall Street success. Moreover, what differentiates Wall Street investment banks from most of corporate America is how they organizationally demonstrate that people are their greatest asset: the majority of their revenue goes toward compensation, with "star performers" and senior bankers and traders of the front office taking the lion's share; compensation is the "single largest expense" for securities firms (Anderson and Thomas 2004). "The standard portion of net revenue (total revenue minus interest expense) earmarked for compensation at Wall Street firms stands at an astonishing 50 percent. That's because talent is the most precious commodity on Wall Street; it's what they sell, so it's also what they have to pay for" (McDonald 2005). Investment banks do not invest much in technology, building infrastructure, or research and development, in part because of the nature of the services industry (although most large U.S. corporations, via outsourcing and delinking from manufacturing and product development, are moving toward the model of the "weightless" corporation which Wall Street interprets as enhancing shareholder value), but mainly because investment banks' identities reside in their front-office workers. During Wall Street's bonus season, lasting from November to February, managing directors spend more than half the work day on matters related to employees' pay (Anderson and Thomas 2004).

How, then, do we reconcile investment banks' identification with, and attachment to, the quality of their front-office workers with the fact that one, they so often treat them as disposable commodities, and two, investment banking's identity also rests (proudly) on an ability to make immediate changes, to move swiftly, decisively, and remorselessly with the market? How does Wall Street bridge and negotiate this contradiction? This question churned in my mind until I began to delineate what it was about their employees that Wall Street continually emphasized: what "qualities" about their people were they committed to? As I've demonstrated, while employees come and go, the elite schools where investment bankers are recruited (and the resultant cultural capital that is imparted to investments banks for continually attracting these highly pedigreed workers) have been unfailingly constant. In other words, investment banking identities cohere around their commitments to employees' pedigrees and university affiliations, *not* individual employees. Not surprisingly, such a way of managing their identity not only contributes to job insecurity but also supports their values and strategy of swift and immediate change. Having a "Stanford" or a "Harvard" as a continual "member" of the group or department is the strategic commitment or identification, not relationships with particular employees. What matters for hiring is not always history or a stable knowledge base, as their businesses are constantly shifting, but the perceived talent and quality of the people, the educational and class identities that are associated with their employees.

Constantly recruiting from "the best," then, is one of the centerpieces of investment banking identity, which in fact, *goes hand in hand with continual downsizing.* As long as Wall Street maintains its intimate and long-standing connection with elite institutions and their constant supply of recruits, banks are able to freely dispose of particular Ivy League employees because they have rendered secure their institutional identity as a place where Ivy Leaguers work. At the level of the everyday, investment bankers regularly refer to themselves by their schools. Julie Cooper, a vice president of High-Yield Bonds at BT, described this phenomenon:

> I think that there's emphasis on our desk [on] where you went to college. I mean, everyone, we have three people who went to Yale, three people who went to Princeton, one who went to Wharton . . . and I really feel that the reason I got the job was I worked with him [her boss] before and I went to Princeton. And so I had the "prereq" to get through the doors. It's funny, they won't even look at resumes that aren't from a top school. I mean, not to say, like John, one of our bosses, I guess he went to—where did he go—it's a good school, it's in the South or somewhere in Ohio, but anyway, he got his JD/MBA at Harvard. So, it's like even if you didn't go to an Ivy League undergrad, [you] have an Ivy League grad degree.

In my conversations with other informants, they, like Cooper, often identified coworkers by their schools, not their names. A litany such as, "We
have two MITs, three Princetons, two Whartons, and a Harvard guy," is
common. Again, individual employees are not only known and referred to
by their universities but are also seen as more or less interchangeable with
others from their school. With investment banking identities lodged in
pedigrees, not people, as their particular "brand," banks unhesitatingly
downsize.

The Culture of High Risk/High Reward

During my fieldwork, I tried to understand the major issues that perme-
ated the workplaces and work lives of investment bankers. What were
their preoccupations? What did they hold most dear? I learned that collectively, their overwhelming concerns were with money and compensation
via bonuses. For front-office workers, perhaps the single most important
topic of discussion with fellow colleagues (during the hiring process, during orientation, in cubicles, in the lunch room, after work) is compensation. In almost all of my conversations with investment bankers, I asked in
some form the questions, "What are the goals of an investment bank?"
and "Why do most people want to work here?" Every answer, with no
exceptions, named "money" as a motivation for both individuals and
institutions. John Carlton, a managing director at BT in high yield, gave
me his interpretation of standard Wall Street thinking:

> If you look at the various categories in this industry, you can get paid very well,
> much better than you can in other industries. One reason that people are in it
> [investment banking] is to get paid very well. A lot of people would be in
> another industry or do something else if they didn't get paid very well. Unlike
> someone who, for example, is a teacher, a musician, who says, "Well, I love to
> teach. I love to work with the students," or "I love to play my instrument."
> They might continue to do it, even if they do not get paid very well. So, if you
> are looking at a sort of hierarchy of satisfaction, being paid well is one reason
> why people are in the business.

Of course, informants often named other factors (such as the excitement
of making deals, working with "smart people," and living in New York),
but money was usually regarded as the most important. In fact, once you
are hired and the interview process is over, most of your colleagues will

think you are "bullshitting" if you claim that money is not your primary reason for working at an investment bank. Carlton went on to identify compensation practices as key determinants of investment banking culture in general: "I think, in this business, [the drive for money] predominates and that predominates [in] why firms organize the way they do—that's why it's viewed as sort of a risky business, because people are paid well, but also can get fired. You can be at a fairly senior level in the organization and be fired tomorrow. It can happen. I lived through the late 1980s and before that. There are cycles to the business. *The importance of compensation has a lot to do with how the business is organized*." These observations helped me to understand that compensation lies at the core of Wall Street's institutional values. Thus an investigation of the ritual of the bonus is crucial to understanding not only the lives and practices of investment bankers but also the organizational structure and strategies of investment banks and their approach to risk.

I begin with a key cultural quandary: how can investment bankers be arguably the most highly compensated workers in the world when their practices so often generate crisis and economic decline?[3] This contradiction has never been so palpable as is in the wake of the subprime debacle and the federal bailout and subsidy of Wall Street financial institutions. Specifically, the divulging of Wall Street's latest bonus numbers ($18.4 billion in 2008, which investment banks understood to be paltry sum) has awakened a firestorm of fury, partly because of the public's surprise that investment bankers and traders are not, in fact, paid for performance in a way that is substantively linked to economic productivity, growth, or stability (New York State Comptroller 2009). At issue here, I argue, is a fundamental misapprehension of Wall Street's practices of compensation (which speaks to the need for local, fine-grained investigations of seemingly mainstream practices such as compensation) and correspondingly, its culture of risk and reward.

First, "pay for performance" is something of a misnomer, at least according to the popular understanding of "performance." Investment bankers measure performance according to the number of deals executed, regardless of their impact on the corporation or society at large. Even in a recession, transactions such as selling off toxic assets or bankruptcy advice count towards the bonus. The essentializing of banker smartness is again important here: despite their roles in failed deals and financial crisis, the discourse of awarding bonuses to retain talent still has traction. Moreover, during a downturn, banks shed employees precisely to preserve the bonus pool, meaning that those who remain continue to command high compensation. Second, the persistence of bonuses despite Wall Street's instigation of global financial meltdown raises the question of who bears the brunt of high-risk practices. In the next few sections and the following chapter, I demonstrate how investment banks' particular approach to risk involves not so much "managing" it as leveraging and spreading it out, in the hopes of both heightening their rewards and delaying the effects of their risky practices. I now turn to the details of Wall Street compensation practices.

Unlike many salaried corporate jobs, investment bankers are mainly compensated through the year-end bonus. The "bonus season" on Wall Street begins after Labor Day, when investment bankers begin to gear up for the "campaign," that is, to advertise, claim, and take credit for every possible transaction in order to boost their bonus number. In November banks announce initial bonus expectations, revealing whether it will be an amazing or a devastating year in relation to previous years, or somewhere in between. The actual bonuses are then paid out in January or February. On the day when investment bankers finally "get their number," all work stops: bankers huddle in small groups trying to guess each other's number, to figure out whether they should go out and buy a Lamborghini or look for a new job. I remember distinctly that during my conversation at a Wall Street café with Will Howard, an associate investment banker of high-yield at Merrill Lynch, he stopped our interview multiple times to observe passersby "who just got their number." He explained that these people were second year associates, and the first year associates were all eager to know what the second years' numbers were because that "kind of sets the bar for next year"—that is, first-years will get some idea of what they might get paid their second year. It was a tough year, though, and he conjectured from their hushed tones and deflated demeanors that they were not pleased. From Labor Day until the end of January, bankers spend countless hours discussing how much they got paid last year, what the percentage markup for bonuses will be for this year, which banks have released "their numbers" ("Have you heard about Goldman's numbers yet?"), and what their own payouts will be. Bankers do not conceive of bonuses as a supplement to their salary, but rather as the substance of their pay.

When I talked to Jacob Carnoy, a financial journalist who used to work as a trader at Datek Securities, he observed that many of his former roommates from Princeton worked on Wall Street in the late 1980s and always defined their identities in terms of their pay:

At the end of the year that's how you tell who's doing the best job—who's made the most money for the firm. And that's also, then, how much money you will make in your bonus. And so when it's all judged on that, you get a skewed version of what life is like because then you judge everybody on how much money they make. And it's not even your fault because that's how you are judged at work every day. So a lot of it is just that you are a product of your environment. So then out in the real world [where] people aren't making that much money, then they don't really matter. They don't really count, so you can treat the guy who gives you coffee as a lesser citizen.

Christine Chang, a high-yield vice president at BT, mentioned that she had left her previous bank, Montgomery Securities, because she was not being fairly compensated, whereupon I asked if compensation was a "big" issue on Wall Street.

CC: Yes. It's the biggest personnel issue on Wall Street—compensation. Compensation is a huge issue, essentially what everybody is here for.

KH: What kind of work environment does that create?

CC: I guess, in the worst-case scenario, it breeds an environment where you may be working on a team for one project, but when it comes to compensation, everybody is trying to shove each other out of the way, saying, "I did the most. I spent the most hours. I did the most work. I made the biggest contribution." So there is a lot of that. There is always the issue of this person made that much money, and I did just as much, so I should be making that much money, too. It is everybody wanting to be paid as much, if not more, than everyone else. That is a very big deal. Most people on Wall Street realize that they are already hugely overcompensated relative to the rest of the population, but when it comes to actually getting their bonus, what matters to them is the fact that somebody else has made this much money and whether you "deserve" it or not, you want that much, too.

KH: Do you know, in general, what other people are making? Isn't that confidential?

CC: Yes, it is confidential, but people hear about it through rumor and folklore and also through headhunters.

KH: So, I guess news spreads because—

CC: Yes, all of a sudden somebody starts looking at you funny. It is supposed to be confidential, and I doubt that anybody ever comes straight out and says, "I made 'x' this year." But people always have this vague sort of notion.

In such a hierarchical context as investment banks, there is much contestation over the definition of performance—who contributed the most, and
what counts as contribution. Senior managing directors will say that after
hearing everyone's story of contribution to the bottom line, it always adds
up to much more than 100 percent. Top executives spend hours each day
during the end of the year "huddled in boardrooms or trapped on endless
conference calls, sparring among themselves to determine how big the
bonus pool will be, how it will be divided among the divisions and, then,
what each employee will receive" (Anderson and Thomas 2004). Such a
compensation scheme, where workers struggle for recognition and "de-
servedness" creates an environment of competitive, even sabotaging, individualism that often cuts along the cleavages of race, gender, and class.

In one of my many discussions with Anthony Johnson, an associate in
M&A at J. P. Morgan, I finally worked up the courage to ask him for an outline of Wall Street compensation scales, so I could contextualize the astronomical numbers that many of my informants threw around. Though the
numbers are now dated, he spoke freely of the "market values on the
Street," as they stood in 1999:

AJ: Well, it's different for each year. So for a first-year analyst to a third-year
analyst, you have the lowest base salary—and it's different also for different firms—so if you work for a big-name firm like Goldman or Morgan
Stanley or J. P. Morgan, the numbers are going to be smaller than if you
work at a DLJ or Lehman.[4] But a first-year analyst coming in will have a
salary of like $45,000, and then the bonus range for a first-year analyst
would be somewhere between $15,000 [and] $35,000. So altogether they
will make somewhere between $60,000 and $80,000. And for a first-year
associate the base salary would probably be around $80,000 to $85,000,
and then the bonus would be $50,000 to $75,000 or somewhere in there.
And for VPs [vice presidents] and MDs [managing directors], it really kind
of depends on how much money you bring in.

KH: And the bonus probably increases more than the salary as you progress.

AJ: Right. When I started at $40,000, and my second year I got a $5,000
raise, so I was at $45,000. And this year I got a $10,000 raise. On the
other hand, my bonus basically more than doubled from my first year.
And next year, you know, my bonus will be the *majority* of my compensation. . . . And as you get more senior, your bonus is some type of multiple
of what your salary is.

Three years at J. P. Morgan and Anthony Johnson, only twenty-four years
old in 1999, had a base salary of $55,000 and a bonus over $70,000. Two

years before, at twenty-two and straight out of college, Johnson made around $75,000, and for the year 2000, at twenty-five, he estimates making close to $200,000. He started as an analyst and was promoted in this third year to associate.

During the recent bull market (2003–7), investment banking associates out of business school made a salary of approximately $110,000, yet his or her bonus ranged from the base salary to double the amount: the total compensation could be $220,000 on the low end to $330,000 on the high end. (Of course, this range is influenced by a whole host of factors from race, gender, and class, to pedigree and networking skills, which in turn frame who gets positioned into the high-profile deals in the first place.) Moving up the hierarchy, most first-year vice presidents started in the $200,000 range, a salary that was usually *less than* their bonus. One of my informants, Raina Bennett, a young second-year analyst, went with her vice president to deposit their bonus checks in 1998, a "down year." As Bennett laughingly tells it, she "inadvertently" glanced at the ATM screen and couldn't help but see that the bonus check looked like $160,000 after tax. She wondered if the ATM would accept such a big deposit! Many other younger informants tell me that their vice presidents often whisper about paying six-figure bonus taxes. In 2000, a high-paying year on Wall Street, the *New York Times* reported that many investment banking vice presidents and senior vice presidents made over a million dollars. Managing directors often received multimillion-dollar bonuses, though a majority of these amounts might be in company stock versus cash. While they have salary "capped" at around $250,000, their bonuses ranged from $1 million on the low end to as high as $10 million. In 2000, the average managing director salary was $240,000 with a bonus of $4 million, a 33 percent increase from 1999 (McGeehan 2000). The *Wall Street Journal* often reports the compensation of star dealmakers and CEOs. In 2003, Merrill Lynch CEO Stanley O'Neal's salary was $500,000, but his bonus amounted to $13.5 million, and he received $11.2 million in "restricted stock." His Goldman Sachs counterpart, Lloyd S. Blankfein, took home a salary of "only" $600,000, but his total compensation was $20.1 million (Anderson and Thomas 2004). In 2006, Blankfein broke the Wall Street bonus record with a $53.4 million bonus, of which $24.7 million was in cash and the rest in stocks and stock options. The record he broke had been set only the week before by John Mack, CEO of Morgan Stanley, with his $40 million bonus (Tong 2006). Such compensation schemes, outrageous compared to most industries, are stratospheric even by Wall Street's historical standards. In 1986, the average bonus for a Wall Street investment banker was

$13,950; in 2006, the average was over $190,000 (Fox 2006, 31; New York State Comptroller 2009)!⁵ A compelling illustration from the 11 December 2006 *New York Post*, titled "Ka-ching!," shows third-year associates, "brash rookies" from the "class of '03," raking in bonuses (not including salaries) that range from "$325K" on the low-end to "$525K" on the high-end, vice presidents from the "class of '00" making "$500K" on the low-end and "$925K" on the high-end, and directors from the "class of '98" with "$600K" on the low-end and "$1.3M" on the high-end (*New York Post* 2006). Investment bankers seemed to have solidified their status as masters of the universe. When estimates of 2006 bonuses leaked, wine stores in Manhattan began to advertise $15,000 bottles of champagne, and car dealerships prepared for BMWs to be driven straight "out of the showroom" (Goldman 2006). Although these bonuses were most likely the highest Wall Street will see for the near-term, they certainly point to extraordinary compensation beyond the imaginings of most workers in the United States. (Of course, bonuses vary according to department and rank: whereas telecom bankers received huge windfall bonuses throughout the late 1990s, their bonuses plunged after the dot-com crash; the same goes for mortgage bankers during the subprime bust). Interestingly enough, the exponentially increasing size of these bonuses since the 1980s (and in particular from 2004 until 2007) can be used as an approximate predictor of crisis; as I explain later, these kinds of stratospheric bonus numbers indicate the frenzy of deal-making that created the bubble in the first place, thus foreshadowing the impending crash.

Bonuses also structure investment bankers' lifestyles and understand of their worth. Anthony Johnson told me the story of his first-year bonus experience to explain why it is important for Wall Streeters not only to compare their bonuses within the firm, but also to judge them against what other investment banks on the Street are paying.

> KH: So how do you know what the Street is paying? Is that just common knowledge?
>
> AJ: In this kind of league there are different types of ways to figure it out. Most people will tell you. Like for analysts, for example, when you sit down with your manager, they will say, we had three buckets in your class. There was a 55, and a 35, and a 25, and you were in the 35. And here were the reasons you were in the 35. And then the person says—well, how many people were in the 55? They try to figure how many people are below me, how many are with me, and how many people did I do better than. And that's how you kind of assess where you are internally. And

then you have the question—like how does this stack up to what's across the Street? You will get that information from the headhunters who are calling and trying to find out. You tell them your numbers, and they'll tell you all the numbers they know. But most people have friends that work at all the different firms, and people kind of share the data. It's important to know—you should always know what your market value is and whether you are getting overpaid or underpaid.

For Wall Streeters, these kinds of money measurements help them gauge how their firm views their performance. Comparing their bonuses with those of their colleagues in other firms gives them incentive, as well as leverage, to leave their own firm if bonuses are not comparable. When I asked Anthony Johnson how his pay affected his lifestyle, he replied:

Your focus shifts from being more kind of balanced to business—from education, family, community, and other things more to business. The shift is more toward business than other things. And then the environment caters to you—like if you do well on Wall Street, then Wall Street does well by you. It pays you more, you have more resources at your disposal, you are able to have more luxuries and benefits in your life than you probably would have in another area. If you think about it, this banker was teasing me the other day because we were at a meeting and he was like you are twenty-four years old and you make over $100,000 a year. That is more money than 95 percent of the people, and it's definitely more money than your parents. It's probably more money than you really know what to do with. Do you know what I mean? All of that, it does change you.

A twenty-four year old making over $100,000 a year was standard practice on Wall Street front offices in the 1990s. With an MBA, most Wall Street associates, usually in their late twenties, would be making in the $200,000–$300,000 range by their second year. This compensation creates such hype around striking it rich that most Wall Streeters stick with jobs and lifestyles that they often do not enjoy. As Jacob Carnoy observes, a few of his friends who graduated from Princeton in 1989 and managed to stay employed on Wall Street are now making windfalls. He describes one friend who "freaked out" when Goldman Sachs decided not to go public in 1998, meaning that he could not cash out his stock options:

The only way he was affected recently [by the current downturn] was when Goldman was going to go public, and he was going to get a monster windfall, and so then he started spending money and bought this house out in East Hampton. And then Goldman didn't go public, so he didn't get the windfall, but then he was made partner, so he will be fine. But he was actually crying poor at that time! I mean here is a partner at Goldman who makes millions a year who is crying poor because he didn't make 30 million or 60 million or 100 million.

Ann Harris, an investment banking associate at Morgan Stanley, is fairly new to the lifestyle that the bonus compensation structure helps to create. Having grown up in a working-class Irish-American household, Harris often commented to me how disconcerting it was to be making so much more money than her parents ever made. I asked her about how bonuses affected Wall Street bankers' lifestyles, especially when the majority of one's compensation is paid on one day.

KH: I always hear stories about how so and so got paid this much, and they totally elevated their lifestyle beyond their means. And the next year they didn't get a bonus as high as the previous year, and now they just don't know what to do. Do people kind of get seduced by the pay and then feel that they don't have any money because they have elevated their lifestyle to such an extent?

AH: I think that there is. It's really easy to see bonuses—and this is something that even one of my managers has told me at one point—*you'll soon get to see your bonus as part of your salary*. And I don't like thinking like that. I like to think of no bonus, and then if I get something it's like, "Ooohh." Because I think when you start planning your expenses and living a lifestyle based on the expectation, when things go badly, it's such a backfire. I think there are people who are seduced by the money. I mean you hear about people who win the lottery and buy two-million-dollar homes and can't pay the property taxes on it after they get the money. Then they have to sell the house three years later. . . . Part of being in that elite club is having the things to show for it. I think people do stretch . . . and many times, if you get a bonus, you'll get $60,000 up front WHAM on one day. People go out and buy a car. People go out and buy all these things. I totally understand it because it is intoxicating. It is intoxicating to suddenly see five figures or six figures suddenly posted in your bank account all at once. It does go to your head. It does make you think, "Oh my God, I can do this. Oh my God I did it. I could fly to Paris. I could get another car. I could take a ski trip in Aspen." And you don't necessarily think, if I really work this out, it is $6,000 a month. . . . You just see five to six figures in your account and then your mind starts to go, "Oh my God, oh my God, this much money." And I think you could get swept away by it.

The consequences of such a compensation strategy on bankers' lives became more apparent in my conversation with John Carlton, who described some of the personal bankruptcies that he witnessed among Wall Street bankers in the 1980s in the context of the stock-market crash of 1987, hyperconsumption, compensation volatility, and job insecurity on Wall Street:

> I know people who literally went bankrupt as a result [of] the overextension in the 1980s. They had a house in Connecticut, a house in Martha's Vineyard, you know, each one leveraged fully. They were not living off their salaries, but *living off the bonus*. Bonus gets cut, they lose their job. The value of their property goes down. I could never imagine property going down in Connecticut, but it [went] flat down, even New York City. Because they maybe bought at the top of the market with an 80 percent mortgage, so suddenly, they are out of a job—so you have difficult problems.

During my fieldwork, I heard countless stories of bankers and traders in investment banks who lived beyond their means, who were on the verge of a nervous breakdown, who "confused" their bonus with their salary; in other words, who spent money as if they were making $300,000, not $90,000, or making $1 million instead of $250,000. Malinda Fan, senior vice president at Lehman Brothers, relayed her own surprise that highly compensated senior colleagues "did not know better" during booms and thus started "going crazy" during downturns, not because they weren't used to the rampant downsizings, but because they were so highly "leveraged" (that is, paying three mortgages with the assumption of constantly rising bonuses and housing prices) that they knew they would have to "sell everything" if their bonus became nil. Maggie Craddock, "a former portfolio manager who now works as an executive coach at some of the top investment banks," argues that bonuses creates "paper millionaires," or what she calls "poor rich people." As an example, she dissected the compensation of a vice president investment banker who made $1 million in a good year. Out of that $1 million, $170,000 is probably salary with the rest of the $830,000 "bonus" divided between stocks and cash bonuses. In a down year, his bonus might be cut 40 percent, with a corresponding restriction on the cashing of stock options; as such, the $1 million dollar VP might "only" receive $200,000 in cash if 60 percent is in stock (Kolker 2003).

But the bonus system does not simply add conspicuous consumption, volatility, and insecurity to investment bankers' lifestyles. It is integrally indicative of how investment banks view their employees, and just as importantly, how they structure their own business and that of corporate America. From an investment bank's point of view, paying the majority of bankers' compensation via their bonuses means that when times are good (which is of course often de-linked from how the larger economy is going), bankers are usually very well paid, yet during off-years, the firm has no commitment to pay everyone bonuses. The bank's bottom line, so to speak, is thus cushioned during leaner times although precisely because bonuses are a core Wall Street value and investment banks have few expenses aside from compensation, totally eliminating bonuses for still-employed bankers would be all but unthinkable. The subtext, then, of "pay for performance" is not simply paying those who "perform," but also paying mainly when the bank is doing well. Such a strategy is similar to outsourcing compensation to the stock market; it works with rampant downsizing to institute payroll flexibility in the employer's favor. The bonus structure, in helping to construct a very high-paying and competitive work environment, creates as well as masks an environment of extreme volatility, insecurity, and lack of commitment.

For example, in 2003, almost three years after the stock market crash, not only had "one out of every ten employees in the securities industry . . . been relieved of responsibility since April 2001," but "for those who have dodged" layoffs, there was a "withering away of Wall Street bonuses." As Robert Kolker (2003) described in an article on "down and out" investment bankers on Wall Street, "In 2000, the financial-services bonus pool was $19.4 billion; last year, it was $7.9 billion. The average bonus dropped from $104,600 to $48,500. Wall Street hasn't seen a two-consecutive-year decrease in bonuses since the eighties. 'What I keep hearing now is base pay of $80,000, and the bonus is eat-what-you-kill,' whispered one once-and-future investment banker at a networking session for unemployed executives in midtown. 'If you don't close a deal, you don't get a bonus'." Kolker interviewed one investment banker who commented that since one only gets paid once a year, if a banker gets fired right before his bonus is paid, it can be devastating. The banker who faced this situation, in addition to feeling anger and betrayal, stated, "It gave me very good perspective on the lack of loyalty and security on Wall Street. I cancelled countless vacations, was on planes for bullshit two-hour meetings on the West Coast. And at the end of the day, there's no consideration" (Kolker 2003).

Investment bankers, however, are not without agency, especially when they are in high demand. Given their high pedigrees and financial training in business schools, many bankers, especially senior ones, have made multiple connections throughout the investment banking world (as well as corporate America) and thus have considerable clout and reputation to draw on when necessary. They can use their connections, their deal-making history, and their clientele to move from one investment bank to another, garnering large salaries and even larger bonuses for themselves and their team. As Raina Bennett, an analyst at Lehman Brothers, explained: "It's very easy, especially for a senior person, to move from company A to company B, which will give them a two-year guaranteed salary and bonus. And once that two years is over, if they don't like the company they're working for or they don't see eye-to-eye on the strategy, don't like the individuals, they can probably move again." In 2000, "with the stock market bulling ahead and multibillion-dollar mergers occurring at a breakneck pace, firms waged a war for talent that sent wages spiraling. To compete, they locked in deal makers with multiyear, multimillion-dollar packages that defied the Wall Street tradition of minimizing fixed costs. As the 1990s boomed on, two-by-fours (two years at $4 million a year) became three-by-fives" (McGeehan 2000). In 2001 and 2002, when bonuses were cut 50 percent, most bankers claimed that they were just happy to have a job. By 2003, high-flying bonuses were coming back, demonstrating that bonuses are not necessarily tied to the investment performance of the stock market, nor the economic recovery of corporate America, but rather to "deal flow," the number and kinds of transactions regardless of whether or not they are "productive."

Across the board, not only for senior bankers—given the norm of job insecurity on Wall Street—investment bankers are well known simply to quit their jobs and move from bank to bank in search of higher bonuses. Julio Muñoz, an associate at DLJ, described Wall Street job-hopping as motivated by a combination of job insecurity and bonus-hunting:

> KH: I know especially that investment banks are good at finding ways to make profits, and they are also good at eliminating people who don't . . .
>
> JM: In a second. They will do it in a second in all areas. That's also another thing about your job security in investment banks—it's very low. I mean they will fire you in a second, whereas in a company it is a little more difficult. The whole incentive structure based on bonuses at the end of the year is also . . .
>
> KH: It gets people to hop whenever they . . .
>
> JM: Yes, a lot of turnover.

Muñoz explained that low bonuses are obvious signs that one's job is in danger, and if you don't want to fall victim to the next round of cuts, you should begin looking for a new job. Thus, the bonus is in multiple ways an incentive to job-hop. Raina Bennett observed that in addition to frequent, periodic layoff cycles, investment banks also have high employee turnover that correlates with the bonus cycle. Just as investment banks often use the bonus cycle as a way to shed workers, investment bankers often leave for another firm immediately after their bonuses are paid.

KH: Would you say that job insecurity is high on Wall Street?

RB: Very.

KH: Why is it so high?

RB: Let me think about this. Well, first of all, it's like you're there for a given purpose, and it's to make money, right, and . . . there's no sense of loyalty from firm to individual or individual to firm. By its very nature, it's very transient. . . . People aren't scared of moving or being fired because you know you can get a job somewhere else, especially in this environment.

KH: So what has the transition been like in your work environment? Is the turnover just continual?

RB: Definitely. I've been in my current position for two years, and there's definitely a cycle, and what the cycle is—and I think it's probably this way for most investment banks right now—is that, especially in sales and trading, bonuses are announced in probably like December or January, and you receive your bonus at the beginning of February, and then every-one starts switching around if they're unhappy with their bonus or in general if they've been unhappy with the group they were in the past year. And there's so much demand right now for talent.

Anthony Johnson described how J. P. Morgan made a strategic mistake in 1998 by assuming that they could get away with paying their younger bank-ers less money. As a result, J. P. Morgan lost many experienced associates.

Last year we had a whole bunch of people who left—I mean a lot of very experi-enced associates—because Morgan's numbers were below the Street numbers in terms of what the top people were getting paid. Even though they were people who were born and raised in Morgan's culture. . . . There were people who left J. P. Morgan, where you had to be an associate for three years [before making vice president], to [go] places where you had to be an associate for four years, purely because the people who had the four-year program were paying more. The title is kind of the stepping-stone format, but it's mostly driven by money. People don't care whether they have an office or whether they have a cube, whether they have an assistant or whether they don't have an assistant. All they care about is whether they're getting paid what their Street value is. And if you are able to do that, you can keep the person who is working there happy. If you don't, they will leave.

Job insecurity, then, at investment banks is not one-sided since investment bankers take advantage of volatile markets to search for the bigger bonus. As Paula Wiley, an associate at J. P. Morgan Chase, observed,
whereas workers in most industries might need to traverse great distances
to "jump around to increase your salary," investment bankers, with countless financial institutions in New York City, "can make more money just by
moving" across the street. Bonus-hopping often leaves other members of
a banker's cohort with more work. As Joseph Tsai, an investment banking
associate at DLJ, bemoaned when I asked him how Wall Street has affected him personally: "Wall Street . . . has opened up my eyes. There are
people out there who don't care about anything else but money and getting ahead. And you know, it sounds like a stereotype, but it's not. It's
really like that. Many times I have heard my coworkers say, 'As long as I get
the bonus that I want, I'll stay. Otherwise, I don't care. I will just leave.'
Always everyone is looking out for himself. I think this has made me grow
and realize that not everything is fair."

   Moreover, not surprisingly, Wall Street investment banks' bonus system is dominantly understood as strictly "paying for performance," a meritocratic system that compensates for hard work and transactions completed, not connections, pedigree, or the distinctions of race, gender, and
class. The fact that bonuses are completely discretionary, unregulated, and
based almost entirely on the whims of senior managing directors is understood as stripping away unnecessary, top-down bureaucratic rules and
"traditional" corporate hierarchies that privilege the entrenched and the
established. I would argue, however, that it is precisely the lack of regulation which allows multiple kinds of transgressions to occur. Studying
gender differences in compensation on Wall Street in 1997, sociologist
Louise Marie Roth—countering the notion that, once one controls for sex
segregation in the workplace and human capital characteristics such as
education, discrimination is a minor factor in gendered earnings asymmetry—argues that the organizational structure of major Wall Street investment banks perpetuates gender discrimination even after all other
factors are "controlled for." In order to control for "human capital, organizational prestige, and market conditions," Roth researched forty-four
women and twenty-nine men (both mainly white) with recent MBAs from
elite programs and similar associate-level jobs at major Wall Street investment banks. She found that not only did "statistically significant"
internal sex segregation occur in the securities industry, but that even in
the "same financial function" with similar job titles, women earned less.[6]
Roth reports:

With respect to compensation, women in the sample earned 60.5% as much as their male peers from graduate business school. That figure compares unfavorably with the earnings inequality ratio for the labor force as a whole, calculated at approximately 75% for the same year (U.S. Bureau of the Census 1998). . . . The gender *difference* in average compensation among financial professionals was an astounding $223,368. . . . [R]ecent cohorts of men and women on Wall Street experience inequality in compensation, independent of human capital and background characteristics and independent of segregation by area, rank, or organization. (Roth 2003, 790, 794)

Comparing her results to a study done on a recent cohort of engineers where there were no significant gender differences in earnings among recent professionals after the equalization of background and sex segregation, Roth argues that gender inequalities in investment banking are starker than those of even the most male-dominated fields because of Wall Street's focus on "client relationships" with mainly white male corporate executives and because of the unique "institutional context" of finance, which attempts to "reward employees on the basis of their performance" (Roth 2003, 785).[7]

Given that for Wall Street's most elite workers, the yearly salary is only a minor part of the total compensation package, the crucial determinant of pay is the variable, year end bonus, determined by participation in profitable, high-profile transactions. As such, this system leaves one's compensation up to "managerial discretion," and in this flexible, unstructured space, as some of my informants recounted, racialized and gendered networks strongly affect who is requested for particular deals, who is perceived as "getting along" with the client, who is automatically seen to be "smart" and "capable," and so on. As Roth points out: "These compensation practices permit differences in total compensation for employees *in the same job* and also allow for much managerial discretion over interemployee differences within each work group. In personal interviews, female securities professionals often claimed that managerial discretion produced gender-biased compensation outcomes" (Roth 2003, 786). Bureaucracy, in this sense, can create a more formalized evaluative process where issues of seniority and job level counter and protect socially disadvantaged bankers from the sorts of privatized deliberation and discretion that privilege white male networks and labor.[8]

The Rationalization of Job Insecurity
through Compensation

Despite their concerns over job insecurity, every Wall Streeter I talked to accepted the notion that working on Wall Street constitutes the more or less "equal exchange" of risk for money. For most of my informants, compensation was integral to how they viewed and experienced job insecurity. For example, Ahmer Gupta, a vice president in trading at Salomon Smith Barney, in speaking about job insecurity as a trader, brought up the issue of compensation. Being on the trading floor, Gupta had perhaps an even more visceral experience of insecurity than many bankers since instead of focusing on transacting deals for corporate America, traders must respond to the constant flux of changes in market prices. He clarified for me the contradiction of job insecurity in times of both boom and bust:

> There are two levels of job insecurity. One is that it is a very competitive, aggressive business, and even when times are going well you are expected to produce. There are constantly younger people coming into the business who are hungry and eager and want to work hard. So there's a little bit of that, but I don't worry about that too much because I think of myself as a hard-working, motivated employee who is just as good as the next guy. There is another level of job instability, especially in my area, where you trade. You can hit a rough patch and just be having a tough time. And when you are losing money for a period of time, then you start to question your confidence and you wonder what other people are thinking about you . . . if you are vulnerable. Then the third level is when the industry goes into a down cycle, which we went through the last several months. Even though the stock market is booming, the bond market has been decimated, and people have lost their jobs. I've had a lot of friends lose their jobs. But the way I look at it is that people in this industry make a lot of money—a ton of money. I do feel that people are compensated for the job insecurity, but it is still unpleasant to deal with.

Gupta reflected that many of his friends lost their jobs, but believed that there was, in the end, an equal exchange between compensation and job insecurity. Because Wall Street front-office workers get paid so much, they do not conceive of themselves as victims, for they have relinquished their complaining rights by accepting their hefty paychecks.

Peter Lucas and I used to work together at BT. Since being downsized in 1997, he has worked for two other investment banks in the span of two years. After a stint with Merrill Lynch (where he went following two more department changes at BT), he is now an investment banking research analyst at Dresdner Bank, based in Germany. We discussed not only the differences between U.S. investment banks and those of Europe (although many have merged with each other), but also the issue of job insecurity in U.S. investment banks in general:

KH: So you were saying American investment banks fire people when things aren't going well. What are the effects on job security due to this restructuring? Do you think that it is definitely part of the culture of U.S. investment banks?

PL: Yes. I think it is part of the culture. It is the nature of the beast. There are a few places that would tend not to do it. I mean, Goldman would probably not—no, that's not true, Goldman laid off a big percentage of its workers right after the '87 crash because they did a huge build up and then the market crashed and they had to lay off. So, every American bank has done it. J. P. Morgan has just laid off another 5 percent. So, within the American banks, absolutely it is part of the culture. It is also the American thing in Europe. But, it is definitely much worse in banking. It is basically, "Here's your money. Thanks. Goodbye." *It's a financial relationship*. If you are not worth more to me *today* than what I am paying you, then I won't pay you. That is the equation. And, I think people know that going in. They really don't have a problem with it, because if they did, they obviously shouldn't be there in the first place. If you get laid off, you tend to get a decent package. I mean, you are basically, you get paid—not only in a severance package but also in a bonus you get while you are working—for that risk. You know, *one reason you get paid so much is because you may lose your job tomorrow.*

How investment bankers view endemic instability and restructuring must be understood in the context of their own environment. Layoffs and job insecurity, according to Lucas, are integral to the fabric of investment banks. The very premise of accepting a job at an investment bank is the understanding that you are "rewarded" for the risk of taking on a job that is not a career, but rather a "financial relationship," where you must be worth more today than what you are being paid today. Stan Clark, another codownsized colleague of mine who had joined Merrill Lynch as a portfolio manager, echoed many of Lucas's observations. Though satisfied with his current job, Clark described Wall Street's approach to downsizing quite frankly:

Wall Street firms . . . could care less about their employees. Easy come, easy go. When times are good, times are great. They hire lots of people who get paid a lot of money. You get big bonus checks. When times are bad, you are gone. They don't care. So, it is a high risk. When things are great, you are going to do well, you get paid well. When things are bad, you have no job. I think that is just a function of the way these companies make money: if things are good, if the economy is strong, they are doing a lot of investment banking deals. The stock market is doing great. People are putting money into the market, so they are making money. Likewise, when everything goes down, they are not making money so they cannot afford to pay the people.

Despite Clark's problematic conflation of downsizings with economic downturns, he spoke with the understanding and the expectation that downsizings will and should happen. It is through job insecurity, the fungibility of employees, that investment banks make money, that is, "I think that is just a function of *the way these companies make money*: if things are good, if the economy is strong, they are doing a lot of investment banking deals." In other words, because investment banking profits can be highly volatile, the risk of these Wall Street businesses is, to an extent, shouldered by highly paid Wall Street workers, who do not complain because they have entered into a contract of high risk and high reward.

Almost all of my informants not only articulated that "no one should be surprised" about their insecurity, but also that high risk is precisely how their jobs *should* be structured. They enter into a "risk-reward" bargain they fully accept, and it is through this experience that investment bankers learn "who is flexible and who can accept change." (It is important to note that what is understood to be at risk is mainly their own jobs, not the systemic risk they inflict on the financial markets.) I thus began to realize that as a result of their highly empowered status, network, and compensation, investment bankers' experiences and the effects of their downsizing diverge from that of most workers. Moreover, Wall Street's compensation strategies allow for flexible employment, an approach to compensation that allows investment banks to immediately hire workers and build departments after large-scale layoffs and continual purges *and* to produce a "strategy of no strategy."

The "Strategy of No Strategy"

Given that the identities of investment banks are wrapped up in their ability to immediately induce change in their people via job insecurity and flexible compensation, it is not surprising that one of their primary strategies—their plans for the future based on their imaginings of "the world and the firm's position in it"—is, simply, to have no long-term plans (Schoenberger 1997, 122). To actualize their central identity as being immediately responsive to their own changing relationships with the market (including employees, products, and so on), their strategy is, in a sense, to have *no strategy*. Ironically, having no long-term strategy is contradictory and potentially self-defeating in that investment banks often find themselves making drastic changes only to realize months or weeks later that those changes were unnecessary, premature, and extremely costly. For example, in chapter 5, I described how investment bankers, in part because of their access to "sensitive, proprietary information," are not only fired in an instant, but must also leave the physical premises of the building within fifteen to thirty minutes. Given how crucial the control of knowledge and the protection of inside information are for Wall Street investment banks, it seems self-defeating that they do not place any premium on loyalty. Despite the fact that firms try above all to enforce secrecy, they accept and maintain this volatility and revolving-door policy.

At first glance, it seems not only improbable, but also "irrational" for investment banks to engage in such practices, for why would a business so focused on profitability and knowledge not engage in practices that always improve its bottom line and its control of information? As many anthropologists have demonstrated, capitalist organizations are not simply motivated by purely instrumentalist quests for profit or governed by perfect rational actors; they are sociocultural organizations with complex, contradictory worldviews and particular organizational practices (Yanagisako 1999, 2002). Profits may be claimed as one of investment banks' primary ideals, but it is mediated, situated, and enacted—along with other values—through the social and cultural lenses of particular organizations, groups, and bankers. How profits are made, what constitute profits, and what amounts are considered "profitable" enough are also culturally, organizationally, and historically variable.

John Carlton, the seasoned investment banker and managing director from BT, described how Wall Street's strategy is to operate without a long-term strategy:

Again, it is a business where there is no tenure. There is no union protection. Basically, if things change, you could be out. That's one reason why people are very flexible. So you need flexible people, and people who can deal with it every day. Some people would hate that. I don't mind that. Some people can't stand it. They can't last. They say, "I like to know where I am going to be five years from now." They like the idea of stability. It is not very stable. I think that is a characteristic. Probably most people you talk to would say that it is not a very stable environment. Most businesses have five-year plans—What are we going to be producing?—and have long product life cycles. [We] have very short product life cycles. How do you plan when you never know what the market is going to do?

Although Carlton attributed the rationale for not having a plan to market unpredictability, my point is that not having a plan is central to the strategy and cultural identity of investment banks. Louis Walter, who is not an investment banker but a facilities vice president at Salomon Smith Barney, ruminated about Wall Street's short-term orientation in the excerpt below:

> All of the Wall Street firms grow at the same time, and they all shrink at the same time. *They do it, really, without a plan so that they are chasing the same people at the same time* [during the rehiring process]. They are usually creating economic depression simultaneously when they all lay off thousands of people. They drive up real estate, and they drive down real estate. After a crash, real estate falls shortly thereafter. Offices are empty, and they lay that way, and a return cycle comes on, and they are all going after the same space, and the price goes up again.

Julie Cooper also argued that many Wall Street bankers not only recognized this short-term strategy but also labeled it as "inefficient." In the conversation below, Cooper had just explained how investment banks make corporate America more efficient by demanding that corporations cut costs to maintain high stock prices and access cheaper capital. However, when I inquired if she understood investment banks themselves to be efficient, her reply surprised me:

KH: Do you think Wall Street itself is efficient?

JC: No, not at all. We have horrible systems. I think that Wall Street is efficient in the sense that it wrings the most that it can out of its people. But I think that given the fact that Wall Street is so dynamic, there [aren't] necessarily a lot of rewards for efficiency. Things grow so quickly before the infrastructure can be put into place to support them. And Wall Street is about making money, and the idea is to be able to charge more for your fees than it costs you to create the product. I think that people tend to just get out of products that they're not efficient in rather than saying how can I be more efficient.

Cooper's insights were not so much a critique of Wall Street's inefficiency as an assertion that the core of investment banking culture and strategy is one of "inefficiency": the point is to be dynamic, to simply get out of products instead of improve them, to grow without planning the proper support infrastructure, to make money immediately. This strategy, despite the fact that it might boomerang after all the waste and mistakes are factored in, is certainly profitable in the short-term. They cannot achieve continual dynamism if they build longer-term businesses, if they strive for efficiency, rationality, or consistency. Instead, they focus their "efficiency" on "wringing the most that they can out of their people" via compensation schemes and the motivation of job loss (and since their people are also short-term, much can be wrung), coupled with a strategic approach that sacrifices "traditional" efficiency for immediate rewards and the next new thing.

In the previous chapter, I described how the emerging markets financial crises of 1998 became a stage for brutal and wholesale downsizings, as well as a convenient time for investment banks to "clean house." Not surprisingly, these immediate and aggressive restructurings often turned out to be premature and are highly indicative of "the strategy of no strategy." Here, I draw from a conversation with Kevin Hwa in September 1998, right after the Russian financial crises. In 1997, he was a currency trader at Caspian Securities, a small Hong Kong firm that traded mostly Asian stocks, and witnessed firsthand how many investment banks reacted during the crisis, especially in terms of employment:

HWA: The first round [of layoffs] was back in February when people announced a slew of cuts and a lot of people, a lot of companies were shut down in Asia, and Caspian Securities was supposed to be one. . . . [T]he minute I joined Caspian, people said it was going down, like going bust. And I said, "Well thanks." And then when I got there, people were like, "Isn't Caspian out of business?" I said, "No, we actually did it right." But it was so funny because through the whole time that I was there, people thought we were out of business, because we were sticking it out. Meanwhile, all of the big firms closed down their Asian operations.

KH: Well, what happened to all of those people? Did they just come back to the United States? Or did they switch industries?

HWA: Some went to other firms that were expanding, and some switched industries, meaning they could have switched out of the financial industry altogether, or they could have gone and done other products like European products or Latin American products rather than Asia. So, the first round of cuts were back in January, February [1998]. A few thousand people got cut. Second round was right about May, June, July. That's when we closed down, as well, and then a few other firms, and so that's another few thousand people. And now [September], this is the third round of cuts. And just this third round Merrill Lynch just announced they are cutting 300 people just in Asia. Nikko Securities and SBC Warburg combined are cutting another 100, 150. And then you have a few other firms . . . just announced that they are closing down all of the Asian operations, another 300 people . . . ING Barings, they are paring down as well. And then Travelers Citicorp just announced that they are going to cut 8,000 people throughout the whole organization. So, if you add all of those people—that's a lot of people! That's like 20,000 to 25,000 people if you add it all up. So, right now is a horrendous time. . . . And, you know it happens every three or four or five years—some other debacle happens, and then people come out of it and things get regenerated.

Hwa's acquaintances assumed that Caspian's only option was to shut down entirely. That they found Caspian's "sticking it out" incredible exemplifies Wall Street's approach to strategy and employment. Investment banks do not "stick it out." As their normative strategy is no strategy, the point is to quickly get out and move on to a new project. Because investment banks have no commitment to workers or even certain businesses, they can freely interpret resources not being used today (or businesses that are losing money) as missed opportunities that can be sought elsewhere. If the point is to get out of certain projects immediately, then, by the same token, it is also to *get into* other projects as quickly as possible. Moreover, to be *in* means to be *in immediately*. It is thus contrary to investment banking culture to "wait out the storm," even if doing so could be shown to save money in the long run.

Samuel Chin, an associate in investment banking at DLJ, told a similar story:

KH: Do you think efficiency is overrated on Wall Street? Wall Street . . . cuts a lot of people's jobs and then they realize, "Oh, a lot of our knowledge is gone and we need to rehire." Does that happen at all?

SC: Yeah, it happened a lot actually. Yeah, within Wall Street, when you have a down year, then a lot of bankers got laid off. Then after a couple of years when the economy picked up, then the people will be rehired. The other thing you can see, there is a *significant waste of resources*. But a lot of things we just cannot get around. When you have a down year just like right now in Asia, a lot of banks, if they don't shut their door, then what should they do? You can only see the balance sheet, and you can only see your loss because you don't get any business going out.

Chin observed that investment banks "can only see . . . loss," and from that standpoint, they are institutionally unable to peer into the future and realize that they will probably have to rehire soon after they have just fired. In the minds of investment banks, keeping Asia open in a downturn would be analogous to staying in a burning building; their identity as being "one" with the market would be jeopardized. Because they understand their employees to be interchangeable and demand them to be intensely mobile, they can fire everyone in their Asia offices, and yet a year later, have it up and running as if nothing happened in order to maintain their global "presence." According to many of my informants, J. P. Morgan "canned" its Asia office after the financial crisis, yet such immediate shutdowns are not always time- or money-saving: firing bankers requires severance pay, and rehiring new bankers necessitates another cycle of lavish compensation and bonus packages. Although many individual bankers readily admit how unstrategic, inefficient, or wasteful such an outlook is, Wall Street's culture of compensation ties them to (as well as helps to create) this institutional view.

A crucial question to ask, then, is how do investment banks start, build, and grow new business ventures without any plans? How are they able to enter new product markets and rival their competitors in a condensed timeframe? Not surprisingly, investment bankers' approach to business "growth" emerges out of the intersection of their strategy (of no strategy) with their compensation and hiring practices, which coconstruct each other. Describing Wall Street culture in general, Lou George, a retired managing director of institutional money management at Salomon Smith Barney, had the following to say about Wall Street's approach to business:

It's very fast moving. It's not like an awful lot of corporate enterprise where you get to make strategic plans, you get to think in a very intellectual way about the future of your business, and you almost have to do it that way because what you decide to do today is going to take a long timeframe to execute. You're going to have to design the product and build the factory and create the distribution channels, and you start to see the results eighteen months or two years from now. On Wall Street, things happen much more quickly, and your ability to marshal the resources of people, people who have customer relationships, to seek opportunity and to throw themselves into it is critical. Transaction by transaction, things move very, very rapidly. There is this sense of common purpose that arises in the roots of people in this business that is generally driven by their self-interest—which is high and executed with a level of almost predatory aggression that makes it work. And they talk in this business in these terms, right?

Like many of my informants, George differentiated corporate America from investment banks by stating that corporations actually design "strategic plans" for the future. When he referred to Wall Street being able to "marshal the resources of people" who "have customer relationships" in order to create immediate opportunities, he hinted at a practice that enables investment banks to enter relationships and develop new products without any plans. For instance, investment banks "develop" new businesses by simply hiring "big names" away from other investment banks, established senior-level investment bankers who bring their own networks of clients in whatever field the bank wants to "build." Such an approach creates a workplace environment of continual exodus and requires little in the way of strategic coordination.

Kate Miller, a former analyst at Morgan Stanley, described this continual buyout and rotating door of teams of executives:

KM: The Street is very small, and people switch firms every three years. And if you're in a particular industry group, it's even more ridiculous [referring to job switching] because you'll find that there will be this mass exodus from companies. Back when I was at Morgan Stanley, everyone in aerospace left Morgan Stanley and went to First Boston. And so, all of the aerospace people that worked at Goldman were then hired in by Morgan Stanley. And then, you know, from Salomon Smith Barney, a mass exodus of people from that industry group went to Goldman Sachs.

KH: Why did that happen?

KM: They just start buying talent. That's what banks do. They have all this money. If there is someone that's really smart about telecom, then, hey, get him. Pay him whatever you need because he's going to increase our business here. So, if he wants two million dollars, give him two million dollars because he's going to bring ten into the company.

In this manner, banks are able to transition "full grown" into their latest priorities. Such practices of instant and aggressive flexibility erase the necessity for "transition," but require that investment banks are also willing and able to fire immediately what is not working today (and hire what is). Not surprisingly, these strategies are supported by the particular allocation (and overabundance) of cash at investment banks, the commodification of "talent," pedigree, and connections, and the abdication of responsibility for the development of employees.

Describing what he did not enjoy about Wall Street, Corey Fisher, a managing director and portfolio manager at Vanguard, explained the shortchanging of employee development:

CF: Another issue that I have, frankly, is that I don't think that people really are, in a lot of these firms, developed. I think that you are really very much on your own. [E]ither you are smart enough to learn enough to survive or you're not, and there is a real sense that if smart people walk in the door, it would all take care of itself. There's a better way of putting this: you can think about it as a sports team. We are really shy a couple of sluggers, someone who can hit a three-point shot, or else we'd be into the playoffs or the World Series or the NBA finals. You have a lot of that around Wall Street firms. But the firms are not particularly good at saying, "Hey, here's somebody who clearly is bright and can do a good job. Maybe we can develop our own stars internally." They tend to look out over the horizon and say, "Where's the next star going to come from?" as opposed to developing their own, and that is pretty frustrating.

KH: It seems like there is no responsibility for the employees that they do have.

CF: Well, it is very short term. It's like, "If you can just keep your fingers in the dam and keep everything from flowing over, then I will go find somebody else who is talented enough to build me a new dam."

Underpinning the continual (re)creation of "instant" teams or product expertise is a corporate culture that values eagerness for change and expediency. The "build a new dam strategy" while the old dam overflows also prefigures waste and even decline. As I learned from informants throughout my fieldwork, these star hires and seven-figure offers are often abysmal failures: stories abound of senior bankers simply pocketing the cash and producing no results, of formerly successful teams that were separated and dislodged from the environments in which they had thrived. Perhaps the biggest debacle was Credit Suisse First Boston's (CSFB) purchase of the prestigious boutique investment bank Donaldson, Lufkin and Jenrette (DLJ) for the explicit purpose of acquiring the "hottest properties in the debt capital markets—the . . . high yield staff" of DLJ (O'Leary 2003). In fall 2000, when the bull market was on the verge of crashing, CSFB bought DLJ for over $90 a share (a total of over $12 billion) in an attempt to rival the biggest investment banks such as Morgan Stanley and Goldman Sachs. "One big void in CSFB was junk bonds, which could be nicely filled by buying DLJ, as the firm had a powerhouse junk franchise headed by Ken Moelis in Los Angeles" (Serwer 2001). Ken

Moelis's team was the jeweled prize that CSFB was willing to sign up at any price; but in 2001, after being poached by other investment banks, Moelis departed DLJ/CSFB for UBS Warburg and "the 30 investment bankers who ended up joining him made CSFB's takeover a hollow victory" (Gorham 2001). Not surprisingly, such a colossal mistake was set into motion via their approach to compensation and the strategy of no strategy. CSFB swiftly acquired DLJ at exorbitant prices for their junk bond team without planning how particular star performers would be integrated into the new structure. To keep key DLJ employees at the onset of the merger, they were given bonus guarantees without thinking through how this would look to CSFB's other bankers, who toiled on for the firm without such guarantees. There were no plans to deal with staffing redundancies created by the merger or any idea how new division and firm names would be negotiated. As a result, a few thousand employees jumped ship, and as a DLJ executive incisively observed, "CSFB did the deal without any due diligence, without any plan, and without any foresight. . . . They're bagging our name and selling our building. What kind of message does that send? Why buy a people business if you are going to alienate the people?" (Serwer 2001). What CSFB also did not anticipate was that other Wall Street investment banks, following a similar employment strategy, would begin luring these former DLJ employees once their retention contracts expired.

Thomas Douglas expertly captured this phenomenon of decline while we were discussing whether or not investment banks—in their continual upsizing and downsizing of people and businesses—were creating value for shareholders and making sustainable business decisions.

> [Upsizing and downsizing], that's the way Wall Street is structured. If I were working on this thesis, I'd want to take a look at the argument that it's better for your shareholders if you do behave like this, you react like this, like cutting the resources and all that sort of thing. Contrary to what Wall Street does, why might you actually want to have a stable human resource plan? In manufacturing, the reason why you strive for stability is you have to bring people in, you have to train them, you're setting up processes, and a process works best when it's going smoothly. If you're bringing somebody new in, you've got plenty of time to train them, so that they don't cause you any quality problems when they put in their widget. . . . You maintain the stability of the process by making sure that all these little pieces all around us, the parts manufacturers, your vendors . . . are all coordinated properly and everything stays nice and steady. . . . Don't have a shock come in because that's gonna impact your

quality. On Wall Street you're zipping it around back and forth all over the place. How much focus has there been on quality control in that environment and are you really losing a lot more money than you think? You know, you think you're being responsive and that's the best thing for the shareholder, but is that really true? Or are there shocks going through that are not necessarily making you go bankrupt, because Wall Street again—you can make a lot of money jumping into a new business first and everything—but could you have made a lot more if you had a real process in place, and you made shifts that were logical and planned where you had the right people, where you paid them the right salary? If J. P. Morgan decided tomorrow to get into some big business, they decided they needed to get in, you know, by tomorrow or by the day after that, I would love to be the guy that they were trying to bring in for that assignment. They'd pay me all kinds of money 'cause all I'd say is now I'm not so sure I want to come, right? That's where you get these ridiculous salaries. Then when you get in there and they figure out, oh, it's not really a business for us, I've already got a contract and they're gonna pay me a hundred million dollars. . . . [W]e talk about this kind of stuff in our meetings all the time. Or you know someone who has been nailed or has been laid off finally, and this person is gonna go retire, and part of it was some firm felt that for whatever reason, they desperately needed to get into a business that, in fact, they didn't. But, you know, they've signed up this guy at any price. And then they had to pay him. Now on Wall Street, that happens all the time.

Douglass pointed out that it is precisely Wall Street's bulimic culture of expediency that is *detrimental* to shareholder value. Time and again, we see Wall Street touting shareholder value, yet its very practices undermine that goal, which only seems to hold in an immediate, short-term timeframe in the context of a bull market. In one sense, Douglass explained, on Wall Street, there is no quality control and no long-range planning, and as a result, they continually lose money. At the same time, because they cut their losses so swiftly and attempt to be the first entrants into new businesses, generating new markets, they also chase windfalls. The crux of the issue here is that their strategy for getting into new businesses "as of yesterday" is simply to pay senior executives overblown salaries with outrageous bonus structures in order to attract these executives immediately. Wall Street's strategy to get these executives to "jump ship" with no time to transition out (or in) is simply to "sign this guy up at any price." An environment of expediency and eagerness for change, where not even medium-term plans are made, produces continual moments of desperation. The consequences of this hurried and harried strategy are multiple.

In many cases, the businesses banks want to enter turn out not only to be overrated, but also incapable of justifying the salary of the executives brought in to lead the effort. So the banks are saddled not only with multiyear, multimillion contracts to pay out but also with the continual necessity of downsizing. Wall Street's culture of expediency can be self-sabotaging.

It is crucial to recognize that one of the primary ways investment banks execute their no-plan strategy is through their people—through the fungibility of their employees *and* their approach to compensating them. The very way that investment banks actualize their strategies and cultural identities is through their approach to compensation and employment. And it is only a constant flow of interchangeable workers that allows banks to turn on a dime, to make "course corrections so swiftly," as the only "things" to shift are people—who fully expect (and in some cases welcome) exactly this instability and two-way lack of obligation or commitment.[9] Compensation, after all, is central to how investment banks measure workers; it is the site of struggle that defines traders' and investment bankers' worth; it is the means by which banks keep the people they want, or let people go; and it is how banks maintain business flexibility through employment fungibility as well as through their own acceptance of that insecurity. It is also damaging to investment banks' corporate clients, as investment bankers are pressured and rewarded to seek out as many deals as possible during the boom times because the compensation structure itself is one where you take what you can get when you can get it. Investment banks' approach to deals is deeply informed by their approach to employment such that corporate America becomes a site for short-term transactions and fee generation. As Andy Kessler, a former Wall Street research analyst, explains, "Wall Street is just a compensation scheme. . . . They literally exist to pay out half their revenue as compensation. And that's what gets them into trouble every so often—it's just a game of generating revenue, because the players know they will get half of it back" (McDonald 2005). Investment bankers realize that the transaction revenue comes directly back to them as pay. In this context, the sky seems virtually limitless, as there is no cap on "pay for performance." As further explicated in an article in the *Economist* (2001): "The investment bankers who make such deals expect also to gain personally. . . . In general, employees share the gains but not the losses both of their 'profit centre' and of their bank. That encourages them to gamble the firm's capital. If things go wrong, there's always another investment bank to move on to." Investment bankers are not compelled to take any responsibility for scandals or bad deals, for compensation has nothing to do with actual investment or client performance (Roane 2005). "Brokers get paid when you buy and when you sell. Almost none of it is linked to how well their customers do," observes Alan Johnson, president of Johnson Associates, which advises Wall Street firms on compensation. "Maybe it should be, but it isn't" (Roane 2005). Nowhere is the disconnect between pay and performance (or rather, the linkage between Wall Street bonuses and the havoc such incentive structures wreak) more stark than in 2007, when Wall Street investment bankers were once again awarded almost record bonuses ($32.9 billion) while the mortgage market was on the verge of collapse, shareholders in the securities industry lost $74 billion, and global economic crisis was beginning to spread (Harper 2007; New York State Comptroller 2009).

The Construction of Crisis: The Social Consequences of Investment Banking Culture

Most of Wall Street's daily values and practices—as constituted through Wall Street's compensation structures, job insecurity, "the-strategy-of-no-strategy," and the adherence to an identity marked by pride in market simultaneity—lead to a corporate culture where reckless expediency is the generalized norm. In this cultural environment, investment bankers, continually threatened with job loss and drastic departmental changes, are motivated to seek out the highest compensation and accept the social contract of high reward/high risk. This Wall Street milieu, however, does more than construct highly unstable organizations and turn investment bankers into compensation mongers. The organizational culture of Wall Street firms creates an approach to business, to corporate America, that continually lays the foundation for the construction *and* the bursting of financial market bubbles. In an environment of job insecurity and compensation for short-term performance, investment bankers are induced to make the most out of the present—practices which often lead to mortgaging the future. Wall Street, then, in helping to construct a market bubble, also negatively affects itself: when the financial bubbles bursts, Wall Street business shifts are even more drastic. In the words of one former informant laid-off during the currently unprecedented subprime layoffs, "By round three [of layoffs this year], everyone was going crazy; the entire floor was decimated."

In this section, I approach the relationality between booms and busts *not* as naturalized cycles and rhythms, but rather as linked consequences of the same cultural practices. The financial culture that produces the boom does so in such a way as to set the stage for the bust. I approach these phenomena not as predetermined but as the outcomes of choices made daily by investment bankers in a highly constrained environment. I problematize the theorizing of dips and recessions (both within and after bull markets) as simply "corrections," market abnormalities, or even separate and autonomous phenomena. Wall Street bubbles and crashes are, as I see them, co-constructed: the normative, everyday practices on Wall Street that constructed the bubble also prefigure, and ultimately create, the "inevitable" bust. Not only are bull and bear markets deliberately made, but the stage of the bust is set in motion by the strategies of the boom. At least in the late twentieth century, Wall Street often took advantage of crash environments to galvanize state support for financial interests such as social austerity programs and governmental deregulation in order to first "hit bottom" and then regenerate the conditions for a market bubble (and ensuing bust).

I begin my explication with John Carlton, whose observations of cycles and cyclical employment on Wall Street led to me think more critically about Wall Street's role in constructing financial market crises:

> What happens is Wall Street tends to go through cycles. Right now it is an up cycle, and so a lot of people are hiring. If in a few years it's a down cycle, it will reverse itself and instead of hiring—let's say we hire a couple dozen college graduates from good schools, that number could be cut to fifty [percent]. It could be cut overnight. What happens is—all the firms do it at the same time. Everybody is hiring, then everybody is cutting back. You have to be able to "take the heat of being in the kitchen" sort of thing. And, you have to react . . .

Attempting to get beyond the explanation of cycles as free market "tendencies" that go up and down autonomously and automatically, I inserted history into the picture by asking if particular market cycles have historically differed.

> KH: Over the past decade or so, has change in the work environment been mostly cyclical or would you say there are distinct differences between twenty years ago and now?
>
> JC: I would say there is sector change and cyclical change. The sector change is consolidation in the [financial services] industry. . . . [P]eople have found that the firms need to be bigger in order to compete with more capital. You know, Salomon taking over Smith Barney in a merger of equals, then being taken over by Travelers, then Travelers merging with Citibank. So one of

the sector trends is just to greater size. At the same time that is going on, there is a reverse: people are spinning out. The people who are not happy with the larger size are forming boutiques [smaller investment banks]. Then, you have this overlay, which are the market cycles. When I joined in '85, I very nearly went to CSFB, Credit Suisse First Boston, and one of the guys there said, *"Well, you are coming in '85. One of the problems is that we have had a good cycle, and you may be getting in at the top of the cycle." He was right, but he was early. The top of the cycle didn't end until '87.* There was a crash in '87. Things went down, and, actually, '88 wasn't a bad year. But then '89, '90, and into '91 were disasters. That was when Wall Street cut back 20 percent. So, by that time, I was a mid-level person and had four or five years' experience. But I had to live through three years at a mid-level of just wrenching change in the business. And then, basically, since about '92, it has been a strong upward market.

In addition to highlighting his "wrenching" experiences of change in the early 1990s (which is a recurring constant), I want to draw attention to his colleague's understanding and concern that Carlton was joining CSFB at the "top of the cycle." *How did he know that 1985 was near the apex? In other words, how did he know that the mid-1980s were unsustainable, and what are the social implications of this knowledge?*

Interestingly enough, except for the youngest and least experienced Wall Streeters I talked to, most of my informants also assumed that in the late 1990s, Wall Street was nearing the top of a cycle, and a major crash was on the horizon. Leaving aside for a moment the crucial question of why they expect or suspect a crash will come, this acknowledgment did not mean that investment banks or bankers became more cautious, for example, by curbing the amount of "risky" deals done based on inflated stock prices, stopping to assess their contributions to unsustainability, or assessing their own overextended lifestyles. The dot-com, "New Economy" discourse of an infinite boom was certainly in the background and caused a few to believe that the boom would simply continue into the foreseeable future (who can forget the prediction in 1999 of the Dow reaching 36,000?),[10] but for the most part, many Wall Streeters realized an "end" was in sight—yet did little to alter the frenzy of transactions. In general, although many bankers realized that they should conserve for a rainy day, they continued with the mentality that they would ride the wave for as long as it took them.

I want to concentrate on the seeming paradoxes: why and how can Wall Streeters expect a crash and yet continue with the values and practices that helped generate the crash? Why are crashes expected in the first place, and why does not the expectation of a bust cause automatic panic about job insecurity? Is job insecurity such a norm that crashes represent only slightly bigger-than-usual jolts? What is the effect on corporate America and people's lives? As Carlton's comments have suggested, investment bankers' temporality, how they conceive of the limited timeframe not only of their own jobs but also of financial booms, offers an important window into their daily organizational terrain. As I have described in previous sections, investment bankers often approach their jobs as fundamentally insecure, as if they could be fired any minute. Consider Thomas Douglass's description of investment banking's hiring and firing: "Here comes the activity and the firms start hiring everybody in sight. MBAs and undergrads lining up and trying to get in on it. All they can see is how many billions of dollars they're gonna make for themselves. And then go retire at the age of 30, you know? And then, boom, everything falls apart. They start laying everybody off." Rachel Aftandilian, an investment banking associate at Citigroup, underscored that job insecurity on Wall Street is like a "plow behind you, constantly pushing you." Investment banks, she said, are "notorious for overspending when they have money and then immediately cutting when they don't." Not only do investment bankers perceive their workplace surroundings as ephemeral, they also negotiate their job insecurity via the bonus-centered compensation system.[11] In an important sense, then, their struggle, dare I say resistance, against job insecurity takes place in the compensation arena.

My Wall Street informants and friends often described their job strategies as holding on as long as they can before the axes fall: do as many deals and get as much experience with transactions as possible while the stock market is rising and deals are much easier to sell to corporations. They will often say that they "hope to ride this wave as long as the good times roll." If they are able to successfully hold on through enough peaks and troughs to get promoted, then they attempt to make the most money out of the new position (the higher the position, the greater the share in the bonus pool) as possible before another layoff comes. Those who successfully weather multiple peaks and troughs often have either made plenty of money to cushion the layoffs or are en route to making more via this pattern. Christine Chang, a vice president at BT, commented on her job strategies:

KH: So, do you see yourself in this industry in the future?

CC: Yes, probably in the foreseeable future, until something happens to force me out of it. The industry is very volatile. *I think the way a lot of people here view it is that you just hold on for as long as you can.* In a bull market you stick around, and when it blows up, at that point you might stop and reassess, figure out if there is something you want to do with your life, something that might be more satisfying. While you are making money, you stick around.

KH: Do you think, in general, most people are satisfied, are happy with the profession?

CC: Not necessarily. A lot of people say about Wall Street that you have to be careful because it sort of sucks you in with the money, and then you find you are unable to do anything else. Whether or not you are happy here, I think that is really true. Whether or not people like the work, once they have started making a million dollars a year, even if they don't like the work, it's very hard to say, "I will do something else and make $250,000 a year." They just can't make that leap. I'd say maybe half the people like it and half the people don't. The half that don't are sort of caught anyway. They have built up a lifestyle around the compensation, and they are unwilling to give up the lifestyle or they can't stomach the idea of making less.

Joseph Tsai, an associate in investment banking at DLJ, had a similar strategy:

KH: Now that we are on the topic of job security, because Wall Street is a kind of dynamic industry, it's always changing, new products are always coming to the forefront, is there a lot of job insecurity on the Street itself?

JT: I think so. My history is really limited, and since I became aware of the market, I really haven't seen a big downturn. But, it does happen. In Asia, part of my sensitivity in going out to Asia is I knew there was a big downturn in '93, '94, probably '94, where a lot of investment banks out there, Goldman Sachs, Merrill Lynch, laid off half of their work force because there was just no market out there. Ideally they transfer people back, but you don't want to be in that situation, so I kind of approach it as pretty insecure. I kind of joke about it because I am at a place in my life where if I lose my job I think I can figure something out. But *the way I approach it is I hope to ride this wave as long as the good times roll but also realizing that if there is a huge market downturn, my job is not secure.* I could lose the job. But, that is one of the trade-offs in leaving law. Law is a very secure job.

While most of my informants in the front office felt an inordinate amount of pressure to seize the deals and increase the bonus before it was too late, they also were confident that they could find jobs on Wall Street were they to be laid off. Monica Choi's observations typified most Wall Streeter's privileged approach to impending unemployment:

KH: It is interesting because job insecurity is not only in other jobs, it is also on Wall Street. They react so quickly. Sometimes a little too quickly. How do you feel about that kind of level of job insecurity?

MC: Absolutely, but I also grew up in that kind of environment. [Monica worked on Wall Street for eight years after college graduation.] Everybody knows. It is really, really sad when one of your colleagues gets fired. We had a massive cut in October, Merrill Lynch did. And, basically, I mean, we had secretaries fired. We are not talking about just professionals. We had a lot of different people at a lot of different levels getting fired. Receptionists getting fired. They are crying. These people are not skilled people. . . . *I don't worry about that because I am just like, I am going to ride this as long as I can.* If I am fortunate enough not to get fired, that will be great. If I do, well, you know what? I have made a lot of money, and I have had a great experience, and I can take this experience into a lot of different things.

In a context of rampant insecurity negotiated through compensation, Wall Street's pay-for-performance bonus system "incentivizes" bankers to compete by doing more deals, bringing in more revenue, finding more profitable trades, convincing more people to invest in funds and the stock market, and so on.[12] Not only are their bonuses directly tied into the amount of deals and revenues that they are able to generate for the bank, but bonuses are also seen as symbols of coming to terms with the riskiness of their jobs. It comes as no surprise, then, that investment bankers, faced with the ever-present specter of layoffs, are motivated to complete as many deals and transactions as possible for their corporate clients. As Paul Flanagan, an M&A associate at Goldman Sachs, articulated, bankers' goals are to "get what you [can] out of it for a short term." The consequences of their behavior for corporate America and the small investor they claim to champion, not to mention the poor, are quite grave. Wall Street investment bankers are motivated to "milk" as much out of the present as possible, regardless of consequence. Given that bonuses depends on the size, amount, and number of deals that bankers bring in and complete, *and* given that their jobs are decidedly short-term and could be eliminated at any time, bankers are structurally primed to generate as many deals as possible whether or not these deals are ultimately "good" for the company by any longer-term, even neoliberal, measure. Since the banker might not even be at his or her job or bank for very long, and the strategy of investment banks is that of no strategy, the question of follow-through is certainly not asked.

I argue that out of the particular culture, strategy, and worldview of investment banks arises this compensation structure, which—when mixed with job insecurity—creates (and is created by) a "bubble" culture of expediency, an approach to people and to corporations (including themselves and their own companies) that is based on generating quick, short-term rewards. Investment bankers, realizing not only that their own jobs are temporary but also that stock prices will not rise forever, rush to advise, convince, and cajole these corporations to engage in as many deals as possible, whether it be buying companies and divisions, selling companies to the highest bidder, refinancing their debt using their stock as collateral or exchange, or issuing more stock. In such a practice of squeezing the most out of the present, the end—the bursting of the bubble—is not only presumed and often expected, but also made possible. In many cases, Wall Streeters expect that their behavior toward corporations, even governments, will in time result in busts, as their strategies are not based on committed relationships to building productive corporations, but rather on selling as much as the current market fads (which they help to construct) will bear. Moreover, many of my informants anticipated not only a crash, but also an *eventual bailout*, on the grounds that Wall Street investment banks were "too big to fail." Such an assumption demonstrates that, contrary to their free market discourses, investment banks embraced risk not because they had successfully hedged their bets or managed their exposure. Rather, they depend on the state and the global interconnectedness of the economy to absorb the risk while they focus on immediate profits. As Peter Felsenthal, a bond trader at Salomon Smith Barney, explained, the government and the IMF won't let them fail. "You have all of the upside when things go well. If you do poorly, you don't owe anybody money, so you might as well take as much risk as possible." Of course, these decisions are not always calculatedly rational: as I develop further in chapter 7, by helping to instigate crashes, investment bankers, especially those caught in the hype through their own boom-time hyperconsumption, do not simply "make a killing" on the bubble, but also help sabotage their own jobs, lifestyles, and future bonuses.

Investment bankers' cultural models of both short-term, relentless deal-making *and* employee liquidity are, in a sense, learned "on the job," imbibed through their own experiences and embodiment of their particular organizational culture. Investment bankers learn to relentlessly push more deals onto corporate America and to transfer their own sensibilities of downsizing and insecurity onto corporate America itself. In such a context, financial crashes and busts are not natural cycles but constructed out of everyday practices and ideologies: the strategies of the boom set the stage for the bust. It is only through the local cultural analysis of investment banking's corporate culture that we can understand how investment bankers reconcile such short-term recklessness with their prevalent worldview that they continually act in the best interests of their corporate clients and shareholders, that is, how bankers can uphold shareholder value as their mission statement and yet participate in its undermining.

While shareholder value is Wall Street's core representation, investment banks' key self-understanding is that they "are" the market. Their model of the market is characterized by immediate responsiveness and an ability to constantly change direction and strategy, and it is precisely by embracing a culture of expediency that investment banks enact their identification with this model. The quickness of investment banks' reaction to market trends signifies their absolute identity with the market; their cultural distinction is the ability to channel the market immediately. Of course, it is their construction of employment fungibility and their approach to compensation that allow investment banks to actualize these key cultural identities and strategies. In chapter 5, I interpreted investment bankers' obligatory resorting to "the market" as the explanation for job insecurity as a sign of their externalization of the market. What I came to realize is that their approach to markets can also be read as evidence of their intimacy and identification with markets, of their attempts to perform and actualize their model of what the market is. While their market shorthand can be interpreted as endowing the market with autonomous features (akin to the paradox of Weber's iron cage, where central actors constructing the market are themselves controlled by, and feel external to, their creation), embedded in their market models are not so much outside forces as explicitly local cultural values and a Wall Street hypercapitalist sense of time, made possible through their institutional arrangements and their central identity as the embodiment of market immediacy.

Today, Wall Street investment banks, as spokespeople for the financial markets, have far-reaching influence over the daily practices of corporate America. Wall Street's financial values, in particular its understandings of temporality which privilege employee liquidity and compressed timeframes to measure corporate performance, have not only encouraged rampant downsizings throughout corporate America, but also realigned corporations from long-term institutions that operate according to their own product and development clocks to the expectations of Wall Street. In so doing, corporate America has been "resocialized," and contrary to the official language of the boom of the late 1990s, championed by Alan Greenspan and most Wall Street advocates, the financial markets did not fuel productive growth but rather spurred short-term, mortgaged productivity which led to bubbles and busts (Brenner 2002). To analyze how financial power gets implemented as well as its effects, my research goal was not only to access and understand the parallel, "para-ethnographic" knowledge and orienting point of view of global experts, but also the very cultural models and mechanisms through which bankers are socialized and from which they enacted their worldviews and practices. To understand how Wall Street imposes and universalizes its influence, I examined the mundane cultural practices of the everyday: the organizational structure of investment banks, their market identities and notions of temporality. While it would have been compelling to argue that the global imposition of Wall Street's theoretical models of shareholder value and market necessity have created these massive shifts in our social economy, such an analysis is incomplete, and it reifies market mystique from the top down. What gets rendered invisible is the way in which a specific corporate culture of investment banks helps to create a model for banker actions, and it is a particular cultural model of work relations designed to be in lockstep with their ideals of the market that is being imposed. It is the interaction, mutual constitution, and gaps between models and effects that are instructive here. While investment bankers say that everyone should follow the dictates of shareholder value, what they do not always recognize is that they enact shareholder value *the way they themselves experience it*—through their own, Wall Street–centric cultural lens—and that this way can actually be detrimental to shareholder value in the long run.

Moreover, continual downsizing further solidifies investment banking's self-identity as the market: in justifying downsizing, my informants constantly uttered, "We're marked to market," meaning that Wall Street people, products, and strategies simply move with the market and as such, bankers' liminal positions are not only temporary, but will improve. Wall Street investment bankers' experiences of employee liquidity, then, only serve to reinforce their greater mettle, efficiency, and smartness compared to the average worker precisely because they are amply compensated, highly networked, and sought after; while their insecurity and conditionality are constant, their misfortunes are assumed to be temporary.[13] As such, the fact that investment bankers get downsized all the time, that they too are vulnerable to downsizing, ironically not only motivates them to recommend this experience as a disciplining "performance enhancement" for corporate America, but also renders them less capable of understanding the suffering of others. These bankers experience downsizing in a way that is often subsidized, empowering, challenging, normal, and productive of their own identities as the market vanguard, the fittest and smartest capitalists. Whereas downsizing continues to be dominantly conceived as abandonment, as being "done to" (the iconic images in American culture of the disgruntled steelworker or liminal middle manager come to mind), this dominant conceptualization ignores a model of worker and workplace— forged on Wall Street—that carries much explanatory power.

I hope my approach to the market challenges anthropology to conduct a thought experiment: what if we approach and conceive of the market as having no externality or abstraction? Given that "the market" has for so long assumed a place of taken-for-granted power in social scientific litera- ture, what would it mean to conceptualize and approach markets only as a set of everyday, embodied practices? After all, it is through investment banking's corporate culture—their approach toward employment, job in- security, temporality, and compensation—that investment bankers can act "like the market" that they espouse and impose on others.

7

Leveraging Dominance and Crises through the Global

The dominance of finance capitalism in the economy of the United States and its influence worldwide depend on the work of investment bankers in claiming and promoting "the global." In this final chapter, I make the case that analyzing investment banks' approaches to "the global," in conjunction with the shareholder revolution, hypercapitalist temporality, and the strategy of no strategy, is crucial in fully understanding Wall Street's market making. Their hyping of their own superior capabilities and financial products breed frenzy and confidence in their latest offerings, which in turn globalize their spread. Far from being immune, investment banks are susceptible to their own global boasting (which is, after all, based on their self-representations as smart and market savvy). This self-confidence, when coupled with an institutional imperative to "milk the present," helps to create a culture of leverage where they literally double down on their latest, most profitable financial instrument. This gamble betrays competing aspects of their cultural milieu: both a realization that a strategy of exponential leverage and the single-minded pursuit of deals is necessary to extract massive short-term profits before the boom turns to bust, *and* a belief in their own capabilities to outsmart and outlast the volatile market they helped to generate. Apprehending how investment banks project their hopes and dreams onto the global, and how they use the global to hype and spread their products, illuminates why and how investment bankers' daily practices engender not only record profits but also financial crises that can have a domino effect globally and, in some instances, threaten the very existence of Wall Street itself.

This chapter seeks to showcase the mutual constitution of the local and the global—the specific techniques, social ramifications, and self-effects of American bankers' promotion of globalization and claiming of the whole world. My argument throughout this ethnography has been premised on the interpenetration of different scales and fields of analysis, between individual biographies, institutional cultures, and larger social transformations. In one sense, I have focused on the historically specific construction and effects of American investment banks on corporate change, inequality, and social life in the United States. In this vein, the habitus of investment bankers and the local, institutional culture of investment banks, coupled with, and framed by, the shareholder revolution, pinnacle status, elite networks, massive insecurity, and a (supposedly) meritocratic culture of hard work, take center stage. In another sense, as I have shown, this particular, homegrown, U.S. financial model does not stay put. Wall Street's rise to dominance—through its smartness, its use of history and shareholder value ideology, its "own" experiences of downsizing as empowerment—has allowed it to project a local model of employee liquidity and financial instability onto corporate America and the financial markets at large, generating globalizing economic crises. In conjunction with the book's analyses of bankers' dispositions and organizational culture, this chapter illustrates that how Wall Street imagines and uses globalization further dramatizes the links between Wall Street's corporate culture (especially employee liquidity and corporate liquidation) *and* wildly gyrating financial markets, prone to stratospheric booms and far-reaching, devastating busts.

Including the global in my analysis demonstrates both the power and the vulnerability of investment banks. On the one hand, Wall Street relentlessly promotes finance-led capitalism through the strategic utilizations of discourses from the shareholder revolution to globalization. As marketing powerhouses in their own right, Wall Street banks spread the doctrine of shareholder value and celebrate their own global financial reach and technological innovations. Their use of the global not only helps to consolidate and confer investment banking dominance and legitimacy, but also fosters the widespread buying and imitation of their products and ideologies, thereby solidifying their reach. Given this context, what additional onus does that put upon a scholar studying up? If the very idea of "inevitable globalization" and worldwide financial integration is precisely the worldview that financial interests desire to construct, then it certainly would not make sense for academics interested in counterhegemonic projects to fixate solely on Wall Street's power.

On the other hand, it turns out that even for the most seemingly globalized and powerful of actors, global ambitions can implode and generate internal contradictions. The very practices (such as global ambition and marketing, and the relentless pursuit of deals) that help to generate and spread Wall Street dominance also create the conditions for its instability, even demise. Wall Street investment banks are not immune to their own hype: in fact, they often internalize and come to believe that which they are peddling, creating massive risk exposures, implosions, losses, downsizings, even bankruptcies for themselves, not to mention gigantic ripple effects throughout the world (we have already seen how Wall Street's contradictory approach to shareholder value and bull markets set the stage for financial crisis).

To bring my analysis up to the present, I am motivated to begin this chapter with a brief description of Wall Street's role in one of the most devastating financial crises of our times—the subprime mortgage debacle —before I turn to analyze investment banks' specific global and rhetorical techniques. I do so because the Wall Street-turned-global meltdown not only encapsulates what the dominance of finance capitalism means concretely for the United States and globally, but also showcases Wall Street's production of worldwide crises through its global hype and corporate culture. Of course, because my focus in this ethnography centers on the relationship between investment bankers and corporate America, and this global crisis implicates Wall Street writ large (from hedge funds to bond traders) and beyond, I do not intend to claim that U.S. investment banking practices single-handedly caused systemic financial crisis, because the causes and players are manifold. However, my findings do point to a broad-based, even generic, financial habitus that emanates from the powerful locus of Wall Street investment banks, and it has become unmistakably evident that this ethos and set of practices have played a key role in the current disaster.

Just as investment banks helped to engender the junk bond debacle of the 1980s, the savings and loan crisis, the emerging market meltdowns of the 1990s, the turn-of-the-millennium dot-com crash, and Enron, they also fueled the subprime boom with the same (or similar) cultural practices, which, not surprisingly, set the stage for their ultimate, almost-catastrophic bust. In this context, it certainly seems as if Wall Street, continually crashing and rejuvenating, has the power to constantly remake the world. While the structuring practices that produce Wall Street's hegemony render these events explainable and in a sense predictable, it is moments like these that also highlight that Wall Street's power (and ultimately its fragility) depends upon constant hype, the marketing of its global prowess and capability, and the restructuring of productive assets from corporations to housing. Although this is not the place to examine in-depth the financing and extensive fallout of the subprime debacle, I illustrate how an investigation of Wall Street's approaches to the global can be relevant to understanding a real-time crisis that has been engendered by the very practices described in this ethnography.

The subprime disaster that began to dominate mainstream news in the summer of 2007 has now, a year later, turned into a global financial crisis, engendering record home foreclosures, a tragic reinvigoration of race, class, gender, and age distinctions, skyrocketing consumer prices, massive job losses, the potential demise of Wall Street itself, and economic crises throughout multiple markets from global equities to credit availability. Although Wall Street investment banks were not the only players constructing this crisis, their role was substantial. According to some of my former informants, investment banks generated a global subprime mortgage market by creating multiple kinds of securities, from highly structured, complex mortgage-backed bonds such as collateralized debt obligations (CDOs) to even more arcane credit-default swaps, based on subprime mortgages. They hyped and sold these instruments to a global network of investors—hedge funds, pension funds, sovereign funds, corporations and banks, wealthy individuals, as well as *themselves* (in effect creating a new market for these investments). As financial journalists report, "Wall Street sold subprime everywhere" "from traders in Hong Kong to small-town mayors in Europe to pensioners in the American Midwest," even "fishing villages in the Arctic circle" (Day 2008; Merle and Tse 2008). The idea was to spread and parcel out the risk globally, not only through myriad investors spread over the globe, but also by slicing and dicing mortgages into multiple levels of risk.

Unusually for Wall Street, investment banks also directly helped to generate the market on the consumer end (as I will explain later). Because investment banks bought pools of mortgages from mortgage lenders to securitize them—structuring them into bonds to sell to investors—these banks provided retail mortgage companies with liquid capital. Unlike federal mortgage lenders who supposedly guarantee the mortgages behind the securitized bonds they sell, Wall Street investment banks bought and bundled mortgages into unregulated, unguaranteed "private-label" mortgage-backed securities, vouched for by the prestige and expertise of such venerable names as Goldman Sachs and Bear Stearns. This meant that Wall Street had no incentive to assess the "risk" of borrowers. In fact, investment banks and direct mortgage lenders deliberately misrepresented subprime loans, selling them to as many borrowers as possible (even those who would have qualified for lower-rate, "conventional" prime loans). They thus generated higher origination fees, future refinancing fees (as it was known many would not be able to pay once interest rates spiked), and higher payments from the borrowers. This also led to higher bond rates upon securitization, which allowed Wall Street to both hype the bonds to investors who clamored for high returns and sell them at a higher fee.[1] Investment banks exerted top-down pressure on mortgage companies (some of which investment banks actually purchased) to constantly generate more subprime loans. Wall Street engineered the proliferation of adjustable-rate mortgages (ARMs) with low teaser rates that skyrocketed after a year or two, along with interest-only loans and loans without proof-of-income documentation from the borrower, all of which allowed the creation of extremely high interest rate bonds that Wall Street marketed to its investors as the hottest new products. To gain investor confidence, "credit-rating agencies, paid by investment banks, blessed the packages, convincing investors they were safe to buy" (Olinger and Svaldi 2007).

Investment banking practices both promoted a surge of predatory lending to originate the loans and created a market to buy the bonds based on them. Bolstered by rising housing prices, low interest rates, and a new worldview of "refinancing" such that predatory and unsound loans could easily be refinanced (often with hidden fees) at the end of a year or two with a higher home valuation, Wall Street investment banks rationalized their behavior. They also claimed that their ingenuity was finally breaking down barriers of race and class, which the traditional "redlining" commercial banker was unable to do with his simple, "vanilla" toolkit of conventional loans that lacked the advantage of global securitization. Again, the discourse of globalization was used: Wall Street investments bankers invoked their creation of a global market of "opportunity finance" and of extending home ownership to those left out of the global market.[2] For example, Corey Fisher, an African American male managing director at Vanguard Investments, subtly linked Wall Street's creativity and aggressiveness with "expanding the pie." By focusing on the best way to make money, the new Wall Street challenged the elaborate and exclusionary protocols traditionally associated with elite banking, creating a new "high-yield" credit market and thus opening monetary access to anyone deserving:

Wall Street has helped to improve the efficiency of the economy, because . . . they have gotten rid of certain middlemen that were highly inefficient players. These inefficient middlemen were the bankers, the commercial lenders. Their pricing and the servicing that was built into that wound up extracting a cost that was exorbitant. What has been beautiful is—and this is one of the things that is good about the high-yield market—is that regardless of what your credit rating is, there is a market for you out there. You may not have the best credit, but because Wall Street is out there creating markets for aggressive markets, and you will pay a relatively higher rate, but it won't be as high of a rate if you—well, frankly, you would not have gotten a loan from the banks, so it is hard to even compare it to that. So, the capital markets have made [borrowing money] much more efficient, so you just have to pay the cost of capital, which is exactly the way it should be. . . . Nobody should be denied access to credit within reasonable means. . . . The cost of that capital should be a function of the earnings capacity and the cash flow capacity of the enter- prise. That is the direction that we are moving in. What that does, from my standpoint, very selfishly, is it allows blacks and other people of color and women to be able to participate in this marketplace.

Of course, as the devastation of the subprime crisis continues to unfold, Wall Street's experiment with broader access and "opportunity finance" has shown itself to be more akin to a short-term creation of a niche market for the purposes of exploiting the poor, creating a bubble real-estate market, and mortgaging the future.

Mortgages were a cash cow for Wall Street, with firms generating record profits and bonuses. "The private-label, subprime bond market grew from $18 billion in 1995 to nearly $500 billion in 2005" (Day 2008). Merrill Lynch, for example, "rose from a bit player in mortgage CDOs in 2003, with just $3.4 billion in underwritings, to the leader from 2004 through 2006, posting $44 billion in deals backed by mortgages" (Tully 2007). Encouraged by former Merrill CEO Stanley O'Neal, Dow Kim, the senior executive in charge of markets and trading operations, increased Merrill's exposure to mortgage-backed securities to "$52 billion in 2006 from $1 billion in 2002" (Thomas 2008). The average Wall Street bonus in 2005 was $150,160, up 38.2 percent from 2004, and 2006 bonuses rose another 33 percent, demonstrating both the speed and extent of the previous bull market's profiteering, fueled in large part by the subprime bubble (New York State Comptroller 2009).

Fast forward another year, however, and "the subprime mess has become Wall Street's version of Hurricane Katrina" (Tully 2007). In the first nine months of 2007 alone, 129,927 financial jobs had been cut, investment banks such as Citigroup, Merrill Lynch, UBS, and Lehman Brothers had seen the evaporation of the majority of their shareholder value, and Wall Street had posted more than $250 billion in losses and mortgage write-downs (Hoffman 2008; Rose 2007; Tully 2007). Of course, the most telling stories are the demise of Lehman Brothers, the near collapse and acquisition of Merrill Lynch, and the near bankruptcy and bailout of Bear Stearns and its two hedge funds that invested heavily in subprime bonds, which signaled for Wall Street the beginning of the end. The managers of those hedge funds were recently indicted for lying and "failing to warn investors" of the gravity of the potential collapse of the mortgage market (Barr 2008).

More to the point, "top guns on Wall Street have spent a lot of time deceiving themselves about the depth of the mortgage mess," and "even as the collapse of the High Grade funds [Bear Stearn's hedge funds] was being dissected in the press, other big subprime-writedown losers . . . remained in denial" (Barr 2008). As with previous crises and missteps, Wall Street investment banks are often deluded by their own ingenuity, hype, deal-making frenzy, and in-the-moment temporality. Simultaneously, of course, investment banks, networked as they are with the wealthiest individuals, institutions, and governments, can often recover from these crashes relatively quickly, often within a year and a half as was the case with the transition from dot-com to mortgage-backed securities as a prime source of profit. In the business of searching out and generating new markets with "innovatively" packaged financial products soon after a bust, Wall Street's pain is often cushioned. In early 2008, investment banking masterminds of subprime loans, from Merrill Lynch's Dow Kim to Citigroup's Thomas Maheras, instead of being tainted by scandal, continue to be hot commodities on Wall Street. The commonsense understanding is that they have demonstrated the ability to create entirely new market opportunities characterized by immediate exploitation and high growth; such is the culture of a presentist strategy of no strategy, where market simultaneity, not wisdom, is a central goal (Thomas 2008).

In the cultural analysis of financial crises, it is crucial to understand how Wall Street investment banks can, in a sense, fall prey to their own "products" (from mergers and acquisitions to global prowess to subprime) in order to ensure, at least, that anthropologists themselves do not "believe the hype" of Wall Street's proclamations. While the egregiousness of predatory lending and the appropriation of subprime as equal opportunity may not fool anthropologists, investment banks' approaches to the global and heralding of global capability might. Regardless, the lessons learned from exploring Wall Street's global claims will shed light on the importance of the techniques of spectacular marketing in the enactment of Wall Street habitus. I now turn to a general investigation of Wall Street's approaches to the global before I return to the subprime crisis in the conclusion of this chapter.

Global Seduction

My initial year on Wall Street working at Bankers Trust (BT) can certainly be characterized as a global seduction. At the various recruiting events I attended as a potential employee, the orientation sessions I participated in as a new employee, as well the various panel discussions, conferences, and social events that attracted investment bankers throughout Wall Street, I was bombarded by proclamations and representations of "the global." Senior investment bankers spoke endlessly about borderless flows of financial capital and finance becoming increasingly "global" as Wall Street investment banks create sophisticated financial products covering new areas and generating new markets, as they enter and dominate the capital markets of various countries. In a marketing and recruiting brochure, J. P. Morgan declares: "We act as a global problem solver for our clients, moving ideas and insights seamlessly across time and space. Our experience in markets around the world gives clients unparalleled access to insights and opportunities" (J. P. Morgan 1995, centerfold). In its 1995 annual report,[3] Merrill Lynch, at that time one of the largest and most profitable investment banks in the United States, proclaims itself "singularly positioned and strategically committed to global leadership as the preeminent financial management and advisory company" (Merrill Lynch and Co., Inc. 1995, 1). In its 1994 annual report, it boasts, "Our global scope and intelligence allow us to respond to opportunities and changes in all markets and in all regions. We serve the needs of our clients across all geographic borders" (Merrill Lynch and Co., Inc. 1994, centerfold).

In August 1996, after completing a two-month training program at BT where I and my cohort learned the basic tools of financial analysis, we were invited to an off-site gala orientation session. What I managed to get out of these three days was how often the global was appealed to, most likely because it resonated with my anthropological norms and assumptions of what Wall Street would be like.[4] In his opening remarks, the CEO stated that investment banks, especially BT, did not simply operate on a "quasi-global" basis by having a single central location with plenty of satellites. Rather, they had multiple locations that were "really integrated." "It just flows," he said proudly. Other senior management speakers spoke generally about the need to combine "global capabilities" with "local relationships," where "the global" referred to financial techniques, products, and resources from New York, and "the local" referred to geographic places, people, business customs, cultural misunderstandings, and branch offices in "developing markets." Such a premise defines the global as mobile technique (eliding where the global is located) and the local as place-bound (eliding the reach of the local), and not only parallels social-scientific conceptual problems but also empowers the global as a world-making force. As such, my experiences during orientation affirmed my beliefs and fears of Wall Street's globalist dreams. I frankly did not understand the nuances of how BT headquarters in New York City used and understood globalization nor how these differed from other offices, not to mention other investment banks. I left the orientation convinced of the seamless global prowess and expertise of investment banks without identifying or contextualizing what was meant by "the global" or how this conception was put into practice.

At every turn during my time at BT, I came across references to the global, from CEO speeches to discussion panels about emerging market trends. Each time the global was emphasized, I often ignored its context and contingency in order to accumulate every mention of the global as evidence of investment banking's power. As I heard about the number of offices investment banks had worldwide, the mobility of their employees and the freedom of their monetary flows, and the number of corporate privatizations and merger deals from São Paolo to Shanghai, I worried about Wall Street's increasing power to make the world in its own image. I understood globality to mean the ability to penetrate the national markets of the world and discipline them according to Wall Street's standards, making the world conducive to financial capital and transnational corporations. Most of my coworkers shared my belief in Wall Street's global influence, but whereas I found globalization to be a negative sign of hegemony, they often took it as a badge of honor, a reason to emphasize their belonging to a particular firm. As employees, we were constantly told how global we were, and we believed it. We didn't just have offices, we had global offices; we did not just understand markets, we had global market access and the capability to exploit all markets.

Given the initial confusion of finding my way in fieldwork, the pressures of employment, and making contacts for future research, I hardly stopped to analyze the particularities of why being global held such an important place in the investment banking imagination; why it was a criterion for prestige, for business, and for attracting employees. Instead of trying to figure out why the global so preoccupied BT (not to mention every investment bank I encountered), I took it at face value. My coworkers and I unselfconsciously used the word "global" to describe BT in particular and investment banking in general: "The investment banking industry is truly global; Bankers Trust is a global investment bank." We uttered such phrases as statements of fact.

Global Fissures: What's in a Name?

It was not until the "name-change" event that I first began to notice the fissures of globalization and its importance for contextualization. A few months after I began working at BT, they announced that they were changing all the names and acronyms for the different sectors of the bank. Most of BT's businesses were previously named with the word "global" as the first descriptor; for example, GIM stood for Global Investment Management and GIB stood for Global Investment Banking. But the debate at hand for senior management was that since the global should be an already understood characteristic, why did they have to mention it at every turn? Instead of naming GIM for Global Investment Management, they would simply call it IM because the "global" was (they hoped) implicit. Moreover, some of the more prestigious investment banks on Wall Street did not use the word "global" in their various business names. This change of names soon became the punch line of many jokes among my coworkers and myself. In our PowerPoint presentations, we would often insert footnotes stating "the global, of course, is understood," or we would continually put the word "global" in parentheses.

This name-changing event alerted me to the always incomplete process of global schemes and claims, the politics of global hierarchies, the uniformity of my approach to the global, and the extent to which BT insisted on and attempted to create its own globalness. I began to notice BT's insecurity as a "global investment bank." For example, the financial media annually ranks the top-tier firms (measured by such criteria as the number and size of deals completed in a variety of industries and stocks and bonds issued); those at the top are known on Wall Street as "the bulge bracket." BT, once a bulge-bracket firm in sales and trading,[5] had recently plummeted in the ranks. It is only in the context of this insecurity that BT's intense concern for global elitism made sense.

BT's reputation among Wall Street investment banks began to falter in 1994 when it was derided on the covers of *Business Week*, the *Wall Street Journal*, and much of the financial media. "Who can trust Bankers Trust?" went the refrain (Holland, Himelstein, and Schiller 1995). BT had been one of the most profitable banks in trading derivatives;[6] it was considered entrepreneurial and technically innovative in constructing and distributing these new financial instruments. But at the height of its success in 1993, it was caught swindling multiple corporate clients, one of which was Procter and Gamble. BT had sold them expensive financial instruments presumably to "reduce their risk exposure" to interest-rate fluctuations, but in practice, these instruments had complex "hidden" caveats which allowed BT, not its clients, to benefit under most monetary conditions; in other words, it had "ripped them off." As a result, these corporations lost millions of dollars.[7]

BT was in the midst of staging a recovery from this major scandal when I arrived. The company had just hired a new CEO, along with a slew of change-management consultants, and launched a campaign to reclaim its reputation and stock price. When I began to think about BT's approach to the global within the context of the campaign waged to restore BT to its former glory, I was better able to discern the differing versions and uses of the global. That investment banking globalisms were not everywhere the same was a revelation for me. BT's practice during orientation and its continual gesturing to the global now started to make more complex sense. Revisiting my observations of orientation, I realized that in addition to proclaiming BT as a "truly global" corporation, another main theme was "building relationships." At the time, I did not understand why the latter was so openly emphasized (nor what it had to do with BT's global imaginings) because I had assumed that relationships were interventions and ties that Wall Street depended on but avidly denied, as is typically the case with most representative free-market institutions. For example, BT's senior management spoke endlessly about how "the hardest thing to earn is relationships," "money is about reputation and relationships," "money is 'client-driven'," and "if you are good to your clients, money is never an issue." This relational emphasis on the link between people and money—especially in a context where most investment banks simultaneously denied the social by assigning agency and responsibility to the market—speaks to the politics of acknowledging the network of relationships that enabled the accumulation of money. Prior to the scandal, BT stood out (even on Wall Street) in its assumption that its financial dealings were so abstract and so transaction orientated, that BT could actually remove itself from the complexities of forming relationships with clients and other banks. Faced with declining profits and forced to realize that their finances were dependent on an array of institutional connections, BT's executives began to speak in terms of clients rather than abstract market mechanisms. The scandal precipitated BT's admission that social networks exist, which can in turn be understood as an effort to negotiate their fall from power.

Just as the emphasis on relationships signified BT's inability to continually claim that its success rested on abstract global capital flows, the ongoing projection of BT as a truly global company reveals the fragility of its global standing. Although these two practices seem at odds (one being a move away from claiming global, nonlocated market objectivity, the other a promulgation of globalness), when seen as interventions by a declining and scandal-ridden investment bank, they both turn out to be gasps for legitimacy. Initially I had inadvertently tuned out BT's emphasis on relationships because of its incongruence with my previous assumptions of Wall Street's global strength and seamlessness. However, BT's very emphasis on global expansion exposed a level of desperation that allowed me to read BT's actions as a set of heterogeneous, even contradictory, strategies within investment banking power relations. Each bank, I realized, has multiple and particular approaches to the global.

In the next section, I explore the complex approaches and uses of the global that Wall Street investment banks share more generally. While I argue for the importance of context and history in ethnographies of the global, I also map out how the systemic collaborations between multiple investment banks create powerful and dominant approaches to globalization. In order to complicate the global, I combine both scales of analysis.

Global Markets—or Global Marketing?

To explore how the global is achieved and used in everyday investment practice, I asked Edward Randolph, a vice president of Risk Management[8] at Merrill Lynch, to explain why major corporations need "global" investment banks:

> If you're going do a big privatization these days of, say, Australia Telecom, you need a big global investment bank to do that. Take Australia Telecom, which they just privatized, and Deutsche Telecom. I mean, these are $5–10 billion deals. There aren't enough people in individual economies in Australia or

Germany to buy all that stock. They're going to issue eight to ten billion dollars worth of shares; there aren't enough people in Australia to buy that. And so you need a global investment bank to kind of distribute [the shares] to different markets around the world, and so as a result, they [the investment banks] will come to the U.S. and say, hey, we've got all this paper, this debt or equity of Australia Telecom.

The importance of maintaining and accessing a transnational network of investors to sell corporate stocks and bonds was further explained by Ken Hu, a vice president in Emerging Markets at J. P. Morgan who was involved in "raising" short-term capital by selling bonds for Latin American governments.[9] "Road shows" are a staple investment banking activity through which banks market their clients' stocks and bonds. As Hu explains, "A road show is when an investment bank goes out to all the key cities and sells a company's story so that investors will buy." To execute a deal, an investment bank has to "go on the road," flying from New York, Boston, Chicago, Houston, and Los Angeles to Frankfurt, Buenos Aires, and London to meet in upscale hotel ballrooms with hundreds of potential investors such as large mutual and pension fund managers to sell them sizeable pieces of the offering.

Investment banks are under pressure to create hype and stimulate "investor appetite." In this context, an investment bank's globalness is measured by its ability to summon the connections and resources necessary to maintain a large transnational network of investors who listen to their advice, believe their stories, and buy the products they sell. To win the deal from a corporate or governmental client in the first place or to convince a particular institution that their investment bank should be entrusted with the deal and reap the commissions, the bank needs to evoke the image of a network global enough to successfully distribute the deal. The global, then, not only refers to a broad network of potential investors, but it is part of the "pitch," a strategic way of marketing necessary to win the business in the first place.

For example, what struck me in March 1998, during my interview with Anthony Johnson, a college graduate who had been working at J. P. Morgan for only a few months, was how smoothly exaggerated "global talk" slid off his tongue. When I asked Johnson how "global" investment banks are and what impact this might have on the global economy, he replied:

> Investment banks, the top investment banks, are in themselves, global. We do the same thing in Hong Kong that we do in the U.S. The hope is that you are

able to supply global strategic advice, which means that we can talk to [our clients] about M&A in the U.S. We can talk to them about M&A in Sri Lanka. We can talk to them about M&A in Kuwait. And I think what you are trying to do is if a company feels like there is value in [being global], having a presence around the world, [then] you want to be in a position to advise them how to gain that presence around the world. And so, you essentially want to be able to seek out global opportunities for your client if you think that is the right way to go.

One of the goals and uses of the global in investment banks and in M&A departments in particular is to project advising capability in multiple markets around the world. What is so striking about Johnson's explanation is that Sri Lanka and Kuwait are two places in the world that investment banks in the United States have not yet entered, despite their global ambitions.[10] In Wall Street's view of the world, they are not "suitable" places for investment activity, and there exists little to no Western investment banking presence there. What was Johnson's purpose in raising Sri Lanka and Kuwait, given that both locations are usually invisible in the investment banking map of the world?

Investment banks must convince the potential corporate client by emphasizing (and sometimes exaggerating) their willingness to search out the best opportunities for a company regardless of place, as well as their ability to anticipate what companies around the world their clients might want to acquire. Johnson's intent was to inspire confidence in the bank's capabilities, by speaking about how capable and knowledgeable it must be to keep up with today's mergers. His narrative use of faraway and unlikely places (places that are characterized by the absence of banks) emphasized how willing, adept, and mobile J. P. Morgan's M&A business could be. The hope of seamless global investment banking invoked by Johnson has become an integral part of Wall Street's strategy for generating deals.

It is of course crucial to understand the larger context in which investment banking pitches and networks operate—a late capitalist economy that encourages spectacular financial accumulation as opposed to steady reproduction, rewards the divestment of labor in favor of financial schemes, and is driven by the production, marketing, and circulation of brands and images.[11] This "economy of appearances," primarily focused on attracting or constructing financial capital, depends on simultaneous "economic performance and dramatic performance" and the "self-conscious making of a spectacle [which] is a necessary aid to [the] gathering of investment funds" (Tsing 2000b, 118). In such an economy,

Wall Street's ability to sell the global is integral to its winning of deals. Wall Street's global marketing skills enable it to execute short-term financial transactions and restructurings and to convince investors to bid up stocks. A bank's capabilities in this regard attract corporate clients who wish to enter into the upper echelons of global competition. However, in an economy so dependent on claims to the global, the line between hype and actual goals becomes blurred. Moreover, the global strategies of investment banks—when seen in action—tend to be context-specific, prone to change, and continually unstable.

Global Contradictions: Simultaneously Here and Everywhere?

In investment banking, the meaning of the global often wavers between being spatially exclusive and being everywhere. In May 1999, I attended a recruitment event cosponsored by Goldman Sachs (also known as Goldman) and the SEO Career Program (Sponsors for Educational Opportunity), an organization geared toward placing undergraduates of color attending prestigious universities into investment banking, asset management, and management consulting. During this presentation held at Goldman's main headquarters in New York City, Goldman's CEO Henry Paulson wanted to impart three kernels of wisdom about the financial services industry and why Goldman excels in this milieu. Without much attention to notes or visuals, he spoke with conviction and comfort as if he had made this speech many times before. His first and overall point? Globalness! "It's about globalness," he stated. "Wal-Mart just signed a deal with Woolco, one of the largest department stores in Canada. We live in a global world; it's a fact, and it's getting more global by the second." His second point: "All the global players, all the leading firms [investment banks] are U.S. firms. We think of ourselves as a global firm." And his third point: "The pace of change in business is accelerating; this change is being led by technology and consolidation. Our deals keep on getting bigger and bigger."

He then began to detail why Goldman, because of its focus, its globalness, its "culture of people," is the leader in this business environment. Most striking was that during the Q&A session afterwards, an African American male college student raised his hand and asked, "What is Goldman Sachs planning to do in Africa? Is it investing in the growth of African economies?" Sitting in the back of the auditorium, I thought to myself, what a perfect question for identifying the potential limits of the global. Paulson answered in detail:

We are not moving or strategizing about moving to other countries in Africa besides South Africa. Similarly, we don't need to be in Russia either. They can wait. We don't need to be in every emerging market. We need to be where the markets are big and real, where our clients are big financial institutions, major companies, wealthy individuals—meaning people with $5 million or more. In South Africa, we were a pioneer, and we pulled out first [because of apartheid]. As soon as Mandela came out from jail, we were there. We worked with the ANC; we trained them. Worldwide, not just Africa, our strategy is paced growth. After the Wall came down, we didn't go to Eastern Europe or Germany. Now, we do more merger deals in Germany than Deutsche Bank [the largest bank in Germany]. We do China. I like India. We can't do it all at once. Once we get better deals, then we'll move on [in]. In Europe and the U.S., people know Goldman Sachs. In the emerging markets, no one knows Goldman Sachs. So we have to show by performance. We do major things that help to credentialize us. We focus on some of the most important families in Asia. We helped to sell Star [a corporation] to [Rupert] Murdoch. We did the first major privatization in China, China Telecom. We did what the Chinese call "the one beautiful flower in the garden," and now we are credentialized. We want to bring U.S.-style integrity. We want to get a strong group of local nationals. So, we have to focus; we can't be everywhere at once.

The question about Africa forced Paulson to delineate what, in particular, the global meant to Goldman. Instead of reiterating that Goldman was everywhere, that it was an expert in all markets, Paulson was quite clear about not needing or wanting to enter multiple markets around the world. He implied that being global is not simply to penetrate all spaces at once but rather to maintain lines of access so that Goldman has the ability to be flexible—to move in and out, to pick and choose as it pleases. Paulson's comment, "We do China; I like India," suggests that if and when he wants to be in India, Goldman could simply "marshal the troops" and move in. The global, here, is not a totalizing strategy; Paulson depicts a situation of choice, flexibility, and focused movement.[12] This notion of globalization as "flexible capability" lies not only at the heart of Goldman's understanding and use of the global but also that of many investment banks.

The verbal exchange in this discussion demonstrated that even those who unreservedly proclaim the globalness of their firm also have specific, tentative, and nationally based notions of what this global is. Why would investment banks claim to be everywhere, even in places where they were not, and yet, when pressed, be quite specific about what the global meant for their firm's strategy? While this discussion helped me to understand the complexities of how the global is understood "on the ground," I was perplexed by how diverging notions of the global were reconciled, if at all. What was the social context that allowed the global to be expressed as both "we are everywhere" and "we focus only on places that produce capital returns"?

Constituting Global Presence and Flexibility

In June 1999, I decided to ask Patty Lin, a college friend and one of my main informants, in hopes that she would help me make sense of conflicting global aspirations. "What does the global mean on Wall Street?" "How global is Wall Street, really?" A vice president who works in the Structured Finance Group[13] at J. P. Morgan, Patty began her response with a reply that I had become very accustomed to: Many investment banks (especially the ones she respects such as J. P. Morgan) are extremely global in that they have full-scale operations and market access in many countries. She cautioned me, however, to make the distinction between "truly" global investment banks that have trading operations in a particular "foreign" locale, that is, a seat on the local stock exchange, and those banks that do not have fully staffed operations, and thus can use only the New York Stock Exchange to trade foreign bonds.

Then, to my surprise, she suddenly remarked, "You need an office to call yourself global. I guess many banks can call themselves global even if they only have an empty office in that country." My jaw dropped. She continued to explain that although these empty offices are occasionally staffed, their resources are minimal, and their operations are cyclical, depending on the boom and busts of financial capital. "Some banks just can't get it right; they open, shut down, open, shut down. . . . They aren't very culturally adept." The more she explained, the more it sounded like all banks—not just "some banks"—were prone to opening and shutting down offices. All banks had the "empty office syndrome." Lin acknowledged that even "truly global" J. P. Morgan had recently laid off most of its Asia operation due to the Asian financial crisis.

Trying to grasp this new revelation—of supposedly global investment banks with empty offices—I asked her, "Wait, so you can have an empty office and still be global? What does being global mean again?" Lin replied emphatically, "Global means as long as you have a presence; it could be an empty office." She reiterated that the crucial factor in being global was "having a presence" and that presence was marked and symbolized by the existence of an office. I revisited the times that I had heard investment banking assertions of "global presence and global capability" and just assumed that they were signs of banking dominance. I had not thought of these assertions as minimalist strategies that enable banks to claim global coverage and generate global confidence.

To further clarify Wall Street's notion of "global presence," I explored this aspect with other informants in a more pointed fashion. Raina Bennett, an analyst in the Emerging Markets Group at Lehman Brothers, explained, "It means having an office in lots of different locations; but at any given time, you might just have a telephone number, fax machine, maybe a receptionist." Sally Han, describing her small investment banking firm, mentioned, "Oh, we always say we're global because we have offices in the U.K. and in Australia, even though it's just two people over there." Although my informants were not advertising to potential recruits or corporate clients that their offices were empty, they were also not embarrassed by the fact.

I then began to reread annual reports to see what investment banks meant by the global in light of these new revelations. Two annual reports are striking in their use of the language of presence and capability: "One obvious opportunity is in the still nascent markets outside the U.S., where we should be able to leverage the firm's global presence along with our considerable asset management expertise. . . . We are committed to meeting the global need for asset management services and thereby hope to capture a large share of the growing global market" (Morgan Stanley, Dean Witter, Discover & Co. 1997, 27). In its 1995 annual report, Merrill Lynch stated that its strategy is one of global presence and local commitment: "Global leadership requires sophisticated cross-border capabilities and a strong presence in select local markets worldwide. . . . With global markets becoming ever more interdependent, cross-border transactions grow in both volume and importance. Global dominance will require strong cross-border competence and presence in select local markets" (Merrill Lynch and Co., Inc. 1995, 7–8). These descriptions of global presence were couched in terms of future requirements or possibility. Instead of proclaiming to be anywhere in particular, they attempted to inspire confidence that they have the necessary potential to capture new business, cross borders, and become global leaders. Perhaps, then, the requirement of being "global" is not simply about how widespread a bank's business is, but rather how it "leverages" its presence and capability.

To understand this concept of "leveraging presence," it is important to delineate the multiple meanings of presence, as this notion is central to

Wall Street understandings and uses of the global. The word "presence" embodies a tension or separation between presence and absence, between one's physical and spiritual states, that is, one's presence is felt although one is not physically there, or although one is physically present, one is not fully there, in spirit. Presence and absence are simultaneously embodied. In *Webster's Encyclopedic Unabridged Dictionary*, the first two definitions define presence as "the state or fact of being present (being, existing, or occurring at this time or now) as with others or in a place." However, further definitions denote an ambiguity: "The ability to project a sense of ease, poise, or self-assurance, esp. the quality or manner of a person's bearing before an audience; personal appearance or bearing, esp. of a dignified or imposing kind; a divine or supernatural spirit felt to be present."[14]

Wall Street's approach toward the global can be understood in terms of these multiple notions of presence: the tension between presence and absence, between existing at a place and being able to project such an impression of self-assurance that one is *felt* to be present at that place. In other words, one of the investment banks' main global strategies is to focus on a few pivotal markets, and yet at the same time project the sense that they are and can be present in many other markets with flexibility. As such, they are focused yet capable of expanding, exclusive yet globally concerned.

To enact this strategy, Wall Street investment banks maintain empty offices in many places throughout the world, and correspondingly, they focus their material infrastructure, people, and energies on even fewer places such as New York, London, and Tokyo. Such an approach allows investment banks to target their resources and be exclusionary in their sites of capital investment while the empty office secures an entry point, a slight foothold, and a particular global image. This flexible arrangement does not incur the cost of maintaining a fully staffed and operationalized infrastructure, especially if the bank does not have any active business in that location. Given the volatility of financial markets and institutions, the empty office is the kind of unfixed presence that facilitates mobility, even as it diverts from view the particularity and exclusivity of investment banking decisions. It is precisely the global boasting which complements (even masks) the existence of empty offices, for such strategies allow investment banks to create "the impression that something is present."[15] It serves as a mask for the spatial practices of Wall Street, as it obscures the partial, incomplete, high-pressured, and ephemeral work of how and what constitutes "global presence." It is a call to look critically at globalization as not simply a fact, but a hope, a strategy, and a triumphalist ideology. Such a call reminds anthropologists that hegemony is not only hard work but also boastful. It would be too facile, however, to read an empty office as simply a sign of weakness, as a puncture in Wall Street's discourses of global seamlessness, as if to state that contrary to what Wall Street discourses say, in practice they have only empty offices. An analysis that positions proclamations of "we are there" against "actual" capabilities creates a misplaced antagonism between the two. Wall Street's constant insistence of total market coverage is part of the same project as its discourse and practice of empty offices, as they are both strategies to construct flexible global presence. Only by emphasizing how many offices they have, how seamless is their ability to respond to clients' needs from New York to Malaysia, can they can afford (literally and figuratively) not to staff offices in Malaysia.

One of the main reasons why "flexible global presence" is an effective strategy is that it blurs the "presences" that are substantial and those that are superficial or absent. It is precisely by exploiting the elusive distinction between real and fake that investment banks are able to sustain and attract more business. This ambiguity is a necessary requirement for their often far-fetched performances of globe-reaching capabilities and potentials.[16] As such, these investment banking projections of the global are not "neutral frame[s] for viewing the world" but are rather specific ways of constructing and imagining scale and movement in order to achieve particular goals and positions in a world of demanding financial flexibility (Tsing 2000b, 120). This flexibility comes at a great price even to the investment bankers who celebrate it. The premise that investment banks must immediately respond to the requirements of a new deal puts the burden directly on the shoulders of investment bankers since the very maintenance of "the empty office" attests to the lack of substantive support. In order to respond quickly and agilely to short-term volatile stock market expectations, investment banks must become "liquid corporations," in the sense that they constantly need to open and shut offices peopled by temporary staff, ultimately heeding only financial measures of success. As anthropologist Emily Martin has observed, the new concept of the worker and the corporation, otherwise known as "You, Inc.," is one where the corporation has relinquished responsibility as a long-term social organization (Martin 1999). The investment banker with laptop, cell phone, and internet connection is the flexible, globe-trotting empty branch office, responsible for maintaining the global image of the investment bank and its flexible lines of access.[17]

Global Ambitions and Instabilities

Although the dominant approach to the global is one of asserting flexible presence and lines of access and retreat (especially aggressive when recovering their power from times of crisis), there are examples of divergences from this practice. Taking seriously the existence of multiple globalisms and refusing to homogenize all Wall Street global practices into one unified strategy, I explore one major investment bank's departure from the flexible strategy of global presence. This example demonstrates that although Wall Street's global performances are usually characterized by claims and proclamations, this does not mean that they are always or singularly about appearances, pretense, or elaborate deceptions, which once uncovered, will be revealed as mere postures or outright lies. For some investment banks, globalism is a deeply believed ideology and praxis with real consequences.

In the late 1990s, during a bull-market period, Merrill Lynch (also known as Merrill) adopted a strategy of widespread global expansion, even saturation, that ultimately failed. I focus on its expansion in 1998 into the brokerage business in Japan and its subsequent withdrawal three years later to highlight how global proclamations of being everywhere can be taken seriously, while global practices can be precarious, not to mention ineffective. By 2002, Merrill had either merged or sold off its global acquisitions and returned to Wall Street's standby strategy of mobile presence in order to stage a recovery.

Merrill's strategy must be understood in the unusual context of the apex of the bull market, a time of overflowing coffers and great hubris for many investment banks, a time when the largest banks gained enormous power as spokespeople and managers for institutional and individual investors. Wall Street investment banks benefited greatly from the discourse of market populism, for this generated large sums of investment capital under their institutional management and strengthened their position as advocates of shareholders. Among top Wall Street firms, Merrill stood out in the late 1990s because of its strengths in investment management and retail brokerage. Unlike many investment banks that focus solely on corporate clients, Merrill has historically also emphasized its retail brokerage side as a way to cultivate investment opportunities and maintain relationships with upper-middle-class and wealthy individuals. Because of its historical institutional structure, Merrill, in Wall Street speak, had fewer "barriers to entry": it was better able to capitalize on this exploding market of everyday investors. Arguing that Wall Street firms could expand into the "Main Streets" of America to capture this growing market, Merrill opened up not empty offices but "brick and mortar" brokerage shops on wealthy main streets across the United States, catering to the (upper) middle class and proclaiming an end to institutional elitism.[18] Such a strategy also allowed Merrill to further differentiate itself from its competitors by drawing attention to its widespread global reach.[19] In 1998, Merrill acquired Yamaichi Securities and Midland Walwyn, the largest brokerage firms in Japan and Canada, respectively (Komansky 1998c).[20] Merrill opened up thirty-three branch offices in Japan to tap into that country's "fabled $10 trillion-plus in household savings" and convince individual "savers" to become investors by purchasing Merrill's financial products (Bremner 2001; McMillan 2001).

In a 1998 interview with CNN's Moneyline, then-CEO David Komansky discussed his company's global expansion strategy, its push to "putting down global roots" during a time when most U. S. investment firms, still reeling from the Asian financial crisis and global market instabilities, stood by their strategy of opening and shutting down offices as needed (Komansky 1998c). Komansky's vision was to build an unmatched on-the-ground global network of "true size, scale, and scope" to achieve a commanding "local presence in all major markets of the world equal to what we have in the U.S." (Komansky 1998b, 1998a). In a series of speeches in 1998, Winthrop Smith, former chairman of Merrill Lynch International, defended this new approach, declaring its long-term commitment to globalization: "We haven't withdrawn, nor do we intend to . . . from any of the countries, markets, or lines of business we're in now. . . . We're now in a financial services 'end game' that will produce institutions of enormous scale and scope . . . active in every major world market." Whereas other firms would resort to "niche strategies, defined by either geography or product," Merrill Lynch was committed to "one of the largest and most ambitious expansions ever undertaken by a financial services company outside of its home-country market" (W. Smith 1998c, 1998b, 1998a). What made Merrill's approach unique was its emphasis on staying the course, on long-term resource commitment to global expansion and establishing roots which required massive direct investment in multiple local operations. In 1999, Rick Fuscone, then COO of Merrill, stated, "Whether it's Asia, Latin America or the Middle East, [we] can't beat a retreat when there's a crisis, then parachute back in and expect to have the trust and confidence of market participants" (Fuscone 1999). Although the bull-market bubble provided a celebratory space for such unorthodox attitudes, Merrill's decisions were still considered controversial and in contradiction to Wall Street's dominant practice of global, rootless flexibility, and its executives found themselves constantly having to justify the firm's global extension.

Merrill was soon to discover that the practice of investing household savings in stocks did not translate well to Japan.[21] Due to such cultural complexities, global over-expansion, not to mention the stock market bust, in May 2001, after an initial startup cost of $200 million and "cumulative losses of at least twice that over three years," Merrill began to announce branch closings and job cuts in Japan (Bremner 2001). By the end of the following year, after only two branches out of thirty-three were left, Merrill completed "full-scale" retreat from the entire venture and merged its Japan operations with those of Hong Kong (Espig 2003, 8). Merrill's global ambitions quickly dissolved in a widely publicized global scale-back, with a change in CEO, the corresponding "ousting of 19 senior executives" and the "erasing [of] more than 23,000 jobs"—almost a third of all Merrill employees (Thomas 2003a). The new CEO, Stanley O'Neal, undertook a restructuring plan that reemphasized leverage, not extension, "disciplined growth," "core strength," "increasing efficiency," "operating flexibility," and global scale only "where it matters" (O'Neal 2002a, 2002b). This seemed in sharp contrast to David Komansky, who committed Merrill to a global empire-building of "enormous scale and scope" to establish roots in multiple local markets, and who soon became "the faded symbol of a global expansion strategy that resulted in the corporate bloat that O'Neal is working so hard to pare" (Thomas 2003b; W. Smith 1998b).

O'Neal began immediately downplaying Komansky's vision, attempting to lead the firm in the opposite direction. In almost every speech O'Neal gave in his first year, he articulated focus, speed, and flexibility. In a speech to Merrill employees in 2002, O'Neal stated, "We are redefining Merrill Lynch as a portfolio of nimble, high-performing opportunities for clients and shareholders with tremendous operating leverage. In each of our chosen sectors, we are able to adapt quickly in a constantly changing landscape and capitalize on new developments as they arise" (O'Neal 2002a, 2002b). Such a quick turnaround in firm strategy and publicity also illustrates how swiftly investment banks, as large corporations, are able to move, as they are willing to immediately fire and replace senior management, reorganize departments, and shift approach, commitments, and even values. By 2002, former CEO Komansky was widely derided in financial media circles as the CEO who took "the global" too far, to the point of excess.[22]

Interestingly enough, coinciding precisely with this shake-up, Jimenez Lee, one of my MBA informants being recruited for an investment banker associate position at Merrill in 2002, noticed that Merrill's investment banking division, previously called the Corporate and Institutional Client Group (CICG), had been renamed Global Markets and Investment Banking (GMI), and its brokerage services for wealthy individuals, U.S. and International Private Client, was now called Global Private Client (GPS).[23] It was unmistakable: Merrill had reverted to the strategy of global presence, changing its core business names to reemphasize globality and to leverage presence while simultaneously retreating from its dreams of global omnipresence and rootedness (Thomas 2003a).

Merrill's case is evidence that Wall Street's approach to global presence is not always so strategic, where they are always able to combine empty offices with global proclamations, absences with the rhetoric of being everywhere. Although these methods are generally practiced, some Wall Street firms are not immune to their own pitches and labeling: the balance between absence and presence can shift to one side, global hype can spark actual ambition and overexpansion. This event demonstrates the flaws and implosions of Wall Street's seemingly foolproof strategy of global presence and the difficulties of successfully implementing globalization strategies. Global proclamations are not simply calculating hegemonic tactics, but they can become actual goals with precarious outcomes.[24]

In this chapter, I have avoided examining the global simply from the "rearview" of what it has left in its wake, that is, as a set of received "effects" or in terms of "impact," in which the causes and motivations are taken for granted. I counter critics' tendencies to "believe the global hype," a tendency that contradicts their own commitment to understanding globalization as a set of constructed events. In this vein, I have demonstrated that Wall Street's global deployments are strategic and based on a variety of proclamations and performances. In the context of a political economy that demands constant change, being global is often more about marketing capability and potential than being fixed in space and time. At the same time, the late capitalist ideal is constantly shifting. For Merrill Lynch, the global shifted to a vision of realizing itself as "truly" global that foundered on the material limitations of overexpansion and on emergent disruptions of the mythology of globalization as a seamless flow of finance capital.

Subprime Coda

In the subprime disaster, though much more far-reaching and socially devastating (for others), investment banks were similarly "caught up" in their own hype of the limitless opportunities of mortgage-backed securities. Whereas Wall Street initially helped to catalyze and spread subprime mania by marketing the returns and the "creditworthiness" of their highly structured bonds to all manner of investors, investment banks decided that they themselves wanted even more expansion into and exposure to mortgages as a way to signal to their fellow Wall Streeters their superior synchronicity with the pulse of the market, their immersion in that which the market had deemed to be one of the most profitable products in the post-dot-com economy. As such, most investment banks on Wall Street took the unlikely steps of not only buying large portions of the high-risk, mortgaged-backed securities they were peddling around the globe for their own balance sheets, but also acquiring actual mortgage-lending outfits so that they could deal directly with customers. In May 2006, Deutsche Bank bought Chapel Funding, a mortgage lender based in California, and shortly thereafter MortgageIT, another mortgage originator, to become a leading player in all aspects of the business and to gain "access to a steady source of product" (that is, the raw materials of actual loans) "for our securitization program" (McCandless 2006). In September 2006, Merrill Lynch announced the purchase of First Franklin, one of the largest originators of subprime residential mortgages in the United States, which has since been named as one of the most notorious practitioners of fraud and predatory lending, and FirstNation, an online mortgage lender. Its rationale was to create a "global mortgage platform" to achieve a "vertical integration" in all aspects of the mortgage business, from wholesale and online origination to securitization and trading (Halldin and Blum 2006). The very next month, Bear Stearns, solidifying its position as the nation's "largest underwriter of mortgage-backed securities" agreed to purchase Encore Credit Corp., a subprime mortgage specialist, to claim "a substantial stake in the subprime lending business" (Bruno 2007; Basar 2006). Hoping to catch up with rivals, in August 2006, Morgan Stanley announced its acquisition of Saxon Capital, a large "non-prime mortgage servicer," in order to "catch up with rivals that have bigger, integrated mortgage businesses" (*Reuters.com* 2006).

These expansions into mortgage lending proved disastrous for Wall Street. As an example, just a few months after Merrill Lynch's purchase of First Franklin, Merrill announced that it had already "lost $111 million through the first half of 2007," and financial analysts questioned the "timing" of Merrill's latest subprime "plunge" (McLaughlin 2007). Merrill, it turns out, was one of the investment banks hit hardest by its own subprime practices. CEO Stanley O'Neal, who lost his job by the end of 2007 in the wake of "$24.3 billion in mortgage-related write-downs," had embarked on an ambitious program to refocus "flabby and complacent" Merrill on high risk/high reward strategies and market simultaneity (Welsch and Craig 2008; Wighton 2007). Like his predecessor Komansky, who took "actual" global expansion too far, O'Neal, so keen on the market nimbleness that was supposed to lend Merrill the flexibility to plunge with little delay into the latest "new developments," took market immediacy, another central aspect of Wall Street institutional culture, too far. (It can certainly be argued that in Merrill's purchase of on-the-ground mortgage lenders, O'Neal also took "actual" globalization too far.) Being "in" subprime, of course, symbolized the pinnacle of "high-performing opportunities" and capitalizing on the newest, hottest growth trend (O'Neal 2003).

In this litany of implosions, the story of Switzerland's biggest bank, UBS, serves as a telling example of Wall Street's cultural identities and practices in formation. In the past few years, UBS "made an astonishingly large bet on risky mortgage securities" amounting to almost "$80 billion," of which they have already written down $37 billion. In protest, "more than 6,000 shareholders" crowded into its central offices in Basel to "vent their fury over tens of billions in losses on American subprime mortgages and what they saw as an insult to traditional Swiss values like prudence and thrift" (Schwartz 2008). UBS, however, especially its American investment banking division on Wall Street, operated under a different set of concerns: its insecurity within Wall Street as a formidable global investment bank and its buy-in of mortgage hype. "Its executives [felt] like laggards in one area that was booming: the mortgage market. They watched enviously as rivals like Bear Stearns and Merrill Lynch practically minted money in the . . . frenzy" (Schwartz 2008). Although UBS did not buy mortgage-lending companies, it bought massive quantities of Wall Street–issued mortgage-backed securities as a way to demonstrate its temporal identification with the latest market fad, to compete with rivals, and to finally garner respect among Wall Street investment banks. " 'In investment banking, UBS doesn't get its due', says J. Richard Leaman III, the joint global head of investment banking. . . . 'If you asked who is in the top five, I'm not sure our name would come up for the uninformed' " (Schwartz 2008). In retrospect, Robert Wolf, president of its investment bank, observed, " 'We like to say we're in the moving business, not the storage business. . . . But we got away from that philosophy' "(Schwartz 2008). For UBS as for Merrill Lynch and most of Wall Street, we see how global ambitions, market identity, mortgage marketing, and the habitus of investment banks led it astray.

Although a full account of Wall Street's role in this crisis is still forthcoming, it has recently come to light that yet another complex financial instrument (beyond mortgage-backed bonds) based on these subprime mortgages has played a central role in Wall Street's decline: credit-default swaps, which further exemplify Wall Street's corporate culture. First, a brief description: according to my former informants, credit-default swaps, constructed by Wall Street "rocket scientists," allowed the very investors who bought Wall Street's subprime bonds to "hedge" against these risky bonds in case they fail, to have the best of both worlds—high-interest bonds for their portfolios and protection against them. Marketed as a quasi-insurance policy to temper risk and ensure reward so that in case the financial institution selling the bonds or the bonds themselves fail or "default," the buyer would recoup some or all of their investment, these financial instruments further exponentialized Wall Street profits and created (yet another) multitrillion dollar market dependent on shaky foundations. Importantly, these swaps were not actual insurance policies; in fact, as they were completely unregulated, most Wall Street investment banks did not bother to set aside sufficient capital reserves or collateral to cover themselves in case of widespread default. And, if the investment banks (and institutions such as AIG that strove to become more like Wall Street) selling these instruments were themselves to fail, the contracts would be nullified. The mutually constituted house of cards thus collapsed: high interest subprime bonds unsustainably demanded predatory mortgages; this in turn instigated widespread defaults and housing foreclosures, thus causing these bonds to become worthless. Credit-default swaps had to be paid on these defaulted subprime bonds, yet minimal reserves were at hand, and simultaneously, swaps sold by investment banks in default (such as Lehman Brothers) were themselves worthless. In the wake of the meltdown, institutional investors also used these swaps to bet that investment banks would default, thereby undermining confidence in the solvency of the banks themselves. In this intricate network of financial dealings, the point is not so much to figure out what was the underlying "real" as opposed to the derivative, but rather to investigate what it means that the very institutions that peddled risky subprime bonds also sold nonguaranteed "insurance" against them, creating a global web of risk that they themselves could not decipher.

Once again, we see the coming together of multiple aspects of Wall

Street's institutional culture. The very structure of Wall Street, which encourages the milking of the present and a strategy of no strategy (that is, full-speed expansion into subprime and buying and selling credit-default swaps without capital reserves, more for the purpose of generating profit than protecting against risk), created the very conditions that render Wall Street's financial modeling, "protection," and predictions obsolete. Moreover, as the smartest financiers in the world, they both helped to construct and expand the subprime mortgage market as well as create a shadow credit-default-swap market that allowed them to further leverage their exposure under the auspices of controlling risk. In one sense, their investments in subprime and the hedging against it demonstrated their smartness in inventing new sources of profit-taking that circumvented and outwitted both governmental regulators and risk managers in their own firm, while seeming to address their concerns. As many investment bankers told me, "We are so much smarter than the folks in risk management and audit." It is important to recall that at most investment banks, risk management is a middle-office function, not part of the prestigious, revenue-generating front office; as such, until the meltdown, traders and bankers in structured finance and mortgage-backed securities were lionized for profiting on both sides of the trade. Unlike conventional risk managers, who were seen as dampening profitability, front-office bankers and traders were able to sell their version of risk management as products. They claimed to manage risk by commoditizing it, selling it, and spreading it around globally. Of course, many Wall Streeters came to believe that they had in fact mastered risk. An informant from Lehman Brothers told me he did not believe that Lehman would go under precisely because the firm's exposure to subprime was offset, "hedged" by purchases of derivatives. A few weeks before Lehman declared bankruptcy, he continued to claim, or perhaps hope, that Lehman was "market neutral," that its risk balance was effectively "zero." The firm was, in his view, smart enough to control its exposure to risk even as it plunged as deeply into the market as possible. Wall Street leveraged claims of its own smartness, and in the end fell victim to its self-representations.

A sense of "the global" galvanized multiple institutions' expansion into these markets and products, promoted Wall Street's dominance, bred confidence in its practices, and contributed both to its own undermining and its potential rescue. Investment banks' belief in their global dominance and risk-spreading techniques prevented them from anticipating the particularities of the crisis or the extent of the collapse. In a 60 *Minutes* examination of credit-default swaps, correspondent Steve Kroft interviewed Frank Partnoy, a former derivatives broker and securities attorney, about the role of these instruments in the current crisis. Partnoy admitted that it was precisely these side bets, which Wall Street claimed to understand yet did not, that brought down the financial system. As Kroft then realized, "You got all these big Wall Street firms; Bear Stearns, Lehman Brothers. You got insurance companies like AIG. Merrill lost a ton of money on this. Everybody's lost a ton of money. They're supposed to be the smartest investors in the world. And they did it themselves." Partnoy nods, "They did it all on their own. That's the most incredible thing about this crisis is that they pushed the button themselves. They blew themselves up." (Kroft 2008)

At the same time, my informants conceived of their institutions as too big and too global to fail; in other words, they used "the global" as subsidy, as insurance policy against their own leveraged practices. All along, many bankers, traders, and fund managers expected the government to step in for Lehman Brothers, just as they "knew" that Bear Stearns, Long-Term Capital Management, and yes, even Wall Street investments in emerging markets such as Mexico, would be bailed out. In fact, it was precisely Wall Street's imbrication in and construction of global interconnection that both generated the crisis and assured its rescue: the more the world bought into Wall Street (from American investors to entire governments), the more leverage it had to hold the globe hostage. Globalization, then, like their culture of expediency, allowed investment banks to both anticipate financial busts (which drives their selling craze during the boom) and continue their risky practices until the very end.

Reflecting on the subprime meltdown, Abigail Hoffman, a former investment banker turned journalist, relates a friend's comment: "For years we have been told that bankers were paid so much because you were cleverer than the rest of us. Now it turns out you were not clever at all, and we are all suffering for your stupidity" (Hoffman 2008). Naming the "corrosive culture of investment banking" as a key instigator of the swindling of marginalized Americans who now sit "amidst the rubble of their dreams," she blames, in particular, Wall Street's "binge culture," which as I have argued rests on the everyday institutional practices of investment banks and bankers (Hoffman 2008). As editor-at-large of *Fortune* magazine Shawn Tully observes:

> Two things stand out about the credit crisis cascading through Wall Street: It is both totally shocking and utterly predictable. Shocking, because a pack of the highest-paid executives on the planet, lauded as the best minds in business

and backed by cadres of math whizzes and computer geeks, managed to lose tens of billions of dollars on exotic instruments built on the shaky foundation of subprime mortgages. Predictable because whether it's junk bonds or tech stocks or emerging-market debt, Wall Street always rides a wave until it crashes. As the fees roll in, one firm after another abandons itself to the lure of easy money, then hands back, in a sudden, unforeseen spasm, a big chunk of the profits it booked in good times. (Tully 2007)

Taken together, Hoffman's and Tully's observations make my point. It is the very privileged subjectivities of investment bankers—their elite biographies, experiences, and hierarchical representations—that empower and legitimate their authority over inefficient corporate America and outdated financial techniques. When enmeshed within the organizational culture of Wall Street, particular dispositions are constructed and investment bankers are motivated to engage in intense deal-making and market responsiveness as signs of their superiority. These structuring practices, which occur without a strategy for the future and are rationalized by a shareholder value ideology, in turn depend on continual global boasting, marketing, and leveraging in order to grow and become dominant. Wall Street–led financial booms are made possible by the very financial ideologies and transactions which eventually implode under the accumulated weight of broken promises, failed shareholder value, and the mining of capital without replenishing it.

It has become painstakingly clear that the practices of U.S. investment banks have global ripple effects, *and* that these financial practices are both created through and constitutive of "the real" economies of the world. In this era of Wall Street dominance, finance—intimately linked to, not decoupled from, the trajectories of corporations, the livelihoods of many, and the nature of work writ large—has produced a highly unequal, new world order. It remains to be seen whether or not the global financial crises of 2008 are seismic enough to radically change the power relations on Wall Street and beyond.

Notes

Introduction: Anthropology Goes to Wall Street

1   Over the past thirty years, what constitutes Wall Street—the number and kinds of institutions, and the amount of investment capital under management —has grown exponentially. From day trading to hedge funds (now numbering in the thousands), Wall Street has expanded so much in both scale and scope that its values and practices have become increasingly diffuse. (Wall Street, of course, is also an actual street, a metaphor for capitalism itself, a "jungle" culture of greed; the list goes on.) My research, however, focused mainly on investment banks and on the worldviews and practices of investment bankers. Claiming to be "the oil that greases the wheels of capitalism," these bankers serve as a bridge, as financial culture brokers between the securities markets, corporations, investors, and the mass media. Because they have helped to fundamentally transform corporate America, studying their daily discourses and practices is essential to understanding the complexities of a finance-capital-oriented vision of the world.

2   From the late 1990s to the present, the telecommunications and media industries, like most industries, have engaged in a merger frenzy, downsizing workers while creating communications monopolies. For example, in 1994, Viacom acquired Blockbuster Video and Paramount Pictures and in 1998, CBS; in 1998, AT&T acquired Tele-Communications Inc. and in 1999, MediaOne Group; in 2000, AOL acquired Time Warner, which had acquired Turner Broadcasting; in 1996, WorldCom acquired MCI; in 2006 BellSouth merged with AT&T; and so on.

3   Two other examples of Wall Street's celebration of downsizing are instructive. When Sara Lee Corporation announced a complete restructuring of its business that would outsource most of its manufacturing capabilities, closing down and spinning off factories and product lines, Wall Street greeted the news with jubilation: "Sara Lee Corp. disclosed a fundamental reshaping of the consumer-products company that would move it away from making the brand-name goods it sells. . . . While the after-tax charge is much more than the $1.01 billion Sara Lee earned in the latest fiscal year . . . it seemed that on Wall Street nobody didn't like Sara Lee's idea. In New York Stock Exchange trading yesterday, Sara Lee jumped $6, or 14%, to close at a 52-week high of $48.5625" (J. Miller 1997). When Unilever, a European, multinational conglomerate, demonstrated, via downsizings, that it was willing to "emulate" the most radical restructurings much more characteristic of American companies, Wall Street "cheered." Its announcement that it would "embark on a severe program of corporate cut-backs, eliminating 25,000 jobs over five years, closing 100 factories and possibly

jettisoning up to 75 percent of its products . . . surprising in its sharpness and scope, reflected a growing trend by European companies to emulate the cutbacks made by big American companies. . . . Today's announcement cheered investors" (Cowell 2000).

4   One strategy of Wall Street bankers, financial analysts, and corporate executives to divert attention from these heightened contradictions was to tout low unemployment statistics for the economy as a whole, with little regard for the fact that the majority of new jobs created were temporary, part-time, underpaid, and without benefits. Many scholars have critiqued the justification of the high employment rate, demonstrating that this new era of work is actually a "postemployment" era, where stable organizations and the notion of a long-term "career" are discarded in favor of rampant insecurity, greater wage inequality, and continuous work and retraining (Reich 2000; Sennett 1998; V. Smith 2002). That Wal-Mart Corporation and the temporary agency Manpower Temporary Services, Inc. are the largest employers of workers in the United States is indicative of the kinds and conditions of "jobs" being created today.

5   It is important to realize that most of the stable jobs in corporate America were available mainly to white, middle-class Americans. While in the past twenty years, white working and middle-class men have experienced a serious decline in earnings and job security, these experiences of downward mobility are even more pronounced among people of color and women. Unfortunately, there is the misplaced tendency to interpret the struggle for equal opportunity by previously marginalized groups as the reason for white middle-class job losses. As David Wellman points out, because white middle-class men have historically experienced their own monopoly on jobs and rights as "fair" and "equal," it comes as no surprise that moving toward "actual" equal opportunity is experienced by the relatively privileged as decline. What gets rendered invisible is a critical interrogation of racism and sexism and, of course, capitalism (Wellman 1997).

6   This ethnography is not so much a totalizing indictment of shareholder value as it is an examination and critique of those who speak in its name. As I will demonstrate, what defines and constitutes shareholder value is historically contingent and dependent on the larger institutional and cultural contexts in which it is embedded. While shareholder value in the past twenty-five years has come to symbolize corporate practices that boost short-term stock prices, this has not always been the case. I will also argue that many of the practices that Wall Street investment bankers construct in the name of shareholder value often result in its decline.

7   I borrow this term "making markets" from Mitchel Abolafia's pioneering ethnographic study of how traders in the stock, bond, and futures markets are embedded in socially constructed institutions (Abolafia 2001).

8   I use the term "corporate America" to reference large public corporations headquartered and operating in the United States, which may include those corporations that are also transnational in their production and delivery of services. (Many of these corporations are incorporated or chartered in the state of Delaware, though not physically located there, because of favorable corporate

tax and disclosure laws.) In particular, I use "corporate America" to convey the normative business values and practices that came to characterize the modern corporation as it was codified and constructed, in conversation with American culture at large, throughout the twentieth century. Corporate America, interestingly enough, ran increasingly afoul of both U.S. corporate law and Wall Street ideology. How Wall Street in the past thirty years worked to restructure and align corporate America to its values and practices is the subject of this ethnography. For most of the twentieth century, public corporations were dominantly defined in corporate law as wholly "owned" by and responsible to their shareholders (who can be located globally, though many corporate shares are owned by institutional investors based in the United States). But in their daily practices, most workers and managers governed and enacted the corporation as a long-tem social institution responsible to multiple stakeholders beyond the shareholder. In this vein, my usage of "corporate America" both refers to public corporations in the United States and emphasizes a particular imagining of those corporations. That corporate America is a contingent term demonstrates that the nature of the corporation—its very definition, meaning, and purpose—is contextual and contested. I would argue that Wall Street has transformed corporate America into a very different kind of institution, one that privileges its financial and legal form.

9 I use the concept "actor-network," derived from the work of Bruno Latour and Michel Callon, as a way to conceive and concretize the space of financial markets as constructed out of a multiplicity of human and nonhuman actors such as investment bankers and traders, financial products and technologies, which together form the complex interactions and "networks" of the market.

10 I use "U.S. capitalism" to demonstrate the cultural particularity and contingency of all economic practices and values. Given that capitalism in the U.S. is routinely conflated with "Western capitalism" or global capitalism, understood as universal, rational, and natural, and represented as the pinnacle of capitalist development, my point is that capitalist actions are always already constructed through complex, contested, and locally specific cultural ethos, motivations, and practices that change over time. All too often, it is "non-Western" capitalisms that are characterized by cultural habits and defined as culturally different from Western capitalism, which remains normative and acultural. In this ethnography, by examining how Wall Street investment banks came to power in the late twentieth century and reshaped the culture of corporate America, I showcase capitalism-in-the-making in the United States and in so doing write against a static and acultural approach to both finance and capitalism. This is not to say that this financially dominant capitalism does not have far-reaching global influence, but rather that it grows out of a particular industry and set of institutional worldviews, subjectivities, and practices, and spreads under certain conditions and at specific moments. I contend that it is precisely this capitalism's location at a distinctly American center of financial power—Wall Street investment banking—that enables its global recognition, spread, and dominance.

11 At the same time, it is important not to homogenize or totalistically

equate market making with investment banks. Markets are not reducible to their dominant voices; they are more multiple, unwieldy, and unpredictable than that. Similarly, the daily workings and values of particular investment banks are not always commensurate with dominant Wall Street "market demands."

12 Investment banks advise major corporations on financial deals and transactions; they do not "do retail," that is, service the mass, consumer market composed of individuals. Their interaction with individuals via their private wealth management departments are limited to "high-net-worth individuals," that is, people with $2 to 5 million in assets. Commercial banks, on the other hand, are the banks with which most Americans are familiar. They have branches, take deposits, maintain accounts, and lend to both individuals and corporations. This separation of commercial and retail banking from the securities industry, of course, occurred with the spate of regulations enacted during the Great Depression when Wall Street was widely discredited and reviled, and commercial banks rebuilt their business only through legal separation and social distancing from financial markets. For most of the mid-twentieth century, commercial banks were considered more reputable institutions than investment banks, yet, since the 1980s, as Wall Street financial values rose to dominance, commercial banks have not had the same cultural cachet as investment banks, which are understood to be elite, prestigious institutions and expert spokespeople for the financial markets. Commercial bankers also receive much lower compensation. Yet, because of Reagan-, Bush-, and Clinton-era deregulations, many commercial banks, through expansions, mergers, and acquisitions, became "hybrid" commercial/investment banks like Bankers Trust, Citigroup, Deutsche Bank, and J. P. Morgan Chase, which are allowed to mix the best of both worlds: their role and expertise in capital markets with access to retail markets.

13 Certainly, concrete legal and policy changes favorable to Wall Street investment banks and the financial markets enabled the dominance of finance capital in the American economy. While mainstream academic and popular discourse describe this restructuring of rules as "deregulation," it is important to point out that in addition to the loosening and removal of controls (the lack of governmental involvement that deregulation connotes), creating "free markets" also necessitated the active re-writing of policy and the hands-on participation of government. As Karl Polanyi long pointed out, free markets were assiduously planned, not organic expressions of natural laws (Polanyi 1944).

14 During the past few decades investment bankers, especially those who worked in the most storied investment banks, were usually quickly rehired at another Wall Street firm, as these institutions all practiced revolving-door employment with constant demand and downsizings. Even if a particular downturn in the financial sector was prolonged, Wall Street dominance and cachet were influential enough such that commercial banks and most corporations relished the opportunity to hire "hot-shot" investment bankers who ostensibly brought the know-how of high finance to the corridors of corporate America. In the current (2009) economic meltdown, Wall Street investment bankers, perhaps for the first time in thirty years, have not quickly found new jobs with comparable

compensation, though many are able to depend on significant bonuses and savings to cushion their transitions. Many of my former informants have received job offers but turned them down because of the sharp decline in pay—a sign that the era of the "big payout" bonus might be over. Given the massive restructuring of the industry and the discrediting (to some extent) of Wall Street practices and incentives, it is unclear if this recession will usher in a new status quo, whether Wall Street will recuperate its standing in a few years, and how investment bankers will weather whatever shifts may occur.

15 Twenty-five years after anthropologist Laura Nader (1972, 289) first issued her call for anthropologists to "study up," to analyze "the colonizers rather than the colonized, the culture of power rather than the culture of the powerless, the culture of affluence rather than the culture of poverty," anthropologist Hugh Gusterson (1997, 114) writes that "these appeals for a critical repatriated anthropology . . . remain substantially unrealized." It is crucial to note, however, that for the past few decades, the anthropology of science and technology has been a long series of encounters of "studying up," beginning with Sharon Traweek's entry into a high energy physics laboratory (Traweek 1992). Eliding this history ignores the recent, important breakthroughs of anthropological inventiveness and dooms anthropology to continually proclaim its inability to study the powerful. As Michael Fischer importantly points out, "anthropologists need legitimation based on our competence, not just always proclaiming 'first contact' " (personal communication).

In part because of lack of access, the "Roger and Me syndrome in ethnography," where the anthropologist is unable to get through the front lines of Fortress, Inc., "there have been few takers" of Nader's challenge to conduct ethnography in "institutions at the heart of capitalist processes of production and stratification" (Gusterson 1997, 115). At the same time, anthropologists are pioneering new strategies to garner access such as developing the requisite set of experiences, connections, and techniques, which allow them to enlist highly placed and privileged individuals as coinvestigators rather than merely informants. See, for example, Holmes and Marcus 2006.

16 Although all of my informants have been given pseudonyms, the investment banks in which they worked have not. Bankers Trust, for example, is not a pseudonym; it is the name of the bank where I worked. I changed the name of bankers' Wall Street affiliations only when their confidentiality could be compromised. It is important to remember that most of my informants are no longer working at the same banks and that many banks have merged or changed their name since the late 1990s.

17 Business divisions such as the Private Bank, Risk Management, and Investment Management hired us to do a variety of projects for them. We analyzed how much market share a group within the bank had in relation to its competitors, documented how the group could implement better "policies and procedures," and streamlined a group's "workflow" so that it could "run a tighter ship." Projects usually lasted a couple of months.

18 Shareholder value is understood by financial economists, Wall Street in-

vestment banks, and members of the investment community as a set of ideas and actions whose primary purpose is to increase the stock price of corporations to generate wealth for shareholders.

19 Although our downsizing was announced in January 1997, I did not leave BT until June 1997 because of an unprecedented deal for transition time our boss struck with the firm's most senior management. I spent the rest of the year writing grants, defending my dissertation prospectus, and garnering human subjects approval.

20 Ironically, precisely because my entire group was downsized, my coworkers dispersed throughout major investment banks, fortuitously solidifying my access to Wall Street more broadly.

21 The canonical fieldwork methodology of single-sited immersion in everyday life might not be the most generative of ethnographic data in an investigation of global financial institutions, nor should it necessarily be the primary tool of fieldwork, given rethinkings in the past two decades of what constitutes "the field," attention to the deterritorialization of culture and place, and increasing realization that cultural formations are characterized as much by change, disjuncture, and movement as by stability or persistence (Gupta and Ferguson 1992; Martin 1997).

22 I borrow this phrase from Joanne Passaro's article "'You Can't Take the Subway to the Field!': 'Village' Epistemologies in the Global Village" (Passaro 1997).

23 Jackson's mission for the Wall Street Project was to partner with large Wall Street investment banks and Fortune 500 companies to provide "access to capital" to "underserved markets, underutilized talent, and untapped capital." Jackson has long maintained that access to capital is the fourth stage of the civil rights movement after the abolition of slavery, the end of legal segregation, and the right to vote (Jackson Sr., Jackson Jr., and Gotschall 1999). Not surprisingly, of the three strategies that Jackson articulated, Wall Street was most interested in the surface multiculturalism of improving diversity.

24 During this speech, what was also striking was his observation of the stark contrast between Wall Street investment banks' approaches to "emerging markets" in Asia and Eastern Europe in relation to Wall Street's nonexistent relationship with Harlem. He questioned, for example, why Wall Street firms and institutional investors lent (short-term) billions to the "Asian Tigers" but could not even support a small business a few blocks away in upper Manhattan.

25 While a rising stock market necessitates exuberant marketing to generate buyers, it is also undermined by this exuberance as the companies the stocks represent often do not "grow" as quickly as the stock price.

26 Although most shareholders should certainly be highly critical and suspicious of Wall Street's and corporate America's breach of "trust" and rhetoric, the very notion of a betrayed investor is itself based on the problematic logic of shareholder value in the first place. The cause of the beleaguered investor, though certainly a compelling one given the extreme losses of the middle classes, often serves to obscure cuts in social programs and other effects of financial

recession on the (nonshareholding) poor and detracts from a deeper interrogation of the ideology of shareholder value.

27 For example, Morgan Stanley's merger with Dean Witter, Discover in 1997
did not capitalize on the purported synergies of cross-selling Wall Street and
Main Street. Daimler-Benz AG's $40 billion purchase of Chrysler Corporation in
1998 has been widely critiqued for "poor integration" and lack of cultural fit.
AT&T's acquisitions of Tele-Communications and MediaOne Group in 1999
were considered not only overpriced but also a strategic waste of money given
that it decided to divest its cable acquisitions to Comcast a few years later in
2002 (Lipin and Deogun 2000). In 2004, AT&T was delisted from the Dow Jones
Industrial Average, due in part to its colossal mismanagement of dozens of M&A
deals throughout the past fifteen years (S. Lynch 2004).

28 I found that these shareholder value origin stories are by and large shared
and retold among all the investment bankers that I met and interviewed. These
myths are reinforced by, intersect with, and are a part of larger narratives passed
down in a variety of sites of economic knowledge production: business schools
(where most investment bankers are trained), undergraduate economics classes,
financial news, and mainstream media.

29 Whereas Wall Street worldviews are grounded in the practices of the stock
market and the values and principles of finance, and largely intersect with neoclassical economic assumptions of ownership and property, managerial worldviews, especially those codified during the post–Second World War era, were
grounded in the bureaucratic practices of the corporation as a long-term social
institution and largely intersected with what might be termed a Keynesian,
paternalistic, or "social entity" conception of corporate governance.

30 Yanagisako argues that "in ethnographic studies, where the subjects are
endowed with sufficient financial and cultural resources to make themselves well
heard, the challenge is less how to give them voice as it is to let others speak as
well." Specifically, she situated the "official histories" of Italian capitalist firms as
told by founder-capitalists "within the broader context of the stories that are
told by other people" so that "critical methods for interpreting individuals'
accounts of their lives and histories" are "part and parcel of cultural anthropology's reflexive critique of ethnographic representations"(Yanagisako 2002, 48).
She analyzed founder narratives alongside those of other family members as well
as archival accounts of the firm from state records.

31 I borrow this term from Anna Tsing's Friction (2005), an ethnography that
provides an incisive anthropological model for approaching the encounters and
interactions between multiple locals and universals.

32 See, for example, Carrier 1995, Granovetter 1985, J. Guyer 1995, Granovetter and Swedberg 2001, D. Miller 1998, and Zelizer 1997.

33 Such a premise builds on a long history of Marxist thinking about the
fetishization of money and capital and its effects on social relations, and a
rich anthropological and sociological literature about the disembedding (and
the concurrent reembedding) of market relations from social relations (Polanyi
1944, 1957).

34 The feminist geographers J. K. Gibson-Graham warned of this potential conflation by pointing out that leftist critics of capitalism have discursively helped to create a "capitalist system" so hegemonic that it is not only omnipresent, but also the only possible economic form (Gibson-Graham 1996).

35 See Abolafia 2001, Buenza and Stark 2005, Goede 2005, Hertz 1998, Knorr Cetina and Preda 2005, MacKenzie 2001, Maurer 2005, Miyazaki 2003, and Zaloom 2006.

36 There are myriad examples of workers being downsized when corporations do not meet Wall Street quarterly stock price expectations, or small loans becoming increasingly impossible as local banks with community ties disappear and money-lending practices are dictated from national or international headquarters (Leyshon and Thrift 1997).

37 See, for example, Tsing 2000a.

38 My informants are often dubbed "masters of the universe," following Tom Wolfe's description of the Wall Street bond trader Sherman McCoy in the bestselling *Bonfire of the Vanities,* by scholars and themselves alike. To compile descriptions from Robert Reich, Rosabeth Moss Kanter, and Saskia Sassen, Wall Streeters are globe-trotting, "world class" knowledge workers; they are the investor elite, the "new monied class"; they are "the labor aristocracy of 'symbolic analysts' who spiral through the weblike structure of the elevated corporation, through workplaces connected across national boundaries, removed from local contexts"; they are the "sky workers . . . detached from those stranded on the ground, production workers and the growing sector of in-person services" (Burawoy et al. 2000, 3). In these representations, Wall Street investment bankers are hyperagents, able to marshal the resources of global institutions and the "transnational capitalist class" to recreate the world in their image and according to their values.

Chapter 1: Biographies of Hegemony

1 Certainly, this idea has currency beyond Wall Street, though I would argue that, as evidenced by Bethany McLean's and Peter Elkind's *The Smartest Guys in the Room* (2003) on the Enron executives and Wall Street advisors, these financiers are so convinced of their own brilliance that they created illusory businesses for short-term stock price appreciation while scamming small investors and their own employees. The culture of smartness is particularly heralded, utilized, and valued in finance capital as productive of spectacular profit accumulation and global dominance.

2 Management consulting is considered a professional service where consulting firms advise corporate America on such "strategic" matters as entering a new business, streamlining existing departments, restructuring and downsizing, outsourcing, and so forth. Projects might include figuring out how to increase a company's market share, how to exit a certain business, where to move and relocate a particular division. At elite universities, becoming a management consulting analyst for some of the top consulting firms such as McKinsey and Bain is

almost as highly sought after as investment banking, though not quite as prestigious or lucrative. The fact that one of the most popular debates on Harvard's and Princeton's campuses are panel sessions entitled "Investment Banking vs. Consulting" is evidence, not only of the production of narrow career "choices," but also of the limiting of what constitutes an acceptable job after graduation. That there are heated debates and panel discussions on campus about whether or not to choose "investment banking or consulting" (not to mention the fact that literally hundreds of students pack auditoriums to hear this topic) is a culturally specific phenomenon. Usually, panelists composed of firm representatives (usually former students) face off about the pros and cons of the two career choices, and use the platform to further recruit students to their "side." Discussion usually ranges from talk of compensation and the "caliber of people" to work hours and the amount of "strategic" responsibility an entry-level employee can have over corporate America. In a *Harvard Crimson* opinion piece, "Avoiding a Path to Nowhere," J. Mehta, a Harvard undergraduate, called attention to this oddness, in a sense, as well as the narrowness of such a debate. He writes, "I-banking and consulting. Consulting and I-banking. I-banking vs. consulting. What more could be on a Harvard senior's mind?" He continues, "We are caught in a vicious cycle, in which the brightest and most ambitious enter fields that most solidify the social status quo—blazing a path to nowhere in which the next generation of equally smart and energetic Harvard graduates are bound to follow" (Mehta 1998).

3 Yale numbers are significantly lower that that of Princeton and Harvard. According to their recruitment office, "30 percent of Yale students chose jobs in non-profits, 30 percent go to graduate or professional school, and 40 percent choose corporate careers in finance, consulting, publishing, communications, manufacturing, even brewing" (Tanenbaum 2005). A survey by the Office of Institutional Research showed that ordinarily around 20 percent of Yale students enter finance, but only 13 percent did in 2002 with the financial downturn (Pryor 2006).

4 Although the recruiting season at elite universities was severely protracted during the 2008–9 academic year, Wall Street banks such as J.P. Morgan and Goldman Sachs maintained their campus presence and continued recruitment, especially for summer internships.

5 Wirzbicki then suggests that "the senior class should form a union," for if "seniors at, say, Harvard, Yale and Stanford all decided tomorrow that they would simply refuse to apply for jobs . . . other firms would immediately gain a substantial competitive advantage. . . . [T]hey would be able to tell potential clients that they employ twice as many Ivy-educated associates as their boycotted competitor." He ends with "Would it be immoral to extort as much as possible from recruiters? I don't think so. . . . These are companies that treat our education like a commodity. And, if we're going to sell out, we might as well go at the highest price we can get. Students of America: We have nothing to lose but our signing bonuses. We have a world to win. Future consultants of all colleges, unite!" (Wirzbicki 2000).

6 Readers of *Liar's Poker* might recall that the author Michael Lewis (1989) was hired at Salomon Brothers in his early twenties and immediately began to engage in million-dollar transactions without any experience mainly because he graduated from Princeton University.

7 The male investment banker is so taken-for-granted especially at the senior levels that such gendered language is commonly used to denote the generic investment banker.

Chapter 2: Wall Street's Orientation

1 Similarly, when Casey Woo landed a coveted position as an analyst with Morgan Stanley after Harvard, "he thought his exhausting undergraduate routine had paid off. He had a hot job, and he had mastered the Harvard lifestyle, which he was sure would serve him well in the workplace. Nearly a year later, he's got a new threshold of pain. 'Imagine you're taking 6 classes, all with deadlines in the next few days, and your professors are standing over you, each asking you to read just a few more pages or complete one more problem set', he says. 'That's kind of what this job is like'" (Widman 2004).

2 From 1994 to 1996, Bankers Trust (BT) was mired in financial scandals, charged with scamming corporate clients such as Procter and Gamble through the use of financial products such as derivatives. Not surprisingly BT's record profits in the early 1990s were constructed via derivatives, and it is in the context of this crisis for BT that senior managers wax nostalgic about BT's regaining its monetary prowess.

3 Although Morimoto never directly recommended layoffs, the costs savings indirectly translates into such a recommendation. These practices are typical for Wall Street: mergers and acquisitions bankers often set a target amount of cost savings that need to be achieved for the merger to "make sense" according to shareholder value. It is then up to corporate managers with the help of change management consultants to do the actual "dirty work."

4 The extreme short-term focus central to investment banking corporate culture (ironically) interfered with the plan to economize through downsizing.

5 The analyst as a job position is not to be confused with the "equity analyst" or the "research analyst," which is a senior position in the research department of banks (as opposed to investment banking or corporate finance). Responsible for tracking all the companies within their particular industry, they wield the power of conferring "buy, sell, or hold" recommendations for the corporations they cover. They were made infamous in the bull market of the late 1990s, as they issued buy and sell recommendations based, not on their "objective" analyses of companies, but on their need to help the investment banking side of the bank generate more deals and transactions. Both investment bankers and research analysts crossed what is known as "the Chinese Wall."

6 Proposed living wage legislation for New York City would have established the city's minimum wage at $10 an hour by July 2006 (after increasing it incrementally over a couple of years). An annual salary of $55,000 for fifty 110-hour

weeks is exactly $10 an hour. The living wage bill can be found at the web site of the Brennan Center for Justice at the New York University School of Law, http://www.brennancenter.org.

7 These direct quotations I have compiled from field notes that aggregate the voices of many analyst and associate informants through observing them "on the job" as well as asking them "what they do" and "what does a typical day (or deal) look like." As such, in this section, although I recorded quotes verbatim, I do not attribute them to individual investment bankers.

8 With the advent of the common server, where documents are accessible to multiple users, such an organizing feat has become unnecessary.

9 See, for example, Fraser 2001, Klein 2000, Newman 2000, Schor 1991.

10 Wall Street's discourse on race is further bolstered by its intersection with the dominant discourse of race in American culture—that of color-blind post-racism, which assumes a discrimination-free, meritocratic present, where people just "happen" to be of a certain color (Gotanda 1996).

11 The National Association of Securities Professionals (NASP) is an association whose stated purpose is to expand the "presence and influence of women and minorities in the Nation's Securities Industry." Based in New York City, NASP's mission statement is to "promote professional excellence, facilitate new business opportunities, and encourage economic empowerment for people of color and women on Wall Street and for our community" (http://www.nasphq.org, accessed 1 March 2006).

12 Since this event was a public forum, and these speakers are well-known figures in the industry, I have not given them pseudonyms. All of my interviewed informants, however, have pseudonyms.

13 Sponsors of Educational Opportunity (SEO) is a program that targets high school and college students from groups underrepresented in the securities industry (mostly investment banking, but also asset management, management consulting, corporate law, and other professions). Through SEO, many students of color from prestigious universities (the only places where investment banks recruit) have access to Wall Street internships during their junior years, and to investment banking analyst jobs after college. Through SEO, for example, banks such as J. P. Morgan and Goldman Sachs distribute interviewing and recruiting schedules. Most of the young analysts of color that I came to know on Wall Street passed through the SEO program.

14 M&A is understood as a "product," a packaged commodity that investment banks market and sell.

15 The departmental hierarchies and the gradations of race and gender, however, do not always run parallel, nor are they always evident or clear-cut. For example, M&A departments, which are also considered extremely prestigious on Wall Street, are—among other characteristics—sometimes imagined to be a site where people of color and women have a better chance at thriving. At the same time, I emphasize the term "imagined," as few women and people of color actually work in M&A, although "product-side" notions of meritocracy can actually influence M&A departments.

16 It is important to keep in mind that product areas are sometimes just as socially exclusionary; for example, product-oriented areas often read women as less technically capable and therefore belie their claims of expertise and objectivity.

17 Deirdre Royster, in her study of how white male working-class networks exclude black men, makes the important point that whereas black male networks are usually confined to coworkers, white male networks are much more extensive and include workers and bosses.

18 "Professional" women often joke that women in administrative positions, such as "Jersey girls," deliberately wear high heels and tight clothing to attract a banker husband for class mobility. In their view, this heightened, "trashy" femininity is indicative of lower-class desperation and lack of education.

19 Those Wall Streeters recruited from less prestigious universities for management tracks in the back office have a different set of struggles, such as attempting to "make it" into the front office, a site of class privilege offered only to graduates of particular universities. Although these experiences are not unique to Wall Street (the boundaries of professionalism are strictly policed everywhere from law to academia to corporate America), investment banks are such tiered and classed spaces in terms of race, gender, and class that they almost seem to demand various kinds of slippage.

Chapter 3: Wall Street Historiographies

1 In later chapters, I explore the workplace organization and institutional culture of Wall Street investment banks to link investment banking biographies and motivations with their everyday cultural milieu to demonstrate how Wall Street investment banks influence and instantiate massive changes in corporate America. To make a compelling ethnographic argument about how Wall Street investment bankers' daily habitus shapes corporations, downsizings, as well as financial market crises, it is crucial to pause at this moment to understand the historical and discursive ways, such as via the shareholder value revolution, in which Wall Street garnered such influence in the first place.

2 See, for example, Aronowitz and DiFazio 1994; Bauman 1998; Bourgois 1995; Wilson 1997.

3 In chapters 6 and 7, I demonstrate the flawed and contradictory assumption that the goals of investment bankers, that is, "making a lot of money today," are actually in sync with the creation of shareholder value. I argue that regardless of intention, such goals structure short-term practices which eventually undermine shareholder value, the stated purpose.

4 Simply presuming the callous and greedy investment banker or a perverse financial market misplaces the locus of analysis, as Wall Street does not rejoice in downsizing for its own sake or "enjoy the spectacle of human suffering." Rather, American business values have radically shifted in the New Economy such that "corporate growth and productivity gains" are thought to be "rightly severed

from wage increases and handed over instead to top management and share-holders" (Frank 2000, 98).

5 Shockingly, when I later discussed this revelation with a friend in business school, he said quite matter-of-factly, "Well, that's the first thing you learn in business school!" In other words, this assumption (that corporate health is a high stock price, that corporations=shareholders) is part of the initial ideological orientation in business school.

6 Scholars investigating massive corporate disinvestment, downsizing, and the neoliberal turn often point to such macrodynamics as global competition, postindustrialization, anti-welfare-state, free-market discourses and practices, not Wall Street and the takeover movement.

7 Such an analogy is reminiscent of what Kathryn Marie Dudley (1994) argues in her ethnography, *The End of the Line: Lost Jobs, New Lives in Post-industrial America*, that the rhetoric of the "culture of the mind" versus the devalued "culture of the hand" justified the downsizing of blue-collar workers, as manual laborers never "deserved" to be middle class in the first place. Although Dudley does not refer to middle managers, much of this same justification is used to delegitimate managers who, in Wall Street's imagination, are usurpers of corporate wealth and untrustworthy agents of shareholder value, and thus unde-serving of their status in corporate America.

8 It is important to note that Gordon Gekko is the film's villain; Wall Street-ers who identify with him are self-consciously identifying with the bad guy, which plays into the hip revolutionary "bad boy" ethos that is central to the formation of macho camaraderie. Through the appropriation of critique or satire by the very people supposedly being attacked, Wall Streeters reframe misogyny and class hierarchy as heroism. I thank Gary Ashwill for bringing these linkages to my attention.

9 Other popular, bestselling titles were Connie Bruck's *The Predator's Ball: The Inside Story of Drexel Burnham and the Rise of the Junk Bond Raiders*, James Stewart's *Den of Thieves*, Tom Wolfe's *Bonfire of the Vanities*, Bryan Burrough's and John Helyar's *Barbarians at the Gate: The Fall of* RJR Nabisco, Sarah Bart-lett's *The Money Machine: How* KKR Manufactured Power and Profits, and Po Bronson's *Bombardiers*, to name a few.

10 My informants almost unfailingly suggested that I read Michael Lewis's *Liar's Poker* (1989) to capture the mood of Wall Street in the 1980s. Although *Liar's Poker* is in one sense a critical satire of Wall Street's misogyny and trad-ing manipulations of American corporations, small banks, and investors in the 1980s, many of my Wall Street informants interpreted it as primarily a hilarious and hip narrative of incredibly intelligent "big swinging dicks" at the forefront of financial innovation, who got "a bit excessive" with money, sex, and greed (Lewis 1989). Of course, I would argue that the figure of "the big swinging dick" demon-strates that monetary accumulation is tied to the performance of sexist mas-culinity, even beyond the notion that men's money making is writ on women's bodies and interpreted in terms of women's subordination in that reproducing

and invigorating gender and racial inequality is a key component of the experience of "getting paid." In other words, gender superiority and inequality
are experienced as pleasure that motivates money-making desire; white male
bankers' and traders' monetary success is "sexy" and properly "sexes" the men
into a hierarchical social context, where unequal racial and gender relations are
felt to be erotic. Monetary success is inextricable from a hypermasculinity that
constructs and derives pleasure from (and therefore naturalizes) gender and
racial asymmetry.

11 Economic and dominant discourses of postindustrialism often portray the
move to a service economy and the shift toward stock market supremacy as
evolutionary, inevitable, and explained by homogenous market logics. It is assumed that these shifts are simply mechanically determined by prices and productivity: for example, although cheap "third world" labor is certainly an important explanatory tool for deindustrialization in the United States, it is crucial to
understand also that such disinvestments in manufacturing bases in the United
States were often deliberate and extremely expensive as continual investments
and upkeep in such industries often cost less than complete relocation or entrance into new industries. In my work, I refuse these assumptions to demonstrate that socioeconomic changes are products of daily investment decisions
and values that are by no means solely instrumental. I conceive of Wall Street's
"solutions" for socioeconomic crisis, not as "necessary" attempts to "fix" socioeconomic problems, but rather as a means and strategy to assert powerful financial interests.

12 David Harvey (2005, 45) points out that the New York City fiscal crisis
of the 1970s was a transformative moment, a staging ground where investment bankers rehearsed and pushed through their particular values and agenda
"against the democratically elected government of New York City." In 1975,
when a "powerful cabal of investment bankers (led by Walter Wriston of Citi-
bank) refused to roll over the debt and pushed the city into technical bankruptcy," New York City was forced to accept the terms of Wall Street's bailout
offer that restructured the city's budget priorities such that bondholders were
privileged and "essential social services," from municipal unions to public universities, had to fight over the leftovers. Harvey (2005, 48) argues that the
"management of the New York fiscal crisis pioneered the way for neoliberal
practices both domestically under Reagan and internationally through the IMF
in the 1980s. It established the principle that in the event of a conflict between
the integrity of financial institutions and bondholders' returns, on the one hand,
and the well-being of citizens on the other, the former was to be privileged. It
emphasized that the role of the government was to create a good business
climate rather than look to the needs . . . of the population at large." Capitalizing
from New York City's fiscal crisis to relandscape the city's institutions and management priorities toward Wall Street helped to set the stage and the mind-set
for the takeover movement and the shareholder value revolution. These developments compellingly parallel structural adjustment practices, where large finan-

cial institutions experience windfalls at the expense of the austerity measures shouldered by "the people."

13 The "property view" held that the company's board of directors' sole obligation was to the shareholders alone, whereas in the "social-entity view," the obligation of the directors was to both the corporation as a long-term social entity and its multiple stakeholder constituents.

14 I use the term "reregulation" interchangeably with "deregulation" to make explicit that "free markets" and a financial system that favors Wall Street is not simply characterized by the absence of governmental and legal regulation, but rather regulatory structures that both deliberately overlook and privilege particular interests and ideological imperatives.

15 The buying and conglomerating of corporations in the 1960s did not lead to massive downsizings, the main reason being that the view of the corporation as an employer and a permanent social institution was still relatively dominant. Moreover, the newly acquired corporation was not "merged" into the parent per se, but rather understood as an autonomous institution.

16 Like the 1990s, the 1960s saw Wall Street promulgate the notion of market populism and participation. For example, a huge proliferation of guides to investment appeared, such as T. A. Wise and E. O. Fortune's *The Insiders: A Stockholder's Guide to Wall Street* in 1962, Charles Rolo's and George Nelson's *The Anatomy of Wall Street: A Guide for the Serious Investor* in 1962, and Janet Low's *Understanding the Stock Market: A Guide for Young Investors* in 1968.

17 The "ruthlessness" of the conglomeration movement in the 1960s "was tame by modern measures." "While they could strip assets like champions, their corporations followed the rules of welfare capitalism, adhering to the prevailing standards when it came to vacations, health benefits, pensions, holidays, sick leave . . . all again scarcely imaginable at the turn of the millennium under the reign of 'shareholder value'. Even the big institutional investors . . . who were caught up in the "go-go" market's sudden raciness were nonetheless Keynesian loyalists" (S. Fraser 2004, 493).

18 As O'Sullivan (2000, 172–73) observes, "It should not be forgotten, however, that to the extent that these transactions [takeovers] responded to deficiencies in corporation organizations' ability to generate innovation, these problems had, in many cases, been created by the previous conglomeration era in which the stock market had played a central and facilitating role. It is, therefore, inappropriate to elevate the market for corporate control to the status of corporate governance solution. . . . Rather, it served as a willing and important accomplice to a management fad that led corporations into . . . a thirty-year detour."

19 For Wall Street, mergers and acquisitions are a constant source of profits: investment banks market them as necessary to keep up with global change. An unsuccessful merger spurred on by an investment bank might simply lead to an "un-merging" and a "re-merging" with a different company, both mediated (once again) by investment banks. In other words, investment banks are continually selling various mergers and acquisitions, depending on what the market trends

are, and as such, are not primarily concerned with the long-term success or stability of the corporation. As a Merrill Lynch mergers and acquisitions specialist Ridge Kiang states, M&A is a "steady revenue stream, less vulnerable to downturns" for banks, because no matter if the market is going up or down, a company can "respond" to the market using M&A.

20 For Wall Street investment banks, "takeovers" are included under their category of M&A.

21 See Bryan Burrough's and John Helyar's description of KKR's rise from relative obscurity to major Wall Street player in the early 1980s (Burrough and Helyar 1990, 140).

22 In a buyout, the new investors, by purchasing a majority of the outstanding stock through debt, transform public joint-stock corporations into privately owned enterprises; then after they have sold off certain assets and restructured the balance sheet to pay off borrowed debt, they resell the company to the "public" stock market again and pocket all the proceeds of the stock offering. The takeover artists, then, without investing much (of their own) money, time, or even effort, manipulated corporations through financial transactions and made billions of dollars by "liquefying" them.

23 Drexel Burnham Lambert went bankrupt in the 1980s in the wake of multiple insider trading scandals.

24 Not surprisingly, the main example we have in the United States of financial capital dominance is that of the days of J. P. Morgan right before the Great Depression, the days when the richest 1 percent owned most of the nation's wealth. As Baker and Smith tell the story, the takeover movement was a success story not simply because it liberated "free cash flows" and improved "equity prices in undervalued companies," but because it signaled a new regime of wealth accumulation through a "more rigorous exploitation of corporate resources" (Baker and Smith 1998, 21–22). Indeed, in the late 1990s, the wealth disparity in the United States returned to the heights of the Great Depression. If achieving the supremacy of financial capitalism is the goal, then, despite the continual busts following takeover booms, shareholder value has certainly succeeded.

25 This is not even to mention the notorious practice of intentional short-term gouging for profitability at the expense of longer-term growth.

26 "A frequently invoked example is Carl Icahn's takeover of TWA in 1985, when the reduction of $200 million in total wages was larger than the entire takeover premium. . . . On the basis of their analyses of a sample of 62 hostile takeover bids . . . between 1984 and 1986, Sanjay Bhagat, Andrei Shleifer, and Robert Vishny concluded that layoffs after takeovers are common and can explain 10–20 percent of the premium" paid to shareholders (O'Sullivan 2000, 169).

27 Cooper openly states that investment banks induce corporations to cater, even manipulate, their balance sheet and other financial numbers to meet Wall Street expectations. Of course, such admissions point to the role of fancy financial accounting and sophisticated packaging of numbers, not "actual" efficiency in producing shareholder value.

28 In a comprehensive review of the multiple effects of corporate downsizing, Jeffrey Pfeffer, professor of organizational behavior at Stanford Business School, found that downsizing "is not a sure way of increasing the stock price over a medium- to long-term horizon, nor does it necessarily provide higher profits or create organizational efficiency or productivity." Drawing from a *Wall Street Journal* article on the effects of downsizing on shareholder value, Pfeffer points out that the stock prices of downsizing firms, following an initial increase, were lagging those of comparable firms in the industry by 5 to 45 percent after two years in two-thirds of the cases, and "in more than half of the cases, stock prices lagged the general market by amounts ranging from 17 to 48 percent" (Pfeffer 1998, 174). He argues that downsizing is strikingly "inefficient" because many firms often immediately bring back laid-off employees as rehired employees or contract workers, as downsizings are spurred by economic fashion, not long-term planning or strategy. Not surprisingly, downsizings also have negative effects on employee performance, productivity, and organizational memory.

29 Unlike most of my informants, Fisher worked on the "buy side" of Wall Street, that is, the institutional investors or money fund managers who buy large amounts of securities for their own or clients' portfolios and make decisions on what to buy based on the marketing or "research" from the investment banking's "sell side," which focuses on making recommendations about stocks (whether to upgrade, downgrade, or create a target price for a stock) for corporate clients and the larger institutional investment community. Whereas the sell side is mainly housed in investment banks, the buy side works either as a part of an investment bank like Morgan Stanley and Merrill Lynch, or for institutions that specialize in managing large investment portfolios, such as Fidelity Investments. Whether or not they are part of an investment bank, money managers are also a part of Wall Street and have many of the same values and priorities.

30 As Fisher points out, however, senior investment bankers and investment managers recognize that Wall Street's short-term cultural parameters do *not* engender long-term shareholder value. "You know, the Street is not totally stupid. They know there are companies that might be reporting in March, knowing damn well that the peak of their earnings won't be until Christmas."

Chapter 4: The Roots and Narratives of Shareholder Value

1 To clarify, although in some contexts shareholder value and neoclassical values can be used interchangeably, for my purposes shareholder value has a more specific meaning, which necessitates the linking of stock-market values with the translation of the corporation into neoclassical terms and priorities. Although the concept of creating value for shareholders has always been in the U.S. financial lexicon, what is today understood as the "shareholder value movement" refers to the systematic restructuring of U.S. corporations, largely promoted by Wall Street in the late twentieth century. Although practices reminiscent of today's shareholder value movement existed in the late nineteenth and early twentieth century in that Wall Street financiers and robber barons con-

trolled many corporations, this control was not always sought in the name of shareholder value, nor did corporations yet occupy such a significant place in U.S. society. Also, today's advocates of shareholder value generally hold what is described as the "finance" position in issues of corporate governance, that is, they believe that the stock markets should govern and discipline corporations. This view argues that rising share prices are synonymous with efficient corporate governance and that corporate control should be left in the hands of the "market."

2 In this chapter, I focus on the crucial importance of narrative, history, nostalgia, and Wall Street fantasies and worldviews as strategic forces in the analysis and shaping of capitalist culture. I also underscore that in the particular case of twentieth-century U.S. capitalism, understanding capitalist narrative constructions and manipulations is crucial, as the narrative fiction and strategy of shareholder value and its effects on the course of U.S. capitalism have been largely ignored outside the business community.

3 The choice of gendered pronoun is deliberate, as classical economists like Adam Smith almost certainly presumed the maleness of their hypothetical entrepreneurs.

4 Although the average shareholder can sometimes benefit from the principle that corporations should be run for them, most individual stockholders do not have the same access to information and technology as Wall Street, nor do they have their fingers on the volatile pulse of the stock market. That individual shareholders can benefit from the tenets of shareholder value conceals more than it reveals, as does "mass" public participation in the stock market. In a world where corporations are foremost concerned with stock prices, the primary beneficiaries of this conflation are the institutions aligned with the stock market and their executives.

5 This is not to say, however, that neoclassical, laissez faire values are espoused and used solely by Wall Street, for throughout the economic history of the United States, many groups have promoted these values for a variety of reasons. Nor is it to presume that Wall Street had long ago foreseen and sown the seed of neoclassicalism for the purpose of begetting the shareholder revolution of the late twentieth century.

6 Certainly, with the unprecedented bull market of the late 1990s, corporations and Wall Street have found it incredibly lucrative to raise money by issuing stocks. Because stock prices were constantly rising, corporations were assured that there would be buyers for their stocks, as the stocks seemed to always rise above their initial offering price. The buyers (that is, large institutional investors as well as individuals) developed an appetite for stocks, so raising money as well as "cashing out" via the stock market had never been easier. Wall Street, which brokers and profits from these transactions, always stands to gain from a rising stock market, as corporations seek to use high stock prices as currency for acquisitions, mergers, and equity offerings.

7 J. P. Morgan and Co. dominated the capital market and helped to create (through consolidations, mergers, and financings) most of the major industrial

giants of the twentieth century: U.S. Steel, General Electric, International Harvester, and AT&T.

8 An economy or sector controlled by such firms, that is, investment banks, has often been termed one of "financial capitalism" (Chandler 1977, 9). By the early twentieth century, "180 bankers and directors of the inner circle served on the boards of 341 financial and other corporations with total resources in excess of $25 billion" (Carosso 1970, 151–54). It is no wonder that this era is often known as the height of finance capitalism, the age of the financier robber-barons and the money trusts. The main beneficiaries of their efforts at consolidation were the corporations' creditors and trustees—that is, the bankers themselves.

9 Illustrating the extent of Wall Street's influence before the Great Depression, Ferdinand Pecora, in *Wall Street under Oath*, a record of the Pecora investigations of 1933–34 conducted by the Banking and Currency Committee of the U.S. Senate that marked the beginning of the New Deal, dubbed Wall Street a "national danger." Pecora, the main Senate investigator, and Rep. Marland, a member of the House of Representatives, blamed Wall Street for contributing to and exacerbating the Great Depression. Describing the extent of J. P. Morgan's control over American finance and business, Pecora (1939) wrote, "The members of the firm of J. P. Morgan and Company and Drexel and Company held twenty directorships in fifteen great banks and trust companies, with total assets of $3,811,400,000. . . . They held no less than fifty-five directorships in thirty-eight industrial corporations, with total assets of $6,000,000,000. In grand total, they held 126 directorships in 89 corporations with total assets of twenty billions— incomparably the greatest reach of power in private hands in our entire history." According to Ron Chernow, at its height "J. P. Morgan held 79 directorships in 112 corporations, spanning the worlds of finance, railroads, transportation, and public utilities" (Chernow 1990, 152). No matter which figures one uses, the sheer magnitude of investment banking's influence was astounding.

10 Although I critique the notion of the stock market as a primary source of funding for corporations, I do not mean to downplay how crucial the stock price has become as the dominant measure of corporate behavior. If stock prices fall, corporations are considered to be poor performers; they lose investors, and usually embark on a rampage of cost cutting and restructuring. Furthermore, today the compensation of most corporations' top executives is tied to the stock market, which further ensures the conflation of the two domains and their values.

11 It was the growth and development of "dominant enterprises" that "made possible the rise of a market in industrial securities, not vice versa" (Lazonick and O'Sullivan 1997, 10).

12 During this time, financiers were popularly assumed to constitute "the most dangerous sub-segment of the non-producing class in a proprietary democracy and a producerist political economy. These moneyed men enjoyed wealth they had not produced; their paper assets represented fictitious capital" (Ott 2007, 54). Furthermore, the corporate enterprise itself had not secured broad political and cultural legitimacy either.

13 It was not until the formation of the Securities and Exchange Commission (SEC) and the passage of a body of regulatory law after the Great Depression that there was an attempt to curb stock market manipulations and monitor securities offerings to "protect" investors.

14 For example, as I have described, the liquidity and exchangeability taken for granted in the stock market is a deliberately constructed practice dependent on everything from local notions of property and temporality to a complex infrastructure of institutions, investors, and technologies.

15 See, for example, Bill Maurer's discussion of Berle and Means in Maurer 1999.

16 Berle's and Means' groundbreaking work critiquing neoclassical logic is today frequently cited as one of the principal intellectual forebears of the shareholder value revolution, a misreading that furthers the "historical" foundation and economic legitimacy of this cause. For example, many scholars of business and finance often foreground their research in Berle's and Mean's observations of the tensions between ownership and control, only to then claim that shareholder value corrects this tension without a corresponding engagement with the complexity of Berle's and Mean's arguments. See, for example, Baker and Smith 1998; Roe 1994; M. Useem 1996.

17 Like most of the business community, Berle and Means were wary of the potential of managerial abuse. Mid-century business expansions and empire-building, not to mention increasingly steep corporate hierarchies, certainly warranted such fears—which shareholder activist critiques of managerial capitalism were quick to exploit. While warning of a "corporate oligarchy coupled with the possibility of an era of corporate plundering," Berle and Means also cautioned against reforming American industry to operate for the "sole benefit of inactive and irresponsible security owners" (Berle and Means 1991, 311).

18 Because I am most concerned with shareholder value as espoused by its dominant spokespeople and proponents (Wall Street investment bankers as opposed to the "average Joe" stockholder), I want to similarly focus on corporate executives as spokespeople who set the tone for the direction and "the vision" of the corporation. I investigate the discourses and representations espoused by the managers and executives of corporations, as well as academic observers, during the 1950s and 1960s, a time when corporations were at the height of their growth and influence in American society. I also realize that the values and locations of "managerialism," especially its articulation of a more inclusive, welfare capitalism, have been largely shaped by the struggle of workers and communities. My interpretation of "managerial values" is not necessarily one espoused by all managers, although for the most part I describe a worldview that was considered to be mainstream.

19 Highlighting the marked difference between the two forms of capitalist organization, Marina Whitman, drawing from Prakash Sethi in *Is the Good Corporation Dead? Social Responsibility in a Global Economy*, echoes this sentiment in her description of the social economy: "America's large corporations became private institutions endowed with a public purpose—indeed, multiple public

purposes. Americans took it for granted that these powerful institutions could fulfill the vision of "a financially successful and economically efficient company that would marry profit-making with social responsibility; provide stable, well-paid jobs with generous benefits; support culture and the arts; encourage employees to become involved in their communities; and be a good corporate citizen" (Whitman 1999, 2).

20 See Margaret Blair's discussion of the regulation of banks and securities markets (Blair 1995, 29–30).

21 Levy is referring to the California state pension fund manager who was fired in 2002 for investing in United States Treasury Bonds.

22 The NYSE also tested the success of recent marketing and advertising efforts via the new medium of television. The survey asked subjects whether or not they could properly identify the current campaign slogans "Own Your Share of American Business" and "The Nation's Market Place" to the NYSE. It was found that whereas merely 4–5 percent of the population could correctly link these campaigns to the NYSE, 63 percent correctly linked "It Floats" to Procter and Gamble and "The Pause That Refreshes" to Coca Cola Company.

Chapter 5: Downsizers Downsized

1 While there are certainly distinctions between the "corporate cultures" of various Wall Street investment banks, I argue that because many investment banks on Wall Street have similar structural locations in the new economic order as well as almost identical organizational arrangements and management priorities, their corporate cultures, experiences, and roles are readily generalized. Because investment bankers throughout Wall Street share similar socioeconomic worldviews, job descriptions and experiences, and compensation structures, these overarching commonalities have shaped my conceptualization of investment banking "corporate culture."

2 Of course, especially during downturns many investment bankers are laid off right before the bonus is paid to preserve, or even increase, the already exorbitant bonus pool for those remaining.

3 Their main competitors are agencies such as Right Management Associates, headquartered in Philadelphia; the Strickland Group, in New York; and the Ayers Group, also in New York. Right Associates describes themselves as "the world's leading career transition and organizational consulting firm," that is, in addition to outplacement services, they also do consulting, change management, and restructuring for corporations (www.right.com). The Strickland Group is "internationally recognized as a leader in Executive Coaching, Career Transition and Communication Services" (www.stricklandgroup.com). Finally, the Ayers Group specializes in recruiting services, career transition, and human resource and technology consulting (www.ayers.com).

4 The outplacement services agency that I had the most interaction with was Lee Hecht Harrison, one of the agencies that Bankers Trust subcontracted to administer our group's outplacement services. Because they sought clients within

the financial services industry, Lee Hecht Harrison's main offices in Manhattan were located in the Wall Street and Park Avenue areas. According to their web site and various brochures, this firm, headquartered in Woodcliff Lake, N.J., is "the leading global career services company specializing in outplacement, career development, leadership development and coaching" (www.lhh.com).

5 One of the major tragedies of the Great Depression was that commercial banks took people's deposits and gambled them in the stock market. The Glass-Steagall Act and FDIC insurance after the Great Depression sought to prevent this from occurring again by separating commercial banks from the securities businesses (that is, from investment banks), and insuring people's deposits.

6 During the time of my fieldwork from 1997–99, many of my informants as well as many observers of my research remarked that the younger analysts and associates had mainly experienced an extended U.S. stock market boom with only one major market downturn—the "emerging market" crisis. Despite the fact that "extended booms" carry within them extended periods of insecurity (and busts), I found it important to include vice presidents and managing directors who have experienced multiple bouts of insecurity and several market cycles.

7 I found his accordion image extremely compelling, for it demonstrated that employment at investment banks expands and contracts not *only* because of market cycles, but because of their approach to employment *in general.* The accordion moves in and out not only at a singluar climactic point in the music, but constantly, as the way the instrument is played.

8 It is important to note that when Wall Street investment bankers experience or claim "not getting paid," such expectations are based on assumptions that would be extraordinary for the average corporate manager. The understanding is that bonuses should continue to climb based on some multiple of salaries (from double one year to triple the next, for example).

9 Andrew Grove, previous CEO of Intel Corporation, wrote a career advice book evocatively entitled, *Only the Paranoid Survive,* in which he asks, "When companies no longer have lifelong careers themselves, how can they provide one for their employees?" In this context, "nobody owes you a career. Your career is literally your business. You own it as a sole proprietor." And "frankly," Grove adds, no one "will care besides you" (Grove 1999, 6). In a much quoted statement from an AT&T executive, there is "no long term" in the workplace today; even the very concept of "job" is being replaced by "projects" and "fields of work" (Sennett 1998, 22).

10 A case in point is that downsizings in corporate America in 2001 (after the stock market crash beginning in 2000) reached unprecedented, stratospheric levels. Coupled with a continued adherence to short-term shareholder value, the dot-com crash of 2000 instigated a bear market and massive, spiraling economic downturns that dwarfed all previous downsizing episodes. From 2000 until 2006, monthly headlines about six-figure downsizings and articles showing how businesses are "no longer afraid" of holiday layoffs continually dramatized a new era in employment practices. As John Challenger, CEO of Challenger, Grey

and Christmas, told CNN correspondent Lisa Leiter in April 2001, "We saw over 600,000 cuts in 2000. We're already at 572,000 through the first four months. This is downsizing of a whole new scale. It's not like anything we've ever seen" (*CNN Moneyline News Hour* 2001). Since Challenger, Grey and Christmas began tracking downsizings in the late 1980s, 2001 with 1,956,876 job cuts destroyed all previous records (Disabatino 2002). 2002, 2003, and 2004 were not far behind with 1,431,052; 1,236,426; and 1,039,176 layoffs respectively (Moeller 2005). Since 2004, these drastic numbers have been interspersed with periodic claims of "economic recovery," however disappointing. In 2005, with Wall Street and the larger business community rejoicing in a stronger economy, Challenger, Grey and Christmas announced that by mid-year, over half a million jobs had been cut.

Chapter 6: Liquid Lives

1   Whereas I was referring to Wall Street's effect on corporate America, interestingly enough, Douglass's reply was to talk about how Wall Street investment bankers themselves were hurt by their firms' organizational priorities.

2   Not missing a beat does not always translate into making the best long- or even medium-term decisions for their own bottom line.

3   To give a sense of the numbers, in 2005, which surpassed 2000 in terms of Wall Street record profits and banker compensation despite the fact that most of America had not yet "recovered," the New York state comptroller's office announced that Wall Street securities firms paid out a record total of $25.7 billion in end-of-year bonuses, $150,160 per employee if it were divided equally. This broke the previous record of $19.5 billion set in 2000. In 2006 the record was shattered again, as the bonus payout reached $34.1 billion (New York State Comptroller 2009).

4   Anthony Johnson's logic here is that the most prestigious investment banking firms can get away with paying new employees lower base salaries because they attract more applicants.

5   Compared to most workers in New York City in 1998, "Wall Street employed 166,000 people, up slightly to 4.7 percent of the city's workforce . . . [but] take home 19 percent of the town's total pay" (Kirkpatrick 2000).

6   Roth argues that race was not a significant variable in determining compensation. I would counter that because there were only seven people of color in the sample (one African American and six of Asian descent), the sample is too small to draw such a conclusion. Moreover, Roth coded race "dichotomously as white/ nonwhite," thus collapsing the differences between people of color, as well as between white women and men of color.

7   Many sociological studies have pointed to how women and people of color are disadvantaged by the "nature and amount of client interaction," which privileges "homosocial" interactions and exclusionary "social closure" based on informal "in-groups" (Browne and Misra 2003; Kantor 1993; Roth 2003).

8   At investment banks (as elsewhere), white male dominance is passed on to

new cohorts of investment bankers because white male networks are the most extensive and dense; those incorporated into these networks tend to be given more opportunities as well as the benefit of the doubt—that is, forgiveness for mistakes is more forthcoming for young white men (Royster 2003, 176–78). Since social location helps to structure one's social and professional network as well as one's access to clients and to particular kinds of departments and jobs—all of which in turn affect the amount of money made—Wall Street's discourse of money meritocracy once again elides the exercise of power. The money meritocracy renders invisible the "visible hands" that control access to the performative stage and shape what constitutes meritorious performance in the first place.

9 As many Wall Streeters have demonstrated, investment banks are in the business of information processing and making connections in order to transact deals with corporate America, and as such, they have very few "fixed" capital assets. Given that people are banks' main assets, to change their strategy/position/profitability would essentially mean changing the people instead of, say, buying new equipment. The change strategy is to rotate in workers with highly profitable connections, knowledge, and reputations, and rotate out workers whose repertoires are out of favor.

10 In 1999, financial journalist James Glassman and economist Kevin Hassett published *Dow 36,000: The New Strategy for Profiting from the Coming Rise of the Stock Market*. This book fit neatly into the hype of the late 1990s, when almost every financial news outlet as well as Wall Street research analysts and spokespeople were proclaiming an infinite boom driven by "supertanker America," a phrase that Goldman Sachs executive Abby Joseph Cohen used in her keynote speech to the Securities Industry Association Conference in 1998.

11 Of course, what constitutes "performance" is usually neither shareholder value nor corporate productivity, but the number of deals closed.

12 Because I focus on such topics as compensation and incentives within a context of rampant insecurity, such terminology certainly parallels the discursive formations of standard *homo economicus* narratives or even rational-choice theorists in that bankers can be interpreted as aculturally optimizing rational behaviors of profit, set in the context of particular labor market conditions. I caution against, however, the simplistic assumption that the topic of "making money" is automatically located beyond the bounds of cultural inquiry, signaling a presumed dichotomy between economic rationality and cultural particularity. What normatively gets called standard economic behaviors and "rational choices" are explicitly cultural and contingent, dependent upon, and constructed out of, specific social institutions and arrangements. Ignoring money and incentives does not make the analysis any more cultural. Investment banking's corporate culture cannot be assumed to be an exercise in rationality merely because it is concerned with making money; it is about specific and intricate local cultural expressions, desires, and experiences.

13 As I have noted, the global economic crisis of 2008–9 could very well restructure the experience and meaning of downsizing for investment bankers.

Chapter 7: Leveraging Dominance

1 Kathleen Day (2008) of the *Washington Post* points out that "a majority of subprime customers—61 percent in 2006 . . . could have qualified for less expensive conventional loans."

2 By 2006, the home ownership rate grew close to 70 percent, and "some 12 million new homeowners emerged, roughly half of them members of racial minorities. The American dream had been extended as never before" (Mallaby 2007).

3 The audience for corporate annual reports consists mainly of the shareholders, potential clients such as Fortune 500 companies, to whom these banks want to "pitch" their services, consulting and information-service firms who use these reports to compile information and generate performance charts, the financial news media, and state regulatory agencies such as the Securities and Exchange Commission (SEC).

4 Many cultural studies theorists and social scientists, by giving emphasis to capitalism's omnipotence, have helped to imagine a world of capitalist totality. In the rush to confront and depict the powerful impact of Western global hegemony, they have often neglected the power-laden political effects of their own representations of this very hegemony. Ironically, these academic representations and critiques sound extremely similar to Wall Street triumphalist discourses of global capitalism, as promulgated in much of the business and financial literature.

5 Sales and Trading is a major division of an investment bank that sells and distributes securities to large investment funds, handles transactions for institutional investors for a commission, and trades in various stocks and bonds for profit.

6 A derivative is a financial instrument or "security whose value is derived from the value of some other asset, called the underlying asset" (Marshall and Ellis 1995, 261).

7 Of course, scandals on Wall Street and in corporate America are commonplace. However, Bankers Trust's transgressions were particularly egregious in the eyes of both investment banks and Fortune 500 companies for the following reasons. First, as in the case of Enron, Wall Street investment banks and the executives of major corporations often act in concert to take advantage of "market opportunities" at the expense of other constituencies such as its employees, the public, or the state. In this case, Bankers Trust very obviously turned on its own client. Second, the victim was Procter and Gamble, one of the most powerful corporations in the United States. Third, the transgressions were captured on tape.

8 Risk Management is the part of the investment bank which attempts to temper and "hedge" the investment bank's technical, strategic, and monetary risk. For example, on the monetary front, they use technical models to measure how much exposure a bank has to an array of scenarios. While touting (even selling) their risk-management capabilities, most investment banks do not heed

their own cautions or recommendations, as deal making and demonstrating market vanguard status are more highly valued.

9 Financial economists assert that Wall Street investment banks provide a crucial function in capitalist economies in that they help corporations and governments raise much-needed capital via linking these institutions with investors. This claim is highly problematic in that for governments, most of the capital raised is short-term and dependent on austerity programs, and for corporations, much of the capital goes to large shareholders and is not necessarily reinvested in long-term corporate growth. Investment banks often "help" corporations "grow" through short-term financial deals and transactions, not through steady, long-term production.

10 It is commonsense knowledge on Wall Street that investment banks mainly have offices and "do deals" in places that have "mature" financial markets and a sizeable number of corporations. Investment bankers tell me that in addition to the United States, these places are "Europe, Japan, Hong Kong, and a few other countries." Although a few local investment banks have opened up in Kuwait since 2000, none of the annual reports of the major Wall Street investment banks list any offices or deals done in Kuwait or Sri Lanka.

11 Journalist Naomi Klein writes that corporations today are "competing in a race toward weightlessness," where "the very process of producing—running one's own factories, being responsible for tens of thousands of full-time, permanent employees" is a "clunky liability" (Klein 2000, 4). Exorbitant profits lie in global marketing via the proliferation of corporate brands, and corporations' expenditures for marketing and "brand management" are growing exponentially (Klein 2000, 483).

12 Dominant academic assumptions of the speed of globalization are put into perspective with Goldman Sachs's emphasis that market building takes time, focus, and local relationships. Paulson speaks about capitalism in national terms, as a reflection of national style and standards: "U.S.-style integrity" must be painstakingly built with "paced" and cautious growth and proven performance, not rapacious global capitalism. The passionate moralism often implicit in neoliberal globalization is an important component of Wall Street's beliefs and motivations.

13 The Structured Finance Groups of investment banks engineer a variety of financial instruments, such as innovative debt instruments based on subprime mortgages, in order to exploit new market opportunities.

14 Webster's Encyclopedic Unabridged Dictionary, 1997, s.v. "Presence."

15 This quotation is another definition of "presence" found on www.diction ary.com, accessed 20 August 2004.

16 Anna Tsing has similarly argued that in contexts and economies (such as the recent dot-com bubble or the Asian miracles) in which "finance capital is the ruling edge of accumulation," accumulation strategies rest on the difficulty of discerning "companies that have long-term production potential from those that are merely good at being on stage" (Tsing 2000b, 127). Those engaged in speculation and financial accumulation rely on the construction of hype to attract

capital; the inability to distinguish between the real and the fake is a competitive requirement of these speculative practices.

17   There exist enormous human as well as corporate consequences of maintaining this particular kind of potential globalism. Emily Martin observes:

> As the mechanical regularity avidly sought from the assembly line worker gives way to the ideal of a flexible and constantly changing worker, what will happen to the value previously placed on stability and conformity? . . . The individual [now] consists in *potentials to be realized and capacities to be fulfilled*. Since these *potentials and capacities* take their shape in relation to the requirements of a continuously changing environment, their content—and even the terms in which they are understood—are also in constant change. The person is made up of a flexible collection of assets; a person is proprietor of his or her self as a portfolio. (Martin 1999, my emphasis)

This notion of the person as potential and capability parallels Wall Street's overall approach to business. Just as the new worker is measured more for his or her potential and capacity to continuously change (rather than the content of the change), Wall Street rewards corporate America (as well as itself) for an ability to respond to the latest market trends to merge, cut, move, upsize, and downsize, regardless of content.

18   Whereas investment banks cater to corporations and large institutional investment funds, "discount brokerages" cater to the "retail market" (that is, middle- and upper-middle-class individuals). Because discount or retail brokerage businesses are not only less prestigious but also have lower profit margins, the strategy is to amass large client bases, often using the Internet. Because of the incredible success of brokerages such as E-trade, Ameritrade, and Charles Schwab in the late 1990s, Merrill attempted to enter this market globally.

19   Although Merrill Lynch's strategy of global expansion was the most explicitly articulated in its own representations and in the financial media, I would also argue that Morgan Stanley, to a lesser degree, was entranced by such an approach. For example, in 1997, Morgan Stanley, a "blue-blood" investment bank, merged with Dean Witter, a retail brokerage, in an attempt to broaden the scope of its services (although in this case entering the market of the individual investor was a greater priority than global saturation).

20   During this time, Merrill Lynch also "entered into acquisitions/joint ventures in Canada, the U.K., Spain, Italy, South Africa, Australia, India, Indonesia, Malaysia and Thailand" (Sievwright 1998).

21   Merrill Lynch attempted what its top executives called a "global/local strategy," where they would not simply impose U.S. business models onto the Japanese and run the business from New York, but attempt to "instill our [global capitalist] value system and meld it with their [Japanese] culture" (Komansky 1998a). Of course, the assumption that capitalist values are global and Japanese culture is local is just as problematic as the model which assumes total assimilation to American business models.

22   Even David Komansky himself, in an interview with *Business Week* invest-

ment banking editor Emily Thornton, responded to the question "Why does Merrill need a dramatic shakeup?" this way: "I look back on the decade of the '90s, and I say that purposefully we started out doing, and in retrospect we did, drive the globalization of the firm into 40 countries and position ourselves as the most global securities firm. In that period of time, we made something in the area of 19 acquisitions ranging from big to small. Any time you grow that much, that you make that many acquisitions, there comes a time when excesses creep into your organization, and the portfolio has to be redressed" (Thornton 2001).

23 I did not investigate this event during my fieldwork, as this case did not resolve until 2002, after I had already left the field. Jimenez Lee inadvertently alerted me to the global implications of this story by narrating this name-change event in passing.

24 As an addendum, it is important to note that according to some business journals, Merrill's investment in Japan was due to become profitable in 2002. Dominant Wall Street notions of global presence, mobility, and short-termism, however, apparently cannot tolerate even a few years of losses; so Merrill pulled out in 2001, arguably going against its own longer-term global interests. Thus globalist proclamations can be seen, not as mere disposable rhetoric, but as an ideology with the force to shape a firm's perceptions and goals.

References

Abolafia, Mitchel. 2001. *Making Markets: Opportunism and Restraint on Wall Street*. Cambridge, Mass.: Harvard University Press.

Allen, William. 1992. "Our Schizophrenic Conception of the Business Corporation." *Cardoso Law Review* 14, no. 2, 261–81.

Anderson, Jenny. 2006. "Wall Street's Women Face a Fork in the Road." *New York Times*, 6 August, www.nytimes.com (accessed 8 June 2008).

Anderson, Jenny, and Landon Thomas. 2004. "The Number Wall St. Crunches the Most." *New York Times*, 29 November, C1–2.

Aronowitz, Stanley, and William DiFazio. 1994. *The Jobless Future: Sci-Tech and the Dogma of Work*. Minneapolis: University of Minnesota Press.

Arrighi, Giovanni. 1996. *The Long Twentieth Century: Money, Power, and the Origins of Our Times*. London: Verso.

Baker, George, and George David Smith. 1998. *The New Financial Capitalists: Kohlberg Kravis Roberts and the Creation of Corporate Value*. Cambridge: Cambridge University Press.

Ball, Jeffrey. 2001. "Unmaking Mistake: Daimler's New Boss for Chrysler Orders Tough, Major Repairs." *Wall Street Journal*, 22 January, A1, A8.

Ball, Jeffrey, Joseph White, and Scott Miller. 2000. "Megamerger No Road to Riches: The Dream Marriage of Daimler-Benz and Chrysler Is Experiencing a Few Nightmares That Could include Some Staff Cutting in the U.S." *Ottawa Citizen*, 28 October, D3.

Baran, Paul A., and Paul M. Sweezy. 1966. *Monopoly Capital: An Essay on the American Economic and Social Order*. New York: Monthly Review Press.

Barr, Colin. 2008. "Crime and Delusion on Wall Street." *Fortune*, 19 June, www.cnnmoney.com (accessed 1 July 2008).

Basar, Shanny. 2006. "Bear Stearns Boosts Mortgage Business." *Financial News Online*, 11 October, www.efinancialnews.com (accessed 2 July 2008).

Baskin, Jonathan Barron, and Paul Miranti, Jr. 1997. *A History of Corporate Finance*. Cambridge: Cambridge University Press.

Bauman, Zygmunt. 1998. *Globalization: The Human Consequences*. New York: Columbia University Press.

Beniger, James. 1967. "Smithies, Walzer, and Peretz Discuss the Five R's: Recruitment, ROTC, Ranking, Research, and Relationship." *Harvard Crimson*, 11 November, www.thecrimson.com (accessed 11 May 2007).

Benn, Melissa. 2001. "Inner-City Scholar." *Guardian* (London), 3 February, www.guardian.co.uk (accessed 27 February 2007).

Bennett, Amanda. 1972. "The Jobless Class of '72." *Harvard Crimson*, 16 December, www.thecrimson.com (accessed 11 May 2007).

Berle, Adolf A., and Gardiner C. Means. 1991. *The Modern Corporation and Private Property*. Revised edition. New Brunswick, N.J.: Transaction Publishers.

Berle, Adolf A., and Victoria J. Pederson. 1934. *Liquid Claims and National Wealth: An Exploratory Study in the Theory of Liquidity*. New York: Macmillan.

Blair, Margaret M. 1995. *Ownership and Control: Rethinking Corporate Governance for the Twenty-First Century*. Washington, D.C.: The Brookings Institute.

Bloomberg, and AP and Staff Reports. 2007. "Shareholders Want 'Chrysler' Out of Name." *Tulsa World* (Okla.), 14 March, E1.

Boudreau, Abbie, David Fitzpatrick, and Scott Zamost. 2008. "Wall Street: Fall of the Fat Cats." *CNN.com*, 17 October, www.cnn.com (accessed 17 October 2008).

Bourdieu, Pierre. 1990. *Outline of a Theory of Practice*. Cambridge: Cambridge University Press.

Bourgois, Philippe. 1995. *In Search of Respect: Selling Crack in El Barrio*. Cambridge: Cambridge University Press.

Bremner, Brian. 2001. "How Merrill Lost Its Way in Japan." *Business Week*, 12 November, www.businessweek.com (accessed 30 July 2004).

Brenner, Robert. 2002. *The Boom and the Bubble: The US in the World Economy*. London: Verso.

Brooks, John. 1987. *The Takeover Game*. New York: Truman Talley Books.

Browne, Dudley E. 1967. "The Institutional Investor and the Corporation." *Commercial and Financial Chronicle*, 19 January, 11, 34.

Browne, Irene, and Joya Misra. 2003. "The Intersection of Gender and Race in the Labor Market." *Annual Review of Sociology* 29, 487–513.

Bruno, Joe Bel. 2007. "Bear Stearns Eyeing Subprime Purchases." *Boston.com*, 15 March, http://boston.com (accessed 30 July 2008).

Buenza, Daniel, and David Stark. 2005. "How to Recognize Opportunities: Heterarchical Search in a Trading Room." *The Sociology of Financial Markets*, edited by K. Knorr Cetina and A. Preda, 2–20. Oxford: Oxford University Press.

Burawoy, Michael, Joseph A. Blum, Sheba George, Zsuzsa Gille, Teresa Gowan, Lynne Haney, Maren Klawiter, Steven H. Lopez, Seán O. Riain, and Millie Thayer. 2000. *Global Ethnography: Forces, Connections, and Imaginations in a Postmodern World*. Berkeley: University of California Press.

Burrough, Bryan, and John Helyar. 1990. *Barbarians at the Gate: The Fall of RJR Nabisco*. New York: Harper and Row.

Business Wire. 1999. "Goldman, Sachs & Company and Salomon Smith Barney's Eduardo Mestre Awarded Investment Dealers' Digest Bank and Banker of the Year." *Business Wire*, 21 January, www.businesswire.com (accessed 30 April 2008).

Caldeira, Teresa. 2000. *City of Walls: Crime, Segregation, and Citizenship in Sao Paulo*. Berkeley: University of California Press.

Callon, Michel. 1998. "Introduction: The Embeddedness of Economic Markets in

Economics." *The Laws of the Markets*, edited by M. Callon, 1–68. Oxford: Blackwell.

Carosso, Vincent P. 1970. *Investment Banking in America: A History*. Harvard Studies in Business History 25. Cambridge, Mass.: Harvard University Press.

Carrier, James G. 1995. *Gifts and Commodities: Exchange and Western Capitalism since 1700*. London: Routledge.

——, ed. 1997. *Meanings of the Market: The Free Market in Western Culture*. Oxford: Berg.

——. 1998. "Introduction." *Virtualism: A New Political Economy*, edited by James G. Carrier and Daniel Miller, 1–24. Oxford: Berg.

Carrier, James G., and Daniel Miller, eds. 1998. *Virtualism: A New Political Economy*. Oxford: Berg.

Certeau, Michel de. 1984. *The Practice of Everyday Life*. Berkeley: University of California Press.

Challenger, Grey & Christmas. 2009. "Financial Cuts Breakdown 2008." Challenger, Grey & Christmas, 1 January, www.challengergrey.com (accessed 12 February 2009).

Chan, Kai. 2001. "A Cacophony of Career Choices." *Daily Princetonian*, 13 February, www.dailyprincetonian.com (accessed 27 February 2007).

Chandler, Alfred D., Jr. 1977. *The Visible Hand: The Managerial Revolution in American Business*. Cambridge, Mass.: Harvard University Press.

Chernow, Ron. 1990. *The House of Morgan: An American Banking Dynasty and the Rise of Modern Finance*. New York: Atlantic Monthly Press.

Cimilluca, Dana, and Marcus Walker. 2007. "DaimlerChrysler Split is Adviser's Second Payday." *Wall Street Journal Asia*, 17 May, 22.

Clark, Gordon. 2000. *Pension Fund Capitalism*. Oxford: Oxford University Press.

CNN Moneyline News Hour. 2001. "Dow Falls 80.03 to 10,796.65; NASDAQ Tumbles 74.40 to 2,146.20; Rise in Jobless Claims Unnerves Investors" (transcript), 3 May, www.cnn.com (accessed 28 May 2006).

Cowell, Alan. 2000. "Unilever Plans Huge Cuts in Jobs, Plants, and Brands." *New York Times*, 23 February, C1, C4.

Craig, Susanne, Charles Gasparino, and Jathon Sapsford. 2001. "Deals & Deal Makers: Wall Street Top Guns Face Layoffs, Too—Cuts Are Expanded from Lower Levels." *Wall Street Journal*, 22 August, C1, C13.

Creed, Jesse. 2003. "Students Face Weak Job Market despite Improvements." *Daily Princetonian*, 26 September, www.dailyprincetonian.com (accessed 27 February 2007).

Crossa, Veronica. 2005. "Converting the 'Small Stories' into 'Big' Ones: A Response to Susan Smith's 'States, Markets and an Ethic of Care'." *Political Geography* 24, 29–34.

Dalton, George. 1961. "Economic Theory and Primitive Society." *American Anthropologist* 63, no. 1, 1–25.

Day, Kathleen. 2008. "Villains in the Mortgage Mess? Start at Wall Street. Keep Going." *Washington Post*, 1 June, B1, B4.

Dilley, Roy. 1992. "Contesting Markets: A General Introduction to Market Ideology, Imagery, and Discourse." *Contesting Markets: Analyses of Ideology, Discourse, and Practice*, edited by R. Dilley, 1–36. Edinburgh: Edinburgh Press.

Diner, Steven. 1998. *A Very Different Age: Americans of the Progressive Era*. New York: Hill and Wang.

Disabatino, Jennifer. 2002. "Report: Jobs Cuts in 2001 Reach Nearly 2 Million." *CNN.com*, 6 January, http://archives.cnn.com (accessed 24 May 2006).

Donaldson, Gordon. 1963. "Financial Goals: Management vs. Stockholders." *Harvard Business Review* 41, 116–29.

Drucker, Peter F. 1972. *Concept of the Corporation*. 2nd edition. New York: John Day Company.

Duboff, Josh. 2005. "Six College Students Create Job-Search Site." *Yale Daily News*, 11 February, www.yaledailynews.com (accessed 19 March 2007).

Dudley, Kathryn Marie. 1994. *The End of the Line: Lost Jobs, New Lives in Postindustrial America*. Chicago: University of Chicago Press.

Dyer, Richard. 1997. *White*. London: Routledge.

Easton, Alice. 2006. "Firms Lure Students with Extravagance." *Daily Princetonian*, 13 March, www.dailyprincetonian.com (accessed 27 February 2007).

Economist. 1998. "Blood on the Street." 10 October, 80.

——. 2001. "Living in Leaner Times." 4 August, 57–58.

——. 2005. "Happy Days." 1 January, 54–55.

Eldridge, Earle, and Thor Valdmanis. 2001. "Daimler Could Sell Some Assets." *USA Today*, 31 January, 3B.

Engler, Steve. 2006. "Don't Let Job Frenzy Overwhelm Your Life." *Yale Daily News*, 18 October, www.yaledailynews.com (accessed 19 March 2007).

Espig, Peter. 2003. "The Bull and the Bear Market: Merrill Lynch's Entry into the Japanese Retail Securities Industry." *Chazen Web Journal of International Business*, 14 May, www.gsb.columbia.edu/chazenjournal, 1–11.

Faludi, Susan. 1992. "The Reckoning." *The Gaga Years: The Rise and Fall of the Money Game, 1981–1991*, edited by B. Fromson, 285–305. New York: Citadel Press.

Fiorini, Phillip. 1995. "Mobil Restructuring Pumps Shares." *USA Today*, 2 May, 3B.

Fischer, Michael. 2003. *Emergent Forms of Life and the Anthropological Voice*. Durham, N.C.: Duke University Press.

Foucault, Michel. 1980. *Power/Knowledge: Selected Interviews and Other Writings*. New York: Pantheon Books.

Fox, Justin. 2006. "Why Wall Street Had a Record Year and You Didn't." *Fortune*, 26 February, 31.

Frank, Thomas. 2000. *One Market under God: Extreme Capitalism, Market Populism, and the End of Economic Democracy*. New York: Doubleday.

Fraser, Jill Andresky. 2001. *White-Collar Sweatshop: The Deterioration of Work and Its Rewards in Corporate America*. New York: W. W. Norton.

Fraser, Steve. 2004. *Every Man a Speculator: A History of Wall Street in American Life*. New York: HarperCollins Publishers.

Fuscone, Rick. 1999. "Global Trends in Investment Banking." Speech delivered at

Merrill Lynch Headquarters, 11 November, www.ml.com (accessed 5 August 2004).

Gibson-Graham, J. K. 1996. *The End of Capitalism (as We Knew It): A Feminist Critique of Political Economy*. Cambridge, Mass.: Blackwell.

Goede, Marieke de. 2005. *Virtue, Fortune, and Faith: A Genealogy of Finance*. Borderlines 24. Minneapolis: University of Minnesota Press.

Goldman, Alan. 2006. "Wall Street Bonuses Flood NYC's Economy." *Washington Post*, 19 December, www.washingtonpost.com (accessed 12 February 2009).

Gomstyn, Alice. 2008. "Wall Street Braces for Huge Job Losses." *ABC News*, 16 September, http://abcnews.go.com (accessed 12 February 2009).

Gorham, John. 2001. "L.A. Story." *Forbes*, 5 March, 56.

Gotanda, Neil. 1996. "A Critique of 'Our Constitution Is Color-Blind.'" *Critical Race Theory: The Key Writings That Formed the Movement*, edited by K. Crenshaw, N. Gotanda, G. Peller, and K. Thomas, 257–75. New York: New Press.

Graham-Felsen, Sam. 2003. "Invest in Life, Not Your Wallet." *Harvard Crimson*, 27 October, www.thecrimson.com (accessed 27 February 2007).

Granovetter, Mark. 1985. "Economic Action and Social Structures: The Problem of Embeddedness." *American Journal of Sociology* 91, no. 3, 481–510.

Granovetter, Mark, and Richard Swedberg, eds. 2001. *The Sociology of Economic Life*. Boulder, Colo.: Westview Press.

Gregory, Steven. 1998. "Globalization and the 'Place' of Politics in Contemporary Theory: A Commentary." *City and Society* 10, no. 1, 47–64.

Grove, Andrew. 1999. *Only the Paranoid Survive: How to Exploit the Crisis Points That Challenge Every Company*. New York: Currency.

Gudeman, Stephen. 1986. *Economics as Culture: Models and Metaphors of Livelihood*. Boston: Routledge and Kegan Paul.

Gupta, Akhil, and James Ferguson. 1992. "Beyond 'Culture': Space, Identity, and the Politics of Difference." *Cultural Anthropology* 7, no. 1, 6–23.

Gusterson, Hugh. 1997. "Studying Up Revisited." *PoLAR: Political and Legal Anthropology Review* 20, no. 1, 114–19.

Guyer, Jane, ed. 1995. *Money Matters: Instability, Values, and Social Payments in the Modern History of West African Communities*. Portsmouth: Heinemann.

———. 2004. *Marginal Gains: Monetary Transactions in Atlantic Africa*. Chicago: University of Chicago Press.

Guyer, Nora. 2003. "There Is More to Life Than I-Banking." *Harvard Crimson*, 28 April, www.thecrimson.com (accessed 27 February 2007).

Haar, Dan. 1998. "Global Mergers Raise Doubts: Skeptics Wonder if Expected Gains Will Materialize." *Hartford Courant*, 10 May, A1.

Hall, Cailey. 2005. "Wall Street: Paradise Found?" *Daily Princetonian*, 25 September, www.dailyprincetonian.com (accessed 27 February 2007).

Halldin, Bill, and Jonathan Blum. 2006. "Merrill Lynch Announces Agreement to Acquire First Franklin from National City Corporation." Merrill Lynch Press Release, 5 September, www.ml.com (accessed 30 July 2008).

Harper, Christine. 2007. "Wall Street Plans $38 Billion of Bonuses as Shareholders Lose." *Bloomberg.com*, 18 November, www.bloomberg.com (accessed 12 February 2009).

Harvard Crimson. 1953. "Finance Industry Needs Graduates, Businessmen Say." 25 February, www.thecrimson.com (accessed 11 May 2007).

——. 1957. "Conference Stresses Greater Opportunities in Financial Fields." 15 February, www.thecrimson.com (accessed 11 May 2007).

——. 1963. "More Jobs Available to '63 College Grads." 21 May, www.thecrimson.com (accessed 11 May 2007).

——. 1995. "Career Forum Could Be Broader." 23 October, www.thecrimson.com (accessed 27 February 2007).

Harvey, David. 1999. *The Limits to Capital*. 2nd edition. London: Verso.

——. 2005. *A Brief History of Neoliberalism*. Oxford: Oxford University Press.

Healey, Tim, and Assif Shameen. 2001. "Submerging Markets." *Asiaweek*, 31 August, www.asiaweek.com (accessed 24 March 2006).

Henderson, Carter, and Albert Lasher. 1967. *20 Million Careless Capitalists*. Garden City, N.Y.: Doubleday.

Henn, Brian. 2001. "Fewer Jobs in Financial Services Worry Class of '02." *Daily Princetonian*, 9 November, www.dailyprincetonian.com (accessed 27 February 2007).

Hertz, Ellen. 1998. *The Trading Crowd: An Ethnography of the Shanghai Stock Market*. Cambridge: Cambridge University Press.

Hiltzik, Michael. 2001. "Giant Cable Deal; AT&T Returning to Basics." *Los Angeles Times*, 21 December, C1.

Hirschman, Albert O. 1997. *The Passions and the Interests: Political Arguments for Capitalism before Its Triumph*. 20th anniversary edition. Princeton, N.J.: Princeton University Press. ·

Ho, Margaret. 2003. "Campus Recruiting Rates Inch Upward." *Harvard Crimson*, 26 September, www.thecrimson.com (accessed 27 February 2007).

Hochman, Dafna V. 1999. "Recruiting Your Career." *Harvard Crimson*, 15 October, www.thecrimson.com (accessed 27 February 2007).

Hoffman, Abigail. 2008. "The Binge Culture of Banking Must Be Changed." *Financial Times*, 28 April, www.ft.com (accessed 1 July 2008).

Holland, Kelley, Linda Himelstein, and Zachary Schiller. 1995. "The Bankers Trust Tapes." *Business Week*, 16 October, 106–11.

Holmes, Douglas R., and George E. Marcus. 2005. "Cultures of Expertise and the Management of Globalization: Toward the Re-Functioning of Ethnography." *Global Assemblages: Technology, Politics, and Ethics as Anthropological Problems*, edited by A. Ong and S. J. Collier, 235–52. Malden, Mass.: Blackwell.

——. 2006. "Fast Capitalism: Para-Ethnography and the Rise of the Symbolic Analyst." *Frontiers of Capital: Ethnographic Reflections on the New Economy*, edited by M. S. Fisher and G. Downey, 33–57. Durham, N.C.: Duke University Press.

Holson, Laura. 1998. "Advisers and Lawyers Stand to Get Richer in Auto Deal." *New York Times*, 8 May, D5.

Houser, Theodore. 1957. *Big Business and Human Values*. New York: McGraw-Hill.

Huber, H. Max. 2006. "Careers 'R Us: Online Recruiting Isn't Just for Aspiring Gordon Gekkos Anymore." *Harvard Crimson*, 5 October, www.thecrimson .com (accessed 27 February 2007).

Jackson, Rev. Jesse L., Sr., Jesse L. Jackson Jr., and Mary Gotschall. 1999. *It's about the Money! The Fourth Movement of the Freedom Symphony: How to Build Wealth, Get Access to Capital, and Achieve Your Financial Dreams*. New York: Random House.

Jensen, Michael. 1976. *The Financiers: The World of the Great Wall Street Investment Banking Houses*. New York: Weybright and Talley.

Jones, Jacqueline. 1998. *American Work: Four Centuries of Black and White Labor*. New York: W. W. Norton.

J. P. Morgan. *Client Focus with a Global Perspective*. 1995. New York: J. P. Morgan.

Kantor, Rosebeth Moss. 1993. *Men and Women of the Corporation*. New York: Basic Books.

Karseras, Hugh. 2006. "Starting Out on the Right Foot." *Daily Princetonian*, 21 November, www.dailyprincetonian.com (accessed 27 February 2007).

Kaysen, Carl. 1957. "The Social Significance of the Modern Corporation." *American Economic Review* 47, no. 2, 311–19.

Keller, John. 1996. "AT&T Will Eliminate 40,000 Jobs and Take a Charge of $4 Billion." *Wall Street Journal*, 3 January, A3, A6.

Kelly, Kate. 2002. "Deals and Deal Makers: Well-Baked: With Its Business So Slow, Wall Shows Hunger for Any Deal." *Wall Street Journal*, 30 October, C1, C5.

Kim, Hoon-Jung. 2000. "So You Want to Work on Wall Street." *Harvard Crimson*, 25 September, www.thecrimson.com (accessed 27 February 2007).

Kirkpatrick, David. 2000. "Street Addict." *New York Magazine*, 24 April, www .nymag.com (accessed 27 February 2007).

Klein, Naomi. 2000. *No Logo*. New York: Picador.

Knorr Cetina, Karin, and Alex Preda, eds. 2005. *The Sociology of Financial Markets*. Oxford: Oxford University Press.

Knox, Noelle. 2002. "Finance Sector in Confusion." *USA Today*, 19 August, 3B.

Kolker, Robert. 2003. "Down and Out on Wall Street." *New York Magazine*, 10 March, www.nymag.com (accessed 24 March 2006).

Komansky, David. 1998a. "Building Value in the Securities Industry." Paper read at the Merrill Lynch Banking and Financial Services Investor Conference, 14 September, New York City, www.ml.com (accessed 5 August 2004).

———. 1998b. "Effectively Serving Clients in Diverse Markets." Paper read at Sanford J. Bernstein Investor Conference, 5 June, New York City, www.ml .com (accessed 5 August 2004).

———. 1998c. "Putting Down Global Roots." Interview by Lou Dobbs, *Moneyline News Hour*, 2 July, www.cnnmoney.com (accessed 5 August 2004).

Kroft, Steve. 2008. "Wall Street's Shadow Market." *60 Minutes*, 6 October, www .cbsnews.com (accessed 6 October 2008).

Landler, Mark. 1997. "Investing It: A Plodding Ma Bell and Her Precocious Child." *New York Times*, 13 April, F1, F7.

Lazonick, William, and Mary O'Sullivan. 1997. "Finance and Industrial Development: Part 1: The United States and the United Kingdom." *Financial History Review* 4, no. 1, 7–29.

———. 2002. "Maximizing Shareholder Value: A New Ideology." *Corporate Governance and Sustainable Prosperity*, edited by W. Lazonick and M. O'Sullivan, 11–35. New York: Palgrave.

Leach, Andrew. 2001. "Merger Most Foul: As Daimler-Chrysler Veers into Another Crisis, Will It Join the 83 Per Cent of Corporate Tie-Ups That End in Failure?" *Mail on Sunday*, 21 January, 9.

Lerer, Justin D. 1997. "New Recruits." *Harvard Crimson*, 5 June, www.thecrim son.com (accessed 27 February 2007).

Levy, Leon. 2002. *The Mind of Wall Street: A Legendary Financier on the Perils of Greed and the Mysteries of the Market*. New York: Public Affairs.

Lewis, Michael. 1989. *Liar's Poker: Rising through the Wreckage on Wall Street*. New York: W. W. Norton.

———. 1991. *The Money Culture*. New York: Penguin.

Lewis, William. 1999. "Year of the Mega-Deal for Wall Street Bankers: US M&A." *Financial Times*, 29 January, 2.

Leyshon, Andrew, and Nigel Thrift. 1997. *Money/Space: Geographies of Monetary Transformation*. London: Routledge.

Lipin, Steven, and Brandon Mitchener. 1998. "Daimler-Chrysler Merger to Produce $3 Billion in Savings, Revenue Gains within 3 to 5 Years." *Wall Street Journal*, 8 May, A10.

Lipin, Steven, and Nikhil Deogun. 2000. "Deals & Deal Makers: Big Mergers of '90s Prove Disappointing to Shareholders: Poor Market Reaction Does Little to Slow Pace of Acquisitions." *Wall Street Journal*, 30 October, C1, C21.

LiPuma, Edward, and Benjamin Lee. 2004. *Financial Derivatives and the Globalization of Risk*. Durham, N.C.: Duke University Press.

Low, Janet. 1968. *Understanding the Stock Market: A Guide for Young Investors*. Boston: Little, Brown and Company.

Lynch, David. 1996. "AT&T Downsizes Estimate of Layoffs by 40%." *USA Today*, 15 March, B1.

Lynch, Stephen. 2004. "Index Face-Lift; Verizon In, AT&T Out as Dow Shuffles Lineup." *New York Post*, 2 April, 35.

MacKenzie, Donald. 2001. "Physics and Finance: S-Terms and Modern Finance as a Topic for Science Studies." *Science, Technology, and Human Values* 26, no. 2, 115–44.

———. 2006. *An Engine, Not a Camera: How Financial Models Shape Markets*. Cambridge, Mass.: MIT Press.

Malinowski, Bronislaw. 1948. *Magic, Science, and Religion and Other Essays*. Prospect Heights: Waveland Press.

Mallaby, Sebastian. 2007. "Pain, Gain of Subprime Meltdown." *Oakland Tribune*, 16 August, www.insidebayarea.com (accessed 2 July 2008).

Marshall, John F., and M. E. Ellis. 1995. *Investment Banking and Brokerage*. Malden, Mass.: Blackwell.

Martin, Emily. 1994. *Flexible Bodies: Tracking Immunity in American Culture—From the Days of Polio to the Age of AIDS*. Boston: Beacon Press.

——. 1997. "Anthropology and the Cultural Study of Science: From Citadels to String Figures." *Anthropological Locations: Boundaries and Grounds of a Field Science*, edited by A. Gupta and James Ferguson, 131–46. Berkeley: University of California Press.

——. 1999. "Flexible Survivors." *Anthropology News* 40, no. 6, 5–7.

Mason, Edward. 1959. "Introduction." *The Corporation in Modern Society*, edited by E. Mason, 1–24. Cambridge, Mass.: Harvard University Press.

Masters, Brooke. 1986. "Harvard Graduates Buck National Trend." *Harvard Crimson*, 25 February, www.thecrimson.com (accessed 27 February 2007).

Maurer, Bill. 1999. "Forget Locke? From Proprietor to Risk-Bearer in New Logics of Finance." *Public Culture* 11, no. 2, 365–85.

——. 2002. "Repressed Futures: Financial Derivatives' Theological Unconscious." *Economy and Society* 31, no. 1, 15–36.

——. 2005. *Mutual Life, Limited: Islamic Banking, Alternative Currencies, Lateral Reason*. Princeton, N.J.: Princeton University Press.

——. 2006. "The Anthropology of Money." *Annual Review of Anthropology* 35, 15–36.

McCandless, Jennifer. 2006. "Deutsche Expands in Mortgages with Chapel." *Financial News Online*, 18 May, www.efinancialnews.com (accessed 2 July 2008).

McDonald, Duff. 2005. "Please, Sir, I Want Some More: How Goldman Sachs Is Carving Up Its $11 Billion Money Pie." *New York Magazine*, 5 December, www.nymag.com (accessed 24 March 2006).

McGeehan, Patrick. 1998. "Wall Streeters Are Preparing for Layoffs." *Wall Street Journal*, 9 October, C1.

——. 2000. "Make a Wish, It's Bonus Time on Wall Street." *New York Times*, 8 December, C1–2.

McLanahan, Sarah. 2003. "Taking the Job Plunge: Stern Seniors Start Search." *Washington Square News*, 23 September, www.nyunews.com (accessed 27 February 2007).

McLaughlin, Tim. 2007. "Merrill Lynch's Painful Lesson in Subprime." *Reuters.com*, 16 August, http://www.reuters.com (accessed 2 July 2008).

McLean, Bethany, and Peter Elkind. 2003. *The Smartest Guys in the Room: The Amazing Rise and Scandalous Fall of Enron*. New York: Portfolio.

McMichael, Philip. 1998. "Development and Structural Adjustment." *Virtualism: A New Political Economy*, edited by James G. Carrier and Daniel Miller, 95–116. Oxford: Berg.

McMillan, Alex Frew. 2001. "Merrill Lynch Cuts Offices in Japan." *CNN.com*, 24 May, http://www.cnn.com (accessed 27 July 2004).

Mehta, Jal D. 1998. "Avoiding a Path to Nowhere." *Harvard Crimson*, 16 October, www.thecrimson.com (accessed 27 February 2007).

Merle, Renae, and Tomoeh Murakami Tse. 2008. "Banks Reduce Bonuses Only

Slightly." *Journal Gazette* (Fort Wayne, Ind.), 3 February, www.journalgazette .net (accessed 2 July 2008).

Merrill Lynch and Co., Inc. 1994. *Merrill Lynch Annual Report*. New York: Merrill Lynch and Co., Inc.

——. 1995. *Merrill Lynch Annual Report*. New York: Merrill Lynch and Co., Inc.

Miley, Marissa. 2000. "Career Fair Provides Exposure for Students and Companies." *Daily Pennsylvanian*, 9 October, www.dailypennsylvanian.com (accessed 27 February 2007).

Miller, Daniel. 1998. *A Theory of Shopping*. Ithaca, N.Y.: Cornell University Press.

——. 2002. "Turning Callon the Right Way Up." *Economy and Society* 31, no. 2, 218–33.

Miller, Glenn. 1968. "Corporate Financing in Today's Turbulent Markets." *Commercial and Financial Chronicle*, 25 April, 3, 26–28.

Miller, James. 1997. "Sara Lee to Retreat from Manufacturing." *Wall Street Journal*, 16 September, A3, A10.

Milne, Richard. 2007. "Sell Chrysler, Urge Daimler Shareholders." *Financial Times*, 5 April, 23.

Miyazaki, Hirokazu. 2003. "The Temporalities of the Market." *American Anthropologist* 105, no. 2, 255–65.

——. 2006. "Economy of Dreams: Hope in Global Capitalism and Its Critique." *Cultural Anthropology* 21, no. 2, 147–72.

Miyazaki, Hirokazu, and Annelise Riles. 2005. "Failure as Endpoint." *Global Assemblages: Technology, Politics, and Ethics as Anthropological Problems*, edited by A. Ong and S. J. Collier, 320–31. Oxford: Blackwell.

Moeller, Tom. 2005. "Challenger Layoffs Up Again in October, Trend Lower." *Haver Analytics*, 7 November, www.haver.com (accessed 28 May 2006).

Morgan Stanley, Dean Witter, Discover and Co. 1997. *Morgan Stanley, Dean Witter, Discover & Co. Annual Report*. New York: Morgan Stanley, Dean Witter, Discover & Co.

Murray, Matt. 1998. "J. P. Morgan to Cut Nearly 5% of Staff through Layoffs, Attrition by Year End." *Wall Street Journal*, 9 November, A4.

Nader, Laura. 1972. "Up the Anthropologist—Perspectives Gained from Studying Up." *Reinventing Anthropology*, edited by D. Hymes, 284–311. New York: Pantheon Books.

Nelson, Julie A. 1998. "Abstraction, Reality, and the Gender of 'Economic Man'." *Virtualism: A New Political Economy*, edited by James. G. Carrier and Daniel Miller, 75–94. Oxford: Berg.

Newman, Katherine 1999. *Falling from Grace: Downward Mobility in the Age of Affluence*. Berkeley: University of California Press.

——. 2000. *No Shame in My Game: The Working Poor in the Inner City*. New York: Vintage.

New York Post. 2006. "Ka-ching." 11 December, www.nypost.com (accessed 31 January 2007).

New York State Comptroller. 2006a. "Wall Street Bonuses Set New Record in 2005." 11 January, www.osc.state.ny.us (accessed 12 February 2009).

New York State Comptroller. 2006b. "Wall Street Bonuses Set New Record." 19 December, www.osc.state.ny.us (accessed 12 February 2009).

New York State Comptroller. 2009. "New York City Securities Industry Bonuses." January 28, www.osc.state.ny.us (accessed 12 February 2009).

New York Stock Exchange. 1955. *The Public Speaks to the Exchange Community*. New York: New York Stock Exchange.

New York Times. 1996. *The Downsizing of America*. New York: Times Books.

O'Boyle, Thomas F. 1999. *At Any Cost: Jack Welch, General Electric, and the Pursuit of Profit*. New York: Vintage.

Oldham, Jennifer. 1999. "A History of the Dow." *Los Angeles Times*, 30 March 1999, C6.

O'Leary, Christopher. 2003. "Poaching Season on CSFB?" *Investment Dealer's Digest*, 5 March, 12–13.

Olinger, David, and Aldo Svaldi. 2007. "The Subprime Lending Crisis: Origins and Consequences." *Denver Post* (Colo.), 2 December, A1, A18–19.

O'Neal, Stanley. 2002a. "Investor Confidence and the Financial Services Industry." Merrill Lynch Banking and Financial Services Conference, New York. 4 September, www.ml.com (accessed 5 August 2004).

——. 2002b. "Merrill Lynch's Platform for Growth." Salomon Smith Barney Financial Services Conference, New York. 31 January, www.ml.com (accessed 5 August 2004).

——. 2003. "Merrill Lynch: Investing for the Future." Salomon Smith Barney Financial Services Conference, New York. 29 January, www.ml.com (accessed 5 August 2004).

O'Sullivan, Mary. 2000. *Contests for Corporate Control: Corporate Governance and Economic Performance in the United States and Germany*. Oxford: Oxford University Press.

Ott, Julia. 2007. "When Wall Street Met Main Street: The Quest for an Investors' Democracy and the Emergence of the Retail Investor in the United States, 1890–1930." PhD diss., Yale University.

Passaro, Joanne. 1997. "'You Can't Take the Subway to the Field!': 'Village' Epistemologies in the Global Village." *Anthropological Locations: Boundaries and Grounds of a Field Science*, edited by A. Gupta and J. Ferguson, 147–62. Berkeley: University of California Press.

Pecora, Ferdinand. 1939. *Wall Street under Oath: The Story of Our Modern Money Changers*. New York: Simon and Schuster.

Peterson, Devon. 2002. "Careers at Princeton: The Allure and Drawbacks of Elite Jobs." *Daily Princetonian*, 16 October, www.dailyprincetonian.com (accessed 27 February 2007).

Pfeffer, Jeffrey. 1998. *The Human Equation: Building Profits by Putting People First*. Boston: Harvard Business School Press.

Polanyi, Karl. 1944. *The Great Transformation: the Political and Economic Origins of Our Time*. Boston: Beacon Press.

——. 1957. "The Economy as Instituted Process." *Trade and Market in the Early*

Empires, edited by K. Polanyi, C. M. Arensberg, and H. W. Pearson, 243–69. Glencoe, Ill.: Free Press.

PR Newswire. 1998. "Breakthrough Deals of the Year Award Winner Announced." *PR Newswire*, 14 December, www.prnewswire.com (accessed 30 April 2008).

Pryor, Christina. 2006. "Future I-bankers Face Grueling Interview Cycle." *Yale Daily News*, 1 November, www.yaledailynews.com (accessed 19 March 2007).

Rahim, Taufiq. 2003. "Recruiting Insanity." *Daily Princetonian*, 15 October, www .dailyprincetonian.com (accessed 27 February 2007).

Rampell, Catherine. 2006. "In the Nation's Financial Service." *Daily Princetonian*, 6 October, www.dailyprincetonian.com (accessed 27 February 2007).

Rappaport, Alfred. 1986. *Creating Shareholder Value: The New Standard for Business Performance*. New York: Free Press.

———. 1998. *Creating Shareholder Value: A Guide for Managers and Investors*. 2nd edition. New York: Free Press.

Ravenscraft, David J., and F. M. Scherer. 1987. *Mergers, Sell-Offs, and Economic Efficiency*. Washington, D.C.: Brookings Institution.

Reich, Robert. 2000. *The Future of Success: Working and Living in the New Economy*. New York: Vintage Books.

Reilly, Katherine. 2003. "Courage to Buck a System That Has Served Us So Well." *Daily Princetonian*, 23 April, www.dailyprincetonian.com (accessed 27 February 2007).

Reuters.com. 2006. "Morgan Stanley to Buy Mortgage Firm Saxon Capital." 9 August, http://www.reuters.com (accessed 2 July 2008).

Right, Jonathan. 2000. "Banking on Future Success." *Daily Princetonian*, 12 April, www.dailyprincetonian.com (accessed 27 February 2007).

Rimer, Sara. 1996. "A Hometown Feels Less Like Home." *New York Times*, 6 March, A1, A16–17.

Ritter, Scott. 1995. "Mobil to Reduce Its Work Force by About 9.2%." *Wall Street Journal*, 2 May, A4.

Roane, Kit. 2005. "Easy Street." *U.S. News and World Report*, 13 November, www.usnews.com (accessed 8 June 2007).

Roe, Mark. 1994. *Strong Managers, Weak Owners: The Political Roots of American Corporate Finance*. Princeton, N.J.: Princeton University Press.

Rosaldo, Renato. 1989. *Culture and Truth: The Remaking of Social Analysis*. Boston: Beacon Press.

Rose, Josee. 2007. "Street's Bonus Outlook Is Mixed." *Wall Street Journal*, 31 October, B5.

Roth, Louise Marie. 2003. "Selling Women Short: A Research Note on Gender Differences in Compensation on Wall Street." *Social Forces* 82, no. 2, 783–802.

Royster, Deirdre. 2003. *Race and the Invisible Hand: How White Networks Exclude Black Men from Blue-Collar Jobs*. Berkeley: University of California Press.

Rubalcava, Alex F. 2001. "Recruit This, McKinsey." *Harvard Crimson*, 26 November, www.thecrimson.com (accessed 27 February 2007).

Sahlins, Marshall. 1972. *Stone Age Economics*. New York: Aldine.

Sassen, Saskia. 1998. *Globalization and Its Discontents: Essays on the New Mobility of People and Money*. New York: New Press.

Schoenberger, Erica. 1997. *The Cultural Crisis of the Firm*. Cambridge, Mass.: Blackwell.

Schor, Juliet. 1991. *The Overworked American: The Unexpected Decline of Leisure*. New York: Basic Books.

Schrader, David. 1993. *The Corporation as Anomaly*. Cambridge: Cambridge University Press.

Schwartz, Nathaniel L. 1999. "I-Banking Ire." *Harvard Crimson*, 7 May, www.thecrimson.com (accessed 27 February 2007).

Schwartz, Nelson. 2008. "The Mortgage Bust Goes Global." *New York Times*, 6 April, BU1, 6.

Senger, Jeffrey. 1984. "A Stampede to the Work Place." *Harvard Crimson*, 7 June, www.thecrimson.com (accessed 11 May 2007).

Sennett, Richard. 1998. *The Corrosion of Character: The Personal Consequences of Work in the New Capitalism*. New York: W. W. Norton.

——. 2006. *The Culture of the New Capitalism*. New Haven, Conn.: Yale University Press.

Serwer, Andy. 1999. "A Nation of Traders." *Fortune*, 11 October, 116–20.

——. 2001. "Swiss-American Bank Mergers—Which One Works?" *Fortune*, 5 February, 201–2.

Shapira, Ian. 1998. "Companies Use Aggressive Tactics to Bolster Employee Recruitment." *Daily Princetonian*, 19 February, www.dailyprincetonian.com (accessed 27 February 2007).

Sherrill, Phillip W. 2004. "Working for the Man." *Harvard Crimson*, 30 September, www.thecrimson.com (accessed 27 February 2007).

Siegal, Dan. 2005. "Goldman Sachs CEO Shares Tale of Banking." *Daily Pennsylvanian*, 13 January, www.dailypennsylvanian.com (accessed 27 February 2007).

Siegel, Matthew L. 2003. "Dress for Success: The I-Banker Has No Clothes." *Harvard Crimson*, 20 October, www.thecrimson.com (accessed 27 February 2007).

Sievwright, John P. 1998. "Merrill Lynch's Strategy in Japan 1998." Speech given at the Japan Productivity Center for Socio-Economic Development, 18 November, Tokyo, http://www.ml.com (accessed 27 July 2004).

Simmel, Georg. 1990. *The Philosophy of Money*. Edited by D. Frisby. London: Routledge.

——. 1997a. "Money in Modern Culture." *Simmel on Culture: Selected Writings*, edited by D. Frisby and M. Featherstone, 243–55. London: SAGE Publications.

——. 1997b. "On the Psychology of Money." *Simmel on Culture: Selected Writings*, edited by D. Frisby and M. Featherstone, 233–43. London: SAGE Publications.

Sklar, Martin J. 1987. *The Corporate Reconstruction of American Capitalism, 1890–1916: The Market, the Law, and Politics*. Cambridge: Cambridge University Press.

Slater, Don, and Fran Tonkiss. 2001. *Market Society*. Oxford: Polity Press.

Sloane, Leonard. 1995. "AT&T Dominates as Dow Climbs 25.65." *New York Times*, 21 September, D12.

Smith, Adam. 2000. *The Wealth of Nations*. New York: Random House.

Smith, George David, and David Dyer. 1996. "The Rise and Transformation of the American Corporation." *The American Corporation Today*, edited by C. Kaysen, 28–73. New York: Oxford University Press.

Smith, Randall. 2001. "Morgan Stanley to Cut Bankers in First Layoffs since Attack." *Wall Street Journal*, 1 October, C1, C19.

Smith, Susan J. 2005. "States, Markets and an Ethic of Care." *Political Geography* 24, 1–20.

Smith, Vicki. 2002. *Crossing the Great Divide: Worker Risk and Opportunity in the New Economy*. Ithaca, N.Y.: Cornell University Press.

Smith, Winthrop. 1998a. "The Asian Crisis: An Investment Opportunity?" Paper read at Asian Venture Forum, 12 November, www.ml.com (accessed 5 August 2004).

——. 1998b. "Expansion of Business into Global Markets." Speech delivered at the Richard Ivey School of Business, University of Western Ontario. 3 November, www.ml.com (accessed 5 August 2004).

——. 1998c. "Welcome to the Family of Merrill Lynch." Speech delivered at Merrill Lynch Japan Securities. 18 April, www.ml.com (accessed 5 August 2004).

Steinbery, Julie. 2006. "Want to Do I-Banking with That English BA?" *Daily Pennsylvanian*, 4 October, www.dailypennsylvanian.com (accessed 27 February 2007).

Stewart, James. 1992. *Den of Thieves*. New York: Touchstone Book.

Stokes, Jeanie. 2000. "Shareholders Dump Stock." *Rocky Mountain News* (Denver, Colo.), 26 October, 7B.

Strauss, Nathan C. 2006. "'Extreme Jobs' Threaten Sex Lives." *Harvard Crimson*, 14 December, www.thecrimson.com (accessed 27 February 2007).

Suleiman, Daniel M. 1998. "Beyond the Good and Evil at OCS." *Harvard Crimson*, 8 December, www.thecrimson.com (accessed 27 February 2007).

Tanenbaum, Jessica. 2005. "I-Banking for Dummies." *Yale Daily News*, 6 October, www.yaledailynews.com (accessed 19 March 2007).

Thomas, Landon. 2003a. "Dismantling a Wall Street Club." *New York Times*, 2 November, BU1, 11.

——. 2003b. "Have Merrill's Bulls Been Led to Pasture?" *New York Times*, 5 January, BU1, 10.

——. 2008. "What's $34 Billion on Wall St.? A Subprime Strategy Implodes But Some of Its Captains are Just Fine." *New York Times*, 27 January, BU1, 5.

Thornton, Emily. 2001. "Online Extra: Q&A with Merrill CEO David Komansky." *Business Week*, 12 November, www.businessweek.com (accessed 16 July 2008).

——. 2002. "More Heads Will Roll." *Business Week*, 1 April, www.businessweek.com (accessed 27 October 2002).

——. 2003. "On Wall Street, 'Layoffs Aren't Over'." *Business Week Online*, 13 February, www.businessweek.com (accessed 24 March 2006).

——. 2004a. "Down Days for Investment Banks." *Business Week Online*, 23 September, www.businessweek.com (accessed 6 June 2006).

——. 2004b. "Wall Street? Thanks, I'll Pass." *Business Week*, 18 October, www .business week.com (accessed 6 June 2006).

Thornton, Emily, Heather Timmons, Mara Der Hovanesian, Ben Elgin, and Pallavi Gogoi. 2001. "Tearing Up the Street." *Business Week*, 26 March, 42–43.

Tong, Vinnee. 2006. "$53.4M Bonus Shatters Wall Street Record." *The Eagle-Tribune* (North Andover, Mass.), 21 December, www.eagletribune.com (accessed 12 February 2009).

Traweek, Sharon. 1992. *Beamtimes and Lifetimes: The World of High Energy Physicists*. Cambridge, Mass.: Harvard University Press.

Tsing, Anna. 2000a. "The Global Situation." *Cultural Anthropology* 15, no. 3, 327–60.

——. 2000b. "Inside the Economy of Appearances." *Public Culture* 12, no. 1, 115–44.

——. 2005. *Friction: An Ethnography of Global Connection*. Princeton, N.J.: Princeton University Press.

Tully, Shawn. 2007. "Wall Street's Money Machine Breaks Down." *Fortune*, 12 November, www.cnnmoney.com (accessed 7 July 2008).

Urken, Nicole B., and May Habib. 2003. "Job Fair Caps off Career Week." *Harvard Crimson*. 10 October, www.thecrimson.com (accessed 27 February 2007).

Useem, Jerry. 2000. "New Ethics or No Ethics? Questionable Behavior is Silicon Valley's Next Big Thing." *Fortune*, 20 March, 82–86.

Useem, Michael. 1996. *Investor Capitalism: How Money Managers Are Changing the Face of Corporate America*. New York: Basic Books.

Vickers, Marcia, and Mike McNamee. 2002. "The Betrayed Investor." *Business Week*, 25 February, 104–15.

Waters, Richard. 1999. "Hungry for More: Man in the News Michael Armstrong." *Financial Times*, 24 April, 13.

Wellman, David. 1997. "Minstrel Shows, Affirmative Action Talk, and Angry White Men: Marking Racial Otherness in the 1990s." *Displacing Whiteness: Essays in Social and Cultural Criticism*, edited by R. Frankenburg, 311–31. Durham, N.C.: Duke University Press.

Welsch, Ed, and Susanne Craig. 2008. "Top Merrill Officers Won't Get '07 Bonus; Brokerage Follows Bear's Example after Loan Debacle." *Wall Street* Journal, 31 January, C4.

Werner, Walter, and Steven T. Smith. 1990. *Wall Street*. New York: Columbia University Press.

White, Joseph, and Carol Hymowitz. 1997. "Broken Glass: Watershed Generation of Women Executives Is Rising to the Top." *Wall Street Journal*, 10 February, A1, A8.

Whitman, Marina. 1999. *New World, New Rules: The Changing Role of the American Corporation*. Boston: Harvard Business School Press.

Widman, Wendy. 2004. "Banking on Pain." *Harvard Crimson*, 15 April, www.the crimson.com (accessed 27 February 2007).

Wighton, David. 2007. "Subprime Crisis Seals O'Neal's Fate at Merrill." *Financial Times*, 29 October, 19.

Wilentz, Amy. 1975. "The Class, Leaving." *Harvard Crimson*, 12 June, www.the crimson.com (accessed 11 May 2007).

Williams, William Appleman. 1966. *The Contours of American History*. Chicago: Quadrangle Books.

Wilson, William Julius. 1997. *When Work Disappears: The World of the New Urban Poor*. New York: Vintage.

Wirzbicki, Alan E. 2000. "Senior Class Consciousness." *Harvard Crimson*, 29 September, www.thecrimson.com (accessed 27 February 2007).

Yanagisako, Sylvia. 1999. "The Cultural Production of Capitalist Accumulation." Paper read at the American Anthropological Association Ninety-eighth Annual Meeting, Chicago.

———. 2002. *Producing Culture and Capital: Family Firms in Italy*. Princeton, N.J.: Princeton University Press.

Zaloom, Caitlin. 2006. *Out of the Pits: Traders and Technology from Chicago to London*. Chicago: University of Chicago Press.

Zelizer, Viviana. 1997. *The Social Meaning of Money*. Princeton, N.J.: Princeton University Press.

Zuckerman, Gregory, Randall Smith, and Susanne Craig. 2004. "Investors Hear a Takeover Wave." *Wall Street Journal*, 14 January, C1, C3.

Zuckerman, Laurence. 1995. "The Second Breakup of AT&T: The Computer Business; The Costly Marriage to NCR Becomes a Vision That Failed." *New York Times*, 21 September, D9.

Index

Abstraction, 31–37
Accumulation. *See* Profit accumulation
Acquisitions: confidentiality agreements and, 96; failures and, 135–36, 154–56; identity and, 6–7; shareholder value and, 25, 128; takeovers vs., 138–39. *See also* Mergers
Actor-networks, 4, 174
Aggressiveness and banking recruitment, 40
Allen, William, 209
Analysts: exploitation of, 76; office space, 90; perks for, 90–91; ranking of, 73–74; roles, 85, 92, 95–96
Anthropology of Wall Street, 1–38; approaches to, 31–38
Anticompetetive mergers, 134
Antimonopoly regulation, 134
Antitrust laws, 134, 136
Aronowitz, Stanley, 162–63
Arrighi, Giovanni, 152
Associates: roles, 85–86, 92, 95–96
AT&T downsizing, 1–3, 24–25

Back-office workers, 16–17, 66, 76, 79, 81
Baker, George, 134
BankersTrust New York Corporation (BT) downsizing, 13–18
Bankruptcies, 6, 266, 297
Baran, Paul, 195
Berle, Adolf, 184–86, 188–89, 191–94, 207
Best and brightest, 11, 55, 58, 64, 69, 256
Boesky, Ivan, 149

Bonuses. *See* Compensation Schemes
Bourdieu, Pierre, 11, 12
Brooks, John, 137
Browne, Dudley, 204–5
BT. *See* BankersTrust New York Corporation (BT)

Caldeira, Teresa, 30
Callon, Michael, 36
Capital investment rules, 136
Capitalism: dominant visions of, 209; managerial, 140, 170, 173, 176, 183, 190, 194–98, 201, 203, 205–7, 209–10; profit accumulation and, 3; shareholder value and, 153; U.S. capitalism, 327 n. 10; welfare, 36, 125, 153, 167, 170, 183. *See also* Globalization, capitalist
Carrier, James, 34–35
Certeau, Michel de, 30
Chrysler merger. *See* Daimler-Benz-Chrysler merger
Clark, Gordon, 136
Class inequality, 58, 77–78, 117–18, 120
Clinton, Bill, 22
Compensation schemes, 11–12, 25, 79–80, 86, 257–71; crisis and, 263; discriminatory, 87; downsizing and, 240; institutional culture and, 252, 255, 284–85, 348 n. 11; job insecurity and, 272–74, 286–94; politics of, 249; stock market ties, 128, 141, 197, 214
Conglomeration: defined, 133–34; downsizing and, 135; failure of, 136
Corporate America, defined, 326 n. 8. *See also* Managerial capitalism

Corporate culture. *See* Institutional culture

Creating Shareholder Value (Rappaport), 150

Credit Suisse First Boston. *See* Donaldson, Lufkin and Jenrette merger

Daimler-Benz-Chrysler merger, 154–56

Deal Decade, 132

Den of Thieves (Stewart), 149

Deregulation, 134, 136

DiFazio, William, 162–63

Dill, James, 181

Disembedding, 32–35, 331 n. 33

Disposition, 11

DLJ. See Donaldson, Lufkin and Jenrette merger

Donaldson, Gordon, 205, 210

Donaldson, Lufkin, and Jenrette merger, 281–82

Dow Jones Industrial Average origins, 178

Downsizing: abstraction and, 34; bear market and, 224–27, 346 n. 10; bull market and, 1–3, 222–25, 238–41; conglomerates and, 135; connection to stock prices, 1, 2; by investment banks, 15–18, 67, 213–48, 251, 293–94; market externalizations and, 238–43; overwork and, 104–5; shareholder value and, 4, 16, 36, 67, 126; stock prices and, 1, 2–3. *See also* Job insecurity

Drexel Burnham Lambert, 10, 139–40, 142, 340 n. 23. *See also* Junk bonds

Drucker, Peter, 123–24, 207

Dudley, Kathryn Marie, 198, 337 n. 7

Dyer, Richard, 37, 195

Economics: culture/society and, 32; neoclassical, 34; real vs. virtual practices, 36

Efficiency, 157–64

Elitism: cross-pollination, 55–66; kinship, 13, 58–62; post-graduation, 56–58; smartness and, 50, 76. *See also* Powerfulness

Emerging market crisis, 223, 232–33

Employment: corporate health and, 4, 127–28; cycles, 162; Fortune 500 companies drop in, 137; fungibility, 274, 284, 291; stock ownership and, 183. *See also* Downsizing; Job insecurity

Empty office syndrome, 311–14

Entrepreneurs. *See* Owner-entrepreneurs

Ethnography: access and methodology, 13–16, 31; of investment banks, 3–4, 15–16, 25–26; of powerful, 19, 30; representation and shareholder value, 22–31

Face time, 98–99

Faludi, Susan, 143–44

Finance capital: abstraction and, 31–37; accumulation and, 72, 350 n. 16; defined, 152; dominance of, 6, 12, 295, 297, 318, 328 n. 13; employment and, 17; height of, 343 n. 8; ideal worker and, 244–48; kinship and, 13; markets and, 17, 179–80; production and, 17, 163, 167, 323; smartness and, 332 n. 1; success and, 74, 121; U.S.-centric, 3, 5–6

Financial models: abstraction of, 33–37; market prices and, 251; relationship with practice, 28–29, 250–51

Fischer, Michael, 38, 329 n. 15

Foucault, Michel, 145, 171

Frank, Thomas, 22

Fraser, Steve, 199–200, 203

Front-office employees, 66, 76, 77–78, 81–82, 85

Gender inequality, 13, 16, 37, 79–80, 107–8, 117, 120, 270–71

Glass-Steagall Act, 7, 199

Globalization, capitalist, 5, 31–38, 75, 184, 295–324; contradictions, 309–11; fissures in, 304–5; marketing of, 296, 298, 306–9; presence and, 311–18

Goldsmith, James, 146–47

Gramm-Leach-Bliley Act, 7

Grubman, Jack B., 3

Gusterson, Hugh, 19

Guyer, Jane, 28

Habitus, 11, 12, 34, 138, 249

Hard work: culture of, 11, 42, 74, 85, 97–99, 99–107, 249; perks, 90–91; politics of, 73–121; relationships vs., 113

Harvey, David, 163, 338 n. 12

Hegemony, 42. See also Powerfulness

Henderson, Carter, 207–8

High-yield bonds. See Junk bonds

Holmes, Douglas, 38

Houser, Theodore, 196–97

Identity: formation, by investment bankers, 55, 256–57; institutional, 6

Inequality. See Gender inequality; Racial inequality; Socioeconomic inequality

Initial Public Offerings (IPOs), 128

Insecurity. See Job insecurity

Instability, culture of, 75

Institutional culture: compensation schemes and, 252, 255, 284–85, 348 n. 11; elite kinship and, 13–21; financial crisis and, 10–11, 285–94, 321–23; growth of, 136–37; of investment banks, 6–7, 11–12, 13–21, 58, 75, 213–48; mergers and acquisitions and, 6–7; social vs. investment cultures, 30; strategy and, 215, 227–28, 249, 274–85

Investment bankers: African American, 21, 108–15, 118–19; Asian American, 20, 110–11, 119–20; identity-formation, 55, 256–57; internships, 53–54; kinship and, 58–62, 67, 72; marked/unmarked, 107–21; ranking of, 73–74; recruitment of, 11, 39, 42–55, 62–67; recruitment schedule, 46–47; smartness and, 11–12, 39–42; white male, 41, 60, 62, 112, 121, 271, 347 n. 7; women, 116–20, 336 n. 18

Investment banks: commercial banks vs., 7, 66, 328 n. 12; as corporate system creator, 27; culture of employment, 17–18, 213–48, 249; downsizing by, 15–17, 67; ethnographic analysis, 3–4, 16; ethos, 11; institutional culture, 6–7, 11–12, 13–21, 58, 75, 213–48, 285–94; making markets, 4; maps, 8–9; as market spokesperson, 5–6; orientation program, 74–77; pinnacle status and, 40, 62–67, 71, 105; process for deals, 106; relationship to corporate America, 5, 27, 131, 243; short-term gains and, 18; stock prices and, 1; strategy and, 215, 274–85; student view of, 53; takeovers and, 139–40. See also Shareholder value

IPOs. See Initial Public Offerings (IPOs)

Jackson, Jesse, 23

Jensen, Michael, 27

Job insecurity: abstraction and, 34; compensation schemes and, 272–74, 286–94; corporate profits and, 4; culture of, 11–12, 80, 213–48, 251; market externalizations and, 238–43, 249; narratives, 215–22, 231–38; shareholder value and, 126. See also Downsizing

Jobless recovery, 162–63

Junk bonds, 131, 138, 140–43, 145, 235

Kaysen, Carl, 195

Kinship, 13, 58–62, 67, 72

Klein, Naomi, 350 n. 11

Kolhberg, Kravis, and Roberts (KKR), 139, 143–45

Lasher, Albert, 207–8
Layoffs. *See* Downsizing
Leveraged buyouts (LBOs), 10, 139–46, 151, 173, 340 n. 22
Levine, Dennis, 149
Levy, Leon, 200
Lewis, Michael, 140–41, 337 n. 10
Lippmann, Walter, 195
Liquidation, 4–13, 129, 142
Liquidity, 183–88, 198, 214, 245
Long Twentieth Century, The (Arrighi), 152

MacKenzie, Donald, 28, 251
Malinowski, Bronislaw, 29
Management consulting vs. investment banking, 43–44, 332 n. 2
Managerial capitalism, 140, 170, 173, 176, 183, 189–91, 194–98, 201, 203, 205–7, 209–10; self-interest, 127–28, 133–34, 189–92
Managing directors, 86–87
Marcus, George, 38
Market formations, 4, 32–33; culture of market simultaneity, 230, 242, 250, 252, 285, 301, 320; market cycles and, 10–11, 235–38, 239
Martin, Emily, 314, 351 n. 17
Mason, Edward, 207
Masters in Business Administration (MBA). *See* MBA programs
Maurer, Bill, 28, 33–34, 251
MBA programs: as channels to Wall Street, 54
Meadows, Lacey, 16
Means, Gardiner, 184–86, 189, 191–94
Mergers: confidentiality agreements and, 96; failures and, 135–36, 154–56; identity and, 5–6; shareholder value and, 25, 128, 177; takeovers vs., 138–39. *See also* Acquisitions

Mergers, Sell-Offs, and Economic Efficiency (Ravenscraft and Scherer), 135
Meritocracy, 55, 58, 60, 71, 77; money, 107–8, 112, 347 n. 7
Merrill, Charles, 200, 202
Merrill Lynch, 315–18
Middle office workers, 66, 77, 78–79
Milken, Michael, 131, 142, 149, 235
Miller, Daniel, 36
Miyazaki, Hirokazu, 28, 34, 250
Modern corporation: legal definition, 206; neoclassical assumptions vs., 188–94, 195; rise of, 176–83; social entity vs. property view of, 209–12; soulfulness of, 195–96
Morgan, J. P., 178, 342 n. 7, 343 n. 9
Morgan Stanley Dean Witter recruitment ad, 70
Mortgages. *See* Subprime mortgages

Nader, Laura, 329 n. 15
Neoclassical economics, 34–35, 129; influence of, 170; modern corporation and, 172–76, 188–94, 195; narratives of shareholder value, 169–212; persistence of, 205–8
Neoliberal discourses, 31, 33–34, 107–8
New Deal, 125, 194, 199, 207
New Economy, 22
New York Stock Exchange, 178, 202–3

Old boys' networks. *See* Kinship
One-stop shopping, 134
O'Sullivan, Mary, 156, 179, 207, 339 n. 18
Ott, Julia, 178–79, 182
Outsourcing, 35
Owner-entrepreneurs, 172–75, 177–79, 183

Pfeffer, Jeffrey, 341 n. 28
Pinnacle status. *See under* Investment banks

Pitch book, 69, 85, 93–94, 100, 105–6
Polanyi, Karl, 32
Polymorphous engagement, 19
Powerfulness: abstraction and, 36–37; ethnography of, 19, 29–30; hegemony, 42; powerlessness vs., 35; shareholder value and, 30–31
Private property: ownership value, 176, 179, 182; rejection of notion, 193; rights, 129, 133, 186
Professional space, 114–15
Profitability crisis, 137
Profit accumulation: desire for, 3, 128; finance capital and, 72, 350 n. 16; flexible, 125, 152; regimes, 152; smartness and, 40, 332 n. 1; socioeconomic inequality and, 35
Property. See Private property
Public corporations: as exchangeable stock, 129–30

Racial inequality, 12, 16, 37, 56–57, 61–62, 79–80, 107–10, 120, 347 n. 5, 347 n. 8
Rappaport, Alfred, 150–51
Ravenscraft, David, 135
Recruitment. See under Investment bankers
Relationship managers vs. product side, 109–11, 113, 114
Reregulation, 134
Restructuring: investment banker habitus and, 34; shareholder value and, 25
Restructuring movement. See Takeover movement (1980s)
Riles, Annelise, 28, 34
Ripley, William, 182
Risk, 250, 259, 291, 321–22
Roth, Louise Marie, 270–71, 347 n. 6

Safeway leveraged buyout, 143–44
Salaries, CEO, 141
Salomon Brothers, 3
Scherer, F. M., 135
Schoenberger, Erica, 214–15

Schrader, David, 172, 174, 175–76
Secrecy, 83
Securities Act (1933), 199
Securities Exchange Act (1934), 199
Segregation: elevators and, 77–83; politics of, 76
Self-confidence and recruitment, 40, 41
Self-interest, 127–28, 133–34, 169–70, 173, 175, 189–92, 205–6
Serwer, Andy, 10
Sexism. See Gender inequality
Shareholder value: capitalism and, 153; corporate interest and, 175; creating, 3, 5, 122; culture of banking and, 12, 36, 152, 251–52, 283; deterioration of, 25; downsizing and, 4, 15–16, 37, 67, 126, 135; ethnographic representation and, 22–31; failures of, 28, 153–56; fixed expenses and, 15; focus on, 137; fungibility and, 150; historiographies, 123; job insecurity and, 126; liquidity and, 183–88; marginalized communities and, 23; as measure of success, 13, 24–26, 28–29; mergers and acquisitions and, 25, 120, 177; narratives of, 30, 157–64, 169–212; neoclassical economics and, 169–212; perfect capitalism and, 169; populism and, 22–24, 138, 315–16; postwar worldviews, 198–205; power elite and, 30–31; problematizing, 169–70; reclaiming, 150–53; rights and, 152, 189; short-term vs. long-term, 210–12; stock market and, 176–83; temporalities, 164–68; transitory nature, 124
Siegel, Martin, 149
Simmel, Georg, 186–87
Sklar, Martin, 205–6
Smartness: banker recruitment and, 11–12, 39–72; culture of, 40–41, 57–58, 59, 67–72, 74, 75, 107, 249, 251; elitism and, 50, 56, 76; use of term, 39

Smith, Adam, 172, 173–74, 176, 191–93
Smith, George, 134
Smith, George David, 195
Smith, Steven, 183–84
Social networks, 33
Social studies of finance, 17, 28, 250
Socioeconomic inequality, 18, 32–33, 35, 37
Stewart, James, 149
Stock market: CEO salaries and, 141; connection to downsizing, 1, 2–3, 126–27; crashes, 135, 138; cycles, 286–87; democratization of, 23; financial models and, 251; fungibility and, 150; price increase as mission, 3, 23–24, 35, 126; shareholder value and, 176–83; takeovers and, 129–30
Stone, Oliver, 132
Subprime mortgages, 7, 10, 235, 297–301, 318–24
Success, culture of, 57, 113
Sweezy, Paul, 195

Takeover movement (1980s), 129–33; deregulation and, 136; historicization, 133–37; key actors, 139–40; mergers and acquisitions vs., 138–39; resistance to, 146, 149; simulated takeover, 146–49; socioeconomic issues, 149–50. See also Leveraged buyouts (LBOs)
Tsing, Anna, 331 n. 31, 350 n. 16
20 Million Careless Capitalists (Henderson and Lasher), 207–8

Underwriting, 137
Universities. See Elitism; Investment bankers, recruitment

Virtualism, 35

Wall Street: defined, 4; during Great Depression, 199–203; habitus, 4–13
Wall Street (film), 132
"Wall Street Project," 23
War bonds, 180
Wealth of Nations, The (Smith), 172
Welfare capitalism, 36, 125, 153, 167, 170, 183
Werner, Walter, 183–84
White-collar sweatshop, 83–87
Whitman, Marina, 133

Yanagisako, Sylvia, 13, 29, 331 n. 30

KAREN HO
is associate professor of anthropology
at the University of Minnesota.

Library of Congress Cataloging-in-Publication Data
Ho, Karen Zouwen, 1971–
Liquidated : an ethnography of Wall Street / Karen Ho.
p. cm.
"A John Hope Franklin Center Book."
Includes bibliographical references and index.
ISBN 978-0-8223-4580-0 (cloth : alk. paper)
ISBN 978-0-8223-4599-2 (pbk. : alk. paper)
1. Securities industry—United States—Employees.
2. Stockbrokers—United States. 3. Investment banking—
United States. 4. Downsizing of organizations—United
States. I. Title.
HD8039.S432U68 2009
331.7'6133264273—dc22   2009007594